Spaces in Late Antiquity

Places and spaces are key factors in how individuals and groups construct their identities. Identity theories have emphasised that the construction of an identity does not follow abstract and universal processes but is deeply rooted in specific historical, cultural, social and material environments. The essays in this volume explore how various groups in Late Antiquity rooted their identity in special places that were imbued with meanings derived from history and tradition. In Part I, essays explore the tension between the Classical heritage in public, especially urban spaces, in the form of ancient artwork and civic celebrations and the Church's appropriation of that space through doctrinal disputes and rival public performances. Parts II and III investigate how particular locations expressed, and formed, the theological and social identities of Christian and Jewish groups by bringing together fresh insights from the archaeological and textual evidence. Together the essays here demonstrate how the use and interpretation of shared spaces contributed to the self-identity of specific groups in Late Antiquity and in so doing issued challenges, and caused conflict, with other social and religious groups.

Juliette Day is University Lecturer and Docent in Church History at the University of Helsinki and Senior Research Fellow in Christian History at Blackfriars Hall, University of Oxford.

Raimo Hakola, Th.D. (2003), is an Academy Research Fellow at the University of Helsinki, Faculty of Theology. His latest publication is *Reconsidering Johannine Christianity: A Social Identity Approach*.

Maijastina Kahlos, Ph.D. (1998), University of Helsinki, has published *Debate and Dialogue: Christian and Pagan Cultures, c. 380–430* and *Forbearance and Compulsion: Rhetoric of Tolerance and Intolerance in Late Antiquity*.

Ulla Tervahauta is post-doctoral researcher in the Center of Excellence Reason and Religious Recognition, at the University of Helsinki. Her publications include *A Story of the Soul's Journey in the Nag Hammadi Library: A Study of Authentikos Logos (NHC VI,3)*.

Spaces in Late Antiquity

Cultural, Theological and Archaeological Perspectives

Edited by Juliette Day, Raimo Hakola,
Maijastina Kahlos and Ulla Tervahauta

LONDON AND NEW YORK

First published 2016
by Routledge
2 Park Square, Milton Park, Abingdon, Oxon OX14 4RN

and by Routledge
711 Third Avenue, New York, NY 10017

Routledge is an imprint of the Taylor & Francis Group, an informa business.

© 2016 selection and editorial matter, Juliette Day, Raimo Hakola, Maijastina Kahlos and Ulla Tervahauta; individual chapters, the contributors.

The right of Juliette Day, Raimo Hakola, Maijastina Kahlos and Ulla Tervahauta to be identified as the authors of the editorial material, and of the authors for their individual chapters, has been asserted in accordance with sections 77 and 78 of the Copyright, Designs and Patents Act 1988.

All rights reserved. No part of this book may be reprinted or reproduced or utilized in any form or by any electronic, mechanical, or other means, now known or hereafter invented, including photocopying and recording, or in any information storage or retrieval system, without permission in writing from the publishers.

Trademark notice: Product or corporate names may be trademarks or registered trademarks, and are used only for identification and explanation without intent to infringe.

British Library Cataloguing in Publication Data
A catalogue record for this book is available from the British Library.

Library of Congress Cataloging in Publication Data
Names: Day, Juliette. | Hakola, Raimo. | Kahlos, Maijastina. | Tervahauta, Ulla.
Title: Spaces in late antiquity : cultural, theological and archaeological
  perspectives / edited by Juliette Day, Raimo Hakola, Maijastina Kahlos and
  Ulla Tervahauta.
Description: Farnham, Surrey, England ; Burlington, VT : Routledge, 2016. |
  Includes bibliographical references and index. | Description based on print
  version record and CIP data provided by publisher; resource not viewed.
Identifiers: LCCN 2016010475 (print) | LCCN 2015045590 (ebook)
  (hardcover : alkaline paper)
Subjects: LCSH: Mediterranean Region—History—476-1517. | Rome—
  History—Empire, 284-476. | Middle East—History—To 622. | Public
  spaces—History—To 1500. | Sacred space—History—To 1500. | Identity
  (Psychology)—History—To 1500. | Group identity—History—To 1500. |
  Identification (Religion)—History—To 1500. | Christianity and culture—
  History—To 1500. | Judaism and culture—History—To 1500.
Classification: LCC DE94 (print) | LCC DE94 .S66 2016 (ebook) | DDC
  937/.09—dc23
LC record available at http://lccn.loc.gov/2016010475

ISBN: 9781472450166 (hbk)
ISBN: 9781315610184 (ebk)

Typeset in Times New Roman
by Swales & Willis Ltd, Exeter, Devon, UK

Printed in the United Kingdom
by Henry Ling Limited

Contents

List of Illustrations   vii
Notes on Contributors   ix
Acknowledgements   xii
List of Abbreviations   xiii

Introduction: Spaces in Late Antiquity – Cultural, Theological and Archaeological Perspectives   1
JULIETTE DAY, RAIMO HAKOLA, MAIJASTINA KAHLOS AND ULLA TERVAHAUTA

PART I
Cultural Perspectives   9

1 **Meddling in the Middle? Urban Celebrations, Ecclesiastical Leaders and the Roman Emperor in Late Antiquity**   11
MAIJASTINA KAHLOS

2 **Classical Culture, Domestic Space and Imperial Vision in the *Cycle* of Agathias**   32
STEVEN D. SMITH

3 **Monastic Space: The Ascetic Between Sacred and Civil Spheres in Theodoret of Cyrrhus**   48
ANDREAS WESTERGREN

PART II
Theological Perspectives   67

4 **Seeing Christ at the Holy Places**   69
JULIETTE DAY

5 Sacred Space, Virginal Consecration and Symbolic Power: A Liturgical Innovation and Its Implications in Late Ancient Christianity 89
DAVID G. HUNTER

6 The City of God and the Place of Demons: City Life and Demonology in Early Christianity 106
JOONA SALMINEN

7 Preaching, Feasting and Making Space for a Meaning 118
ANNA-LIISA TOLONEN

PART III
Archaeological Perspectives 139

8 Galilean Jews and Christians in Context: Spaces Shared and Contested in the Eastern Galilee in Late Antiquity 141
RAIMO HAKOLA

9 Performing the Sacred in a Community Building: Observations from the 2010–2015 Kinneret Regional Project Excavations in the Byzantine Synagogue of Horvat Kur (Galilee) 166
JÜRGEN K. ZANGENBERG

10 Thrown into Limekilns: The Reuse of Statuary and Architecture in Galilee from Late Antiquity onwards 190
RICK BONNIE

Bibliography 212
Index 239

Illustrations

Figures

3.1 The 'Mountain' of Divine Ascent (diagram by author; image of Mount Ararat by NASA/JPL/NIMA [public domain], via Wikimedia Commons) — 58

4.1 The apse mosaic at Santa Pudenziana, Rome (photograph: © Robin M. Jensen. Used with permission) — 85

9.1 Aerial photograph of synagogue at the end of the 2013 campaign (© Skyview Ltd. and Kinneret Regional Project) — 169

9.2 Plan of synagogue (drawing by A. Rheeder: © Kinneret Regional Project)
   a) schematic plan — 171
   b) stone plan — 171

9.3 Stone basin found in secondary use as installation in Area C (© Kinneret Regional Project, reg. nr. 16364/1, database photo nr. 1010777) — 175

9.4 Stone seat and benches in southwestern corner of synagogue, situation at the end of the 2012 campaign (© Skyview Ltd. and Kinneret Regional Project) — 180

9.5 The *bemah* from the air (© Skyview Ltd. and Kinneret Regional Project) — 184

10.1 Reconstruction of a limekiln ready for firing (after Dix, 'The Manufacture of Lime', Fig. 2, courtesy of Brian F. Dix) — 195

10.2 Ground plan of Sepphoris. The limekilns are numbered as in Table 10.1 (after Weiss, 'From Roman Temple to Byzantine Church', Fig. 1, courtesy of Zeev Weiss, The Sepphoris Expedition, The Hebrew University of Jerusalem; drawings by Anna Iamim) — 201

10.3 Sepphoris, circular limekiln found at the east end of the theatre's stage area (Waterman, *Preliminary Report*, pl. XVIII, Fig. 2, courtesy of the Kelsey Museum of Archaeology) — 203

10.4 Cornelis Visscher, after Pieter van Laer, *The Large Limekiln*, engraving (RP-P-1904-723; Rijksmuseum, Amsterdam). Van Laer's original painting has been lost; this engraving is probably a mirror-image of it   209

Table

10.1 Limekilns and associated evidence in Galilee, alphabetically ordered   196

Contributors

Rick Bonnie is a postdoctoral researcher in the Centre of Excellence in Changes in Sacred Texts and Traditions, Department of Biblical Studies, University of Helsinki. He holds degrees in archaeology from Leiden University and the KU Leuven. At the latter, he recently completed his PhD research on the archaeology of second-century CE Galilee. His current research focuses on investigating private and communal religious practices in Galilee during the Late Second Temple period (*c.* 100 BCE–CE 70) through three archaeological features: ritual baths, stone vessels and synagogues.

Juliette Day is University Lecturer and Docent in Church History at the Faculty of Theology, University of Helsinki, and Senior Research Fellow in Early Christian Liturgy at Blackfriars Hall, University of Oxford. Her research and teaching focuses on early Christianity and liturgical history. Her most recent publications include *Reading the Liturgy* (T&T Clark, 2014) and, as editor, volume 71 of *Studia Patristica*, papers on Early Roman Liturgy (2013). She is editor of the journal *Anaphora* and a co-editor of the forthcoming *Oxford Handbook of Early Christian Ritual*.

Raimo Hakola is an Academy Research Fellow at the Faculty of Theology, University of Helsinki, Finland. He has published on the Gospel of John, the Pharisees, ancient Galilee and social identity in the New Testament. His latest publication is *Reconsidering Johannine Christianity: A Social Identity Approach* (Routledge, 2015). Hakola is a co-director of the archaeological excavations conducted by the Kinneret Regional Project at Horvat Kur, Galilee.

David G. Hunter is Cottrill-Rolfes Professor of Catholic Studies at the University of Kentucky. He is the author of *Marriage, Celibacy, and Heresy in Ancient Christianity: The Jovinianist Controversy* (Oxford University Press, 2007) and co-editor of the *Oxford Handbook of Early Christian Studies* (Oxford University Press, 2008). Hunter has served as President of the North American Patristics Society (2006–08) and is active on the advisory boards of *Vigiliae Christianae*, the *Journal of Early Christian Studies*, the *Journal of Late Antiquity*, *Augustinian Studies* and *Augustiniana*. He currently serves as the Editorial Director of the translation series, *The Fathers of the Church*, published by The Catholic University of America Press and on the editorial board of the forthcoming *Brill Encyclopedia of Early Christianity*.

Maijastina Kahlos is an historian and a classicist at the University of Helsinki. She works currently as a research fellow in the Centre of Excellence 'Reason and Religious Recognition', funded by the Academy of Finland. She is the author of *Vettius Agorius Praetextatus: Senatorial Life in Between* (AIRF, 2002), *Debate and Dialogue: Christian and Pagan Cultures, c. 360–430* (Ashgate, 2007) and *Forbearance and Compulsion: Rhetoric of Tolerance and Intolerance in Late Antiquity* (Duckworth, 2009) and the editor of *The Faces of the other: Religious Rivalry and Ethnic Encounters in the Later Roman World* (Brepols, 2012).

Joona Salminen (MTh) is a doctoral candidate preparing his dissertation on Clement of Alexandria and early Christian asceticism at the Faculty of Theology, University of Helsinki. He is also a member of the Centre of Excellence 'Reason and Religious Recognition' funded by The Academy of Finland. His previous publications include edited academic volumes, translations and peer-reviewed articles.

Steven D. Smith is an Associate Professor of Classics and Comparative Literature at Hofstra University in New York. He is the author of *Greek Identity and the Athenian Past in Chariton: The Romance of Empire* (Barkhuis, 2007) and *Man and Animal in Severan Rome: The Literary Imagination of Claudius Aelianus* (Cambridge University Press, 2014).

Ulla Tervahauta is a post-doctoral researcher in the Center of Excellence Reason and Religious Recognition, at the University of Helsinki. Her publications include *A Story of the Soul's Journey in the Nag Hammadi Library: A Study of Authentikos Logos (NHC VI,3)* (Vandenhoeck & Ruprecht, 2015).

Anna-Liisa Tolonen (MTh) is a doctoral student employed by the Finnish Academy funded Centre of Excellence, 'Reason and Religious Recognition'. Her dissertation is a historical comparative analysis of the popular traditions of the story of the mother and her seven sons, common to all the three monotheistic religions. Currently, she works at the Faculty of Theology, University of Helsinki, but she has also studied abroad at the Hebrew University of Jerusalem and attended several research seminars around the Eastern Mediterranean.

Andreas Westergren (PhD 2012) is a research fellow in the research programme 'Early Monasticism and Classical Paideia' at the University of Lund, Sweden. He works with images of schooling in hagiographical literature. Westergren's doctoral thesis, *Sketching the Invisible: Patterns of Church and City in Theodoret of Cyrrhus' Philotheos Historia* looks at Late Antique saints' stories that on the surface depict the saint as separate from the world, yet at the same time paint 'classical' civil ideals, so that the eremite can become a symbolical figure for both the city and the church. In addition to research, Westergren is co-ordinator for the Master's programme 'The Religious Roots of Europe', which investigates the early sources of Christianity, Judaism and Islam in a comparative perspective. In his teaching he has dealt both with the rise of monasticism and with the contemporary situation of Christians in the Middle East.

Jürgen K. Zangenberg is Professor for the History and Culture of Ancient Judaism and Early Christianity at Leiden University in the Netherlands and serves as co-director of Kinneret Regional Project (www.kinneret-excavations.org). His research focuses on the literature and material culture of the various forms of ancient Judaism and early Christianity in their Mediterranean context. Apart from studies on the archaeology of Qumran, Mount Gerizim and Jerusalem his main research focus is ancient Galilee and especially the Byzantine synagogue at Horvat Kur http://www.hum.leiden.edu/history/organisation/staff-history/zangenberg.html.

Acknowledgements

The core of this volume is based on papers presented at the XXII Finnish Symposium on Late Antiquity in 2013 on the theme 'Spaces Past and Present'. A number of papers from the XXI FSLA on the theme 'Popular and Elite' have been added to the volume. The Finnish Symposium on Late Antiquity (FSLA) has been organized annually since 1992 with the aim of bringing together students and scholars of Late Antiquity from a variety of universities and disciplines. These symposia have stimulated interdisciplinary dialogue between philology, archaeology, history, theology, religious studies, art history and other disciplines that deal with Late Antiquity.

The Finnish Symposium on Late Antiquity started as seminars for postgraduate students, but over the years more and more papers were presented by established scholars from universities in Europe, the United States and Israel. The editors wish to thank all the guest speakers and participants in the FSLA symposia where the original papers were discussed. Our special thanks go to Dr Ville Vuolanto (University of Oslo/University of Tampere) who has been part of the organizing committee of the FSLA meetings in recent years, along with two of the editors of this volume, Maijastina Kahlos and Ulla Tervahauta.

The FSLA meetings have recently been funded by various sponsors: the *Ancient Mediterranean and the Near East* (AMNE) network, the Faculty of Arts and the Faculty of Theology at the University of Helsinki, the Academy of Finland research projects headed by Antti Marjanen, Raimo Hakola and Maijastina Kahlos, and the Centre of Excellence 'Reason and Religious Recognition' (headed by Risto Saarinen and funded by the Academy of Finland). Raimo Hakola's research funds have been used for the final editing of this book.

Last but not least, we want to thank Dr. Nina Nikki for her meticulous work in the final copyediting of the manuscript and Routledge, especially Michael Greenwood, for their patience.

Helsinki 16 October 2015,
Juliette Day, Raimo Hakola,
Maijastina Kahlos and Ulla Tervahauta

Abbreviations

AASOR	Annual of the American Schools of Oriental Research
AB	The Art Bulletin
ACW	Ancient Christian Writers
ADAJ	Annual of the Department of Antiquities of Jordan
AES	Archaeological Exploration of Sardis
AH	Art History
AIVM	Archeologie in Vlaanderen, Monografieën
AJA	American Journal of Archaeology
AJSR	Association for Jewish Studies Review
AMSCEU	Annual of Medieval Studies at CEU
AnBoll	Analecta Bollandiana
AntTard	Antiquité Tardive
AP	Anthologie Palatine
AS	Anatolian Studies
ASMA	Aarhus Studies in Mediterranean Antiquity
ASOR	American School of Oriental Research
AUB	Annales de l'Université de Besançon
BASOR	Bulletin of the American Schools of Oriental Research
BJS	Brown Judaic Studies
BRLJ	Brill Reference Library of Judaism
ByzZ	Byzantinische Zeitschrift
CBET	Contributions to Biblical Exegesis and Theology
CCSL	Corpus Christianorum: Series latina.
CSEL	Corpus Scriptorum Ecclesiasticorum Latinorum
CTh	Codex Theodosianus
DHR	Dynamics in the History of Religion
DOP	Dumbarton Oaks Papers
DOS	Dumbarton Oaks Studies
EPRO	Etudes préliminaires aux religions orientales dans l'empire romain
ESI/HA	Excavations and Surveys in Israel/Hadashot Arkheologiyot
FA	Forum Archaeologicae

xiv *Abbreviations*

FCh	Fathers of the Church
GNO	Gregorii Nysseni Opera
GRBS	Greek, Roman and Byzantine Studies
HA (ESI)	Hadashot Arkheologiyot (Excavations and Surveys in Israel)
HABES	Heidelberger althistorische Beiträge und epigraphische Studien
HeBAI	Hebrew Bible and Ancient Israel
IAA	Israel Antiquities Authority
IEJ	Israel Exploration Journal
IJCT	International Journal of the Classical Tradition
IOS	Israel Oriental Studies
ISACR	Interdisciplinary Studies in Ancient Culture and Religion
JAC/ZAC	Journal of Ancient Christianity/Zeitschrift für Antikes Christentum
JAS	Journal of Archaeological Science
JbAC	Jahrbuch für Antike und Christentum
JBL	Journal of Biblical Literature
JBV	Journal of Beliefs and Values
JECS	Journal of Early Christian Studies
JGLGA	Jahrbuch der Gesellschaft für Lothringische Geschichte und Altertumskunde
JGS	Journal of Glass Studies
JHS	Journal of Hellenic Studies
JJS	Journal of Jewish Studies
JLA	Journal of Late Antiquity
JQR	Jewish Quarterly Review
JRA	Journal of Roman Archaeology
JRASup	Journal of Roman Archaeology Supplement
JRitSt	Journal of Ritual Studies
JRS	Journal of Roman Studies
JSJ	Journal for the Study of Judaism
JSPSup	Journal for the Study of the Pseudepigrapha Supplement Series
LAA	Late Antique Archaeology
LCL	Loeb Classical Library
LSJ	Liddell-Scott-Jones Greek-English Lexicon
MEFR	Mélanges d'Archéologie et d'Histoire de l'École Française de Rome
MEPR	Meiron Excavation Project Reports
NCE	New Catholic Encyclopedia
NEAEHL	New Encyclopaedia of Archaeological Excavations in the Holy Land
NHMS	Nag Hammadi Manuscript Studies
NPNF	Nicene and Post-Nicene Fathers
OECS	Oxford Early Christian Studies

OLD	Oxford Latin Dictionary
PAM	Polish Archaeology in the Mediterranean
PBA	Proceedings of the British Academy
PG	Patrologia Graeca. Edited by J.-P. Migne.
PH	Theodoret of Cyrrhus, Philotheos Historia
PL	Patrologia Latina. Edited by J.-P. Migne.
PLRE	Prosopography of the Later Roman Empire
PMS	Patristic Monograph Series
PO	Patrologia Orientalis
QDAP	Quarterly of the Department of Antiquities in Palestine
RA	Recherches Augustiniennes et patristiques
RGRW	Religions in the Greco-Roman World
SBF	Studium Biblicum Franciscanum
SBFCM	Studium Biblicum Franciscanum Collectio Maior
SCh	Sources Chrétiènnes
SCJ	Studies in Christianity and Judaism
SJ	Studia Judaica
SNTS	Society of New Testament Studies
STAC	Studien und Texte zu Antike und Christentum
STJHC	Studies and Texts in Jewish History and Culture
StPatr	Studia Patristica
StPB	Studia Post-Biblica
TBAW	Tübinger Beiträge zur Altertumswissenschaft
ThH	Théologie historique
TSAJ	Texts and Studies in Ancient Judaism
VC	Vigiliae Christianae
VCSup	Vigiliae Christianae Supplement
WGRWS	Writings from the Greco-Roman World Supplements
WUNT	Wissenschaftliche Untersuchungen zum Neuen Testament
ZAC	see JAC
ZDMG	Zeitschrift der Deutschen Morgenländischen Gesellschaft

References to rabbinical sources are abbreviated according to the recommendations in the SBL Handbook of Style.

Introduction
Spaces in Late Antiquity – Cultural, Theological and Archaeological Perspectives

Juliette Day, Raimo Hakola, Maijastina Kahlos and Ulla Tervahauta

The so-called 'spatial turn' has provided a stimulating impetus to late antique studies, a period during which considerable social, political, religious and economic changes can be charted over many centuries. The introduction of space into the field of historical studies has meant that scholars have realized that the questions of how and why certain historical events took place cannot be examined apart from those tangible material environments where these events took place. As a result of this turn, space is increasingly seen across arts and humanities as 'a social construction relevant to the understanding of the different histories of human subjects and to the production of cultural phenomena'.[1]

Space, geographical and built, is no longer taken as just the container for human action, but also, as shall be seen, as a tool for the creation of personal and collective identity exercised concretely and rhetorically.[2] Places and spaces are not approached as neutral categories but as key factors in how individuals and groups construct their identities. Tim Cresswell has expressed this by saying that 'value and meaning are not inherent in any space or place – indeed they must be created, reproduced, and defended from heresy'.[3] Various identity theories

---

1 See Barney Warf and Santa Arias, 'Introduction: The Reinsertion of Space into the Social Sciences and Humanities', in *The Spatial Turn: Interdisciplinary Perspectives*, Barney Warf and Santa Arias (eds) (Routledge Studies in Human Geography 26; London: Routledge, 2009): 1.
2 For a discussion with relevant references, see Halvor Moxness, *Putting Jesus in His Place: A Radical Vision of Households and Kingdom* (Louisville: Westminster John Know Press, 2003): 1–17. In the field of New Testament and early Christian studies, Moxness has been one of the first to apply various spatial theories.
3 Tim Cresswell, *In Place/Out of Place: Geography, Ideology, and Transgression* (Minneapolis: University of Minnesota Press, 1996): 9. As Creswell notes elsewhere, the distinction between the terms 'place' and 'space' has been common in scholarly literature dealing with human geography. A space is seen as a realm without a specific meaning; when people attach to a space unique meanings (e.g. name), it becomes a place (Cresswell, *Place: A Short Introduction* [Oxford: Blackwell, 2004]: 10). In this terminology, the meaning of place comes close to what Henri Lefebvre has called 'social space' that is distinct from 'natural' or 'absolute' space. The concept of social space emphasizes different modes of production that turn a natural space into a social construction. See Henri Lefebvre, *La production de l'espace* (Paris: Anthropos 1974. English translation: *The Production of Space*. Donald Nicholson-Smith (trans), Oxford: Blackwell, 1991). The chapters in this volume approach spaces and places as social constructions but do not adhere to a strict

have recently emphasized that the construction of an identity does not follow abstract and universal processes, but is deeply rooted in specific historical, cultural, ecological, social and material environments.[4] In the context of the late Roman empire, space as the arena for personal and communal activity became contested in both overt and covert ways, and the evidence for this exists in the physical remains brought to light by archaeologists and architectural historians and in the extensive literature.

The starting point for any investigation is the existence of binaries such as sacred and profane, public and private, urban and rural, Christian and pagan or Hellenistic and Jewish, as these are present most clearly in the physical and literary remains. None of these are absolutes and the exploration of one element leads us to consider signs of boundary crossing and merging. The creation of sacred space, in synagogues, temples, churches, shrines and so forth, attempts to provide places unambiguously demarcated from the non-sacred by architectural features such as walls, doors and places for ritual purification, and also by theological conceptions of the presence of the divine or the exclusive locus of divine action.[5] The remaining urban space was not thereby neutralized, but was affected by the location of the sacred, and by the ways in which dominant religious culture was promoted publically – statues and iconoclasm, the changing content of inscriptions, buildings and the destruction of buildings. In the late empire, as it became increasingly Christianized, the church's dominance of the public space through these means was accompanied by ritual acts of appropriation (processions, martyr shrines) and a rhetoric which extended God's authority out of the private into the public sphere. These historical developments illustrate how spaces and places should not be taken as finished, but as processes whereby they are reimagined and reconstructed through reiterated performance of various social practices.[6]

---

terminological distinction of the terms but mostly use them interchangeably. The exception is Andreas Westergren, who makes a distinction between space and place in his chapter.
4 Cf. Maijastina Kahlos, 'Introduction', in *The Faces of the Other: Religious Rivalry and Ethnic Encounters in the Later Roman World*, Maijastina Kahlos (ed.) (Cursor Mundi 10; Turnhout, Belgium: Brepols, 2011): 4–5; Raimo Hakola, Nina Nikki and Ulla Tervahauta, 'Introduction', in *Others and the Construction of Early Christian Identities*, Raimo Hakola, Nina Nikki and Ulla Tervahauta (eds) (PFES 106; Helsinki: Finnish Exegetical Society, 2013): 10–15.
5 For the concept of holy places, see Sabine MacCormack, '*Loca Sancta*: The Organization of Sacred Topography in Late Antiquity', in *The Blessings of Pilgrimage*, Robert Ousterhout (ed.) (Urbana: University of Illinois Press, 1990): 7–40. See further various contributions in *Les frontières du profane dans l'antiquité tardive*, Éric Rebillard and Claire Sotinel (eds) (Collection de l'École française de Rome 428; Rome: École française de Rome, 2010). For instance, Emmanuel Soler ('Sacralité et partage du temps et de l'espace festifs à Antioche au IVe siècle'), Carlos Machado ('The City as Stage – Aristocratic Commemorations in late antique Rome') and Claire Sotinel ('La sphère profane dans l'espace urbain'). Claire Sotinel has also discussed the sphere of the sacred in her articles 'The End of Pagan Holy Places in the West: Problems and Method', and 'Places of Christian Worship and their Sacralization in Late Antiquity', both now in Claire Sotinel, *Church and Society in Late Antique Italy and Beyond* (Aldershot: Ashgate, 2010).
6 For places as processes, see Tim Cresswell, *Place: A Short Introduction*: 33–9; Doreen Massey, *For Place* (London: Sage, 2005): 11.

Public spaces can be constructed to promote the sense of sameness and solidarity among those who use and inhabit them, but, at the same time, they may be used as instruments of marginalization by the ruling elite. Spaces give an expression to specific social relations and structures and so it is necessary to ask who dominates the organization and production of the material environment. Attention must therefore be paid to the ways in which the internal arrangement of space, especially in religious structures, displays divine authority but also acts as a source of social, political and religious power for bishops, synagogue leaders, etc. Patronage is only one way of exerting social power in these contexts: the arrangement of people within them also reflects social power structures outside. In the religious context, the explicit rejection of this by emergent monasticism, which transplanted the locus of divine activity to areas that were, at least theoretically, uninhabited, interestingly maintained the rhetoric of power just as it eschewed the socially normative expressions of that power. Now the desert and the mountain provide a new sacred topography to be exploited by habitation, cultivation, and by a rhetoric of estrangement.[7]

Despite rhetorical and physical constructions of separateness, such as the designation of sacred or profane, there has been a shift to nuance these absolute categories by showing how late antique populations moved quite easily between spaces, or between different interpretations of the same space. Attention to the 'spatial turn' alerts us to the ways in which late Romans negotiated competing cultures as they moved around their cities and engaged in religious activities; the rhetoric of difference is often just rhetoric and we find cultural assimilation and boundary crossing to be much more prevalent. Paula Fredriksen has spoken about 'the strong and prevailing patterns of social and religious interaction' and 'the tradition of openness' that shaped ancient urban life until Late Antiquity and which annoyed various Christian theologians. This tradition is evidenced in various public celebrations, processions and local and imperial festival days that created venues for various interactions between distinct segments of cities' populations.[8] This aspect of urban public space in Late Antiquity could perhaps be characterized by the concept of 'throwntogetherness' which Doreen Massey has used to define spaces as arenas where unexpected neighbours are brought together and negotiation is forced upon them.[9]

Alongside several shared public spaces, various groups in Late Antiquity rooted their identity in special places that were imbued with meanings derived

---

7 For the interdependence of urban centres and rural communities in Late Antiquity, see Thomas S. Burns and John W. Eadie (eds), *Urban Centers and Rural Contexts in Late Antiquity* (East Lansing, MI: Michigan State University Press, 2001).
8 Paula Fredriksen, *Augustine and the Jews: A Christian Defence of Jews and Judaism* (New York, Doubleday, 2008): 98–9. It seems that public *fora* and *agorai* remained an important part of urban life into the latter half of the fifth century and retained many of their traditional political, social, and religious functions. See Luke Lavan, '*Fora* and *Agorai* in Mediterranean Cities during the 4th and 5th c. A.D.', in *Social and Political Life in Late Antiquity*, William Bowden, Adam Gutteridge and Carlos Machado (eds) (LAA 3.1; Leiden: Brill, 2006): 195–249.
9 Massey, *For Places*: 149–62.

4 *Introduction*

from history and tradition; memories of the classical past remained visible in public spaces for a long time, for example in the form of ancient artwork and civic celebrations and in the literary corpus.[10] It is not possible to ignore ways in which places and the rhetoric of place transmitted the distinctive values and ideas of specific groups, particularly religious groups; what is right and appropriate is frequently conveyed through material or imagined spaces.[11] On the one hand, spaces can be seen as to have provided a sense of secure identity for a specific community; on the other hand, they may have been understood as a challenge or a threat by outsiders. While different communities lived side by side and interacted in shared spaces, their claims for specific spaces may have become the source of controversy and conflict.[12]

The chapters in this book reflect the scholarly trends summarized above in a variety of ways. The first three chapters approach cultural perspectives of spaces in Late Antiquity. Maijastina Kahlos investigates urban space and traditional celebrations in 'Meddling in the Middle? Urban Celebrations, Ecclesiastical Leaders and the Roman Emperor in Late Antiquity'. She inquires into the differing meanings given to festivals connected to the cults of the old gods by church leaders (Petrus Chrysologus and Augustine of Hippo in particular), the imperial government and ordinary people. Kahlos takes part in recent scholarly discussions on the religious and the non-religious in the late antique context and is inclined to avoid these terms as problematic in the analysis of late Roman society. Although the late antique disputes from the viewpoint of discursive boundary marking were between pagan and Christian, cultic, civic and neutral, Kahlos shows how the meaning and content were under continuing cultural negotiation.

Steven D. Smith's 'Classical Culture, Domestic Space, and Imperial Vision in the *Cycle* of Agathias' approaches the combination of classical and Christian through an epigram by Agathias of Myrina, published in Constantinople around 567. Agathias' epigram summarizes an ascent through a narrow staircase to the wide view of the sea from a rooftop in Constantinople. Smith provides a stylistic reading of this multi-layered poem and considers its cultural implications in the sixth century context. The epigrams of Agathias' *Cycle* connected the overwhelmingly Christian environment with the rich cultural and literary traditions of the past. Smith argues that Agathias' poem, as a poetic representation of a lived

---

10 Cf. Carlos Machado, 'Building the Past: Monuments and Memory in the Forum Romanum', in *Social and Political Life in Late Antiquity*, eds Bowden, Gutteridge and Machado: 157–92.

11 Cf. Cresswell (*In Place/Out of Place*: 14) who argues that places can play an important role 'in the constitution of ideology' because they may define what is good, just and appropriate. Cf. also Moxness, *Putting Jesus*: 15.

12 Cf. Ulrich Schmitzer, 'Raumkonkurrenz. Der symbolische Kampf um die römische Topographie im christlich-paganen Diskurs', in *Rom und Mailand in der Spätantike: Repräsentationen städtischer Räume in Literatur, Architektur und Kunst*, ed. Therese Fuhrer (Topoi; Berlin Studies of the Ancient World 4; Berlin: De Gruyter, 2012): 237–62. This collection is a part of the research carried out by a research network *Topoi – The Formation and Transformation of Space and Knowledge in Ancient Civilizations* that investigates how space and knowledge were formed and transformed in ancient civilizations (see https://www.topoi.org/, accessed 9 January 2016).

Introduction 5

space in the imperial city, is also the site where the classicizing philosophical tradition harmonizes with both Christian thought and an imperial conceptualization of *oikoumene*.

Classical and Christian encounter is also discussed in Andreas Westergren's 'Monastic Space: The Ascetic Between Sacred and Civil Spheres in Theodoret of Cyrrhus'. Starting with Libanius' lament for the glorious, pagan past of the countryside and his view of the countryside as a space that is closely entwined both with city and empire, Westergren then inquires into Theodoret of Cyrrhus' conception of extra-urban space. Westergren argues that Theodoret of Cyrrhus, not unlike Libanius, creates mythological relations between the city and the countryside. A particular place emerges in Theodoret's text that functions as a space where virtue may be achieved: the mountain. Westergren suggests that, in Theodoret's thought, life in community and life in solitude form a continuum that is reflected in Greek authors. Westergren's key argument is that the cells of the ascetics exist on a continuum between civil and sacred spheres in Theodoret's work and the various locations of the ascetics are exhibited along a graded scale, which situates them differently between the poles of human and divine realms and where there is room for movement in both directions.

The second section of this book offers reflections on theological perspectives of space in Christian authors and their works. In the first chapter of this section, Juliette Day in 'Seeing Christ at the Holy Places' discusses late antique pilgrim accounts and pilgrims' experiences of holy places. A relationship exists between the place, the visits, the pilgrimage accounts and the text of scripture, but how these relate to each other is not always obvious. Day inspects accounts and discussions of pilgrimages and the verbs employed to describe the act of seeing at specific holy places. Very different interpretations of what was seen emerge and Day suggests that these alert us to multiple modes of perception in pilgrimage texts. To support her investigation Day examines Galen, Plotinus and Origen and their ideas on sight that formed part of the cultural consensus. Reflecting on these theories, she asks what sort of seeing took place at the holy places and concludes that what the pilgrims saw was not simply conditioned by what they had read in the Bible, or heard in church, nor even just by what was physically seen at the holy places; rather, what they saw was determined by how sight was considered to relate to knowing and where truth was to be found.

David G. Hunter approaches the nature of sacred space in 'Sacred Space, Virginal Consecration and Symbolic Power: A Liturgical Innovation and its Implications in Late Ancient Christianity'. He discusses the ritual of virginal consecration and how it unfolded within the space of a fourth century church, with special attention to the ways in which the ritual actions served to generate sacred space and to produce distinctive identities. He then turns to Ambrose of Milan and the theological or ideological implications of this ritual, and how this liturgical practice provided late antique Christians, especially their bishops, with the language and images to construct a distinctive social space. Hunter argues that the sacred space of the church was the site at which the identity of the consecrated virgin was instituted and a hierarchy of social relations was generated. In this ritual space the virgin was afforded a distinctive identity superior to the ordinary married layperson and, simultaneously, instituted in a role subordinate to the Christian bishop. The ritual action both empowered her and constricted her, but it was not only the virgin whose status depended on consecrations, as Hunter points out, virginal consecration was connected to enhancing the bishop's authority.

In 'The City of God and the Place of Demons: City Life and Demonology in Early Christianity' Joona Salminen examines the city as an early Christian context and the role of demons in emerging Christianity by analyzing Clement of Alexandria and Tertullian, Athanasius and Evagrius, and finally Augustine, on their views of demons in city life. Salminen suggests that the demonologies of these authors affect their idea of a good city life and especially their view of public and private spaces. Their instructions on dealing with demons differ depending on whether the writer is talking about the actual city or the new city in the desert.

Communal feasting is a well-represented practice in late ancient sources, and ancient Christian homilies provide a variety of perspectives on feasting. In 'Preaching, Feasting: Making Space for a Meaning', Anna-Liisa Tolonen discusses the homily *On Eleazar and the Seven Boys*, ascribed to John Chrysostom, and seeks to contextualize the argumentative environment of the work. Tolonen suggests that the festival space constructed in the homily is above all a theological space which reflects the homilist's ideological objective of educating the minds of the people who participate. The homilist's view exposes Christian perceptions of the martyrdom of the Maccabees that could be used for bridging the gap between the pre- and post-Christ events.

The third section of the book discusses questions of shared space and offers archaeological perspectives focused on late antique Galilee. While this region has often been regarded as a cultural hinterland, it actually provides much evidence for the continuing co-existence of Jewish and Christian communities, as well as the longevity of various features of the classical past in Late Antiquity.

This section opens with Raimo Hakola's 'Galilean Jews and Christians in Context: Spaces Shared and Contested in the Eastern Galilee in Late Antiquity' in which he examines Jewish and Christian groups in eastern rural Galilee in relation to synagogues and churches that can be dated to Late Antiquity. Hakola first provides an overview of recent scholarly discussions about Jewish–Christian relations elsewhere in the ancient world. Building on this, he discusses Galilean synagogues and their diversity, and proposes that the building and renovation of rural Galilean synagogues in Late Antiquity attests to the vitality of village settlements in the region. The Christian churches and communities surrounding them that had connections with pilgrimage were also part of this diversity. Hakola suggests that local Jewish and Christian communities in late antique Galilee cherished their particular traditions by constructing specific spaces which set them apart from the rest of the society and reinforced their collective identity. These buildings, synagogues and pilgrim churches, share much in the details of their art and architecture, but they also epitomize the need of these communities to present themselves as different from one another. Despite these attempts at separation, Hakola claims that there were also social and cultural interactions between different local communities.

Jürgen K. Zangenberg continues the discussion of Galilee by considering how space reflects the sacred and its many aspects. 'Performing the Sacred in a Community Building. Observations from the 2010–2015 Kinneret Regional Project Excavations in the Byzantine Synagogue of Horvat Kur (Galilee)' takes as its starting point the category of the sacred that has remained both central and difficult to grasp, especially as far as material culture studies are concerned. Zangenberg highlights aspects of the sacred and its material and spatial expressions through his observations from the Byzantine synagogue of Horvat Kur in Galilee. Going through what remains of the building, its walls, floors, doors, and special features such as its bemah and the seating, and by reconstructing functions and hierarchies that community members apparently wished to see expressed during liturgical service, Zangenberg demonstrates how the local community created and organized the sacred space in that synagogue.

In 'Thrown into Limekilns: The Reuse of Statuary and Architecture in Galilee from Late Antiquity Onwards' Rick Bonnie challenges the assumption that during the second and the third centuries CE most of the Jewish population in Galilee obeyed prohibitions on displaying idolatrous images and that, as a consequence, during this era Galilee was largely vacant of freestanding statues. Bonnie examines archaeological evidence for limekilns and associated marble deposits in Galilee from Late Antiquity onwards, with a special emphasis on urban regions, and suggests nuancing the earlier picture. In particular, the excavations at Sepphoris indicate that limekilns were common in the urban areas of Galilee during the Byzantine and Early Islamic periods. This evidence suggests that stone statuary was a more common phenomenon than has been hitherto suggested, and that more caution needs to be shown about an alleged absence of evidence.

The different chapters in this collection demonstrate how ancient individuals and groups were involved in various ways in the production of spaces filled with special meanings. This production took place both through literary representations and through the material transformation of existing structures, or construction of new buildings. In both cases, the production of distinct spaces is closely connected to the ways people tried to create and maintain clearly defined identities that separate them from others in their surroundings. However, the writers of this book show how both symbolic and material spaces were produced in a world that too often frustrated attempts to set up clearly defined hierarchies between sacred and profane, public and private, urban and rural, or Christian and pagan. Not only did individuals move across imagined or real boundaries, but the past continued to influence the ways people experienced and saw their surroundings. To navigate through the uncertainties of their world, people needed to reproduce and renegotiate not only the sense of who they were, but also the spaces in which they lived.

Part I
Cultural Perspectives

Part 1

Cultural Perspectives

1 Meddling in the Middle? Urban Celebrations, Ecclesiastical Leaders and the Roman Emperor in Late Antiquity

Maijastina Kahlos

Introduction

Ecclesiastical naysayers complaining about Christians eating and drinking, dancing and singing in local celebrations are commonplace in the fourth and fifth centuries. Bishops used much of their time and energy in disparaging their parishioners' waywardness, whether it was taking part in local traditional festivals, enacting funerary rites, attending theatrical spectacles, games and races or sharing practices with Jews and 'pagans'.

During the fourth and fifth centuries, Christian festivals gradually developed and were merged into the life of cities and country villages. At the same time, a number of traditional celebrations, important to the communal life of these localities, continued. Many of these festivities and spectacles had been closely connected with the cults of the old gods and were still, in the minds of many people, more or less associated with these. Nonetheless the connection was no longer very clear for all who participated in these celebrations. Traditional local festivals, games, races and theatre spectacles were also popular among Christians who seem to have understood their celebrating as merely partaking in the public life of local communities. However, a number of ecclesiastical leaders took a stricter stance, interpreting these celebrations as idolatry and consequently prohibiting Christians from attending them.[1]

---

1 The bibliography on Christian attitudes to traditional spectacles and feasts is vast. See, for example, Robert Markus, *The End of Ancient Christianity* (Cambridge: Cambridge University Press, 1990); Michele Renee Salzman, *On Roman Time: The Codex Calendar of 354 and the Rhythms of Urban life in Late Antiquity* (Berkeley: University of California Press, 1990); Timothy D. Barnes, 'Christians and the Theater', in *Roman Theater and Society*, William J. Slater (ed.) (Ann Arbor Michigan: University of Michigan Press, 1996); Marguerite Harl, 'La dénonciation des festivités profanes dans le discours épiscopal et monastique en Orient chrétien à la fin du IVe siècle', in *La Fête, pratique et discours* (Annales de l'Université de Besançon 62; Paris, 1981); Theodor Klauser, 'Der Festkalender der Alten Kirche im Spannungsfeld jüdischer Traditionen, christlicher Glaubensvorstellungen und missionarischen Anpassungswillens', in *Kirchengeschichte als Missionsgeschichte* I, Heinzgünther

12 *Maijastina Kahlos*

In this chapter I discuss late antique disputes about local celebrations. What was at stake was whether late antique Christians should regard these celebrations as connected with the old cults ('pagan', 'idolatrous') or as something common to all ('mere celebration'). The meanings and contents of festivities and rituals were under continuing cultural negotiation and, hence, I examine the bishops' condemnations from the viewpoint of discursive boundary marking in which the borders of the 'pagan', 'Christian', 'cultic' and 'civic' are constantly shifting.

Similar cultural negotiations are constantly going on in modern societies. Just to take a few examples from the European context: every year in Finland, as the Christmas season approaches, there is a public discussion about the meaning of the feasting. What kinds of carols may be sung and what kinds of productions can be staged in kindergartens and schools? Are these to be regarded as mere merriment common for all or are these emphatically confessional Christian ceremonies? A similar dispute emerges every year concerning the summer hymn (*suvivirsi*), sung at the end of the school year. Is this a religious ritual, a part of the cultural heritage or mere rejoicing at the summer vacation?

All societies negotiate the meanings and contents of their rituals and institutions. Many of the terms used in modern debates have also been employed in the research to describe late antique celebrations. These terms – religious and neutral, sacred and secular – are doomed to be anachronistic and hence problematic for Late Antiquity. Can we speak of 'secular', 'neutral' or 'civic' when they are not only anachronistic but also elusive concepts?

Robert Markus has analysed late Roman society by using the division between sacred and secular.[2] The term 'secular' has been used to designate anything that has nothing to do with a religious context.[3] For instance, Wolf Liebeschuetz speaks of late antique public entertainments in Antioch that had been 'completely secularized'.[4] The term 'secular' is of course anachronistic and not particularly

---

Frohnes and Uwe W. Knorr (eds) (München: Kaiser, 1974); Heiko Jürgens, *Pompa diaboli: Die lateinischen Kirchenväter und das antike Theater* (*TBAW* 46; Stuttgart: W. Kohlhammer, 1972); Werner Weismann, *Kirche und Schauspiele: Die Schauspiele im Urteil der Kirchenväter unter besondere Berücksichtigung von Augustin* (Würzburg: Augustinus Verlag, 1972); Georges Ville, 'Les jeux gladiateurs dans l'empire chrétien', *MEFR* 72 (1960); more recently also John Curran, *Pagan City and Christian Capital: Rome in the Fourth Century* (Oxford: Clarendon, 2000): 236–58; Leonardo Lugaresi, '*Regio aliena*. L'atteggiamento della Chiesa verso i luoghi di spettacolo nella città tradoantica', *Antiquité tardive* 15 (2007); Emmanuel Soler, 'Sacralité et partage du temps et de l'espace festifs à Antioche au IVe siècle', in *Les frontières du profane dans l'antiquité tardive*, Éric Rebillard and Claire Sotinel (eds) (Rome: École française de Rome, 2010).

2 Markus, *End of Ancient Christianity*: 1–17.
3 Ithamar Gruenwald, 'The Other Self: Introductory Notes', in *Concepts of the Other in Near Eastern Religions*, Ilai Athon, Ithamar Gruenwald and Itamar Singer (eds) (IOS 14; Leiden: Brill, 1994): 11.
4 Wolf Liebeschuetz, 'The View from Antioch: from Libanius to John Chrysostom to John Malalas and Beyond', in *Pagans and Christians in the Roman Empire: The Breaking of a Dialogue (IVth–VIth Century A.D)*, Peter Brown and Rita Lizzi Testa (eds) (Wien: Lit Verlag, 2011): 310–11; see also Beatrice Caseau, 'Polemein Lithois: La désacralisation des espaces et des objects religieux païens durant l'antiquité tardive', in *Le sacré et son inscription dans l'espace à Byzance et en occident*, Michel Kaplan (ed.) (Paris: Publications de la Sorbonne, 2001): 110 on 'la sécularisation des statues païennes' and Claude Lepelley, 'De la reaction païenne à la sécularisation:

fitting to describe late antique social life. Modern secularization theories (since Max Weber) imply shifts from the sacred to the secular and often fail to take into account that many (especially pre-modern) societies have not maintained strict distinctions between what we consider to be sacred and secular.[5] Hartmut Leppin suggests that a more suitable way of depicting the late antique urban and rural spaces shared by religious groups is the term 'neutral'.[6]

Richard Lim has criticized the assumptions based on the terms 'pagan', 'secular' and 'Christian'.[7] Éric Rebillard, furthermore, has questioned the division between sacred and secular or between religious and nonreligious because it presupposes 'a model of behavior that is too rigid and too dependent on a Christian theological point of view'. Speaking of sacred and secular, religious and neutral, is to adopt the criteria of the late antique bishops, who wanted to propagate it to their parishioners and make them divide their activities into straight lines of sacred and secular. Rebillard argues that, in Late Antiquity, people did not necessarily separate their activities according to rigid and distinct conventions of what was religious and what was secular unless they were forced to do so.[8] Instead, he offers the situational approach that explains variations

---

le témoignage d'inscriptions municipales romano-africaines tardives', in Brown and Testa (eds), *Pagans and Christians in the Roman Empire*: 288 on 'la sécularité exprimée par les inscriptions municipales'. Nicole Belayche, 'Des lieux pour le "profane" dans l'Empire tardo-antique? Les fêtes entre koinônia sociale et espaces de rivalités religieuses', *AntTard* 15 (2007): 35–46 analyzes the spaces in the late Roman Empire, and Claire Sotinel, 'La sphere profane dans l'espace urbain', in Rebillard and Sotinel (eds), *Les frontières du profane*, 320–49 analyzes urban spaces, using the term 'profane' (in French).

5 For problems concerning the concept of secularization, see the excellent discussion by Richard Lim, 'Christianization, Secularization, and the Transformation of Public Life', in *A Companion to Late Antiquity*, Philip Rousseau (ed.) (Oxford: Wiley-Blackwell, 2009): 503 and 'Inventing Secular Space in the Late Antique City: Reading the Circus Maximus', in *Rom in der Spätantike: Historische Erinnerung im städtischen Raum*, Ralf Behrwald and Christian Witschel (eds) (HABES 51: Stuttgart: Franz Steiner, 2012): 65–7. He nonetheless continues to use the terms 'secularization' and 'secular' but as 'part of the ongoing negotiation over the status of public life in a Christianizing society' (Lim, 'Inventing Secular Space': 78).

6 The term 'Neutralisierung' is used by Hartmut Leppin, 'Christianisierungen im Römischen Reich: Überlegungen zum Begriff und zur Phasenbildung', *ZAC* 16 (2012): 247–78; also Hartmut Leppin, 'Christianisierung, Neutralisierung und Integration: Überlegungen zur religionsgeschichtlichen Entwicklung in Konstantinopel während des vierten Jahrhunderts', in *Christentum und Politik in der Alten Kirche*, Johannes van Oort and Otmar Hesse (eds) (Leuven: Walpole, 2009): 17–19. Furthermore, H. A. Drake, 'Constantinian Echoes in Themistius', *StP* 34 (2001): 48 speaks of 'religiously neutral public space' that Emperor Constantine favoured; see also Isabella Sandwell, *Religious Identity in Late Antiquity: Greeks, Jews and Christians in Antioch*, (Cambridge: Cambridge University Press, 2007), especially 31 on John Chrysostom, who attempted to 'erase any possibility of a neutral non-Christian or non-religious sphere that could be free from religious conflict'.

7 Richard Lim, 'People as Power: Games, Munificence, and Contested Topography', in *Transformations of Urbs Roma in Late Antiquity*, William V. Harris (ed.) (JRASup 3; Portsmouth, RI: Journal of Roman Archaeology, 1999): 267.

8 Éric Rebillard, *Christians and Their Many Identities in Late Antiquity, North Africa, 200–450 CE* (Ithaca: Cornell University Press, 2012): 62, 70, 96. Rebillard, *Christians and Their Many Identities*:, 96, 107 n. 8, also retracts from his earlier delineations of 'religious' and 'secular' in Éric Rebillard and Claire Sotinel, 'Introduction', in Rebillard and Sotinel (eds), *Les frontières du*

within each individual's action and conduct more adequately. The idea of situational identities has been advocated by Rogers Brubaker in *Ethnicity without groups*.[9] Furthermore, Bernard Lahire in *The plural actor* has demonstrated that an individual has various identities and tends to activate (and de-activate) these identities according to changing situations.[10]

In the realities of late antique communal life, this means that Christians tended to make their decisions on a situational basis – in situations in which they felt their sense of belonging to their Christian community was important enough, they 'activated' their Christian 'identity'. The same persons are seen to take part both in 'pagan' (or what was seen as pagan) and Christian festivities probably without any particular scruples, or they would have had no scruples if bishops had left them to continue their celebrations in peace. The much discussed identity crisis of late antique Christians was, therefore, mainly a headache for ecclesiastical leaders, rather than a problem for ordinary people.

The central contention in this chapter is to continue the analysis of the late antique debates from the viewpoint of situational identities. I argue that the same local celebration may have had different meanings and contents for different persons and even for the same person depending on the situation. For one person, a festival constituted a cultic act, while for another it was simply a civic celebration that enhanced a sense of belonging to the city community; for a third person, it meant just having fun (for instance, getting good food, getting drunk and perhaps even finding company or sex partners); for a fourth person, it was all these things. There was no single or identical meaning for all. Neither did the celebrations mean the same thing for a person all the time, for their meanings were situational and dependent on life circumstances.

Therefore, I do not take any stand here on whether a late antique festival was religious ('pagan') or secularized: the issue lies outside my discussion. What is discussed here is the content and connotations with which *ecclesiastical writers* endowed these celebrations and how these contents were questioned, disputed and negotiated in the debates within the community. The content and significance of celebrations, their 'paganness' or neutrality, are discursive categories that are defined according to the writer who delineates them.

First, I discuss how two late antique bishops, Augustine of Hippo and Petrus Chrysologus reproached their parishioners for attending traditional local celebrations. These rebukes are compared with other disputes in which bishops condemned local urban festivities. Then I will investigate the attitudes of the imperial government towards popular feasting in imperial legislation. Finally,

---

profane, discussing the situational identities of North African Christians with examples from the writings of Tertullian, Cyprian and Augustine. The demarcation between 'sacred' and 'secular' space is also criticized by John Curran, 'Moving Statues in Late Antique Rome: Problems of Perspective', *Art History* 7 (1994): 50.

9 Rogers Brubaker, *Ethnicity without Groups* (Cambridge MA: Harvard University Press, 2004).
10 Bernard Lahire, *The Plural Actor*, David Fernbach (trans.), orig. *L'homme pluriel*, 2001 (Cambridge: Polity, 2011): especially 11–31.

I examine how the role of the emperor in the middle of religious disputes was outlined in late antique discussions, especially by the Constantinopolitan rhetorician Themistius.

Petrus Chrysologus on New Year Celebrations

In the 440s, Petrus Chrysologus, the Bishop of Ravenna, complained of Christians who participated in the festivities of the New Year, *Kalendae Ianuariae*. Ravenna was at the time the imperial residence of the West Roman emperor, Valentinian III and his mother, Galla Placidia Augusta.[11]

The *Kalendae Ianuariae* had been celebrated from Republican times onwards as the first day of the year on which the consuls entered their office and public vows (*vota publica*) were made to Jupiter Optimus Maximus to ensure the welfare of the state. During the imperial period, the senate and the army took their oath of allegiance to the emperor on the *Kalendae Ianuariae, and* the emperor received different kinds of offerings (*strenae*) as signs of loyalty from his subjects. Besides this clearly state-run element of the festival, there was a private side to the New Year celebration. In addition to the *vota publica* on behalf of the state, there were private vows and prayers, especially to Janus, the god of beginnings and endings. The New Year was a time for mutual visits and gifts and interpreting omens for the whole year.[12]

The celebration of the *Kalendae Ianuariae* remained popular throughout the centuries, even in the Christianizing Empire, as numerous complaints by Christian writers imply.[13] Christian emperors did not prohibit festivals of this kind, which they defined as gatherings of citizens and a common pleasure for all[14] (see my discussion below). The solemn festivities of the *Kalendae Ianuariae*, such as the appointment of the consuls, vows and offering gifts to the emperor, continued. In 323, Emperor Constantine ordered that Christians could not be forced to make vows and sacrifices

---

11 Petrus Chrysologus or Petrus of Ravenna (c. 380–450) held his bishopric c. 425–450. He maintained good relations with the imperial family and, in the first sermon after his consecration as bishop, praised Galla Placidia, 'the mother of the Christian, eternal and faithful Empire herself' for her works of mercy, holiness and reverence for the Trinity. For the relationship between Petrus Chrysologus and Galla Placidia, see Hagith Sivan, *Galla Placidia: The Last Roman Empress* (Oxford: Oxford University Press, 2011): 162–3.

12 For the development and different elements of the *Kalendae Ianuariae*, see Michel Meslin, *La fête des kalends de janvier dans l'empire romain* (Collection Latomus 115; Bruxelles: Latomus, 1970): 23–46, 73–5; Lucy Grig, 'Interpreting the Kalends of January: A Case Study for Understanding Late Antique Popular Culture?', in *Popular Culture in the Ancient World,* Lucy Grig (ed.) (Cambridge: Cambridge University Press, forthcoming). I thank Lucy Grig for allowing me to see a copy of her article before publication.

13 Tertullian (*Idol.* 10) had also criticized the practice of offering gifts of money (*strenae*) to teachers during the *Kalendae Ianuariae*. From the viewpoint of a twenty-first century university lecturer, it would be a splendid idea to return to this custom.

14 *CTh* 16.10.17 (in 399): '*ita festos conventus civium et communem omnium laetitiam non patimur submoveri*'.

in the ritual of the 'alien superstition', that is, as Roman magistrates were expected to do according to the traditional rites.[15]

Fourth- and fifth-century ecclesiastical writers who disapproved of the New Year feasting could not openly attack the state-run imperial side of the *Kalendae Ianuariae*, but directed their energies towards scolding private practices such as dancing, drunkenness, obscene spectacles and revelries, as well as covering the dinner table with the greatest possible variety of courses and delicacies in the last evening of the old year in order to guarantee prosperity for the next. A number of sixth- and seventh-century writers continue to criticize these private practices.[16]

One example of these reproaches is Petrus Chrysologus' sermon on the New Year. There he reproves his cityfolk who, despite being Christians, take part in the festivities of the *Kalendae Ianuariae*. For Petrus the festivities are clearly idolatrous: 'the pagans bring out their gods today'.[17] Petrus starts his attack by representing these traditional religious practices as a distortion made by the devil and goes on to attack the immoral myths in which the gods of pagans are presented as monstrosities who commit incest and adultery (Mars and Venus are named). He explains that this was how Antiquity proclaimed idols to be gods, but posterity showed that they were only shameful humans and they should be avoided rather than worshipped.[18]

This exposition is a relevant part of Petrus' demonstration of the New Year celebrations as sacrilegious and idolatrous. Furthermore, he wants to represent them as a product of the antiquity that has been forsaken. Petrus Chrysologus admonishes his parishioners to weep for those who follow such things and to

---

15 *CTh* 16.2.5 (in 323): '*Quoniam comperimus quosdam ecclesiasticos et ceteros catholicae sectae servientes a diversarum religionum hominibus ad lustrorum sacrificia celebranda compelli, hac sanctione sancimus, si quis ad ritum alienae superstitionis cogendos esse crediderit eos, qui sanctissimae legi serviunt, si condicio patiatur, publice fustibus verberetur, si vero honoris ratio talem ab eo repellat iniuriam, condemnationem sustineat damni gravissimi, quod rebus publicis vidicabitur.*' For the continuation of the New Year festivities, see Meslin, *La fête des kalends*: 53–70.
16 Jerome, *Comm. Isa.* 65, v.11 (*PL* 24, 639): people decorate the table and drink a cup of wine with honey, *futuri fertilitatem auspicantes*. Caesarius of Arles, *Sermo* 192 (*CCSL* 104, 779), reproves the practice of covering the dinner table with all the food and drink that was to be needed in the following year. Martin of Braga, *Corr. rust.* 11; 16, also castigates the habit of taking auspices from the abundance of the New Year's Eve dinner table: '*si in introitu anni satur est et laetus ex omnibus, ita illi et in toto anno contingat*'. For the continuation of such rebukes, see Meslin, *La fête des kalends*: 71.
17 Petrus Chrysologus, *Sermo* 155.1 (*CCSL* 24B): '. . . *hodie gentiles . . . deos suos videndos trahunt, distrahunt, pertrahunt, quos faciunt non videndos*'.
18 Petrus Chrysologus, *Sermo* 155.1–3: '*eos, quos vetustas aris, incenso, victimis, gemmis, auro deos esse mentita est, posteritas turpi cultu homines fuisse turpissimos indicaret, et . . . ac doceret tales fugiendos esse potius quam colendos . . .* '. The representation of the traditional cults as a diabolic distortion, the critique of the immorality of the gods and the Euhemeristic interpretation of gods as former humans were commonplace in Christian apologetics of the preceding centuries: Jean-Marie Vermander, 'La polémique des apologistes latins contre les dieux du paganisme', *RA* 17 (1982): 21–30.

rejoice for having themselves escaped them.[19] He states that he has explained these matters in order to make it understandable why people today still do such things and 'why they make their gods such as to cause horror and shame for those who see them'.[20] Consequently, Petrus warns his listeners not to pollute themselves with such spectacles. They should rather avoid showing approval of these spectacles. For to approve these things, Petrus Chrysologus stresses, is the same as to do these things.[21]

In his sermon, Petrus Chrysologus describes a fictive protest by his parishioners who explain the festivities of the New Year as harmless celebrations without 'sacrilegious' content:

> But someone says: 'These are not practices of sacrilegious rites, these are vows of entertainment. And this is the merriment for the new, not the error of the old. This is the beginning of the year, not a pagan transgression.'[22]

According to the fictive protest of these Christians, the celebrations were not religious ('not practices of sacrilegious rites'; 'not a pagan transgression') but merely societal entertainment in a neutral sense. How reliable can we consider these voices described by the Bishop of Ravenna? Are these the voices of ordinary Christians who preferred to participate in local festivals and imbued these events with meanings that differed from those assigned to them by their Christian

---

19 Petrus Chrysologus, *Sermo* 155.3: '*Defleamus, fratres, et eos qui talia sunt secuti, et nos evasisse talia caelitus gaudeamus.*'
20 Petrus Chrysologus, *Sermo* 155.4: '*Haec diximus, fratres, ut proderemus causam, quare facientes hodie quae talia sustinemus, faciant gentiles deos suos, et faciant tales, qui videntibus et horrori sint et pudori.*'
21 Petrus Chrysologus, *Sermo* 155.5: '*. . . si modo non eorum exspectaculis polluantur, si eorum non inquinentur adtactu, si huiusmodi fugiunt de adsensione discrimen, quia factis semper est aequalis adsensus . . .*' Petrus enhances his admonition with the exhortation from the Apostle Paul (Rom 1:32). In a similar way, another bishop, Maximus of Turin (c. 380–465), maintained that the silent approval of 'idolatry' defiled the entire community, not only those who performed the rites (*exercentes*), but also those who lived nearby (*habitantes*) and those who watched (*intuentes*) them. The pollution penetrated those who are involved in idolatry, those who are aware of idolatry and those who keep quiet. Maximus Taurinensis, *Sermo* 107. 2 (*CCSL* 23): *Grande igitur est idolatria: polluit exercentes polluit habitantes polluit intuentes; penetrat ad ministros penetrat ad conscios penetrat ad tacentes.* Maximus' reproach is particularly targeted at landlords, who should prevent their tenants from engaging in idolatrous practices. Similar rebukes are found in Maximus' *Sermo* 106. For further discussion, see Maijastina Kahlos, 'Polluted by Sacrifices: Christian Repugnance at Sacrificial Rituals in Late Antiquity', in *Ancient and Medieval Religion in Practice*, Ville Vuolanto and Sari Katajala-Peltomaa (eds) (Rome: Acta Instituti Romani Finlandiae, 2013): 161–3, and for traditional practices in Maximus' sermons in general, see Andreas Merkt, *Maximus I. von Turin: Die Verkündigung eines Bischofs der frühen Reichskirche im zeitgeschichtlichen, gesellschaftlichen und liturgischen Kontext* (Leiden: Brill, 1997): 111, 139, 198.
22 Petrus Chrysologus, *Sermo* 155.5: '*Sed dicit aliquis: non sunt haec sacrilegiorum studia, vota sunt haec iocorum; et hoc esse novitatis laetitiam, non vetustatis errorem; esse hoc anni principium, non gentilitatis offensam.*'

leaders? We have similar protests in other bishops' sermons, as we will see in the discussion of Augustine below. These views are conveyed by ecclesiastical writers who probably portray the opposing views in a selective way – a straw man that can be conveniently refuted. Therefore, protesting voices of ordinary Christians can sometimes be heard, though inexorably as caricatures, from the sermons and treatises of fourth- and fifth-century bishops. The perspective is constantly that of the bishop who formulates the wording according to his dichotomous worldview of sacrileges and entertainments. However, these straw men construed by ecclesiastical writers needed to appear credible, at least to some extent, in order to function effectively in their rhetoric. Thus, even though sermons construct the voices of parishioners that do not have an exact reflection in social reality, they needed to have some point of comparison. As Rebillard points out in his discussion of the North African ecclesiastical writers, Tertullian, Cyprian and Augustine, the arguments needed to sound plausible to the audience: 'in order for the process of communication to happen, interaction must take place'.[23]

Petrus Chrysologus replies to these protests, maintaining that these people were in error; these celebrations were not mere enjoyments, but crimes. He labels them *impietas*, *sacrilegium* and *piaculum*. Consequently, in Petrus' interpretation the *Kalendae Ianuariae* falls outside the category of neutral or societal merriment. Instead, he insists upon a choice between joking with the devil and rejoicing with Christ.[24] Furthermore, he admonishes – as an indication of humanity and brotherly love – his listeners to restrain those who are running to perdition in this way. The father must restrain his son and the master his servant, but from this traditional hierarchy Petrus Chrysologus widens the perspective even to the mutual duty among relatives, citizens and humans to restrain one another and to the overall duty of Christians to restrain all who err with these celebrations.[25]

What were people actually doing in these practices that Petrus Chrysologus condemns? He does not reveal them in detail but only refers to them with the eloquence of repudiation. As mentioned above, he depicts the practices vaguely as horror and disgrace, and connected with the old gods and myths. Furthermore, towards the end of his sermon, he describes people making themselves comparable to beasts, putting themselves equal to draught animals, turning themselves to cattle and presenting themselves as demons.[26] Is this equation with animals a general rebuke, of a type that was so abundant in ancient polemic against religious

---

23 Rebillard, *Christians and Their Many Identities*: 6, 75.
24 Petrus Chrysologus, *Sermo* 155.5: '*Erras, homo! Non sunt, non sunt haec ludicra, sunt crimina. Quis de inpietate ludit? De sacrilegio quis iocatur? Piaculum quis dicit risum? Qui iocari voluerit cum diabolo, non poterit gaudere cum Christo, Nemo cum serpente securus ludit: nemo cum diabolo iocatur inpune.*'
25 Petrus Chrysologus, *Sermo* 155.6: '... *abstrahamus eos, qui sic ad perditionem currunt ... Abstrahat ergo pater filium, servum dominus, parens parentem, civem civis, homo hominem, christianus omnes qui se bestiis conpararunt, exaequarunt iumentis, aptaverunt pecudibus, daemonibus formaverunt.*'
26 See n. 25.

and ethnic groups, or is it meant as a concrete reference to the practices? Peter Brown has connected Petrus Chrysologus' rebukes with the procession accompanying the nomination of the new consuls in which actors were dressed as planets (hence Petrus' reference to the old gods); in this interpretation, the target of the bishop's attack would be the state-run imperial side of the New Year celebrations.[27] Petrus may have been speaking of theatrical performances held on the *Kalendae Ianuariae*. Another possibility lies with the processions of masquerades often reproved in other late antique bishops' writings. In these processions, people danced and sang, masked as various gods and animals; we have references to people acting as Saturn, Jupiter, Hercules, Diana and Vulcan, but also as domestic animals and wild animals, especially elk.[28]

Whatever people were doing, the essential point in this discussion is that Petrus interprets and condemns the practices as idolatrous and sacrilegious, thus investing them with religious content, while the fictive voices of the ordinary people have a divergent interpretation: they see the celebrations as neutral societal merriment.

Augustine of Hippo on Urban Celebrations

Similar construed responses of ordinary Christians are found in Augustine's sermons in which he condemns his parishioners for resorting to traditional healing practices, as well as for taking part in urban celebrations. For example, Augustine reports on some Christians who defend themselves, insisting that they are good Christians and that the sign of cross that they have received on their foreheads as catechumens protects them from the pollution of idolatry.[29] In another example, Augustine reports on Christians who think that they can visit idols and consult

---

27 Peter Brown, 'The Problem of Christianization', *Proceedings of the British Academy* 82 (1993): 99; Peter Brown, 'Aspects of the Christianisation of the Roman World', The Tanner Lecture on Human Values, Delivered at Cambridge University, 22, 23 and 24 November 1993. Available online at http://www.tannerlectures.utah.edu/_documents/a-to-z/b/Brown95.pdf : 129–30 (accessed 23 October 2014). Petrus' reference (*Sermo* 155.4) to people who make themselves images of god (*qui simulacra faciunt semet ipsos*) might corroborate this interpretation.

28 E.g. Maximus Taurinensis, *Sermo* 16: *pecudes portenta*; Caesarius Arelatensis, *Sermo* 192.2: '*qui cervulum facientes in ferarum se velint habitus commutare*'. Pacian of Barcelona, *Par.*, PL 13 1081, '*Puto nescierant cervulum facere nisi illis reprehedendo monstrassem!*' According to Jerome (*Vir. ill.* 106), this Pacianus wrote a (no longer extant) tractate called *Cervus* against the habit of using masks in the New Year celebrations. Ambrose of Milan (*Job* 2.1.5) condemned the habit of elk masks in the New Year festivities. Ecclesiastical writers saw these processions as the pomp of the devil. Grig, 'Interpreting'; Meslin, *La fête des kalends*: 74–82.

29 Augustine, *Sermo* 301A.8. For the social life of North African pagans and Christians in Augustine's time, see Claude Lepelley, 'Formes païennes de la sociabilité en Afrique au temps de Saint Augustin', in *Sociabilité, pouvoirs et société: Actes du Colloque de Rouen 24/26, novembre 198*, Françoise Thélamon (ed.) (Rouen: Publications de l'Université de Rouen, 1987): 99–103; Claude Lepelley, 'Le lieu des valeurs communes. La cité terrain neutre entre païens et chrétiens dans l'Afrique romaine tardive', in *Idéologies et valeurs civiques dans le Monde Romain: Hommage à Claude Lepelley*, Hervé Inglebert (ed.) (Paris: Picard, 2002): 278–83; Ramsay MacMullen, *The Second Church: Popular Christianity, A.D. 200–400* (WGRWS; Atlanta: SBL, 2009): 51–67.

magi and soothsayers but who, at the same time, consider themselves good Christians. They claim: 'I have not abandoned the church for I am *catholicus*'.[30] Furthermore, in a sermon on the resurrection of the dead, Augustine confronts the counter-arguments raised within his congregation. Some people had appealed to a passage from the Book of Tobit (Tob. 4:18: *Lay out thy bread and thy wine upon the burial of a just man*) as a justification for food and wine offerings at the tombs. With all his authority as bishop and interpreter of Scripture, Augustine sets out to refute this challenge by his parishioners and show that offerings to the deceased were a habit of pagans (*consuetudinem hanc esse paganorum*).[31]

Here again we can presume that, even though these voices are Augustine's rhetorical constructions, they have some vague point of comparison with North African social life. The responses of ordinary Christians to the rebukes of their bishops varied. Some were distressed, whereas others saw no contradiction between urban entertainment and their Christian faith. What probably caused more anxiety were the reproaches of bishops who invested traditional urban celebrations with categorically cultic 'pagan' meaning and forced their parishioners to make either/or choices.

These choices are often described with intense expressions and violent metaphors. As Augustine (in *Enarratio in psalmum* 96 in 399) sets himself against attending theatrical performances and insists upon abstaining from them, he enhances his admonitions by speaking of the sword for separation (*gladius ad separationem*) and the fire for burning (*ignis ad ustionem*). The sword will separate Christians from evil habits, their past life and even ancestry, whereas the fire will burn their adversaries who have abandoned God and cling to idolatry. In Augustine's preaching it is stressed that every Christian is more or less attached to the pagan past of which one should rid oneself – and not only oneself but also one's fellow Christians. Like Petrus Chrysologus, Augustine admonishes his listeners to direct other Christians away from the theatre spectacles.[32] This kind of help for fellow souls was not always very welcome: we hear of disturbances that broke out when more zealous Christians tried to prevent other Christians from taking part in urban spectacles and celebrations.[33]

---

30 Augustine, *Enarrat. Ps.* 88.2.14.
31 Augustine, *Sermo* 361.6: '*Et quod obiciunt quidam de Scripturis: "Frange panem tuum, et effunde vinum tuum super sepulcra iustorum, et ne tradas eum iniustis"; non est quidem de hoc disserendum, sed tamen posse dico intellegere fideles quod dictum est. Nam quemadmodum ista fideles faciant religiose erga memorias suorum notum est fidelibus.*' For the debate on the practices at the tombs, see Maijastina Kahlos, '*Comissationes et ebrietates*: Church leaders against Banqueting at *Martyria* and at Tombs', in *Ad itum liberum: Essays in honour of Anne Helttula*, Outi Merisalo and Raija Vainio (eds) (Jyväskylä: University of Jyväskylä, Department of Languages, 2007): 13–23 and Rebillard, *Christians and Their Many Identities*: 70–1.
32 Augustine, *Enarrat. Ps.* 96.7–10.
33 For the conflicts between pagans and Christians in North Africa, see Michele Renee Salzman, 'Rethinking Pagan-Christian Violence', in *Violence in Late Antiquity: Perceptions and Practises*, H. A. Drake (ed.) (Aldershot: Ashgate, 2006): 274–77; David Riggs, 'Christianising the Rural Communities in Late Roman Africa', in H. A. Drake (ed.), *Violence in Late Antiquity*: 297–308.

Augustine also worried about the popular celebrations during the *Kalendae Ianuariae:* in a sermon on that very day he warns his listeners against taking part in what he describes as an outright pagan celebration (*sollemnitas gentium*). He highlights, furthermore, the worldly and carnal character of the festival:

> Now, if this feast of the pagans which is celebrated today with such joy of the world and of the flesh, with the singing of meaningless and base songs, with banquets and shameful dances, if these things which the pagans do in the celebration of this false festival do not please you, then you shall be gathered from among the nations.[34]

Augustine encourages his listeners to separate themselves from pagans in their beliefs, hopes and love: if one does not believe what the pagans believe, if one does not hope for what they hope for, if one does not love what they love, one is congregated (*congregaris*) apart from pagans, segregated (*segregaris*) and separated (*separaris*) from pagans. Augustine reminds his listeners that it is far more important to keep a separation of minds (*separatio mentis*) than to worry about any physical mixture (*commixtio corporalis*) with pagans.[35] He construes this separation by distinguishing practices as characteristic to pagans and proper to Christians: during the *Kalendae Ianuariae*, the pagans offer presents (*strenae*), but Christians should give alms. Similarly, pagans relish extravagant ditties but Christians should cherish the lessons of the Scripture; pagans run to the theatre but Christians should go to the church; when pagans get drunk, Christians should fast.[36]

Augustine remarks that he is addressing the *true* Christians, who should live in a different way (*aliter*) to pagans and show their distinctive faith, hope and love by divergent customs. The celebrations and spectacles delight demons, Augustine states, giving an exhaustive list of them: the songs of vanity, the worthless spectacles,

---

34 Augustine, *Sermo* 198.1: '*Et modo si sollemnitas gentium, quae fit hodierno die in laetitia saeculi atque carnali, in strepitu vanissimarum et turpissimarum cantionum, in conviviis et saltationibus turpibus, in celebratione ipsius falsae festivitatis, si ea quae agunt gentes non vos delectent, congregabimini ex gentibus.*' (Muldowney (trans.) 1959: 55). A slightly different version of the sermon is found in Augustine, *Sermo* 198augm. = 62 Mainz = 26 Dolbeau (in which *in conviviis et saltationibus turpibus* is missing).

35 Augustine, *Sermo* 198.1–2 augm. = 62 Mainz = 26.1–2 Dolbeau: '*Si non credis quod credunt gentes, non speras quod sperant gentes, non amas quod amant gentes; congregaris de gentibus, segregaris, hoc est separaris de gentibus.*' Augustine stresses his admonition concerning separation with the repeated pairs of words *congregari – segregari, misceri – separari, commixtio – separatio* and enhances his argument with the recurrent references to the psalm verse 105.47: '*Salva nos, domine deus noster, et congrega nos de gentibus, ut confiteamur nomini sancto tuo.*' Cf. Augustine, *Civ.* 1.35 in which the mingling of the *civitates* is stressed.

36 Augustine, *Sermo* 198.2: '*Dant illi strenas, date vos eleemosynas. Avocantur illi cantionibus luxuriarum, avocate vos sermonibus Scripturarum: currunt illi ad theatrum, vos ad ecclesiam: inebriantur illi, vos ieiunate.*' Augustine stresses *strenae*, playing dice and drunkenness as pagan characteristics: '*Acturus es celebrationem strenarum, sicut paganus, lusurus alea, et inebriaturus te …*' For *strenae*, see n. 13.

the shamefulness of theatres, the madness of circus and the violent competitions. Taking part in the shows and feasts is the same as offering incense to demons in one's heart.[37]

Ecclesiastical leaders such as Augustine understood that different people invested urban celebrations with different meanings. In a sermon from 399 or later, referring to the Apostle Paul's discussion in *1 Corinthians* 8, Augustine acknowledges that festivals and spectacles could be invested with diverse significations according to the strength of one's faith. 'Firm' brothers knew that the gods connected with the festivals were not real deities and thus, for them, these celebrations were not idolatry. In modern terminology, they did not regard the communal celebrations as religious or sacral. However, this caused problems for 'weaker' brothers who could go astray by thinking that their firm brothers venerated idols in these celebrations, that is, invested the feasts with religious or sacral content.[38]

Here it is the interpretation of the content and intention of activities that causes the problems, not participation as such. This is by no means a new issue: the debate about participation in pagan activities can be traced as far back as the Apostle Paul. In *1 Corinthians* 8, the dispute concerns eating the food offered to the gods. According to Paul, those Christians ('the stronger brothers') who had already reached *gnosis* encountered no harm in eating sacrificial food because they knew that idols were not real gods. However, those Christians ('the weaker brothers') who had not yet attained *gnosis* were in danger of understanding participation in eating sacrificial food as a cultic act and, consequently, risked falling back into idolatry. Paul mainly worries about the weaker brothers' lapse into idolatry but is also concerned about the pollution caused by the cultic communion (*koinonia*) with gods – for him, demons.[39] What is at stake here is the intention

---

37 Augustine, *Sermo* 198.3: '*Ego nunc Christianis veris loquor . . . aliter vivite, et distantem fidem, spem, et charitatem vestram distantibus moribus approbate . . . Etenim illa daemonia delectantur canticis vanitatis, delectantur nugatorio spectaculo, et turpitudinibus variis theatrorum, insania circi, crudelitate amphitheatri, certaminibus animosis eorum qui pro pestilentibus hominibus lites et contentiones usque ad inimicitias suspiciunt, pro mimo, pro histrione pro pantomimo, pro auriga, pro venatore. Ista facientes, quasi thura ponunt daemoniis de cordibus suis.*' Augustine enhances his admonitions with 2 Cor 6:14–16 on the opposition of light and darkness and 1 Cor 10:20 on the separation from demons (*Nolo vos socios fieri daemoniorum*).
38 Augustine, *Sermo* 62(4).7. Peter Brown, 'St. Augustine's Attitude to Religious Coercion', *JRS* 54 (1964): 266 dates sermon 62 to the years 399 to 401.
39 For a discussion and a survey of the abundant scholarship on Paul's attitudes, see Johannes Woyke, 'Das Bekenntnis zum einzig allwirksamen Gott und Herrn und die Dämonisierung von Fremdkulten: Monolatrischer und polylatrischer Monotheismus in *1. Korinther* 8 und 10', in *Gruppenreligionen im römischen Reich*, Jörg Rüpke (ed.), (STAC 33; Tübingen: Mohr Siebeck, 2007): 104–9 and Peter Lampe, 'Die dämonologischen Implikationen von I Korinther 8 und 10 vor dem Hintergrund paganer Zeugnisse', in *Die Dämonen: Die Dämonologie der israelitisch-jüdischen und frühchristlichen Literatur im Kontext ihrer Umwelt*, Armin Lange, Hermann Lichtenberger and K. F. Diethard Römheld (eds) (Tübingen: Mohr Siebeck, 2003): 594–9. For *koinonia* in the ancient Greek context, see, Folkert T. van Straten, 'Ancient Greek Animal Sacrifice: Gift, Ritual Slaughter, Communion, Food Supply, or What? Some Thoughts on Simple Explanations of a Complex Ritual', in *La cuisine et l'autel: Les sacrifices en questions dans les sociétés de la*

and interpretation of the activity: Christians were allowed to eat anything as long as no cultic communion with 'pagan' gods was implied.

Paul's distinction between stronger and weaker brothers was used by later Christian leaders in their discussions of the boundaries between being a proper Christian and participation in the celebrations of the surrounding society in general: what should be regarded as a mere presence in everyday life rituals and thus harmless for a Christian, and what should be seen as active involvement and thus detrimental?[40] Tertullian represents the hard line: strictly speaking, Christians should not even see idolatrous acts, but as they cannot avoid living in the 'pagan' world, their presence in festivities was to be seen as a service to a human (that is, the host of the feast), not to an idol.[41]

The Apostle Paul's words on sacrificial food offered a way of discussing the proper Christian conduct of life, as the homilies of John Chrysostom in late fourth-century Antioch show. John Chrysostom condemned Christian attendance at the races, comparing the Antiochians, who considered it innocuous to go the races, to the Corinthians who saw no problem in eating sacrificial food.[42]

As we can see in these debates on Christian participation, defining and constantly redefining the content and signification of urban celebrations was an issue of authority.[43] Church leaders used their episcopal and spiritual authority to enhance their stricter interpretations of what was to be considered proper Christian behaviour and what idolatry (that is, pagan activity).[44] We hear the fictive voices of Christians defending their attendance at what they thought

---

Méditerranée ancienne, Stella Georgoudi, Renée Koch Piettre and Francis Schmidt (eds) (Turnhout: Brepols, 2005): 24. For Paul's views and their interpretation in early Christian contexts from the viewpoint of commensality, see Éric Rebillard, '"To Live with the Heathen, but not Die with Them": The Issue of Commensality between Christians and non-Christians in the First Five Centuries', in *Transformation of Religious Practices in Late Antiquity,* Éric Rebillard (ed.) (Farnham: Ashgate Variorum, 2013): 115–41.

40 For further discussion, see Kahlos, 'Polluted by Sacrifices': 164–5.
41 Tertullian, *Idol.*16–17. However, in the case of 'pagan' sacrifices, there was compromise for Tertullian. For everyday urban life and Tertullian, see also the contribution of Salminen in this volume.
42 E.g. John Chrysostom, *Hom. 1 Cor.*, 24.3–5 (*PG* 61, 201–5); *Hom. 1 Cor.,* 20. 11, PG 61, 168; *Catech. ult.* 6. 16 (in Jean Chrysostome, *Huit Catéchèses baptismales inédites, Sources Chrétiennes* 50, A. Wenger (ed.), Paris 1957: 223). For a discussion on John Chrysostom, see Sandwell, *Religious Identity,* 79: 192–3. See also the contribution of Anna-Liisa Tolonen in this volume.
43 For the issue of authority, see Peter Brown, 'Christianization and religious conflict', in *The Late Empire, A.D. 337–425: The Cambridge Ancient History vol. 13,* Averil Cameron and Peter Garnsey (eds) (Cambridge: Cambridge University Press, 1998): 662–3; Peter Brown, *Authority and the Sacred: Aspects of the Christianization of the Roman World* (Cambridge: Cambridge University Press, 1995): 23–4; and Todd E. Klutz, 'The Rhetoric of Science in *The Rise of Christianity*: A Response to Rodney Stark's Sociological Account of Christianization', *JECS* 6.2 (1998): 183–4.
44 Aptly summed up by Peter Garnsey and Caroline Humfress, *The Evolution of the Late Antique World* (Cambridge: Orchard Academic, 2001): 142: 'To a Christian "over-achiever" like St Augustine the boundaries between proper and improper theology and religious worship appeared clear-cut; to his Christian parishioners in Hippo who danced and drank their way through the traditional religious calendar, less so.'

were mere amusements (that is, neutral activities) and even challenging their bishops' authority.[45]

The contents and meanings of practices were contested and negotiated amid conflicting and divergent interpretations. The same person could take part both in traditional ('pagan') and Christian celebrations and see no difficulty there. The notion of situational identities within an individual explains what outwardly may look like an inconsistency in an individual's behaviour. An individual does not have one unambiguous identity but different identities that are 'activated' according to varying situations.[46] As Rebillard argues, late antique Christians did not necessarily understand their activities as being distinguished along the two lines of the religious and the secular.[47] However, many bishops insisted upon a choice made between these lines and upon identity building that diminished the space in which Christians acted. The reactions of ecclesiastical leaders were connected with the contested situations in which urban space and time were competed for. Individual Christians often found themselves in the middle of pressures coming from various directions: their bishops, city councillors in the cities and landowners in the countryside, as well as local magistrates. Pressure also came from the central government and the emperors.

The Emperor and the Needs of the People

The imperial government defined the content and significance of urban celebrations in a manner which diverged from the delineations of ecclesiastical leaders. For emperors and their administrations, many festivities were valuable for maintaining societal cohesion, as fourth-century imperial legislation shows. In many cases they wanted to retain traditional festivities. For example, in a law of 399, it was declared that emperors would not accept the abolition of the celebrations of citizens and the common merriments of all people (*festos conventus civium et communem omnium laetitiam*); therefore, these amusements could continue according to custom, but without sacrifices or condemned superstition (*absque ullo sacrificio atque ulla superstitione damnabili*). The continuation of the festivities was justified by the antiquity of the custom (*vetus consuetudo*) and the popularity of the merriments (*communis omnium laetitia*; *populo voluptates*).[48]

---

45 To be specific, the dividing line did not necessarily always go between strict leaders and temperate ordinary Christians but it is more accurate to speak of degrees of moderation. Some so-called ordinary Christians could speak in favour of more austere attitudes towards worldly merriments and several bishops might advocate a more permissive stance on celebrations.
46 Lahire, *The Plural Actor*: 11–31; Brubaker, *Ethnicity without Groups*.
47 Rebillard, *Christians and Their Many Identities*: 62, 70, 96; see also Lim, 'Inventing Secular Space': 77–8 who speaks of multiple and ever-changing meanings.
48 *CTh* 16.10.17 (in 399) addressed to the proconsul of Africa: '... *ut profanos ritus iam salubri lege submovimus, ita festos conventus civium et communem omnium laetitiam non patimur submoveri. Unde absque ullo sacrificio atque ulla superstitione damnabili exhiberi populo voluptates secundum veterem consuetudinem, iniri etiam festa convivia, si quando exigunt publica vota, decernimus.*' See also n. 14. See also Lim, 'Christianization': 508.

Meddling in the Middle? 25

In another edict of 382, addressed to the *dux* of Osrhoene, it was declared that a temple in the region of Osrhoene was to be permitted to stay open and the cult images in it were to be left untouched. It is specifically mentioned that the *dux* would take care of the preservation of all festivities (*omni votorum celebritate servata*). Again, the festivities were allowed to continue but without sacrifices. The emperors justify the preservation of the temple and its images in light of the popularity of festivities as well as the artistic value of the images.[49]

That is not to say that the emperors did not set limitations on popular celebrations. Theodosius I and his successors Honorius, Arcadius and Theodosius II set limitations for games and theatre shows on Sundays and Christian feast days. One of the reasons was to prevent rivalry between the traditional entertainments and the Christian rituals by avoiding coinciding feasts and holidays. A law of 392, forbidding circus races on Sundays, states in a straightforward way that the prohibition is given 'in order that no gathering to the spectacles may divert people from the reverend mysteries of Christianity'. The emperor and his power nonetheless sat outside all restrictions since the birthdays of emperors were an exception to this rule.[50] A law of 425 forbade games and theatrical performances on Sundays, Christmas, Epiphany, Easter, Pentecost and a few other Christian feast days, and reminded even those still 'enslaved by the madness of Jewish impiety or the error and insanity of senseless paganism' that there was 'a time for prayer and a time for pleasure' (*aliud esse supplicationum noverint tempus, aliud voluptatum*).[51]

Furthermore, as these laws show, festivities were permitted only when divested of sacrificial rituals. In fourth- and fifth-century legislation, many practices and rituals were allowed to continue (even encouraged when loyalty to the emperor would be shown) when stripped of sacrifices, especially blood sacrifices. For instance, in the consular games in the circus, imperial images were habitually

---

49 *CTh* 16.10.8 (in 382): '*Aedem olim frequentiae dedicatam coetui et iam populo quoque communem, in qua simulacra feruntur posita artis pretio quam divinitate metienda iugiter patere publici consilii auctoritate decernimus neque huic rei obreptivum officere sinimus oraculum. Ut conventu urbis et frequenti coetu videatur, experientia tua omni votorum celebritate servata auctoritate nostri ita patre templum permittat oraculi, ne illic prohibitorum usus sacrificiorum huius occasione aditus permissus esse credatur.*' Similarly, *CTh* 16.10.3 (in 346) speaks of 'the regular performance of long established amusements for the Roman people'. See also Lim, 'Inventing Secular Space': 72.
50 *CTh* 2.8.20 in 392: '*Festis solis diebus circensium sunt inhibenda certamina, quo christianae legis veneranda mysteria nullus spectaculorum concursus avertat, praeter clementiae nostrae natalicios dies.*' See also *CTh* 15.5.2 in 386 (forbidding spectacles on Sundays).
51 *CTh* 15.5.5 (in 435): '*Dominico, qui septimanae totius primus est dies, et natali adque epifaniorum Christi, paschae etiam et quinquagesimae diebus, quamdiu caelestis lumen lavacri imitantia novam sancti baptismatis lucem vestimentis testantur, quo tempore et commemoratio apostolicae passionis totius christianitatis magistrae a cunctis iure celebratur, omni theatrorum adque circensium voluptate per universas urbes earundem populis denegata totae christianorum ac fidelium mentes dei cultibus occupentur. Si qui etiamnunc vel Iudaeae impietatis amentia vel stolidae paganitatis errore adque insania detinentur, aliud esse supplicationum noverint tempus, aliud voluptatum.*'

venerated. In a law of Emperor Theodosius II aimed at regulating the rituals connected to imperial images, the magistrate should not employ 'any vainglorious heights of adoration' (*sine adorationis ambitioso fastigio*).[52] What the 'vainglorious heights of adoration' meant was left to a magistrate to decide in each case.

With these decrees the imperial government aimed at balancing the demands of ecclesiastical leaders and the needs of the urban and rural populations. The attempts to 'clean up' those features of traditional celebrations that were disturbing to many Christians, usually sacrifices, can be depicted as a compromise. This cleaning up could also involve eradicating 'superstition', as in the above mentioned law of 399, or in the rescript of Hispellum in 333/335 concerning the veneration paid to Emperor Constantine's family.[53] This superstition (*superstitio*) was a vague term that could be interpreted to mean almost anything from traditional sacrifices to illegal magic. Its interpretation on the local administrative level was obviously a matter of authority.[54]

A similar 'cleaning up' is connected with the idea of divesting temples and shrines of their cultic content but preserving their aesthetic value. In the early fifth-century *Contra orationem Symmachi*, the Christian poet Prudentius encourages his contemporaries to purify pagan monuments:

> Wash you the marbles that are bespattered and stained with putrid blood, you nobles. Let your statues, the works of great artists, be allowed to rest clean; let these be the fairest ornaments of our country and let no debased usage pollute the monuments of art and turn it into sin.[55]

---

52 *CTh* 15.4.1 (in 425): '*Si quando nostrae statuae vel imagines eriguntur seu diebus, ut adsolet, festis sive communibus, adsit iudex sine adorationis ambitioso fastigio, ut ornamentum diei vel loco et nostrae recordationi sui probet accessisse praesentiam. Ludis quoque simulacra proposita tantum in animis concurrentum mentisque secretis nostrum numen et laudes vigere demonstrent; excedens cultura hominum dignitatem superno numini reservetur.*' For the allegiance paid to the emperor or emperor's image, see Kahlos, 'The Emperor's New Images: how to honour the Emperor in the Christian Empire,' in *Emperors and the Divine: Rome and Beyond*, Maijastina Kahlos (ed.). Helsinki: Helsinki Collegium for Advanced Studies', forthcoming.

53 *CIL* XI 5265=*ILS* 705. The inscription was an imperial response to a petition from the inhabitants of Hispellum; Constantine approved the continuation of emperor worship, with restrictions ('should not be defiled by the deceits of any contagious *superstitio*') which have usually been interpreted as referring to sacrifices. For a discussion, see Lee, *Pagans and Christians*: 92–3 and Cecconi, 'Il rescritto di Spello: Prospettive recenti.' In *Costantino prima e dopo Costantino: Constantine before and after Constantine*, Giorgio Bonamente, Noel Lenski and Rita Lizzi Testa (eds), (Bari: Edipuglia, 2012): 273–90.

54 Michele Renee Salzman, '*Superstitio* in the *Codex Theodosianus* and the Persecution of Pagans', *VC* 41 (1987): 172–88; Maijastina Kahlos, *Forbearance and Compulsion: Rhetoric of Tolerance and Intolerance in Late Antiquity* (London: Duckworth, 2009): 101; Garnsey and Humfress, *Evolution of the Late Antique World*: 163–4.

55 Prudentius *C. Symm.* 1.501–5: '*marmora tabenti respergine tincta lavate / o proceres! Liceat statuas consistere puras, / artificum magnorum opera; haec pulcherrima nostrae / ornamenta fiant patriae nec decolor usus / in vitium versae monumenta coinquinet artis,*' H. J. Thomson (trans.) (modified), *LCL* 387.

These words belong to a fictional speech of Emperor Theodosius I in which he admonishes the senate to convert to Christianity. Prudentius – with the Emperor as his mouthpiece – insists that ancient temples must be allowed to remain, but cleansed of their original cultic purposes. The temples and images within them now stand for their artistic value, no longer as cultic objects.[56] Similar discussions were held on the aesthetic value of the old literature and education for Christians; in these debates Basil of Caesarea and Augustine of Hippo took a moderate stance, emphasizing the 'correct use' of the 'pagan' achievements.[57]

As mentioned above, the emperors tried to achieve a balance between the various forces that pulled in many directions. Bishops representing divergent Christian inclinations and regions exerted pressure on the imperial government, defending their own interests. Ecclesiastical councils made demands to the emperors to limit 'pagan' feasting and even to put an end to many traditional celebrations. For instance, the Council of Carthage (in 401) insisted that the emperors should forbid public banquets (*convivia*) that originated from 'pagan' error. It was declared that 'pagans' forced Christians to celebrate these banquets and this even looked like a second persecution in the era of Christian emperors.[58] The disapproving tone of the church council reminds us of the condemnations by Augustine and Petrus Chrysologus discussed earlier. Local bishops defined public banqueting as a religious activity – originating from 'pagan' error and being imposed upon Christians by 'pagans' – whoever these 'pagans' were, adherents of old polytheistic cults or 'weak' Christian brothers.

The Emperor and the Middle Ground?

Were Christian emperors looking for a neutral or even secular space with their compromises and attempts to find a balance between different interest groups? As I argued in the introduction to this chapter, the terms 'neutral' or 'secular' may be anachronistic in depicting late Roman society. Nonetheless, the emperor's position in

---

56 On the preservation of temples and images, see Claude Lepelley, 'The survival and fall of the classical city in Late Roman Africa', in *The City in Late Antiquity*, John Rich (ed.) (London: Routledge, 1992): 59; Salzman, 'The Christianization of sacred time and sacred space,' in *Transformations of Urbs Roma in Late Antiquity*, W. V. Harris (ed.), *JRASup* 33. Portsmouth, RI: JRA 1999: 131–2; Alan Cameron, *The Last Pagans of Rome* (Oxford: Oxford University Press, 2011): 348; Luke Lavan, 'Political Talismans? Residual "Pagan" Statues in Late Antique Public Space', in *The Archaeology of Late Antique 'Paganism'*, Luke Lavan and Michael Mulryan (eds) (Leiden: Brill, 2011): 442.
57 Philip Rousseau, 'Christian Culture and the Swine's Husks: Jerome, Augustine, and Paulinus', in *The Limits of Ancient Christianity: Essays on Late Antique Thought and Culture in Honor of R. A. Markus*, William E. Klingshirn and Mark Vessey (eds) (Ann Arbor MI: University of Michigan Press, 1999): 172–87.
58 *Concilium Carthaginense* can. 60–1 (in 401) (*CCSL* 149: 196–7): '*Illud etiam petendum ut, quoniam contra praecepta divina convivia multis in locis exercentur, quae ab errore gentili adtracta sunt, ita ut nunc a paganis christiani ad haec celebranda cogantur – ex qua re temporibus christianorum imperatorum persecutio altera fieri occulte videatur.*'

the middle ground in the inter-religious and inter-sectarian disputes was intensely discussed in the late fourth century.

In his account of Emperor Valentinian I (364–375), the Roman historian Ammianus Marcellinus writes in a positive tone about the remarkable moderation of his reign. Valentinian remained in the middle between the divergences of religions (*inter religionum diversitates medius stetit*); he did not harass anyone or order anyone to worship this or that divinity, nor did he try to bend the necks of his subjects with intimidating edicts in favour of his own religion, but rather let religious issues be as he found them.[59] Ammianus' appreciation for Valentinian here is worth noting since he otherwise depicts Valentinian as a paranoid ruler, especially in connection with the magic trials of the 370s.[60] We know that at the beginning of their reign in 364, Valentinian I and his co-emperor and brother Valens (364–378) issued a (no longer extant) law in which they granted everyone the freedom to embrace any form of worship they wished.[61] Furthermore, the fifth-century ecclesiastical historian Socrates Scholasticus states that, even though Valentinian was Nicene Christian, he did not set out to pressurize 'Arians'. Socrates emphatically contrasts Valentinian with his co-ruler Valens, whom he depicts as the 'Arian' oppressor of Nicene Christians.[62]

R. Malcolm Errington is probably correct in suggesting that labels such as 'Nicene' and 'Arian' hardly fit the emperors Valentinian and Valens who, above all, were interested in retaining social order and discipline in the Empire. It is the ecclesiastical writers for whom doctrinal issues were the main concern and who interpreted the policies of Valentinian and Valens along sectarian lines. Valentinian in the West succeeded better than his brother in the East: in the West, dominated by Nicene bishops, there were fewer disputes to solve, while in the East doctrinal disputes were impossible to control.[63] In the East, the emperor was in a position in which, as Noel Lenski puts it, 'no one would envy Valens the woes he faced with the Christian church'.[64] Valens' policy of exiling Nicene bishops

---

59 Ammianus 30.9.5: '*Postremo hoc moderamine principatus inclaruit, quod inter religionum diversitates, medius stetit, nec quemquam inquietavit, neque ut hoc coleretur, imperavit aut illud: nec interdictis minacibus, subiectorum cervicem ad id quod voluit, inclinabat, sed intemeratas reliquit has partes, ut repperit.*'

60 For Ammianus, criticism of Valentinian's reign, see Mark Humphries, '*Nec metu nec adulandi foeditate constricta*: The Image of Valentinian I from Symmachus to Ammianus', in *The Late Roman World and Its Historian*, Jan Willem Drijvers and David Hunt (eds) (London: Routledge, 1999): 117–26. For accusations of magic in the reign of Valentinian I and Valens, see Noel Lenski, *Failure of Empire: Valens and the Roman State in the Fourth Century A.D.* (Berkeley: University of California Press, 2002): 25–6, 105–6, 211–13; Rita Lizzi, *Senatori, popolo, papi: Il governo di Roma al tempo dei Valentiniani* (Bari: Edipuglia, 2004): 209–35; John F. Matthews, *The Roman Empire of Ammianus Marcellinus* (London: Duckworth, 1989): 210–25; Hermann Funke, 'Majestäts- und Magieprozesse bei Ammianus Marcellinus', *JbaC* 10 (1967): 165–75.

61 The proclamation is not extant but Valentinian I and Valens refer to it in another law (in 371): CTh 9.16.9: '*Testes sunt leges a me in exordio imperii mei datae, quibus unicuique, quod animo inbibisset, colendi libera facultas tributa est.*'

62 Socrates, *Hist. eccl.* 4.1; cf. Sozomen, *Hist. eccl.* 6.6 and 6.21; Theodoret, *Hist. eccl.* 5.20.

63 R. Malcolm Errington, *Roman Imperial Policy from Julian to Theodosius* (Chapel Hill: The University of North Carolina Press, 2006): 188–9.

64 Lenski, *Failure of Empire*: 234.

was a continuation of the age-old Roman tradition of keeping order in the cities by banishing troublemakers.[65]

In addition to Ammianus, another writer who makes a statement about the medial position of the Roman emperor is Themistius (c. 317–388), a Constantinopolitan polytheist philosopher and rhetorician. In early 364 Themistius gave a speech to Emperor Jovian (27 June 363–17 February 364), the predecessor of the Emperors Valentinian I and Valens.[66] Themistius praises the Emperor for his policy of religious moderation.[67] He contrasts Jovian's moderate religious policy with the strict attitudes and abrupt changes of previous emperors. These emperors are not named but the allusions are probably targeted at Constantius II and Julian, who implemented austere policies, the former against pagans and the latter against Christians.[68]

Speaking of the coexistence of different religions, Themistius uses the metaphor of many paths and states, with not just one path, *hodos*, leading to the divine. Linked to the metaphor, Themistius also introduces the idea of the utility of competition: Emperor Jovian does not prevent the religions of the Empire from rivalling one another in piety because mutual competition and rivalry is beneficial. Here Themistius builds a comparison with races in which all competitors speed towards the same Judge (*Athlothetes*) but along different routes. If there were no competition at all between religions, people would be filled with lethargy and boredom. In competition 'the spirit is always easily galvanized by opposition to take pleasure in toil'. If the Emperor allows only one path and prohibits the rest, he 'will fence up the broad field of competition'.[69]

Themistius suggests that this competition be held under imperial tutelage. Is he advocating emperors' occupation of a neutral space in religious affairs? The medial position of the emperor is evoked when Themistius uses the metaphor of scales to describe the social tranquillity of the Empire. The emperor should not

---

65 Garnsey and Humfress, *Evolution of the Late Antique World*: 143–4. In the apologetics of the exiled Nicene bishops, Valens' discipline was, of course, considered persecution. Errington, *Roman Imperial Policy*: 188–9.
66 Themistius, *Or.* 5 was first delivered in honour of Jovian's consulship in Ancyra, 1 January 364 and was given again later in Constantinople. Jovian became emperor after Julian's death in 363 and was forced to make a peace with the Persians after Julian's disastrous Persian campaign.
67 As Peter J. Heather and David Moncur, *Politics, Philosophy, and Empire in the Fourth Century: Select Orations of Themistius* (Translated Texts for Historians, vol. 36; Liverpool: Liverpool University Press, 2001): 34–5, 157–8 argue, Themistius, *Or.* 5 was a justification and support of the new emperor's existing policy rather than an appeal for moderation. Themistius' depiction of Jovian's policy is reinforced by the account of Socrates (*Hist. eccl.* 3.25) on Jovian's moderate attitude towards religious deviants. See also Errington, *Roman Imperial Policy*: 173–5. John Vanderspoel, *Themistius and the Imperial Court, Oratory, Civic Duty, and Paideia from Constantius and Theodosius* (Ann Arbor: The University of Michigan Press, 1995): 152 interprets Themistius' speech as a plea.
68 Especially Themistius, *Or.* 5.67d-69c.
69 Themistius, *Or.* 5.68c; 5.69a, (Heather and Moncur (trans), *Politics* cit.: 168–9). For a more thorough discussion of Themistius' speech, see Maijastina Kahlos, 'Rhetoric and Realities: Themistius and the Changing Tides in Imperial Religious Policies', in *Politiche religiose nel mondo antico e tardoantico*, Giovanni A. Cecconi and Chantal Gabrielli (eds) (Collana Munera 33; Bari: Edipuglia, 2011): 287–304, and on the metaphor of many paths, see Kahlos, *Forbearance and Compulsion*: 131–3.

attempt to disturb the balance, letting one side go down or forcing the other side to go up. Themistius also declares that the emperor ought to let prayers on behalf of his imperial rule rise to heaven from all sides.[70]

Themistius' assertions led Lawrence J. Daly to propose that the orator may have spoken for the secularized role of the emperor in religious issues. The emperor was *pontifex maximus*, the head of the most important priestly college of the traditional Roman religion and therefore, during the imperial period, a symbolic head of Roman religious life. According to Daly, Themistius tried 'to solve the dilemma of a Christian cult-lord in a pagan state by substituting humanism for sectarianism' and attempted to shift 'the context of that royal function from the cultic to the cultural, from the theological to the philosophical'. Furthermore, 'Themistius' emphasis on the cultural rather than the religious aspect of the cult-lord function secularized the pontifical role traditionally associated with the monarchy'. Daly even suggested that Themistius spoke for the separation of 'the historical association of throne and altar'.[71] This is a tempting suggestion; however, I would like to remain cautious in order to avoid interpreting Themistius anachronistically and seeing him in too modern a light. Themistius may have endorsed the middle position of the emperor but this does not necessarily imply the neutrality of the state in religious issues; it does not even imply secularization.

Emperors Jovian, Valentinian I and Valens emphasized religious moderation in their policies.[72] Their successors, however, took a more authoritarian and coercive tone in their religious policies.[73]

Conclusion

During the long process of the Christianization of the Roman Empire in the fourth century, Christian festivals were gradually consolidated into urban frameworks. Researchers even speak of the conquest of time and place.[74] Many traditional urban celebrations nonetheless continued and were also attended by Christians which, from time to time, led ecclesiastical leaders to condemn these festivities.

These disputes about late antique celebrations exhibit significant discursive boundary marking between 'pagan', Christian, cultic, 'civic', and 'neutral'. But where does religion end and where does neutral space begin? I have argued that meaning and content are subject to continuing cultural negotiation, especially during

---

70 Themistius, *Or.* 5.69c.
71 Lawrence J. Daly, 'Themistius' Plea for Religious Tolerance', *Greek, Roman and Byzantine Studies* 12 (1971): 68–71, 76–7.
72 For further discussion, see Kahlos, 'Rhetoric and Realities': 287–304.
73 Ambrose of Milan made an authoritative remark on the position that the emperor should take in religious issues by stating that the emperor's voice had to ring out with the name of Christ: Ambrose *Ep.* 18.10 Maur. = *Ep.* 73.10: *Vox imperatoris nostri Christum resultet*. See Klaus Rosen, 'Fides contra dissimulationem: Ambrosius und Symmachus im Kampf um den Victoriaaltar', *JbaC* 37 (1994): 34–6.
74 Salzman, 'Christianization': 123–34.

periods of social and religious transformation. Boundaries are not to be taken at face value since they have a cultural, rather than a natural, character. Drawing boundaries and establishing clear demarcation lines usually reveals that the boundaries a writer wants to enforce are far from self-evident and unambiguous.

What I wish to point out is that the same celebration may have had different meanings for different persons: for one, a feast was emphatically a cultic act; for another, it was simply a communal celebration; for a third, it was having fun; for a fourth, it was all these things and so on. There was not one identical meaning for all. This applies to the late antique disputes as well as to modern discussions of Christmas carols or end of school term hymns.

The approach according to which people are understood as having many situational identities (Brubaker 2004) explains why the same people are seen to take part in traditional and Christian celebrations without further complications. We could speak of degrees of allegiance rather than either/or decisions. Urban celebrations were not necessarily a problem for ordinary people (certainly they were for some, but not for all of them). What eventually tended to cause anxiety were the reproaches of bishops, who invested traditional urban celebrations with categorically cultic 'pagan' meaning and insisted upon these either/or choices. The strong reactions of ecclesiastical leaders were connected with the contested situations in which urban space and time were in competition.

Nor were urban celebrations a problem for Christian emperors. The imperial government can be seen to balance different interest groups, the leaders of different Christian sects and ordinary Christians, landowners and common people. For emperors, many traditional celebrations were valuable for maintaining societal coherence and they therefore wished to retain many of these festivities. Therefore, compromises were made. For instance, festivals were 'cleaned up' of what was regarded as 'pagan', especially the rituals of sacrifice. Even the possibility of the emperor keeping out of inter-religious and inter-sectarian disputes was discussed in the late fourth century. The philosopher Themistius was the most conspicuous spokesperson in favour of the emperor retaining the middle ground; however, the idea of the emperor as remaining 'neutral' in religious disputes was eventually discarded in Late Antiquity.

2 Classical Culture, Domestic Space and Imperial Vision in the *Cycle* of Agathias

Steven D. Smith

Introduction: an Inscription from a House in Constantinople

The ninth book of the *Greek anthology* contains the following epigram by Agathias of Myrina about the view from a rooftop of a house in Constantinople:[1]

'Τῆς ἀρετῆς ἱδρῶτα θεοὶ προπάροιθεν ἔθηκαν,'

ἔννεπεν Ἀσκραῖος, δῶμα τόδε προλέγων.

Κλίμακα γὰρ ταναὴν περόων κεκαφηότι ταρσῷ,

ἱδρῶτι πλαδαρὴν ἀμφεδίηνα κόμην·

ὑψόθι δ' εἰσενόησα θαλασσαίην περιωπήν.

Ναὶ τάχα τῆς ἀρετῆς πιστότατος θάλαμος. (*AP* 9.653 Agathias)

'The gods placed sweat before virtue', said the man from Ascra, prophesying this house. For climbing the long staircase on wearied heel with sweat I made my hair moist all over. But on high I looked upon a wide view of the sea. Yes, maybe it is a most faithful chamber of virtue.

The lofty quotation from Hesiod with which the epigram begins contrasts humorously with the earthy details of the poet's physical exertion – wearied heel, sweat-soaked hair – as he climbs the stairs to the roof. But the rooftop's panoramic view of the sea, such as any visitor to modern Istanbul can still appreciate, is worth the effort. Beneath the humour, though, is a sophisticated commentary by an adroit *pepaideumenos* about the cultural implications of how space may be experienced and interpreted. In only six verses, the epigram provokes philosophical contemplation of vertical ascent and horizontal epiphany, harmonizes the apparently disparate cultural frames of classicism and Christianity, and shows how epigrammatic intimacy is dependent upon an expansive, epic vision of Empire.

---

1 The lemma reads 'for a house situated on a height in Byzantium' (εἰς οἶκον κείμενον ἐν ὕψει ἐν Βυζαντίῳ), Pierre Waltz, Guy Soury, Jean Irigoin and Pierre Laurens (eds), *Anthologie Grecque, Tome VIII: Anthologie Palatine, Livre IX, Épigrammes 359–827* (Paris: Les Belles Lettres, 1974, repr. 2002): 126

The poem originally appeared in the second book of the anthology that was called, according to the *Souda*, the *Kyklos*, or *Cycle*, a collection of epigrams by contemporary poets that Agathias himself arranged and published in Constantinople around 567; though the collection appeared early in the reign of Justin II, most of its poems were composed during the reign of Justinian and reflect a Justinianic cultural context.[2] In the verse preface to the *Cycle*, the poet writes that the second book contains,

ὅσσαπερ ἢ γραφίδεσσι χαράξαμεν ἤ τινι χώρῳ,

εἴτε καὶ εὐποίητον ἐπὶ βρέτας, εἴτε καὶ ἄλλης

τέχνης ἐργοπόνοιο πολυσπερέεσσιν ἀέθλοις. (*AP* 4.4.72–74)

as many of the things that we inscribed either on paintings or in some place, whether upon some well-made statue, or for the widely strewn prizes of another labour intensive craft.

The 'inscribing' posited by Agathias suggests poetic composition not merely for private entertainment among a cultured elite, but for monumental display for an imperial public. Indeed, while many of the epigrams from Book Two of Agathias' *Cycle* need not have been actual inscriptions lifted from public monuments or works of art,[3] many others probably were publicly displayed in Constantinople and its environs. These include poems on baths (9.614–33), the Sangarius bridge (641), a public latrine in Smyrna (642–4, 662), the palace built for the Empress Sophia by Justin II (657), and the newly renovated Praetorium (658–9). A number of surviving honorific poems also accompanied statues and paintings of distinguished individuals of the age, including Gabriel, prefect of Constantinople; the antecessor Julian; Philip, prefect of Smyrna; the sophist Heraclamon; Peter Barsymes; the lawyer and victorious general Synesius; Longinus, prefect of Constantinople; and the financial minister, Thomas.[4] The

---

2 For the title, see *Souda* α 112; for the date, see Averil Cameron, *Agathias* (Oxford: Clarendon Press, 1970): 12–15; Barry Baldwin, 'Four Problems in Agathias', *ByzZ* 70 (1970): 295–305; and Barry Baldwin, 'The Date of the *Cycle* of Agathias', *ByzZ* 73 (1980): 334–40. For the Justinianic context, see Ronald C. McCail, 'The *Cycle* of Agathias: New Identifications Scrutinised', *JHS* 89 (1969): 94–6. See also the excellent overview of the collection by Lynda Garland, 'Public Lavatories, Mosquito Nets and Agathias' Cat: The Sixth-Century Epigram in its Justinianic Context', Geoffrey Nathan and Lynda Garland (eds), *Basileia: essays on imperium and culture in honour of E. M. and M. J. Jeffreys* (Virginia, Queensland, Australia: Centre for Early Christian Studies, Australian Catholic University): 141–58.
3 The poets of the *Cycle* were well aware of the sophisticated conceits of Hellenistic epigram. On the origins of ecphrastic epigram, see Kathryn Gutzwiller, 'Art's Echo: The Tradition of Hellenistic Ecphrastic Epigram', in *Hellenistic Epigrams*, M. Annette Harder, Remco F. Regtuit, and G. C. Wakker (eds) (Leuven, Belgium; Sterling, VA: Peeters, 2002).
4 On Gabriel, see *AP* 16.32 (Leontius Scholasticus) and *PLRE* IIIA Gabrielius 1. A nobleman esteemed by Justinian, Gabriel is also the author of *AP* 16.208, on an image of Eros sleeping. John the Lydian dedicated to him his works *de mensibus* and *de ostentis*. On Julian, see *AP* 16.32b (Theaetetus) and *PLRE* IIIA Iulianus 10. This Julian, a noted jurist and professor of law, is also the

imperial city of the sixth century was, in other words, replete with verse inscriptions composed by Agathias and his friends. These epigrams gave the urban landscapes of Byzantium a classicizing gloss, connecting the public spaces of an overwhelmingly Christian environment with the rich cultural and literary traditions of the Hellenic past.[5]

Verses inscribed on the walls of public baths regularly announced the presence of Aphrodite, Eros and the Graces – a concession to continuity with the pagan past in the most sensual of Roman cultural spaces.[6] All of the other public epigrams listed in the previous paragraph, however, represent an interesting balance struck by the poets of Agathias' circle between the traditional motifs of classical culture on the one hand and on the other hand a tempering of those motifs to make them palatable within a Justinianic context.[7] While they all adhere to the formal and linguistic conventions of classical epigram, none, apart from the bath epigrams, offer any explicit reference to the pagan religious culture that was the foundation of the poetic tradition. And yet the rest of the *Cycle* of Agathias is filled with epigrams that would have scandalized conservative Christians of the sixth century, both for their explicit eroticism and for their refusal to represent the world through the lens of an orthodox Christian Hellenism. Not every expression of classical culture was acceptable in Constantinople in the sixth century, and those epigrams that displayed an unrepentant sexuality or provoked orthodox sensibilities with their constant references to the old gods and goddesses would have found a receptive performance space only in the private homes of the poets themselves or their patrons. The poem on the view from a rooftop in Constantinople quoted at the beginning of this chapter, if it was inscribed at all, could only have been inscribed

author of three epigrams from the *Cycle* (*AP* 11.367–9). If the poem by Theaetetus did not accompany a statue of Julian, it may commemorate his Latin epitome of Justinian's *Novellae*. On Philip, see *AP* 16.34 (Theodoretus) and *PLRE* IIIB Philippus 1. On Heraclamon, see *AP* 16.36 (Agathias) and *PLRE* IIIA Heraclammon. On Peter Barsymes, see *AP* 16.37 (Leontius Scholasticus) and *PLRE* IIIB Petrus *qui et* Barsymes 9. On Synesius, see *AP* 16.38 (John Barbucallus) and *PLRE* IIIB Synesius 2. On Longinus, see *AP* 16.39 (Arabius Scholasticus) and *PLRE* IIIB Longinus 2. On Thomas, see *AP* 16.41 (Agathias) and *PLRE* IIIB Thomas 20. On all of these figures, see also Alan Cameron and Averil Cameron, 'The *Cycle* of Agathias', *JHS* 86 (1966): 9–20 and Robert Aubreton and Félix Buffière (eds), *Anthologie Grecque, Tome XIII: Anthologie Planude* (Paris: Les Belles Lettres, 1980, repr. 2002): 238–43.

5 Christian ideology would increasingly dominate the urban landscape over the following century; see Jean-Michel Spieser, 'La christianisation de la ville dans l'Antiquité tardive', *Ktèma* 11 (1986).

6 On the poetry of the Roman baths, see Stephan Busch, *Versus Balnearum: die antike Dichtung über Bäder und Baden im römischen Reich* (Stuttgart: Teubner, 1999).

7 On the rise of Christian ideology, class-related cultural conflicts, and the complex relationship between Christianity and Hellenism in the sixth century, see Peter N. Bell, *Social Conflict in the Age of Justinian: Its Nature, Management, and Mediation* (Oxford and New York: Oxford University Press, 2013): 213–66; on the poetry of Agathias and his peers in particular, see 220–21; Bell concludes that 'the frequent shrillness of the official Christian tone towards [Pagans] ... reflected the painful – largely unmentionable – fact that the dragon, if gravely wounded, was not actually dead – and that in places, classical culture, sometimes practiced by Christians, actually flourished': 262.

inside the house that it celebrates, and therefore was accessible only to those readers granted access to this private space.[8]

The *Cycle* of Agathias and Domestic Space

In fact, Agathias himself reveals, both in the verse preface to the *Cycle* and in his later preface to the *History,* that the poems of the collection had their origins in the intimate spaces of private homes. At the opening of the *Cycle*, Agathias imagines the collection as a banquet and its audience as well-fed guests:

Οἶμαι μὲν ὑμᾶς, ἄνδρες, ἐμπεπλησμένους

ἐκ τῆς τοσαύτης τῶν λόγων πανδαισίας,

ἔτι που τὰ σιτία προσκόρως ἐρυγγάνειν·

καὶ δὴ κάθησθε τῇ τρυφῇ σεσαγμένοι.

λόγων γὰρ ἡμῖν πολυτελῶν καὶ ποικίλων

πολλοὶ προθέντες παμμιγεῖς εὐωχίας,

περιφρονεῖν πείθουσι τῶν εἰθισμένων.

τί δὲ νῦν ποιήσομεν; τὰ προὐξειργασμένα

οὕτως ἐάσω συντετῆχθαι κείμενα,

ἢ καὶ προθῶμαι τῆς ἀγορᾶς ἐν τῷ μέσῳ

παλιγκαπήλοις εὐτελῶς ἀπεμπολῶν;

καὶ τίς μετασχεῖν τῶν ἐμῶν ἀνέξεται;

τίς δ' ἂν πρίαιτο τοὺς λόγους τριωβόλου,

εἰ μὴ φέροι πως ὦτα μὴ τετρημένα; (*AP* 4.3.1–14)

I think, gentlemen, since you are quite full from so great a banquet of words, that you are still perhaps belching out the food in satiety. And indeed you sit there stuffed with delicacies. For many men, having set before us mixed feasts of extravagant and varied words, make us disdain what has become customary. And what will I do now? Should I allow what has been prepared to lie there and rot, or should I even set it forth in the middle of the *agora*, selling it cheap to retail grocers? And who will endure to have a share of what I have to offer? And who would pay three obols for my words, unless I suppose it were someone whose ears are blocked up?

---

8 For a survey of domestic inscriptions from Late Antiquity, see Veronika Scheibelreiter-Gail, 'Inscriptions in the Late Antique Private House: Some Thoughts about their Function and Distribution', Stine Birk and Birte Poulsen (eds), *Patrons and Viewers in Late Antiquity* (Aarhus, Denmark: Aarhus University Press): 135–65).

In Aristophanic mode, the poet envisions his guests as so sated by the feast of poetry that has come before that they now have no room in their stomachs for what he has prepared. But his collection is too good simply to let it go bad and spoil, and so he is forced to imagine what it will be like to sell his wares on the open market. Publication means that Agathias' collection must emerge figuratively from the intimate gatherings of private dinner parties to public scrutiny in the *agora*. If the private, domestic sphere is the site where his audience may savour or even over-indulge in refined delicacies, then the poet questions whether the wider public will even have a taste for what he has to offer.

Later in his career, Agathias turned from poetry to prose and in the preface to his *History* of events from the 550s, as he looks back on his earlier career as a poet, he writes,

> ἔδοξε δέ μοι πρότερον κἀκεῖνο ἀξιέπαινόν τι εἶναι καὶ οὐκ ἄχαρι, εἴ γε τῶν ἐπιγραμμάτων τὰ ἀρτιγενῆ καὶ νεώτερα, διαλανθάνοντα ἔτι καὶ χύδην οὑτωσὶ παρ' ἐνίοις ὑποψιθυριζόμενα, ἀγείραιμί τε ὡς οἷόν τε εἰς ταὐτὸ καὶ ἀναγράψαιμι ἕκαστα ἐν κόσμῳ ἀποκεκριμένα. (Agathias *Histories*: 4, ll. 24–8 Keydell)

> And I thought previously that that too was something worthy of praise and not unpleasant – if I should both collect, as far as is possible, the recently produced and newer epigrams, which were still escaping notice and which were being whispered softly in some people's houses in such a complete flood of disorder, into the same volume and record each of them after they had been classified in orderly manner.

Even later in life, therefore, Agathias still thought about his publication of epigrams by contemporary poets as a bringing-to-light of material that had hitherto been confined to the private sphere. The spatial dimension of the language and imagery that Agathias uses here indicates both how privately the epigrams of his peers were circulating prior to publication and how important his own role was in bringing order to the collection for public consumption. The participial phrases describing the epigrams as 'still escaping notice' (διαλανθάνοντα ἔτι) and 'whispered softly in some people's houses' (παρ' ἐνίοις ὑποψιθυριζόμενα) evoke an atmosphere of secrecy.[9] It is not hard to imagine that the increasing public hostility in Justinian's Constantinople towards all forms of traditional Hellenic culture would occasion guardedness on the part of this community of poets and their readers. Regardless of what their own personal religious beliefs were, their epigrams are frankly sensual and often explicitly pagan in their outlook, and so it makes sense that they were circulating behind closed doors. Furthermore, that

---

[9] It should be noted that the only other appearance of the participial form ὑποψιθυριζόμενα in Greek literature is in the (much later) *Alexiad* of Anna Komnene, regarding 'the things that were being whispered against him [the Emperor] in the crossroads and corners' of Constantinople (6.3.1 Reinsch and Kambylis). The word has a conspiratorial flavor.

the epigrams were being muttered 'in such a complete flood of disorder' (χύδην οὑτωσί) on the one hand indicates the indiscriminate manner in which the poems were circulating among the *literati*. On the other, the liquid metaphor suggests also the natural inevitability with which the poems would overflow the confines of the private sphere and pour out into the streets of Constantinople. This stream of new epigrams – a powerful expression of classical culture in Justinian's Christian city – became a torrent that could not be contained.

Harry Maier, in his investigation of the use of domestic spaces as redoubts for heretical Christian sects throughout the fourth and fifth centuries, writes that, 'outside the walls of officially recognized meeting places we may imagine a 'heterodox' mosaic of more private conventicles, a diverse series of movements oriented around particular figures, ideas and practices, in varying degrees exotic and virtually impossible to control.'[10] While Maier is concerned exclusively with diverse Christian communities in the century and a half before the reign of Justinian, I think that his conclusion is applicable also to the community of classicizing poets in Constantinople in the sixth century. I do not claim that the poets of Agathias' *Cycle* shared a common religious belief or that they were engaged in pagan cult practice, only that their cultivation of classicizing epigram identified them as a literary community at odds with the orthodoxy of early Byzantine culture. In an environment that was becoming increasingly hostile to traditional forms of Hellenism, Agathias and his poets found their audience among each other and within the private homes of Constantinople's cultured elite. This in turn consolidated their group identity as *pepaideumenoi*, even as they played their roles as *scholastikoi* or members of the imperial court in a devoutly Christian context.[11] Various forms of classical culture undoubtedly continued to find public expression in the sixth century. One thinks especially of the mimes and pantomimes of the theatre. But these were under imperial control and were framed within court ceremonial, in spite of which they never lost their association with sin.[12] The refined epigrams of Agathias and his peers,

---

10 Harry O. Maier, 'Religious Dissent, Heresy and Households in Late Antiquity', *VC* 49.1 (1995): 59. The use of domestic space for religious practices that were foreign or that did not conform to those of the dominant culture was not new in Late Antiquity; see L. Michael White, *Building God's House in the Roman World: Architectural Adaptation among Pagans, Jews, and Christians* (Baltimore and London: The Johns Hopkins University Press, 1990): 26–59.

11 Cf. the evidence of John of Ephesus for the arrest in 545–46 of '*grammatici*, sophists, *scholastici* and physicians' accused of being pagans (Pseudo-Dionysius of Tel-Mahre, *Chronicle*, 71). Despite persecution and despite whether they were actually engaged in pagan cultic activities, this communal identity among the urban cultured elite continued at least into the following generation: in 580, there was another round of arrests of patricians, magistrates, scribes and lawyers (the Syriac historian uses the Greek loan-words *patrikioi*, *archontes*, *antigraphoi*, and *scholastikoi*), against whom even the urban masses rioted demanding their deaths; see John of Ephesus, *Hist. Eccl.* 3.3.31, Ernest Walter Brooks (ed.), *Iohannis Ephesini Historiae Ecclesiasticae Pars Tertia* (Leuven: Peeters, 1935), as well as Glen Warren Bowersock, *Hellenism in Late Antiquity* (Ann Arbor: The University of Michigan Press, 1990): 1–4, and Bell, *Social conflict in the Age of Justinian*: 95–6, 242–3.

12 Procopius, *Hist. Arc.* 26.6; on imperial control of theatrical performances, see Bell, *Social Conflict in the Age of Justinian*: 126; on Christian polemic against theatrical performances, see Ruth Webb,

however, which were neither explicitly Christian in their outlook nor grounded within a strong Christian social context, could only have been met with hostility by the orthodox flock of Justinian's New Jerusalem.[13] This was poetry more suitable for recitation in the salon than for declamation in street corners, and although Paul the Silentiary, poet of the famous *ekphrasis* of Hagia Sophia, is also one of the collection's most frequent contributors, he could never have performed his sensuous, provocative epigrams within the vast space of the great church.[14]

The epigrams of Agathias' *Cycle* can therefore be said to have occupied at the time of their composition and early circulation a vertical, seclusive space. Paradoxically, however, the seclusion that gave birth to and nurtured classical epigram in sixth century Constantinople also accommodated an expansive vision that looked outward to distant horizons. This paradoxical doubling of seclusive and expansive, vertical and horizontal is best illustrated in the epigram with which this chapter began and which I quote again in full:

'Τῆς ἀρετῆς ἱδρῶτα θεοὶ προπάροιθεν ἔθηκαν,'

ἔννεπεν Ἀσκραῖος, δῶμα τόδε προλέγων.

Κλίμακα γὰρ ταναὴν περόων κεκαφηότι ταρσῷ,

ἱδρῶτι πλαδαρὴν ἀμφεδίηνα κόμην·

ὑψόθι δ' εἰσενόησα θαλασσαίην περιωπήν.

Ναὶ τάχα τῆς ἀρετῆς πιστότατος θάλαμος. (*AP* 9.653 Agathias)

'The gods placed sweat before virtue,' said the man from Ascra, prophesying this house. For climbing the long staircase on wearied heel with sweat I made my hair moist all over. But on high I looked upon a wide view of the sea. Yes, maybe it is a most faithful chamber of virtue.

Agathias' poem on the panoramic view of the sea from a private house in Constantinople[15] offers compelling evidence of a dynamic ideology in the

---

Demons and Dancers: Performance in Late Antiquity (Cambridge, Massachusetts and London, England: Harvard University Press, 2008): 197–216.

13 Sarah Bassett, *The Urban Image of Late Antique Constantinople* (Cambridge and New York: Cambridge University Press, 2004): 135–6.

14 On Paul the Silentiary as a crypto-pagan and political dissident, see Peter N. Bell, *Three Political Voices from the Age of Justinian* (Liverpool: Liverpool University Press, 2009): 14–7, 79–95. For the influence of classical culture on the creation of Hagia Sophia, see now also Anthony Kaldellis, 'The Making of Hagia Sophia and the Last Pagans of New Rome', *JLA* 6.2 (2013), who argues that Anthemius of Tralles and Isidorus of Miletus were pagans who encoded their neo-Platonist cosmology within the architecture of Justinian's great church. By contrast, I make no claims here about the religious identity of Agathias and his peers; only that their dedication to increasingly dangerous forms of classical literature required them to perform and circulate their works in private.

15 On similar poems from the *Cycle*, see *AP* 9.648 and 649 (Macedonius the Consul); 650 (Leontius); 651 (Paul the Silentiary); 652 and 654 (Julianus Aegyptius); 677 (Agathias), on a house built by

classicizing conceptualization of private space. In what follows, I argue that this epigram, as a poetic representation of a lived private space in the imperial city, is also the site where the classicizing philosophical tradition harmonizes with both Christian thought and an imperial conceptualization of the *oikoumenē*. An eloquent expression of a transformative spatial experience that is both vertical and horizontal, the poem offers a shrewd argument for the ongoing role of *pepaideumenoi* as theoreticians of an imperial vision that harmonizes Christian thought with traditional forms of Hellenism.

AP 9.653 and the Classical Tradition

Agathias' poem declares its affiliation with classical literature in the very first line by quoting a verse from Hesiod's *Works and Days*. The poet from Ascra had once been a familiar presence in the urban landscape of Constantinople, as his bronze statue could be found in the collection of classical sculptures from the Baths of Zeuxippos before its destruction in the Nika riots of 532.[16] Here is the relevant passage from Hesiod to which the speaker in Agathias' poem alludes:

τῆς δ' ἀρετῆς ἱδρῶτα θεοὶ προπάροιθεν ἔθηκαν

ἀθάνατοι· μακρὸς δὲ καὶ ὄρθιος οἶμος ἐς αὐτὴν

καὶ τρηχὺς τὸ πρῶτον· ἐπὴν δ' εἰς ἄκρον ἵκηται,

ῥηιδίη δὴ ἔπειτα πέλει, χαλεπή περ ἐοῦσα. (Hesiod, *Op.* 289–92)

And the immortal gods placed sweat before virtue, and long and steep is the path to it and rough at first, and when it reaches the top, easy indeed then it is, though it was difficult.

Agathias' quotation of Hesiod is apt, for just as Agathias' poem describes the ascent from ground floor to the rooftop of the house in question, so Hesiod's aphorism about the sweat that must be expended in striving for virtue prefaces a metaphorical elaboration of moral excellence as the goal at the end of a path that is long and steep. Hesiod's proto-philosophical musings about the labour of virtuous ascent were prophetic, from Agathias' perspective; with the participle 'prophesying' (προλέγων), Agathias figures the archaic poet of didactic epic as an oracle for the late Roman house in Byzantium.[17] In the world of Agathias the poetry of the ancient past still had the power to reenergize the apparently mundane in surprising ways, and,

---

a certain Musonius; and 808 (Cyrus), on the house of a certain Maximinus. See Cameron and Cameron, 'The *Cycle* of Agathias', 9, 16–17 and Heinrich Schulte, *Die Epigramme des Leontios Scholastikos Minotauros: Text, Übersetzung, Kommentar* (Trier: Wissenschaftlicher Verlag Trier, 2005): 31–2. On the humorous interpretation of 9.653, see Giovanni Viansino, *Agazia Scolastico: Epigrammi* (Milan: Luigi Trevisini, 1967): 93–4.

16 See *AP* 2.38–40 and Bassett, *Urban Image of Late Antique Constantinople*: 173.
17 Thus Viansino, *Agazia Scolastico*: 94; cf. Herodotus, *Hist.* 1.53, 8.136.

conversely, the apparently mundane could offer surprising portals for the imagination to access the classical past. Relevant in this respect are several other poems from the *Cycle* on personal objects from everyday life – a mosquito net (9.764–6), a gaming table (767–9), a drinking cup (770–71), a water-clock (782), a pepper grinder (16.208) – objects that, once absorbed within the conceptual schemata of Greek epigram, become suffused with the numinous power of the classical past. The speaker of Agathias' poem, having experienced for himself the sweaty ascent up the ladder to the rooftop of the house in Constantinople, reads this particular private space as a manifestation of Hesiodic wisdom, which is confirmed in the poem's final verse, in which the speaker declares that 'Yes, maybe it is a most faithful chamber of virtue' (Ναὶ τάχα τῆς ἀρετῆς πιστότατος θάλαμος).

But whereas Hesiod speaks of a 'steep path' (ὄρθιος οἶμος), the journey up towards *aretē* in Agathias' poem is upon a 'staircase' (κλίμακα). The staircase as a metaphor for philosophical ascent is of course familiar from Socrates' speech in Plato's *Symposium*. At a critical moment in the dialogue, Diotima describes Eros as a *daimōn* that guides human souls upward towards true Beauty, at which point the soul 'suddenly will see something wondrously beautiful in its nature – this is that very thing, Socrates, indeed the reason why even all the previous labours existed' (ἐξαίφνης κατόψεταί τι θαυμαστὸν τὴν φύσιν καλόν, τοῦτο ἐκεῖνο, ὦ Σώκρατες, οὗ δὴ ἕνεκεν καὶ οἱ ἔμπροσθεν πάντες πόνοι ἦσαν, Plato, *Symp.* 210e2–6). Shortly after, Diotima summarizes the soul's properly guided journey: it begins by loving one, then two, then all beautiful bodies, and then from beautiful bodies to beautiful activities, and thence to beautiful knowledge, and from there to knowledge of the Beautiful itself (*to kalon*), a journey achieved, she says, 'as if using the steps of a stairway' (ὥσπερ ἐπαναβασμοῖς χρώμενον, 211c3).

While Agathias' poem must certainly have evoked in any contemporary learned reader this *locus classicus* of philosophical ascent, nowhere in the immediate vicinity of this passage does Diotima speak of *aretē*. She likens the soul's journey to an ascent upon the 'steps of a stairway' (*epanabasmoi*) leading to the beautiful (*to kalon*). At the very end of her speech, Diotima says that it is only within sight of what is truly beautiful that one can give birth to true *aretē* (212a), but this comes almost as an afterthought, and in the earlier description of the soul's journey the goal was emphatically not *aretē* but the Beautiful itself, *to kalon*. Agathias' *klimax aretēs* is thus a literary blending of the Hesiodic 'path toward virtue' (*oimos es aretēn*) with the Platonic simile of philosophical ascent as if upon the 'steps of a stairway' (*epanabasmoi*).

While Hesiod and Plato offered the philosophical background, the first century poet Nicarchus provided the epigrammatic model for Agathias' poem:[18]

---

18 For the background on this poem, see Robert Aubreton, *Anthologie Grecque, Tome X: Anthologie Palatine, Livre XI* (Paris: Les Belles Lettres, 1972, reprinted 2002): 281 and Gideon Nisbet, *Greek Epigram in the Roman Empire: Martial's Forgotten Rivals* (Oxford and New York: Oxford University Press, 2003): 29.

Ἐκλήθην ἐχθές, Δημήτριε· σήμερον ἦλθον

δειπνεῖν. Μὴ μέμψῃ, κλίμακ' ἔχεις μεγάλην·

ἐν ταύτῃ πεποίηκα πολὺν χρόνον· οὐδ' ἂν ἐσώθην

σήμερον, ἀλλ' ἀνέβην κέρκον ὄνου κατέχων.

Ἦψαι τῶν ἄστρων· Ζεὺς ἡνίκα τὸν Γανυμήδην

ἥρπασε, τῇδ' αὐτόν, φαίνετ', ἔχων ἀνέβη.

Ἔνθεν δ' εἰς Ἀίδην πότ' ἀφίξεαι; Οὐκ ἀφυὴς εἶ·

εὕρηκας τέχνην πῶς ἔσῃ ἀθάνατος. (*AP* 11.330 Nicarchus)

I was invited yesterday, Demetrius; today I arrived to dine. Don't blame me: you have a long stairway on which I spent a long time. Nor would I have gotten here safely today, but I came up holding onto the tail of an ass. You touch the stars. Zeus, when he stole Ganymede, came up holding onto him this way, it seemed. But from here when will you reach Hades? You aren't without natural talent: you've found out a way to be immortal!

The Platonic background obviously informs Nicarchus' figuration of the stairway (*klimax*, the same word used by Agathias) as a *technē* for ascending to divinity, but whereas the point of Diotima's imagery was a gradual transcendence of bodies, the speaker in Nicarchus' poem remains obsessed with the corporeal, even to the point of obscenity. Demetrius' abode may touch the stars, but Nicarchus' speaker seeks only a banquet up there. According to Diotima's scheme, Eros is a *daimōn* that will guide human souls properly toward the Beautiful, but the ascent of Nicarchus' speaker is parodic, as he is guided by holding onto the tail of an ass. The word 'tail' (*kerkos*) is slang for the phallus,[19] and an obscenity is surely implied in the comparison of the speaker's ascent holding onto the tail of an ass with Zeus' similar ascent holding onto Ganymede 'in this way' (τῇδ'). Plato's Socrates emphasized the spiritual aspects of *paiderastia*, but Nicarchus' speaker suggests that the motivations of the *erastēs* are more sexual than spiritual. Nicarchus thus anticipates similarly ironic treatments of Platonic *erōs* in the satiric literature of the following century, such as the quasi-philosophical erotic dialogue in Achilles Tatius' *Leucippe and Clitophon* and at the conclusion of the Lucianic *Erotes*.[20] Needless to say, Agathias in his own epigram achieves a light comic tone but avoids entirely his model's obscene homoerotic innuendo, as one would expect of a poet writing during the reign of

---

19 Jeffrey Henderson, *The Maculate Muse: Obscene Language in Attic Comedy* (second edition; Oxford and New York: Oxford University Press, 1991, orig. 1975): 128.
20 Achilles Tatius, *Leuc. Clit.* 2.35–8; Lucian, *Am.* 54; see Simon Goldhill, *Foucault's Virginity: Ancient Erotic Fiction and the History of Sexuality* (Cambridge and New York: Cambridge University Press, 1995): 46–111.

the emperor Justinian.[21] Also unlike the speaker in Nicarchus' poem, Agathias' speaker seeks a vision of the beautiful: 'But on high', he says, 'I looked upon a wide view of the sea' (ὑψόθι δ' εἰσενόησα θαλασσαίην περιωπήν), a sublime vista that is more consistent with the tenor of Platonic philosophy.

AP 9.653 and the Christian Tradition

Despite the parodic nature of his epigrammatic model, Agathias invests his own poem with a reverential tone. This is an epigram commemorating a domestic space that the poet imagines as accessing the divine,[22] for his image of a *klimax aretēs* evokes what had become by the sixth century a commonplace among early Christian writers. One such writer is the third century theologian Origen. The Book of Proverbs declares that, 'nests of wisdom are preferable to those of gold, and nests of understanding are preferable over silver' (νοσσιαὶ σοφίας αἱρετώτεραι χρυσίου, | νοσσιαὶ δὲ φρονήσεως αἱρετώτεραι ὑπὲρ ἀργύριον, *Prov* 16:16). In his allegorical commentary on this verse, Origen writes that the 'nests of understanding' are 'the practical virtues (*aretai*) ... through which, like the steps of a stairway (*klimakos*), those wishing to ascend and dwell there enter unhindered into the tents of wisdom' (αἱ πρακτικαὶ ἀρεταί ... δι' ἃς ὡς κλίμακος βαθμίδας, εἰς τὰς τῆς σοφίας σκηνὰς εἰσιέναι ἀκώλυτον τοὺς ἀνιέναι καὶ οἰκῆσαι βουλομένους).[23] Origen's connection of the 'practical virtues' (πρακτικαὶ ἀρεταί) with the 'steps of a stairway' (κλίμακος βαθμίδας) clearly anticipates Agathias' poetic *klimax aretēs*.

Other instances of a *klimax aretēs* in Christian literature refer to the Old Testament story of Jacob and his dream of a stairway ascending to heaven. In the Septuagint version with which Agathias would have been familiar, Jacob 'dreamed, and behold there was a stairway (*klimax*) firmly planted on the earth, the top of which reached into heaven, and the angels of God were ascending and descending upon it' (ἐνυπνιάσθη, καὶ ἰδοὺ κλίμαξ ἐστηριγμένη ἐν τῇ γῇ, ἧς ἡ κεφαλὴ ἀφικνεῖτο εἰς τὸν οὐρανόν, καὶ οἱ ἄγγελοι τοῦ θεοῦ ἀνέβαινον καὶ κατέβαινον ἐπ' αὐτῆς).[24] Jacob's stairway to heaven became a commonplace among Christian writers of the fourth century. Ephraim, bishop of Cherson, in the preface to his narrative about the miracle of St. Clement, writes that the holy man was

---

21 Axel Mattsson, *Untersuchungen zur Epigrammsammlung des Agathias* (Lund: Håkan Ohlssons Boktryckeri, 1942): 57–8; Averil Cameron, *Agathias (*Oxford: Clarendon Press, 1970): 27, 106; Steven D. Smith, 'Agathias and Paul the Silentiary: Erotic Epigram and the Sublimation of Same-Sex Desire in the Age of Justinian', in *Sex in Antiquity: Exploring Gender and Sexuality in the Ancient World*, Nancy S. Rabinowitz, James Robson and Mark Masterson (eds) (Abingdon and New York: Routledge, 2015) offers a more nuanced interpretation.
22 On conceptions of divine space in the early Christian world, see Ann Marie Yasin, *Saints and Church Spaces in the Late Antique Mediterranean: Architecture, Cult, and Community* (Cambridge and New York: Cambridge University Press, 2009): 14–45.
23 Origen, *Exp. prov.*, *PG* vol. 17: 196, lines 6–14.
24 Gen 28:12 (Rahlfs).

τῆς ἀληθοῦς κλίμακος, τῆς οὐ πρὸς γεώλοφόν τι ὕψος ἐπαναγαγούσης ἡμᾶς, ἀλλὰ ταῖς τῶν ἀρετῶν ἀναβάσεσιν, ὥσπερ τισὶ βαθμίσι, πρὸς οὐρανόν τε καὶ τὰ οὐράνια ἡμᾶς διαβιβαζούσης· κλίμακος, καὶ τῆς Ἰακὼβ ὁραθείσης οὐδὲν ἀποδεούσης, οὐκ ἀγγέλους δι' αὐτῆς ἀνιόντας καὶ κατιόντας ἡμῖν δεικνυούσης, ἀλλὰ ἀνθρώπων ψυχὰς ταῖς θειοτάταις παραινέσεσιν, ὡς ἐκ βαθμῶν εἰς βαθμοὺς δι' ἀρετῶν τῷ Θεῷ συνεισφερούσης. (Ephraim, *Mir. Clem. Rom.*, *PG* vol. 2: 636, lines 5–13)

the true stairway (*klimakos*), one leading us not to some terrestrial height, but by means of the ascensions of the virtues (*tōn aretōn*), like certain steps, conveying us toward both heaven and the heavenly things; a stairway in no way inferior even to the one seen by Jacob, not showing us angels ascending and descending along it, but introducing the souls of men to God through virtues (*di' aretōn*) by means of the most divine exhortations, as if from step to step.

In Ephraim's conception, the goal at the top of the *klimax* is heaven itself and God, and the virtues (*aretai*) serve as the steps by means of which one gradually makes one's ascent. Though the language is similar, Agathias' *klimax aretēs* is somewhat different: for Agathias, *aretē* is the goal at the top of the stairway, achieved only by a sweaty labour on wearied heel.

Gregory of Nyssa begins his oration on the fifth beatitude – 'Blessed are the merciful, because they themselves will receive mercy' (Μακάριοι οἱ ἐλεήμονες, ὅτι αὐτοὶ ἐλεηθήσονται, Matt 5:7) – by likening the teaching of the beatitudes as a whole to Jacob's vision of a stairway leading to heaven:

Καὶ γὰρ ἐκεῖ τῷ πατριάρχῃ τὸν κατ' ἀρετὴν οἶμαι βίον τῷ εἴδει τῆς κλίμακος διατυποῦσθαι, ὡς ἂν αὐτός τε μάθοι καὶ τοῖς μετ' αὐτὸν ὑφηγήσαιτο, ὅτι οὐκ ἔστιν ἄλλως πρὸς τὸν Θεὸν ὑψωθῆναι, μὴ ἀεὶ πρὸς τὰ ἄνω βλέποντα, καὶ τὴν τῶν ὑψηλῶν ἐπιθυμίαν ἄληκτον ἔχοντα, ὡς μὴ ἀγαπᾶν ἐπὶ τῶν ἤδη κατορθωθέντων μένειν, ἀλλὰ ζημίαν ποιεῖσθαι, εἰ τοῦ ὑπερκειμένου μὴ ἅψαιτο. (Gregory of Nyssa, *Orat. VIII beat.*, *PG* vol. 44: 1248, lines 45–52)

For even there I think that the life according to virtue (*aretē*) is represented to the patriarch in the form of the stairway (*klimakos*), both so that he himself might learn it and that he might be the guide for those who come after him, because it is not possible otherwise to rise towards God, unless one looks always towards the things above, and possesses the unceasing passion for the things on high, with the result that one is not content to rest on past successes, but considers it a punishment if one does not touch that which lies above.

As in the preceding passage, God is the goal of the ascent, and Gregory interprets the stairway as a metaphor for the life lived in accordance with virtue (*kata aretēn*). Likewise evoking the story of Jacob, though without explicitly mentioning him, Gregory asserts that he has composed his encomium of Ephraim the Syrian, 'so that we might only set before the sight of the many how our Ephraim reached to the very top of the spiritual stairway of virtues (*aretōn klimakos*), and was more a teacher for the whole world' (ὡς ἂν δὲ μόνον ὑπ' ὄψιν τοῖς πολλοῖς παραστήσωμεν, ὡς ἐπ' αὐτοῦ τοῦ ἄκρου ἔφθασε τῆς πνευματικῆς τῶν ἀρετῶν κλίμακος ὁ ἡμέτερος, μᾶλλον δὲ τῆς οἰκουμένης διδάσκαλος Ἐφραΐμ).[25] Gregory of Nazianzus too employs the figure of the *klimax aretēs* in an evocation of the Old Testament story; in his funeral oration for St. Basil, Gregory writes that, 'I praise Jacob's stairway (*klimaka*) . . . But I praise also this man's stairway (*klimaka*), with its gradual steps upward toward virtue (*aretēn*), one that was not only seen but also traversed' (Ἐπαινῶ τὴν Ἰακὼβ κλίμακα . . . ἀλλ' ἐπαινῶ καὶ τούτου τὴν οὐχ ὁραθεῖσαν μόνον, ἀλλὰ καὶ διαβαθεῖσαν κλίμακα ταῖς κατὰ μέρος εἰς ἀρετὴν ἀναβάσεσι).[26]

In conceiving of the stairway to the rooftop of the house in Constantinople as a *klimax aretēs*, not only does Agathias allude to the classical writers Hesiod, Plato, and Nicarchus, but equally he evokes a Christian tradition represented in the writings of Origen, Ephraim of Cherson, Gregory of Nyssa, and Gregory of Nazianzus, for whom Jacob's dream of a stairway to heaven in the Old Testament served as a symbol of the virtuous ascent towards God. The figure of the *klimax aretēs* had become so much a commonplace within Christian thought by the late sixth century (a generation after Agathias) that a monk named John at Mt Sinai would conceive of his famous exhortation to monastic life in thirty steps as the *Klimax*. The monk would come to be known as John Climacus, after the title of his book, which became a classic of Byzantine ascetic literature.

In his far-reaching study of *Hellenism in Byzantium*, Anthony Kaldellis concludes that, 'what Christian Byzantium inherited from Hellenic antiquity was a set of tensions rather than a resolution.'[27] While this is true for much of late antiquity, Agathias' epigram represents an anomalous attempt to find a unified, common ground between the classical and the Christian. In Agathias' imagination, Hesiod becomes a prophet not only of Platonic philosophy but also of Christian spiritual ascent. Furthermore, Agathias was not the only writer in the sixth century to harmonize the classical and the Christian by means of a combined evocation of both Hesiod and Jacob. In the third book of his universal history, John Malalas juxtaposes two seemingly unrelated etiological notices. He states first that,

> Ὁ δὲ Ἀβραὰμ ἦν ἐτῶν ρ', ὅτε ἐγέννησε τὸν Ἰσαάκ, καὶ Ἰσαὰκ τὸν Ἰακὼβ τὸν λεγόμενον Ἰσραήλ. ἐκλήθησαν δὲ οἱ Ἰουδαῖοι ἀπὸ Ἰούδα τοῦ τετάρτου υἱοῦ τοῦ Ἰακώβ· ἔσχεν γὰρ υἱοὺς δώδεκα. ἡ δὲ τοῦ Ἰούδα φυλὴ ἐκράτει τῶν Ἰουδαίων καὶ διώκει· ὅθεν καὶ τὸ ὄνομα ἔσχον. (Malalas, *Chron.* 3.4 Thurn)

---

25 Gregory of Nyssa, *In sanct. Ephr.*, PG vol. 46: 828, lines 44–57.
26 Gregory of Nazianzus, *Or. Bas. (Or. 43)*, 71.3.1–4.6 (Boulenger).
27 Anthony Kaldellis, *Hellenism in Byzantium: The Transformations of Greek Identity and the Reception of the Classical Tradition* (Cambridge and New York: Cambridge University Press, 2007): 165.

Abraham was 100 years old when he begat Isaac, and Isaac begat Jacob, who was called Israel. And the Jews took their name from Juda, the fourth son of Jacob, for he had twelve sons. And the tribe of Juda had power over the Jews and managed them, for which reason they also took his name.

Then in the very next paragraph, Malalas notes that,

Ἐν δὲ τοῖς χρόνοις τούτοις ἐκ τῆς φυλῆς τοῦ Ἰάφεθ ἀνεφαίνετό τις ὀνόματι Ἡσίοδος· ὅστις ἐξεῦρεν τὰ Ἑλλήνων γράμματα, καὶ συντάξας γράμματα ἐξέθετο τοῖς Ἕλλησι πρῶτος. (Malalas *Chron.* 3.5 Thurn)

At this time, from the tribe of Iapheth appeared someone named Hesiod who invented the letters of the Greeks, and having arranged the letters was the first to exhibit them to the Greeks.

Malalas thus synchronizes the birth of the Jews with the birth of Greek literature, connoted by the simultaneous appearance in history of Jacob and Hesiod, respectively. Agathias would certainly have appreciated this, since the Old Testament patriarch and the archaic poet both speak in his epigram, the latter explicitly, and the former indirectly through his dream of a *klimax aretēs*.

Conclusion: Distant Horizons

The quotation from Hesiod at the beginning of the poem connects the intimacy of epigram with the comprehensive vision of epic, and the expansive rooftop vista in Agathias' epigram finds its analogue in the imperial gaze with which the poet surveys the world in the hexameter panegyric that opens his collection. In his preface, the poet looks to the limits of the known world, which all now have fallen under the power of the Roman emperor. He sings that Hesperia, recovered from the barbarians, may breathe freely 'to the far edge of Cadiz and to the Iberian strait and Oceanic Thule' (ἐς κρηπῖδα Γαδείρων | καὶ παρὰ πορθμὸν Ἴβηρα καὶ Ὠκεανίτιδα Θούλην, *AP* 4.4.7–8). In the East, the poet imagines dancing 'on the Caucasian ridge and Kytaian shore' (Καυκασίῳ δὲ τένοντι καὶ ἐν ῥηγμῖνι Κυταίῃ, 12), a reference to Lazica, the site of ancient Colchis on the eastern shore of the Black Sea, recently pacified by Justinian.[28] Scanning the world from North to South, the poet declares that,

οὐκέτι μοι χῶρός τις ἀνέμβατος, ἀλλ' ἐνὶ πόντῳ

Ὑρκανίου κόλποιο καὶ ἐς βυθὸν Αἰθιοπῆα

Ἰταλικαῖς νήεσσιν ἐρέσσεται ἥμερον ὕδωρ. (*AP* 4.4.28–30)

No longer is any space inaccessible to me, but in the sea of the Hyrcanian gulf and to the bottom of Ethiopia calm water is traversed by Italian ships.

---

28 Agathias describes Roman affairs among the Lazoi extensively in his *History*.

All the world is open to the 'Ausonian traveller', whom the poet encourages to 'leap as you journey over the entire continent' (ὅλην ἤπειρον ὁδεύων, | Αὐσόνιε, σκίρτησον, ὁδοιπόρε, 31–2). The Roman tourist may travel safely from India to the pillars of Heracles, commonplaces for celebrating the extent of imperial geography (34–7). The emperor 'has surrounded the world with his sovereignty' (κυκλώσατο κόσμον | κοιρανίῃ, 49–50).[29]

The 'wide view' (περιωπή) at the top of the house is therefore an epigrammatic counterpart to the imperial vision that Agathias celebrates in the hexameters of the panegyric. Combining vertical ascent with horizontal expansiveness and harmonizing the classical and Christian traditions, Agathias' epigram also weds the seclusive, esoteric space of a cultured elite to the open, exoteric realm of empire. The poet envisions leaving behind the concealment of the cloistered cell and moving about in the world, and the panegyric of the verse preface to the *Cycle* is an important strategy in that transition. The kind of poetry that he and his peers compose must find a place in the imperial milieu: by making a prologue beginning with the emperor, he says, 'my entire enterprise will get off on the right foot' (ἅπαντα γάρ μοι δεξιῶς προβήσεται, *AP* 4.3.44). He wants his book to become as horizontally mobile as the hypothetical Ausonian tourist whom he imagines crisscrossing the Mediterranean.

By way of conclusion, I wish to consider briefly the significance of the final verse of Agathias' epigram, when the poet says, 'Yes, maybe it is a most faithful chamber of virtue' (Ναὶ τάχα τῆς ἀρετῆς πιστότατος θάλαμος, *AP* 9.653.6).[30] Viansino interprets the adjective πιστότατος (πιστότατον in his edition) as contrasting 'the difficulty of reaching the virtue that stays far from easy paths, with that which is met by reaching a well guarded and secret chamber' (*la difficoltà di giungere alla virtù, che si tiene lontana dalle facili strade, con quella che si incontra per giungere in una stanza ben custodita e nascosta*).[31] Viansino's identification of the contrasting spatial conceptualizations of *aretē* in Agathias' poem is consistent with the paradoxical coupling of intimacy and expansiveness that runs throughout the epigram. But there is more to the curious description of the airy rooftop as a 'most faithful chamber'. The phrase was inspired by a similar phrase from Nonnos' *Dionysiaka*: when Hera tries to make Semele reveal which god impregnated her, she provokes her with the suggestion that it was Apollo, in which case he should offer the girl his harp as a 'faithful sign of his chambers'

---

29 The Emperor in question is Justin II, not Justinian, though of course Justinian's wars provide the historical background for the empire that Justin II inherited: 'Nowhere here does Agathias specifically say that the Emperor in question had himself won these victories; he is describing not a process but a state of affairs – a reasonable account of how things might have appeared at the start of Justin's reign' (Cameron, *Agathias*: 14).

30 I follow the Budé edition of Waltz and Soury, who print πιστότατος θάλαμος, which is the reading in Planudes. The Palatine manuscript reads πιστότατον, which Beckby, Paton, and Viansino all preserve in their editions.

31 Viansino, *Agazia Scolastico*: 94.

(πίστον ἑῶν θαλάμων σημήιον, *D.* 8.231).[32] Adapting and transforming Nonnos' half-line into the climactic image of a πιστότατος θάλαμος,[33] Agathias invokes myths of marriage between gods and mortals. From the perspective of the epic predecessor, the epigram's 'most faithful chamber' becomes the conjugal bedroom where the human bride and her divine consort, subjects disparate in nature, unite in *erōs*. It is therefore a fitting space also for harmonizing vertical and horizontal orientations, classical and Christian cultural traditions, domestic intimacy and imperial grandeur. But the poet is not held in thrall to a sacred mystery, as he qualifies his profound description of the rooftop as a most faithful chamber with the wry expression 'yes, maybe' (Ναὶ τάχα).[34] In the end, his paradoxical coupling of horizontal expansiveness with seclusive intimacy remains provisional, and this indeterminacy reflects the ongoing struggle of the *pepaideumenos* as he seeks to find his place in the shifting cultural landscape of the sixth century.

---

32 Nonnos, poet of both mythological epic and author of a paraphrase of the Gospel of St. John, was himself interested in giving new expression to both the Christian and the classical traditions; see Bowersock, *Hellenism in Late Antiquity*: 41–53; Robert Shorrock, *The Myth of Paganism* (New York and London: Bloomsbury Academic, 2011); and David Hernández de la Fuente, 'Parallels Between Dionysos and Christ in Late Antiquity: Miraculous Healings in Nonnus *Dionysiaca*', in *Redefining Dionysos*, Alberto Bernabé, Miguel Herrero de Jáuregui, Ana Isabel Jiménez San Cristóbal, and R. Martín Hernández (eds) (Berlin: De Gruyter, 2013). On Nonnos' influence on Agathias and his circle of poets, see Cameron, *Agathias*: 24–6.

33 The phrases πίστον ἑῶν θαλάμων and πιστότατος θάλαμος each measure two and a half dactylic feet (–⏑ ⏑ – ⏑ ⏑ –), with adjectival and nominal stems occupying identical positions (πιστ ⏑ ⏑ – θαλαμ–). The metrical structure shows great versatility: Nonnos used it as the first half of an hexameter verse, while Agathias repositions his variation of the phrase to the second half of his final pentameter.

34 Paul the Silentiary uses the same phrase to humorous effect at the beginning of *AP* 5.235, as he imagines that 'yes, maybe' (Ναὶ τάχα) his own erotic suffering is worse than the torture endured by Tantalus in the underworld.

3 Monastic Space

The Ascetic Between Sacred and Civil Spheres in Theodoret of Cyrrhus

Andreas Westergren

Introduction[1]

The countryside is 'blinded and lies murdered', Libanius wails to his auditors, among them the emperor.[2] The farmland, he cries out, has been laid waste by an overflowing force as strong as the torrents in the winter-time.[3] The extra-urban temples, situated in 'some beauty spot',[4] have been swept away by the wave, and people, yes, countless innocent people have been killed by the flood. No longer are there any happy feasts where farmers can gather and celebrate in the surroundings of long-standing sacred shrines, these monuments of the very creation of cultivated land. These temples were the first buildings built by humans – in a time when they were recovering from another flood – and what is presently happening, Libanius seems to insist, is no less a catastrophe.

In his thirtieth oration, Libanius bewails the loss of a glorious but recent pagan past, and he points the finger accusingly at those who are responsible for the destruction of the rural temples, and therefore also for the ruin of the countryside: the famous 'black-robed tribe',[5] i.e. the Christian monks. What looks like a tidal wave crushing the countryside in one image is portrayed as a barbarian army ravaging the land in another; these monks 'wage war in peace time against the peasantry'.[6] Because the temples are 'the soul of the countryside' and 'to the benefit of humankind', these runaway rustics, robbers, and rebels threaten the authority of the emperor.[7] In the long run, the 'stability of the empire' is threatened because it 'depends on sacrifices' being performed in places such as these.[8]

---

1 This chapter brings together ideas that are also articulated in Andreas Westergren, 'Sketching the Invisible: Patterns of Church and City in Theodoret of Cyrrhus' Philotheos Historia' (PhD dissertation, Lund University, 2012): especially chapters 2.3 and 3.2.
2 Libanius, *Or.* 30.9: οὗτος τετύφλωταί τε καὶ κεῖται καὶ τέθνηκε, Richard Foerster (ed.) in vols. 1–4 of *Libanii opera* (Leipzig: Teubner, 1906); A. F. Norman (trans.) in vol. 1 of *Libanius: Selected Orations*, LCL 452 (Cambridge, MA: Harvard University Press, 1977).
3 For the image of a torrent (χειμάρροος) and its effect, see Libanius, *Or.* 30.9 and 20.
4 Libanius, *Or.* 30.17: τι φαιδρὸν χωρίον.
5 Libanius, *Or.* 30.8: οἱ μελανειμονοῦντες.
6 Libanius, *Or.* 30.13: ἐν εἰρήνῃ πολεμεῖσθαι τοὺς γεωργούς.
7 Libanius, *Or.* 30.9: ψυχὴ . . . τοῖς ἀγροῖς, 30.36: τοῖς ἀνθρώποις συμφέρειν, and in general 30.13–15.
8 Libanius, *Or.* 30.33: ἐν ταῖς ἐκεῖ θυσίαις κεῖται τὸ βέβαιον τῆς ἀρχῆς.

What is most apparent in Libanius' use of natural images is the polemic involved. By depicting a temple beautifully, he wishes to reinforce a negative sentiment toward those who destroy it. While character depictions involve value judgments it is also clear that natural images function to create emotion: 'Values . . . are also conceptualized in spatial and local terms.'[9] That space can be employed as a 'characterization device'[10] is something the ancients already knew, and characters were either good or bad. These matters are reflected in the rhetorical exercises that governed any educated writer's examination of a place, whether in its praise or blame of someone (or of a place).[11] To mention a person's hometown was to say something about her nature, and if someone had no origin to boast about, this gave added reason for praise of an achievement (or reason for a failure). In addition, the rhetorical exercise next to *ethopoeia*, literally the 'making of character', is the *ekphrasis*. Once you have learned to invent what different characters might *say* in a particular situation, you learn to present vivid pictures of them and/or their surroundings. A depiction of space can therefore be more or less 'naturalizing', thus either presenting a character's location only as a 'place of action', or rather making it into the 'acting place' which changes the course of the story.[12] Nevertheless, even a careful presententation of a specific place, one which seems to depict a location as it is, changes the presuppositions for story-telling, slowing down the pace of the narrative and inviting the character or the reader to meditate upon its impact.

The value-laden nature of space is even more noticeable when there are conflicting interpretations of a given environment. Christine Shepardson has considered how differently Libanius and Christian authors mapped the same Antiochene landscape according to religiously charged agendas that were at odds with one another.[13] A specific feature of this competition was the distinction between city and countryside. The perceived dividing line between urban and rural was age-old, she observes, and a commonplace in writings from the Roman and late Roman period. While the people of the *polis* expected country dwellers to be depicted as less intelligent, rhetors sometimes challenged the expectations to prove a specific point. John Chrysostom, for example, often inverted the logic to claim Christian superiority over pagan culture. Although Libanius generally defended a civic point of view, he also knew how to praise farmers while ridiculing drunkards in

---

9   Ineke Sluiter and Ralph M. Rosen, 'General introduction', in *City, Countryside, and the Spatial Organization of Value in Classical Antiquity*, Ralph M. Rosen and Ineke Sluiter (eds), (Mnemosyne Supplementa 279; Leiden, Boston: Brill, 2006): 3.
10 Gerald Prince, *A Dictionary of Narratology* (Lincoln: University of Nebraska Press, 2003): 90.
11 See, for example, the guidelines by Hermogenes, or Aphthonius, who was contemporary with Libanius in Antioch, in *Progymnasmata: Greek Textbooks of Prose Composition and Rhetoric*, George A. Kennedy (trans.) (WGRW 10; Atlanta: SBL, 2003).
12 Mieke Bal, *Narratology: Introduction to the Theory of Narrative* (third edition; Toronto: University of Toronto Press, 2009): 133–45, 139.
13 Christine Shepardson, *Controlling Contested Places: Late Antique Antioch and the Spatial Politics of Religious Controversy* (Berkeley: University of California Press, 2014): 171–90.

the city taverns.[14] In the above example, however, the contrast is quite different. The rural scenery that Libanius laid out before the eyes of his audience in the thirtieth oration is surely a space of its own, but still closely entwined both with city and with empire. In this instance, there seems to be a deep symbolic interrelation between the city and the countryside through the temples. The negative counterpart, the monks, come from a place even further away.

One might ask, therefore, how the defenders of asceticism responded to Libanius' scenic view and explicit criticism?[15] Were the only means a rhetoric of inversion, which contrasted the life of the world with that of the monastery? Until recently, scholarly interpretations of a monastic milieu have put a one-sided emphasis on remoteness. However, the picture is changing and James E. Goehring, for example, has remarked how the stories about Antony and the desert fathers created an *impression* of separateness, which was not always reflected by real circumstances. Not only were several desert settlements close to the Nile and thereby in the vicinity of villages and towns, but there were also many urban expressions of asceticism. The desert monk became the 'icon of renunciation', and exactly like an icon, this model was going to have an impact.[16] Lillian I. Larsen has gone a step further, arguing that we must re-direct the study of the desert saints into one which pays closer attention to the literary means through which these 'larger than life figures' and their surroundings are depicted and put them in conversation with the material remains. Reading the 'simple stories' about monks against an educational background, she has traced a trajectory which is parallel to the ways in which civic virtues are highlighted in ancient school texts. 'The caricatures that claim the foreground in texts like the *Life of Antony* and the *Apopthegmata Patrum*', she writes, 'offer a lucid record of explicit investment aimed at turning "the raw material of humanity" into model citizens and leaders of society'.[17]

These insights should be borne in mind when attention is directed to what is possibly an even stranger climate than the desert of Egypt, namely, the hinterland of Libanius' Antioch, a place where Christian monks were famous for both taking over temples and raising pillars. Keeping Libanius' portrait of catastrophe in mind, we shall see in the *History of the Monks of Syria* how the bishop Theodoret of Cyrrhus (CE 393–ca 460) is as careful as Libanius to create mythological relations between the city and the countryside, and how he in fact depicts the rise of monasticism according to a pattern that follows the rise of society. Expressions of remoteness, I will argue, are balanced by a civic perspective, a 'rhetoric of

---

14 Shepardson, *Controlling Contested Places*: 131–36.
15 Shepardson compares Libanius with John Chrysostom and Theodoret in *Controlling Contested Places*: 171–90.
16 James E. Goehring, 'The Encroaching Desert: Literary Production and Ascetic Space in Early Christian Egypt', *JECS* 1 (1993): 296.
17 Lillian I. Larsen, 'Re-Drawing the Interpretative Map: Monastic Education as Civic Formation in the *Apophthegmata Patrum*', *Coptica* 12 (2013): 21.

proximity'.[18] While the text certainly offers a rhetoric of distance and separateness, by which the saint is lifted out of the ordinary, I will highlight a rhetoric of adaptation to a human milieu. In the end, I will suggest that we do well to think of this literary presentation as a 'one-space-model', where divine and human realms are interrelated, rather than simply opposed, and where the monks, therefore, are contextualized on a continuum rather than being isolated in a place that is wholly different from the human world.

The Monks of Syria

If there is one 'icon of renunciation' in Theodoret's portrayal of the rising monastic movement in the Syrian milieu, it is certainly Symeon the Stylite. Among the 30 Lives in Theodoret's collective biography entitled *Philotheos Historia (PH)*,[19] the Life of Symeon has a key role as one of the last and longest narratives. Theodoret and Symeon were contemporaries, and Theodoret takes pride in having met the pillar saint before his work was published in CE 444. At least on the surface of these stories, there is little that recalls the theological and political turmoil of which Theodoret was a part as one of the defenders of the Antiochene position. In the hagiographical discourse, we are seemingly in another, more divine territory. Not only in Theodoret, but also in the history of scholarship, Symeon's long lifetime spent 20 metres in the air on a pillar seems to be the ultimate symbol of a world-renouncing tradition that privileges heaven over earth to the extent that it leaves the world out of the picture.

Recently, Niketas Siniossoglou has argued that, for Theodoret, Hellenic and Christian ascetical ideals are 'incompatible', citing examples from the *Philotheos Historia* about 'monks chaining themselves to rocks, living in cages, carrying weights around their necks and wearing heavy iron belts'.[20] According to Siniossoglou, such an emphasis on extreme suffering reflects an absence of social and political dimensions in the Christian asceticism depicted by Theodoret. However, Siniossoglou's interpretation is not uncontested.[21] Cristian Gaşpar,

---

18 Cf. Georgia Frank, *The Memory of the Eyes: Pilgrims to Living Saints in Christian Late Antiquity* (Berkeley: University of California Press, 2000): 76, who compares a rhetoric of displacement with a 'rhetoric of reconciliation'.
19 The critical edition of the *PH* is Pierre Canivet and Alice Leroy-Molinghen (eds), *Théodoret de Cyr: Histoire des moines de Syrie, Histoire Philothée*, two vols. (SCh 234, 257; Paris: Cerf, 1977, 1979). See also Canivet's groundbreaking study, *Le monachisme syrien selon Théodoret de Cyr* (ThH 42; Paris: Beauchesne, 1977).
20 Niketas Siniossoglou, *Plato and Theodoret: The Christian Appropriation of Platonic Philosophy and the Hellenic Intellectual Resistance* (Cambridge: Cambridge University Press, 2008): 127–46, 133.
21 Adam Schor's interpretation of how Theodoret is networking through his texts, above all through his letters, but also the *PH*, reveals an author who is keenly aware of his place in the world and who employs complex patronage strategies, such as humility, to become an indispensable bishop in civic, ecclesial, and monastic milieus. Adam M. Schor, *Theodoret's People: Social Networks and Religious Conflict in Late Roman Syria* (Berkeley: University of California Press, 2011). See also the important contributions by Canivet, *Le monachisme syrien*, especially 235, 248–53,

for example, has suggested that we can even identify a change of mind within Theodoret's own *corpus*, marked by his transition to the episcopacy. Where the ascetics seem lost in a flight to God in the earlier apologetic writing, the *Cure of Hellenic Maladies*, they come back to the world in the *Philotheos Historia*, and have developed civil manners. Like a public rhetor, Theodoret wields the panegyric speech to defy the explicit critique of ascetics by non-Christian intellectuals, notably Libanius. Now Theodoret consciously presents models that are well-known to a civic audience: heroes and philosophers. The desert model is exchanged for a city model.[22]

Gaşpar's analysis invites further scrutiny of the refined ways in which Theodoret paints the ground on which the ascetics stand. Theodoret had not only seen it with his own eyes but he had spent a considerable part of his life in this milieu. If we are to believe his own words, he stayed in the monastery of Agapetus and Symeon in Nikerte, not far away from Apamea, before being appointed a bishop.[23] What he does not mention, but rather displays, is the kind of traditional *paideia* he must have attained already while growing up in Antioch; in passing, Diodore of Tarsus and Theodore of Mopsuestia are referred to as teachers. Their connection to Libanius itself suggests that Thedoret probably knew the writings of the sophist.[24] So when Theodoret sat down to draw up his own picture of the monastic geography in Syria, he surely had the rocky topography of the Syrian hinterland before his eyes, but perhaps not only or even primarily this landscape. A trained eye such as Theodoret's was accustomed to catch sight of the details that linked a physical landscape with the literary world, both biblical and classical. To catch the attention of his readers or listeners, he knew how to make the images vivid with colours from a glorious past. In the *Prologue*, Theodoret makes an explicit comparison between the heroes of times gone by, who were remembered as literary models and statues on the city streets, and the living saints. If so many different people have received a place of honour before, he argues, do not the 'athletes of virtue' or 'god-loving humans' even more deserve emulation?[25] The juxtaposition makes clear that Theodoret painted the present with the past before his eyes, and that this involved not only the characters, but also the landscape of which they were a part.

Philip Wood, *'We Have No King but Christ'*: Christian Political Thought in Greater Syria on the Eve of the Arab Conquest (c.400–585) (Oxford: Oxford University Press, 2010): 39–66, and Arthur Urbano, *The Philosophical Life: Biography and the Crafting of Intellectual Identity in Late Antiquity* (North American Patristic Society, PMS 21; Washington, DC: The Catholic University of America Press, 2013), especially the introduction and ch. 7.

22 See Cristian Gaşpar, 'An Oriental in Greek Dress: The Making of a Perfect Philosopher in the *Philotheos Historia* of Theodoret of Cyrrhus', *AMSCEU* 14 (2008): 193–229, and Cristian-Nicolae Gaşpar, 'In Praise of Unlikely Holy Men: Elite Hagiography, Monastic Panegyric, and Cultural Translation in the *Philotheos Historia* of Theodoret, Bishop of Cyrrhus' (PhD dissertation, Central European University, 2006).

23 Theodoret, *Ep. (Collectio Sirmondiana)*: 81, 119; cf. Theodoret, *PH* 3.3.

24 Theodoret, *Ep. (CS)*: 16.

25 *PH* Pr. 1 τῶν . . . τῆς ἀρετῆς ἀθλητῶν . . . τῶν φιλοθέων ἀνδρῶν.

The Mountains

A key passage displaying the complex, conscious rhetorical skill that Theodoret employs when he discusses the monastic space is the introductory scene to the fourth Life. Theodoret is about to examine the saints of Teleda, a major monastery, and also a stepping stone for Symeon the Stylite on his rise to the pillar. In this short passage, the many ways of making a place into space are displayed, and illustration gives way to allusion and interpretation, sometimes by means of paradox. The previous narratives have been set in a well-known ideal terrain, the desert, which is now alluded to in a way that recalls the paradisal garden. However, the reader also learns that the desert is not the only place where piety can be practiced, since 'virtue' is not 'circumscribed in place (τόπος)'. As the limitless Godhead cannot be traced to a specific location – a point that is repeated – so virtue is not bound to place.[26]

> Ὁποίους μὲν ἡ ἄκαρπος ἔρημος καρποὺς τῷ θεῷ προσενήνοχεν, ὡρίμους καὶ πεπείρους καὶ πολυτίμους καὶ τῷ φυτουργῷ προσφιλεῖς καὶ τοῖς εὖ φρονοῦσι τῶν ἀνθρώπων ἐρασμίους καὶ τριποθήτους, ἐν τοῖς ἤδη συγγραφεῖσιν ὑπεδείξαμεν διηγήμασιν. Ὡς ἂν δὲ μή τις ὑπολάβῃ τόπῳ περιγεγράφθαι τὴν ἀρετὴν καὶ μόνην εἶναι τὴν ἔρημον εἰς τοιαύτης προσόδου φορὰν ἐπιτηδείαν, φέρε λοιπὸν εἰς τὴν οἰκουμένην μεταβῶμεν τῷ λόγῳ καὶ δείξωμεν τῇ τῆς φιλοσοφίας κτήσει ἥκιστα ταύτην ἐμποδὼν γιγνομένην. (*Philotheos Historia* 4.1)

> Which fruits are offered to God by the fruitless desert, ripe and mature and precious, dear to the gardener and beloved and thrice desired by men of good judgment – these we have displayed in the narratives we have already written. But lest anyone should suppose that virtue is circumscribed in place and that only the desert is suitable for the production of such a yield, let us now in our account pass to inhabited land, and show that it does not offer the least hindrance to the attainment of virtue.[27]

This passage contains a strong emphasis against anyone who assumes that the desert – presumably the Egyptian desert – should be a more saintly milieu. The narrator insists that virtue can be achieved in proximity to people, in the world of humans (τὴν οἰκουμένην), just as readily as in the wilderness. But what is the place signifying this human connection? Following directly upon the above passage, a vivid *ekphrasis* of another mythic space is suddenly elaborated: the mountain.[28]

---

26 See *PH* 6.8, 9.2 and the discussion in Westergren, *Sketching the Invisible*, ch. 3.3.3.
27 Translation by R. M. Price (ed.), *Theodoret of Cyrrhus: A History of the Monks of Syria* (Kalamazoo, MI: Cistercian, 1985), slightly revised.
28 As described by Aphthonius, an ecphrasis (at least of persons) should go from top to bottom, which is exactly what is happening here. Aphthonius, *Prog.* 36–42.

Ὄρος ἐστὶν ὑψηλὸν, πρὸς ἔω μὲν τῆς Ἀντιόχου, Βεροίας δὲ πρὸς ἑσπέραν διακείμενον, τῶν παρακειμένων ὀρῶν ὑπερκείμενον, κατὰ τὴν ἀκροτάτην κορυφὴν κωνοειδὲς μιμούμενον σχῆμα, ἀπὸ τοῦ ὕψους τὴν προσηγορίαν δεξάμενον· Κορυφὴν γὰρ αὐτὸ οἱ περίοικοι προσαγορεύειν εἰώθασιν. Τούτου πάλαι κατ' αὐτὴν τὴν ἀκρωνυχίαν τέμενος ἦν δαιμόνων ὑπὸ τῶν γειτονευόντων λίαν τιμώμενον. (*Philotheos Historia* 4.2)

Lying East of Antioch and west of Beroea, there is a high mountain that rises above the neighbouring mountains and imitates at its topmost summit the shape of a cone. It derives its name from its height, for the local inhabitants are accustomed to calling it *Koryphê* (Summit). On its very peak there was a precinct of demons much revered by those in the neighbourhood.

In the words of André-Jean Festugière, this panoramic description – which continues to describe the plain and the village below the summit before closing in on the narrative's ascetics – is 'très précise'.[29] Lying above the Dana Plain in northern Syria, *Koryphê* (today Sheikh Barakat), still has an imposing presence in this area. Even the 'precinct of demons' can easily be identified as a *temenos* to Zeus Malbachus and Salamanes.[30] That mountains come to play such an important role as a setting for the saints in the *Philotheos Historia* is not surprising, given the stony nature of the Syrian environment.[31] The reflection of a real habitat should not divert one's attention away from how these portraits also refract this landscape, so that it is cast in a particular light.[32]

Philip Rousseau has attracted attention to the symbolic role of mountains in the *Philotheos Historia*.[33] As he has pointed out, ascetics do not only climb mountains, they also scale the 'summit of virtue'.[34] Rousseau has suggested that the

---

29 André-Jean Festugière, *Antioche païenne et chrétienne: Libanius, Chrysostome et les moines de Syrie* (Paris: E. de Boccard 1959): 258.
30 Georges Tchalenko, *Villages antiques de la Syrie du Nord: Le massif du Bélus à l'époque romaine* (three vols; Paris, 1953–1958), cf. 1:154–5.
31 See for example the Life of James of Nisibis (*PH* 1), Macedonius (13), Maron (16), James of Cyrrhus (21), and not least, Symeon the Stylite (26), who also passed through the monastery of Teleda on the way to his own hilltop.
32 Susan Ashbrook Harvey has remarked that the Syrian geography was different from Egypt, and that these actual conditions are reflected in the texts. The fact that Syria lay on the border between the Roman and the Persian Empires made it necessary to develop a monastic culture that lay closer to protected places. 'The Syrian terrain and its vulnerable position as a border country made it necessary for the early Syrian anchorites either to remain near to fortified villages, as Jacob of Nisibs had done, or to bond together as a community, however loosely, as in the case of Julian Saba. These factors marked Syrian asceticism with its own distinctive style.' Susan Ashbrook Harvey, *Asceticism and Society in Crisis: John of Ephesus and the Lives of the Eastern Saints* (Berkeley: University of California Press, 1990): 14.
33 Philip Rousseau, 'Moses, Monks, and Mountains in Theodoret's Historia Religiosa', in *Il monachesimo tra eredità e aperture,* Maciej Bielawski and Daniël Hombergen (eds) (Rome: Centro Studi S. Anselmo 2004): 323–46.
34 *PH* 30.8: τὸ ὕψος τῆς ἀρετῆς

basic framework for this imagery is Moses as lawgiver on Mount Sinai. Moses provides an almost living arch between the age of the patriarchs and the lives of the Syrian ascetics. The power and authority of the latter mimic and reproduce the power and authority of the great lawgiver himself.[35] The association of place is important and Rousseau's interpretation is clearly correct; nonetheless, to say that the 'broader context' of a mountain peak is 'beyond doubt' an 'allusion to Sinai' seems to limit the case.[36] The attention that mountains have attracted in different cultures and Zeus' typical residence atop a mountain, reflected in the temple on *Koryphê*, suggests that the context is even broader. Even if Theodoret deliberately alludes to Mount Sinai when talking about a mountain peak, many of his readers would still be able to see Mount Olympus on the skyline.

What makes the 'pagan' connection especially valid is the way in which Theodoret rhetorically frames the whole story. Not only does he begin the narrative with the image of the mountain, he returns to the topic in the final paragraph. While the site is pagan in the first depiction, it is a 'holy mountain'[37] in the last, since it has become the symbolic centre for the growth of monasteries in the area. This spatial *inclusio* marks the transformation of this space from pagan to Christian. This is not the only instance when Theodoret points out that ascetics chose to live in or near sacred enclosures dedicated to the 'old' gods.[38] On several occasions, this detail is mentioned, as a brief nod to a sacred past that is recognized, albeit undermined. In contrast to Libanius, who lived a generation earlier, this recognition is detached in tone, as if there were no struggle anymore. Yet it is no less apologetic, and the rhetorical structure gives weight to Theodoret's demonstration of the grand tradition of both this particular monastery and the whole Syrian monastic tradition.

Since Theodoret invites the reader into the world of humans with the image of *Koryphê*, it may be worth spelling out some of the traits of a mountain in Greek mythology. An interpretation by Richard Buxton points to three main aspects: the *oros* was 'outside and wild', it was 'before', and lastly, it was a 'place for reversals', such as between gods and humans, possibly leading to metamorphoses.[39] All of these reflect the basic idea of a place set apart from the city and its cultivated surroundings. In this sense, there is no decisive difference between the desert and the mountain as formative milieux.[40] In both spaces, the ascetic may be seen as a wild outsider, as one who is primordial in his elementary way of living. Still, there are important differences in nuance between the desert and the mountain. The first concerns the gods. As symbolized by Mount Olympus, a mountain was the paradigmatic abode of the gods. Like no other place, the mountain was a place of revelation and intrinsically bound up

---

35 Rousseau, 'Moses, Monks, and Mountains': 331. Cf. *PH* 2.4,13.
36 Rousseau, 'Moses, Monks, and Mountains': 326.
37 *PH* 4.13: τὸ ὄρος . . . τὸ ἱερόν.
38 See for example *PH* 4.2, 6.4, 16.1 and 28.1 for ascetics living on temple sites. Cf. Theodoret, *Cur.* 10.52.
39 Richard Buxton, 'Imaginary Greek Mountains', *Journal of Hellenistic Studies* 112 (1992): 7–10.
40 In the Egyptian setting, an *oros* can even designate the desert. Buxton, 'Imaginary Greek Mountains': 2.

with Greek mythology. A second difference concerns distance from society. Unlike the desert, the mountaintops were visible, and in this way, comprehensible and accessible. The city/mountain boundary is not as sharp as that between city and desert, since many cities were built on or near mountainous terrain. An acropolis, for example, was the highest part of a city, serving as an easily defended refuge, and sometimes as a religious centre.[41] In times of trouble, the mountains surrounding a city could also serve as a temporary acropolis.[42] Moreover, temples on the hills surrounding a city were sites for processions, and so maintained living contact with the *polis*.[43] What is said about ancient Greece in the following passage also bears on later Antiquity – especially when we see the ascetics replacing the gods as the *locus* of holiness: 'Religious processions visibly illustrate interconnections between local sacred places, between gods within the local pantheons, and between people of the community; they ultimately achieve the overall goal of connecting people to their local gods and land.'[44] The processional route is a vivid reminder of the second difference, namely, that the relationship between a city and its surrounding mountain area can be seen as a continuum. Reading Theodoret, these fine distinctions are significant. In general, the vocabulary that he employs is atticizing, and he avoids, for example, the common words for a monastery (μοναστήριον) and a cell (κελλίον), replacing them with words that recall philosophical or more general religious contexts.[45] Consequently, Theodoret is concerned not only with picking the right words, but with evoking environments. In fact, there is another intriguing passage in the *Philotheos Historia* to which we should turn because it effectively organizes the various ascetic practices according to a long-standing spatial pattern that is associated with the mountains. Having recognized this design, we will be able to see how it is reflected throughout Theodoret's many stories.

The Rise to Heaven

In a collective biography, the organization of Lives is one way of creating overarching themes that help give sense to individual narratives. The *Philotheos Historia* loosely follows both a chronological development, from dead to living saints, and a geographical outline, from Nisibis and Edessa to Antioch, and finally to Theodoret's own diocese, Cyrrhus. In this scheme, the prologues and epilogues often serve the purpose of transition between otherwise more or less disconnected narratives. The

---

41 See for example the portrayal of the Serapeum in Alexandria as an acropolis in Aphthonius, *Prog.* 38–42.
42 Buxton, 'Imaginary Greek Mountains': 4.
43 Buxton, 'Imaginary Greek Mountains': 10–11.
44 Irene Polinskaya, 'Lack of Boundaries, Absence of Oppositions: The City-Countryside Continuum of a Greek Pantheon', in *City, Countryside, and the Spatial Organization of Value in Classical Antiquity*, Ralph M. Rosen and Ineke Sluiter (eds), Mnemosyne Supplementa 279 (Leiden, Boston: Brill, 2006): 90.
45 μοναστήριον is used once in the *PH*, in 3.14, and then as part of a quotation. See Canivet and Leroy-Molinghen, *Histoire des moines*, 1:277, n.3 and Westergren, *Sketching the Invisible*: ch. 2.3.3.

prologue to the fourth Life is one such example, signifying the transfer of holiness and virtue from the desert to the world. At the end of the *Philotheos Historia*, there is another case in point in the prologue to the Life of Baradatus, an ascetic who spent part of his life in a box mismatched to his size. In the face of such radical measures, Theodoret seeks to clarify that a plurality of ways (of life) lead to heaven. What makes this passage so captivating, apart from the strange milieu that is portrayed, is its careful ordering of space. In fact, if we watch closely, it is possible to compare this arrangement with Libanius' depiction of the rise of society after the flood, which was mentioned at the outset. Theodoret introduces a variety of ascetic abodes with a vertical image, the ladder, highlighting an upward orientation. The lifestyles of these saints, he says, are the 'many and various ladders for the ascent into heaven'.[46] Although the image conveys the ascent to heaven of all these ascetics, one should not miss the graded scale of their earthly dwellings.

Οἱ μὲν γὰρ κατὰ συμμορίας ἀγωνιζόμενοι – μυρία δὲ τοιαῦτα συστήματα καὶ ἀριθμὸν νικῶντα –, τῶν ἀγηράτων στεφάνων ἀπολαύουσι καὶ τῆς ποθουμένης ἀνόδου τυγχάνουσιν. Οἱ δὲ τὸν μοναδικὸν ἀσπαζόμενοι βίον καὶ μόνῳ προσλαλεῖν τῷ θεῷ μελετῶντες καὶ παραψυχῆς ἀνθρωπίνης οὐδεμιᾶς μεταλαγχάνοντες οὕτω τῆς ἀναρρήσεως ἀπολαύουσιν. Ἄλλοι δὲ ἐν σκηναῖς καὶ ἕτεροι ἐν καλύβαις διάγοντες τὸν θεὸν ἀνυμνοῦσιν. Οἱ δὲ τὸν ἐν ἄντροις καὶ σπηλαίοις ἀσπάζονται βίον. Πολλοὶ δέ, ὧν ἐνίων ἐμνήσθημεν, οὐκ ἄντρον ἔχειν, οὐ σπήλαιον, οὐ σκηνήν, οὐ καλύβην ἐπείσθησαν, ἀλλὰ γυμνῷ τῷ ἀέρι τὰ σφέτερα σώματα δεδωκότες τῶν ἐναντίων ποιοτήτων ἀνέχονται, ποτὲ μὲν τῷ κρυμῷ τῷ ἀκράτῳ πηγνύμενοι, ποτὲ δὲ τῷ πυρὶ τῆς ἀκτῖνος φλεγόμενοι. Καὶ τούτων δὲ αὖ πάλιν ὁ βίος διάφορος· οἱ μὲν γὰρ ἑστᾶσι διηνεκῶς, οἱ δὲ εἰς καθέδραν καὶ στάσιν τὴν ἡμέραν μερίζουσι. Καὶ οἱ μὲν ἐν θριγκίοις τισὶ καθειργμένοι τῶν πολλῶν τὰς συνουσίας ἐκκλίνουσιν, οἱ δὲ οὐδενὶ τοιούτῳ καλύμματι χρώμενοι πρόκεινται πᾶσι τοῖς βουλομένοις εἰς θεωρίαν. (*Philotheos Historia* 27.1)

Some, contesting in *companies* – myriad are such communities, defeating enumeration – enjoy ageless crowns and attain the desired ascent; others, embracing the *solitary life*, practising conversation with God alone and receiving no human consolation, enjoy in this way the proclamation [as victors]. Some living in *tents* and others in *huts* praise God with song; others embrace the life in *caves* and *grottoes*. Many, of whom I have recalled some, have not been induced to have a cave or hole or tent or hut, but giving their bodies to the *naked air* endure contrasts of temperature, sometimes frozen by unrelieved frost, sometimes burnt by the fire of the sun's rays. Of these again the life is various: some *stand* all the time, others divide the day between *sitting* and *standing*; some, *immured in enclosures*, shun the company of the many; others, with no such covering, are *exposed to all* who wish to see them.

---

46 *PH* 27.1: τῆς εἰς οὐρανὸν ἀνόδου πολλὰς καὶ διαφόρους . . . κλίμακας.

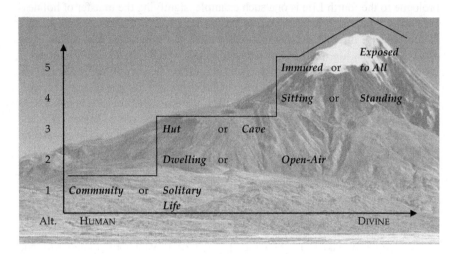

Figure 3.1 The 'Mountain' of Divine Ascent (diagram by author; image of Mount Ararat by NASA/JPL/NIMA [public domain], via Wikimedia Commons)

Following the order of the alternatives that are given in the passage, a structure is evoked that spans life in community to life in solitude. In its turn, the solitary life is systematically depicted as a movement from life in human-built abodes (σκηνή, καλύβη) to life in natural shelters (ἄντρον, σπήλαιον), while the last saints, having fled even these refuges, are living with little or no protection. Since these last saints also live on the mountains the idea of virtuous ascent is fused with the visible topography. In a diagram we can see how the passage is structured as five alternatives, which also depict a movement from a human to a divine environment.

Even if it should not be treated as a fixed system, Figure 3.1 depicts a pattern that is logically consistent with the narratives in the *Philotheos Historia*. Saints who live in the open-air are often depicted as having started their career in a community, or at least with some kind of shelter, before going to extremes. These steps could therefore describe a kind of training, whereby an ascetic proceeds to more severe practices. If so, community life is conceived as the starting point for ascetic life, and only a small number of recluses attain the highest and most rigorous degree of solitary life. Residence inside a dwelling, then, constitutes a preparatory phase. Through the walls of a cell, ascetics can turn to themselves, according to the philosophic maxim, contemplate God, and so be purified.[47]

As I see it, the chart does not represent an opposition between irreconcilable poles so much as a continuum, where it is possible to move in both directions.

---

47 *PH* 15.1.

Just as there is a way towards transcendence of nature, the model exhibits a way to adjust ascetic practice to human nature by endorsing a more civilized monastic setting. Sometimes, therefore, an open-air ascetic needs to take a step back on the scale to a life better adapted to human conditions. One story tellingly describes how an ascetic had to return to the safe harbour of a monastery. Living in an unprotected enclosure, he was increasingly disturbed by visitors. Since 'intercourse with the multitude exhausted him completely', as the story goes, he tried to shut himself in. Notwithstanding this attempt to restructure his open-air life as a life in a secluded dwelling, the burnt-out ascetic finally ran off to a monastery and was left alone – with God.

This story reveals how an ascetic might reconcile his intention and ability with God's economy. In my interpretation, the story of the monk who finally reverts to the life of the monastery exhibits the motif of balance between a more divine life and a life adapted to human conditions in the *Philotheos Historia*. In other stories, the same adaptation is needed because the saint is sick or getting old.[48] It is clear that Theodoret cautions against extremes. As is clearly said in one Life: suicide is not a virtue.[49] To more clearly indicate how profoundly this second trajectory – from a divine to a human way of life – influences the depiction of monasticism, I will give two further examples, first a well-known legend about the rise of society, and then the story of the rise of monasticism as depicted in the *Philotheos Historia*.

The Rise of a Monastic Society

In the beginning of the thirtieth oration, Libanius recounts the legend with which we began concerning the rebirth of civilization after a great flood. The story was widespread, being found already in Homer, and later also in Plato and Strabo among others.[50] In it, the symbolic role of the mountain as a place of origin for human and civil existence is displayed. A direction emerges: downwards, from the tops of the mountains to the plain.

> Οἱ πρῶτοι φανέντες ἐπὶ γῆς, ὦ βασιλεῦ, τὰ μετέωρα καταλαβόντες σπηλαίοις τε καὶ καλύβαις αὐτοὺς διασώζοντες θεῶν εὐθὺς ἔννοιαν λαβόντες καὶ γνόντες ὁπόσον ἡ 'κείνων εὔνοια τοῖς ἀνθρώποις, ἱερά τε οἷα εἰκὸς τοὺς πρώτους φύντας, καὶ ἀγάλματα σφίσιν αὐτοῖς ἐποίησαν. τῶν πραγμάτων δὲ εἰς πόλεις προελθόντων ἤδη τῆς περὶ ταῦτα τέχνης εἰς τοῦτο ἀποχρώσης πολλαὶ μὲν ἐν ὑπωρείαις, πολλαὶ δὲ ἐν πεδίοις ἐφάνησαν, ἐν ἑκάστῃ δὲ μετὰ τὸ τεῖχος ἀρχὴ τοῦ λοιποῦ σώματος ἱερὰ καὶ νεῴ. παρὰ γὰρ δὴ τῶν τοιούτων κυβερνητῶν ἡγοῦντο μεγίστην αὐτοῖς καὶ τὴν ἀσφάλειαν ἔσεσθαι.[51]

---

48 Cf. *PH* 13.2 and 3.
49 A priest and abbot warned Symeon against the severity of his practice, and 'urged him not to think suicide [lit. 'a violent death'] a virtue', *PH* 26.7: παραινοῦντος μὴ νομίζειν ἀρετὴν εἶναι τὸν βίαιον θάνατον.
50 Homer, *Il.* 20.216–218, Plato, *Leg.* 677a–681e, Strabo, *Geogr.* 13.1.25.
51 Libanius, *Or.* 30.4 (Norman (trans.), slightly revised).

The first men who appeared on earth, Sire, occupied the high places and protected themselves in caves and huts, and soon gained a notion of gods and realized how much their goodwill means to humankind. They raised the kind of temples to be expected of primitive man and made idols for themselves. As their accomplishments advanced towards urbanization and building techniques became adequate for it, many cities made their appearance at the mountain's foot or on the plains, and in each and every one of them the first civic bodies to be erected after the wall were shrines and temples, for they believed that from such governance they would have the utmost protection also.

The flood's only survivors, the legend says, were those who had lived on the high mountains, and who continued to live their very simple way of life in caves and huts (σπηλαίοις τε καὶ καλύβαις). Only after much time did the people dare to descend in stages. Strabo summarizes the long discussion in Plato:

Εἰκάζει δὲ Πλάτων μετὰ τοὺς κατακλυσμοὺς τρία πολιτείας εἴδη συνίστασθαι· πρῶτον μὲν τὸ ἐπὶ τὰς ἀκρωρείας ἁπλοῦν τι καὶ ἄγριον, δεδιότων τὰ ὕδατα ἐπιπολάζοντα ἀκμὴν ἐν τοῖς πεδίοις· δεύτερον δὲ τὸ ἐν ταῖς ὑπωρείαις, θαρρούντων ἤδη κατὰ μικρόν, ἅτε δὴ καὶ τῶν πεδίων ἀρχομένων ἀναψύχεσθαι· τρίτον δὲ τὸ ἐν τοῖς πεδίοις.[52]

Plato conjectures, however, that after the time of the floods three kinds of civilization were formed: the first, that on the mountain tops, which was simple and wild, when men were in fear of the waters which still deeply covered the plains; the second, that on the foothills, when men were now gradually taking courage because the plains were beginning to be relieved of the waters; and the third, that in the plains.

Only after this slow development, occurring over generations, did the first cities eventually arise. On the plain, the founder of Troy, Ilus, was born. This example, recalling a downward process of civilization, exhibits the same motion as the previous examples from the *Philotheos Historia*, and is even more compelling if we also take into account the way in which Theodoret depicts the rise of monasticism as the rise of a new society.

The two first ascetics, James of Nisibis and Julian Saba, resemble the 'first' people in the legend, James 'occupying the high places' and Julian 'protecting himself in a cave'.[53] These saints are cast in a legendary light where their pristine ways of life are in the foreground. James does not have a settled place, but wanders around the mountains nearby, sustained only by what nature provides, not even using fire.[54] Julian conducts his life in similar fashion, although bound to one place. And yet, even these

---

52 Strabo, *Geogr.* 13.1.25 (Jones (trans.)).
53 Cf. the previous quotation from Libanius, *Or.* 30.4.
54 *PH* 1.2; cf. 2 Cor 3:18.

saints are not portrayed as entirely uncivilized. Both saints are 'metamorphosed' in the encounter with God, an encounter that is expressed with mimetic and erotic imagery.[55] In the case of Julian, it seems that the portrayal of his location echoes the oracle cult. The act of seeking out a secluded place, such as a *cella* or a cave, was commonplace also in Greek religion, and to an 'astonishing' degree,[56] the oracle cult was connected precisely to caves, exemplified most famously by the temple grotto at Delphi, where Apollo was manifested through the Pythia. In Theodoret's early writing, the *Cure of Hellenic Maladies*, this practice was severely criticized, but precisely against this background the presentation of Julian Saba becomes even more remarkable.[57] In his cave, Julian is depicted as an 'inspired man' (τὸν θεσπέσιον ἄνδρα), a description partly linked to oracles.[58] The whole scene is carried out in what Pierre Canivet has termed 'le style poètique',[59] with the *Psalms of David* serving as a new kind of oracle. Julian is an enthusiast, divinely possessed and intoxicated (μεθύειν), not by the fumes at Delphi, but by his desire for the Beloved, to the extent of dreaming dreams (ὀνειροπολεῖν) and seeing visions (φαντάζεσθαι).[60] Under these circumstances, it follows that Julian's life is related to human life inasmuch as any oracle would be, and as a result, he soon attracts disciples.

In the course of the first two narratives we can trace the downward movement in the diagram, from life in the open-air to a natural shelter, to a dwelling made by human hand. While James lived on the mountain, and Julian in a natural cave, the latter is soon involved in a discussion with his disciples about building a hut. They ask Julian for permission to build it, but the saint is hesitant at first. A negotiation between the saint and his disciples begins, which takes on almost mythic proportions. Throughout the story the saint travels between an isolated place where he can turn to God in solitude and the camp of his monks. Recalling the dialogue between Moses (who is mentioned) and his people, Julian lays down rules with a transcendent paradigm in mind, but these are not fully accepted. On repeated occasions, Julian therefore chooses to concede, 'for he had been taught by the great Paul not to seek his own will but to accommodate himself to the lowly'.[61] Living without a hut would be the 'more perfect way',[62] he states, and

---

55 James not only receives a vision of God, but *becomes* vision, and is transformed (μετεμορφοῦτο) completely. Cf. *PH* 1.3 and 2.2.
56 Yulia Ustinova, *Caves and the Ancient Greek Mind: Descending Underground in the Search for Ultimate Truth* (Oxford: Oxford University, 2009): 53, 121–53 and 189.
57 Theodoret, *Cur.* 10.4. Porphyry explains the mysterious and symbolic meaning of the cave, referring to how the 'ancients' consecrated caves as temples and how they have been used as places for initiation. The reference to the 'caves and grottoes' of the ancients is expressed with the same doubling of words that was seen in the diagram. Porphyry, *Antr. nymph.* e.g. 5, 6, 8, 20.
58 See LSJ, θεσπέσιος. For an inspired singer at an oracle-site being called a θεσπιῳδός, see Ustinova, *Caves*: 111.
59 Canivet and Leroy-Molinghen, *Histoire des moines*, 1:197: n.4.
60 For all these expressions, see *PH* 2.2.
61 *PH* 2.4: ἐδιδάχθη γὰρ ὑπὸ τοῦ μεγάλου Παύλου μὴ τὰ ἑαυτοῦ ζητεῖν, ἀλλὰ τοῖς ταπεινοῖς συναπάγεσθαι. Cf. Rom 12:16 and 1 Cor 10:33.
62 *PH* 2.4: τὰ τελεώτερα.

closer to heaven, but this is not for everyone. The passage displays the necessity of accommodating human conditions.[63] The related idea of *synkatabasis*, or 'condescension to the level of the audience' was an important and popular motif in Antiochene exegesis.[64] It took as its paradigm the God who dwelt among humans, and Paul was considered to be a strong advocate for this kind of thinking, which involved a pedagogical way to salvation for everyone according to their level of understanding. A constructed building is just such an adjustment to human conditions, but exactly as such can also be a means for rising above these conditions. As a soteriological response to human needs, this civilizational logic constitutes something good. It is not the goal of the journey, but a necessary starting point and a continuous reference point on the way to heaven.

In a later narrative, the Life of Publius (*Philotheos Historia* 5), the monastic building project is brought to a new stage, with an even stronger stress on civilization. The beginning of the narrative describes a group of ascetics who live in cells under a supervisor. Only after some time does the ascetic leader, Publius, realize that the construction of a single building, the first coenobitic monastery, would actually help their cause. From that point on, the ascetics live in a perfect *koinônia*, helping each other to even more perfect virtue.

> Καθάπερ γὰρ ἐν ταῖς πολιτικαῖς ἀγοραῖς ὁ μὲν ἄρτων ἐστὶ πρατήρ, ὁ δὲ λαχάνων, ὁ δὲ ἱματίων ἔμπορος, ἄλλος δὲ ὑποδημάτων δημιουργός, παρ' ἀλλήλων δὲ τὴν χρείαν ἐρανιζόμενοι θυμηρέστερον βιοτεύουσιν, ὁ μὲν γὰρ ἱμάτιον διδοὺς ἀντιλαμβάνει ὑπόδημα, ὁ δὲ λάχανον ὠνούμενος ἀποδίδοται ἄρτον· οὕτως ἡμᾶς ἀλλήλοις ἀντιδιδόναι προσήκει τῆς ἀρετῆς τὰ πολυτίμητα μόρια. (*Philotheos Historia* 5.4)

> Just as in city markets one sells bread, another vegetables, one trades in clothes while another makes shoes, and so supplying their needs from each other they live more contentedly – the one who provides a piece of clothing receives a pair of shoes in exchange, while the one who buys vegetables supplies bread – so it is right that we should give each other the highly honoured pieces of virtue in return.

This is life lived in utmost harmony, with a remarkable comparison to life in a city: civilized life here constitutes the positive example for coenobitic life.

There is at least one further stage in the monastic evolution towards civilization. The Life of Theodosius (*Philotheos Historia* 10) begins in a familiar manner, with an ascetic retreating from the world in search of God. After a while, he attracts disciples, but he does not only pray with them. Instead, he strongly advocates

---

63 Cf. e.g. *PH* 3.12, 26.4.
64 LSJ: συγκατάβασις, and Jutta Tloka, *Griechische Christen – christliche Griechen: Plausibilisierungsstrategien des antiken Christentums bei Origenes und Johannes Chrysostomos* (Tübingen: Mohr Siebeck, 2005): 130.

taking care of guests and even develops something resembling an industry.[65] The building of a sea port fulfils an important function as a place for a new encounter. If the monastery served as a place where their respective needs could be met in community, their landing-place offers a similar opportunity with respect to the wider world: the monastery's community's commercial trade testifies to a mutual dependence between the two. They can blend their contribution with their need, and the purposefulness of this civic life is underlined by Scriptural quotations. The grandeur of a monastery with its own harbour comes close to the depiction of a city, and the ascetic is also told to be the patron saint of many sailors.

In four successive stages, then, a monastic society is evolving, from the mountain of James, to the cave and hut of Julian, to the monastery of Publius, and finally to the 'city' of Theodosius. From a simple, basic life in the early stories, constituting one kind of ideal, civilization gradually emerges, in the later stories, in a fully developed life in the service of others. In short, it is the same development that was depicted in the chart, and which was reflected in Libanius' legend about the rise of society.

The Rise of a Stylite

My main argument has been that the many cells of the ascetics exist on a continuum between civil and sacred spheres in the *Philotheos Historia*. The contrast between the cell of an eremite and human society should not be thought to constitute an opposition so much as distinct, but related spheres of a common environment. A rhetoric of proximity, or civilization, occurs next to one of separateness, or sacralization. In a way, the structure of the *Philotheos Historia* as a whole follows the two trajectories that I have outlined. Whereas the first part of the *Philotheos Historia* follows a pattern of civilization, from James of Nisibis to the evolving monasteries, this development seems to come to a halt with the stationary saints, who embody the most extreme practices of the saints in the second half. This tradition, which reaches a climax in the life of Symeon the Stylite, was native to Cyrrhus, the diocese of Theodoret. When the *Philotheos Historia* depicts this as the most divine way of asceticism, it could thus be seen as a form of self-promotion, but perhaps also as a limit for ascetic idiosyncrasy. These ascetics' late arrival on the scene indicates that they had developed out of the greater Syrian and coenobitic tradition, and reflects an awareness of the preparation that was needed before an ascetic could become like Symeon such an open window to a more divine life.

This takes us back to the Stylite, and the question of a 'social and political dimension' to these texts. The first half of Theodoret's Life of Symeon (*Philotheos Historia* 26) is modelled very closely along the patterns of the chart, from life in a community to a life in full exposure, and it is no coincidence that the interpretative passage that we employed for the diagram is inserted immediately after

---

65 PH 10.3-4. For another story stressing hospitality, see *PH* 3.20.

the Life of Symeon. Having been chased out of a monastery, Symeon resides in two dwellings: first, a natural shelter (a dried pond or cistern), then a human-made structure (a hut).[66] After a while Symeon decides to lead his life in the open air, staying first inside an unroofed enclosure, then tearing that down and living 'exposed to all'.[67] By this point he has also climbed a mountain, which again fuses the ideas of physical and spiritual ascent.

Symeon's life elucidates the tension between a preparatory practice inside a cell, where the saint is hidden from the world, and a life exposed, which is only possible as the result of an initial purification. However, it is also crucial to note that the Life of Symeon does not end with his ascent; in a way, it begins anew with stories that testify to his positive influence on barbarian tribes.[68] Perhaps the link between the saint's deification and the divine actions that are performed by the saint is the one most easily missed. After all, the depiction of a life that is spent in solitude, sometimes in the strangest of ways, creates an impression of difference, or displacement. However, one must also take account of the panegyrical structure of the stories, where *êthos* is followed by *praxeis*. This is a biographical commonplace with moral consequences: an acquisition of virtue constitutes the condition for action in the world. The pattern is given already by Plato, where the deification of society first required a deification of the soul.[69] In the *Philotheos Historia*, this arrangement is developed with an accent on the actions of the saint as worked out by the grace of God.

Conclusion

This journey has taken us from Libanius' portrait of a devastated farmland to the temples on the highest mountains and back to society again – with the monks. With Libanius as travel companion we were able to identify an apologetic concern in a real struggle over space, but also a more general depiction of a cultivated landscape of which both the city and the countryside were a part. The temples were signifiers for both milieux and the road in between a sign of their interrelation, serving as reminders that before imposing dichotomies we should attempt to view these poles on a continuum.

Once Theodoret took over as a guide it seemed, at first sight, that he preferred a transcendent to a civic paradigm, heaven over earth, the mountain instead of the city. Nevertheless, it has became clear that he offers a very similar approach to Libanius, both in his apologetic concern (against the 'pagans' that Libanius defended) and in the endeavour to integrate the divine with the human without allowing one of them to be swallowed by the other. Although he surely offers a

---

66 *PH* 26.5–7.
67 *PH* 26.22: Πρόκειται πᾶσι.
68 *PH* 26.13–14, with metaphors of light and descent.
69 Cf. Dominic J. O'Meara, *Platonopolis: Platonic Political Philosophy in Late Antiquity* (Oxford: Oxford University Press, 2003).

divine trajectory, which is symbolized by the ascetics leaving the world behind and climbing the ladders to heaven, he also depicts a second, downward trajectory, reflected in the ancient myth of civilization, which was employed in the depiction of the growth of the monastic movement. There, the monasteries developed to the point of resembling cities. In these narratives, the tension between the perfect human who seeks only God and society where human needs are met reflects two poles on a continuum. According to this scheme, which was visualized in the diagram, deification and civilization are parallel trajectories rather than contradictions. There is movement between human and divine which goes in both directions.

In conclusion, I suggest that we call this scheme a 'one-space-model' inasmuch as the different locations of ascetics are exhibited along a graded scale, which situates them differently between the poles of human and divine realms and where there is room for movement in both directions. The model is not general in the sense that it could be applied to any context or text. It emerges from a simple observation of structure within a specific text-passage and continued reflection on how this structure relates to other narratives in the *Philotheos Historia*, displaying a general understanding of the relation between the sacred and civil. Rather than saying that Symeon's life is to be imitated, the chart indicates that there are many routes to becoming virtuous, because, as is said in another key passage, virtue is not 'circumscribed in place'. Virtue is not even a privilege of the monks, but rather available to everyone, men and women, rich and poor, whether in the city or in the countryside. Moreover, the chart's reflection of a mythic landscape, which connects the heroes of the past with a new, monastic society, suggests that its conceptual world is accessible both to believers and to non-believers (and those in-between). It places the strange saints within the frame of a civilized world.

However, even if the model does not permit general conclusions beyond the *Philotheos Historia*, it may be used as point of comparison for depictions of space in other texts, and may serve as a reminder that one should be careful not to apply binary options too readily to monastic texts, even when the texts themselves seem to have adopted them.

Part II
Theological Perspectives

Part II

Theological Perspectives

4 Seeing Christ at the Holy Places

Juliette Day

Late antique pilgrims travelled to the Holy Land to see the Holy Places where biblical events took place, the most important of these were connected with the birth, death and resurrection of Christ. These pilgrims engaged in a whole body sensory experience. They walked, or travelled uncomfortably in carriages or on donkeys, to the places themselves. They touched the Holy Places with their feet, their hands, their lips. They smelt sanctity in oil and incense, or even from the monks. They heard the relevant scriptures read, as Egeria frequently noted, in the very places where the events described took place.[1] They tasted holy water and the 'apples from John the Baptist's orchard'.[2] But, above all, they saw. As Georgia Frank has demonstrated, sight was the privileged sense through which sense, that is meaning, was conveyed and understood.[3] Most studies of these pilgrimages concern themselves with the places, the itinerary, and the devotional actions at each place, but here I wish to take Frank's observations a little further and reflect on the different ways in which sight conveyed meaning, and how the reports of 'seeing' in the pilgrimage narratives function to reveal truths about Christ, about the place and about the pilgrim herself.

There is clearly a relationship between the place, the visits, the pilgrimage accounts and the text of scripture, but how these relate to each other is not always so obvious and a number of factors come into play. These are important because they help explain why pilgrims saw differently and reported what they saw quite differently, which cannot be explained simply by their exegetical skills, or lack thereof. First, the selection of places to be visited is not necessarily determined in relation to the scriptural narrative, and this is evident when pilgrims visit places out of sequence, or appear to ignore some significant places while making detours to visit other, quite obscure, places. The journeys are, to a large extent,

---

1 Egeria, *Itinerarium* (henceforth *It. Eg.*).
2 *It. Eg.* 15.6 (John W. Wilkinson (trans.), *Egeria's Travels* [second edition; Warminster: Aris & Phillips, 1981]: 111).
3 See especially, Georgia Frank, *The Memory of the Eyes: Pilgrims to Living Saints in Christian Late Antiquity* (Berkeley: University of California Press, 2000) and 'The Pilgrim's Gaze in the Age before Icons', in *Visuality Before and Beyond the Renaissance: Seeing as Others Saw*, Robert S. Nelson (ed.) (Cambridge: Cambridge University Press, 2000): 98–115.

determined by pragmatic factors – the roads, the memorials or churches, and the monks or deacons who act as guides and interpreters of the topography and of scripture. Liturgical commemorations offer another interpretation, in which psalms, readings from the Old and New Testaments and prayers present a theology of the place and/or of the event, and ritual participation situates the pilgrim typologically in that event; as Jonathan Z. Smith has observed it is the particular focus on the place through ritual which causes a place to take on a sacred character.[4] In Jerusalem, the participation of the bishop, and gathered around him the whole church – presbyters, deacons, the faithful, catechumens, monks and virgins, amongst whom were also pilgrims – raised the status of the commemoration and thus of the place. Thirdly, there may well be other literature supporting the pilgrimage which is not mentioned in the accounts, but which surely lies behind them: Eusebius' *Onomasticon,* a gazetteer of biblical places, with Jerome's additions; the *Itinerarium* of the anonymous Pilgrim of Bordeaux; even Jerome's *epitaphium* of Paula, which we will study here, may well have served as a guide to future pilgrims.[5] Thus what they saw was interpreted not just through Scripture; Scripture itself was interpreted through a variety of other texts, as Frank has asserted of Egeria, 'She knew that travel writing both represents what has been seen and creates what can be seen.'[6] A most obvious example of this is Jerome's *Ep.* 46 to Marcella, in which he, purportedly on behalf of Paula and Eustochium, described what Marcella might see if she came to the Holy Land, and much of that is indeed what he reported (in *Ep.*108) that Paula had seen during her pilgrimage.

What the pilgrims were doing and their interpretative methods have, of course, come under scrutiny, but none of these seem applicable to the specific ways of seeing which the late fourth and early fifth century reports indicate. Thus Sabina MacCormack suggested that it was the concrete relationship between Scripture and the place which was primary, and that seeing was a way of validating the place;[7] or Kenneth G. Holum, that the pilgrim sought to 'make Scripture vivid', that is to bring it alive;[8] or Gary Viken, that we should focus on *mimesis*, that is how the pilgrims imitate the (biblical) participants at specific holy places.[9] Patricia Cox Miller, in two thought-provoking books, focusses our attention on the role

---

4 Jonathan Z. Smith, *Imagining Religion: From Babylon to Jonestown* (Chicago; University of Chicago Press, 1982): 54–5.
5 See Rodney Aist, *The Christian Topography of early Islamic Jerusalem: The Evidence of Willibald of Eichstätt (700–787 CE)* (Turnhout: Brepols, 2009) for a discussion of the re-use of pilgrimage literature.
6 Frank, *Memory*: 102.
7 Sabina MacCormack, 'Loca Sancta: The Organisation of Sacred Topography in Late Antiquity', in *The Blessings of Pilgrimage*, Robert Ousterhout (ed.) (Urbana: University of Illinois Press, 1990): 7–40.
8 Kenneth G. Holum, 'Hadrian and St. Helena: Imperial Travel and the Origins of Christian Holy Land Pilgrimage', in Ousterhout, *Blessings*: 66–81, especially 69.
9 Gary Viken, 'Pilgrims in Magi's Clothing: The Impact of Mimesis on Early Byzantine Pilgrimage Art', in Ousterhout, *Blessings*: 97–107.

of imagination and of the visual in late antique culture, a focus which extends to ways of writing,[10] and on what she termed the 'material turn', where 'the material world was suffused with divine presence', so that 'matter could provide an intercessory conduit for human access to spiritual power'.[11] Thus *phantasia* (imagination) is, following Plotinus, an essential aspect of cognition which may be displayed in, for example, *ekphrasis*, '"a descriptive speech bringing the thing shown vividly before the eyes", turning listeners into spectators'.[12] *Ekphrasis* was more than just a description, it was intended to place the listeners in the situation being described, so that they might respond emotionally, see in their mind's eye and therefore comprehend, just as the writer had done.

Thus we are invited to consider the literariness of the pilgrimage accounts, to regard them not simply as descriptions of what one pilgrim saw, but as a means to enable readers and hearers to see the holy places while being far removed from them. In this way, reporting what was seen or could be seen is an essential element in the pilgrimage genre, although one does note that the descriptions of the places are often too lacking in detail to enable any sort of imaginative reconstruction of the place itself, so that the focus seems rather to be on the act of seeing them.

Seeing the Holy Places

One of the earliest references to the benefit of seeing the Holy Places is from Cyril, Bishop of Jerusalem (c. 350–86) whose episcopate witnessed the first flourishing of devotional and liturgical commemorations at the biblical sites, especially those in the city itself. Speaking to those preparing for baptism, he emphasized their privileged position, 'For others merely hear, but we see (βλέπομεν) and touch.'[13] Seeing confirmed the truth of the biblical narrative and, by extension, the truth of Christian doctrines: 'The Lord was crucified; you have received the testimonies. You see (ὁρᾷς) this place of Golgotha. With a cry of praise you assent (συντιθέμενος).'[14] In asserting and demonstrating the truth of the resurrection, Cyril presents prophecies of the Old Testament in conjunction with the gospel accounts, and then situates the candidates as witnesses to these events, just as they are witnesses to the very places as he speaks, therefore 'even the stone which was rolled back, lying there to this present day, testifies to the Resurrection'.[15] Any doubts they have about the truth of Christian doctrines can be set aside because of the plentiful evidence which is before their eyes:

---

10   Patricia Cox Miller, *Corporeal Imagination: Signifying the Holy in Late Ancient Christianity* (Philadelphia; University of Pennsylvania Press, 2009) and *Dreams in Late Antiquity: Studies in the Imagination of a Culture* (Princeton: Princeton University Press, 1994).
11   Cox Miller, *Corporeal Imagination*: 9.
12   Cox Miller, *Corporeal Imagination*: 10.
13   Cyril of Jerusalem, *Cat.* 13.22 (FCh 64,19; PG 33, 800B).
14   Cyril of Jerusalem, *Cat.*13.23 (FCh 64, 19; PG 33, 800D). The editor of the Greek text suggests that the assent was given by an acclamation (PG 33, 799 n2).
15   Cyril of Jerusalem, *Cat.*19.22 (FCh 64, 47).

You have many witnesses, therefore; you have this place of Resurrection itself; you have to the east the place of His Ascension. You have as witnesses the angels, also, who bore his testimony at His Resurrection, and the cloud on which he ascended, and the disciples who came down from the place of the Ascension.[16]

Gregory of Nyssa visited the holy places in Jerusalem when sent as an envoy to the church of Palestine from the council of Constantinople in 381. In a letter written almost immediately afterwards to three women ascetics whom he had met there,[17] he too seems to assert the moral and spiritual benefits of seeing the holy places: 'So when I saw the holy places with the senses (εἶδον ... αἰσθητῶς) and saw too the signs of these places manifested in you, I was filled with a joy so great that it cannot be described in words.'[18] However, when asked to assess the merits of pilgrimage for monks and nuns from Cappadocia, he was much more hesitant about the concrete benefits. He acknowledges that, 'some of those who have undertaken the solitary and retired life have made it a law of their piety to see (ἰδεῖν) the places in Jerusalem where the tokens of the Lord's sojourn in the flesh may be seen (ὁρᾶται)'.[19] But, they are mistaken if they think there is a direct connection between piety (εὐσεβείας) and seeing:

> For we confessed that the Christ who was made manifest is true God both before we arrived in the place and afterwards. Our faith was neither diminished nor increased. We knew that he was made man through the Virgin – before we saw (ἠπιστάμεθα) Bethlehem; we believed in his resurrection from the dead – before we saw (ἐπιστεύσαμεν) his memorial-rock; we confessed the truth of his ascension into heaven – without having seen (ἰδεῖν) the Mount of Olives. We benefited only this much from our travelling there, that we came to know by comparison that our own places are far holier than those abroad.[20]

What is important is 'receiving Christ into yourself', a spiritual state not related to sense-perception, which is brought about by virtue:

> if you keep your inner man full of wicked thoughts, even if you were on Golgotha, even if you were on the Mount of Olives, even if you stood on the memorial-rock of the Resurrection, you will be as far away from receiving Christ into yourself, as one who has not even begun to confess Him.[21]

A similar dissenting voice was Paulinus of Nola who never visited the Holy Places despite the encouragement of Jerome and Melania the Elder, and he also makes a

---

16 Cyril of Jerusalem, *Cat.*19.23 (FCh 64, 47–8).
17 Anna Silvas, *Gregory of Nyssa: The Letters* (Leiden: Brill, 2007): 123.
18 Gregory of Nyssa, *Ep.* 3.3 (Silvas, *Gregory*, 125; GNO VIII/2, 20).
19 Gregory of Nyssa, *Ep.* 2.2 (Silvas, *Gregory*, 118; GNO VIII/2, 13).
20 Gregory of Nyssa, *Ep.* 2.15 (Silvas, *Gregory*, 121; GNO VIII/2, 18).
21 Gregory of Nyssa, *Ep.* 2.17 (Silvas, *Gregory*, 121; GNO VIII/2, 19).

connection between piety and pilgrimage. In 409, he wrote a letter in support of a returned pilgrim, Valgius, whose miraculous delivery from shipwreck earned him the status of a living saint.[22] The motivation to 'see and touch the places where Christ was physically present' was piety,[23] but that to be gained by sight, or indeed touch, is considerably less significant than having received living proof of Christ through the miracle: Valgius is 'walking proof of divine Truth'.[24] Paulinus asserted the role of sight to provide proof of the scriptures but in themselves the holy places are lifeless and do not reveal the living Christ:

> If the manger of his birth, the river of his baptism, the garden of his betrayal, the palace of his condemnation, the column of his scourging, the thorns of his crowning, the wood of his crucifixion, the stone of his burial, the places of his resurrection and ascension are famed as recalling God's former presence, and if living proofs in lifeless objects demonstrate the ancient truth for today's belief, then with what reverence must this man be regarded, with whom God deigned to converse, before whom God's face was not concealed, to whom Christ revealed now His martyr and now His own person?[25]

Thus, for Paulinus, one might surmise, seeing the places is a pious act by the pilgrim, but one which has no spiritual returns; it is instructive only so far as it confirms what is already believed. It is the living saints that reveal Christ if one regards *them* with 'the eye of faith and spiritual sight' (*fidelibus oculis et acie spiritali*).[26]

Not long after Gregory's visit, the western nun, Egeria made a comprehensive pilgrimage throughout the region, including extended periods in Jerusalem itself where she participated in the rich liturgical commemorations at the sites connected to Christ's life, death and resurrection.[27] In what purports to be a journal (the *Itinerarium*) prepared for her 'sisters' back at home, she describes the places visited and the devotions carried out there. The places to be visited are determined by the biblical narrative as her extensive travels in Sinai indicate, even though she does not always follow the biblical chronology.[28] At the end of this stage of her journey she thanks God that the monks had shown her all the places she wanted to see '*semper iuxta Scripturas sanctas*',[29] although she had already wearied of recounting all the places to her readers and instead tells them to consult the books

---

22 Paulinus of Nola, *Ep.* 49 (CSEL 29, 390–404; ACW 36, 258–75). Walsh dates the letter to after 409 (358, n.1).
23 Paulinus of Nola, *Ep.* 49.14(ACW 36, 273).
24 Paulinus of Nola, *Ep.* 49.14 (ACW 36, 273).
25 Paulinus of Nola, *Ep.* 49.14 (ACW 36, 273).
26 Paulinus of Nola, *Ep.* 49.14 (ACW 36, 273; CSEL 29, 403).
27 Egeria's pilgrimage is usually dated to c.384, that is during the episcopate of Cyril. See Paul Devos, 'La date du voyage d'Égerie', *AnBoll* 85 (1967): 165–84.
28 Egeria is first taken up Mount Sinai 'where Moses received from the Lord the Law for the children of Israel' and then to the 'place of the Bush (which is still alive and sprouting)'. *It. Eg.* 4.4 and 4.7 (Wilkinson, *Travels*: 96).
29 *It. Eg.* 5.11 (SCh 296, 148).

74   *Juliette Day*

of Moses.[30] Scripture is corroborated by a direct correlation between the viewer and the text, and the connection is made all the more evident by the reading of relevant passages at each location accompanied by suitable prayers.[31] There is, though, very little sense of Egeria's personal religious response except where she says how excited she was to be shown the biblical sites: at Nebo she records,

> The presbyters and the monks who were familiar with the place asked us, 'Would you like to see (*videre*) the places which are described in the books of Moses? If so, go out of the church door to the actual summit, the place which has the view, and spend a little time looking at it. We will tell you which places you can see.' This delighted us and we went straight out.[32]

Also during this journey, we are presented with a paradox of seeing and not-seeing. Egeria remarks upon an elevated platform in the church at Nebo and was informed that this was the place where Moses was laid by the angels, although she then quotes Deut 34:6, 'no man knows his burial place'. She trusts what she has been told by the monks because they asserted, 'Our predecessors here pointed out this place to us, and now we point it out to you (*qui hic manserunt, ubi ostensum est, ita et nos vobis monstramus*). They told us that this tradition came from their predecessors.'[33] Shortly after, she was shown the place where Scripture says the pillar of Lot's wife was located, although

> what we saw was not the actual pillar but only the place where it had once been. The pillar itself, they say, has been submerged in the Dead Sea – at any rate we did not see it, and I cannot pretend we did (*Certe locum videremus, columnam nullam vidimus*).[34]

It is most surprising how rarely Egeria tells the readers what she saw (*videre*), overwhelmingly she tells them what she was shown (*ostendere* or *monstrare*) and it does appear as if this has greater authority than the evidence of her own eyes. In a sense the 'eyes of faith' are not required; she has the authority of tradition and of the holy men who guard it, just as they guard the holy places. *Videre* is used for not-seeing the pillar of Lot's wife, or for unverified seeing which is awaiting corroboration. Thus, she reports that she saw (*vidimus*) Elijah's town of Thesbe and shortly after saw (*vidimus*) a hermitage; she asked why the hermitage was there and on being told that it was located where Elijah was fed by a raven she 'gave thanks to God' (*qui nobis non merentibus singula, quae desiderabamus, dignatur*

---

30 *It. Eg.* 5.8. '*Quae quidem omnia singulatim scribere satis fuit, quia nec retinere poterant tanta; sed cum leget affectio vestra libros sanctis Moysi, omnia diligentius peruidet, quae ibi facta sunt*' (SCh 296, 146).
31 See *It. Eg.* 4.4–5; 4.8, etc.
32 *It. Eg.* 12.3–4, (Wilkinson, *Travels*: 107).
33 *It. Eg.* 12.2 (Wilkinson, *Travels*: 107; SCh 296, 174).
34 *It. Eg.* 12.7 (Wilkinson, *Travels*: 107; SCh 296, 178).

ostendere).³⁵ It is even more remarkable that when she describes the liturgical events at the christological sites in and around Jerusalem she never uses a verb of seeing³⁶ and one might speculate that this may be because she participated ritually in the biblical texts at these places, and thus the demonstration of their veracity occurred quite differently. At Bethany they commemorate liturgically the raising of Lazarus because, she tells us,

> They do it on this day because the Gospel describes what took place in Bethany 'six days before the Passover', and it is six days from this Saturday to the Thursday night on which the Lord was arrested after the Supper.³⁷

This statement is further indicative of the lack of imagination in Egeria's connections between the text and what she sees in each place, which we noted also in connection with the pillar of salt: Egeria's concern is to make a concrete identification of each place without much interpretation.

Jerome and Paula visited the holy sites within a few years of Egeria's visit and he described the journey in his *epitaphium* on Paula (*Ep.* 108) written after her death in 404, as well as in a letter to the Roman lady Marcella (*Ep.* 46) to encourage her to join them in the Holy Land. Jerome describes Paula's particularly powerful response to the sites and in doing so employs a rich vocabulary of vision and perception. Two visits stand out: that to the Holy Sepulchre and that to the cave of the Nativity in Bethlehem. In Jerusalem,

> She prostrated herself before the cross and worshipped as if she beheld (*cernerat*) the Lord hanging there. She entered the Sepulcher of the Resurrection and repeatedly touched her lips to the stone that the angel had rolled away from its door and as if thirsting for waters longed for by faith, she passionately kissed the very place where the Lord's body had been laid.³⁸

On the visit to Bethlehem, Jerome says,

> she entered the cave of the saviour and beheld (*vidit*) the virgin's sacred inn and the stall where the ox knew its owner and the donkey its master's crib ... I heard her swear that she could see, with the eyes of faith, (*me audiente iurabat cernere se fidei oculis*) the infant wrapped in swaddling clothes crying in his crib; the Magi worshipping him as God; the star shining down from on high; the virgin mother; the attentive foster father; the shepherds coming

---

35 *It. Eg.* 16.3 (SCh 296, 192).
36 There is one incidental, but not active, use of *videre* as part of her description of the Epiphany decoration at the basilicas in Jerusalem and Bethlehem (*It. Eg.* 25.8).
37 *It. Eg.* 29.6 (Wilkinson, *Travels*: 132).
38 Jerome, *Ep.* 108.9,2 (Andrew Cain, *Jerome's Epitaph on Paula: A Commentary on the Epitaphium Sanctae Paulae*, edited with an introduction and translation [Oxford: Oxford University Press, 2013]: 53).

by night both to see the Word which had come to pass and to affirm right then and there the beginning of John's Gospel 'In the beginning was the Word', and 'the Word became flesh'; the slaughtered infants; Herod in his rage; and Joseph and Mary fleeing to Egypt.[39]

The distinctiveness of her seeing at these places can be shown by the different verbs Jerome chooses when referring to other locations. Thus, after a journey to Sodom and Gomorrah, she is recorded as saying 'I will return to Jerusalem and ... I will gaze upon (*aspiciam*) the glistening cross on the Mount of Olives.'[40] At Gilgal, she 'gazed (*intuita*) upon the camp'.[41] At the Jordan, at sunrise, 'she *called to mind* (*recordata*) the sun of righteousness and how the priests left dry footprints in the middle of the riverbed ... She also recalled (*recordata*) how the Lord by his baptism cleansed the waters that had been defiled by the flood ... '[42]

In complete contrast to Egeria, Paula's own sight is not verified by guides or even by the biblical text. Jerome has not chosen verbs of physical sight, but rather verbs of perception which demonstrate that Paula's physical sight is either supplemented or supplanted by cognitive and reflective practices. Thus, at Jerusalem and Bethlehem, he uses *cernere* – to perceive, see with the mind's eye, discern with the intellect[43]; he uses *aspicere* – to observe, but also 'to see by visiting' or 'to see mentally, perceive'[44]; *intueri* – look at or contemplate.[45] Although these verbs can function as synonyms for *videre*, their meaning is much broader. He does a similar thing in the letter to Marcella: on visiting the Holy Sepulchre, he says, 'As often as we enter it we see (*cernimus*) the Saviour in His grave clothes, and if we linger we see (*videmus*) again the angel sitting at His feet, and the napkin folded at His head.'[46] At the end of the letter, Marcella is given an itinerary which they might do together if she came to the Holy Land, and now Jerome uses *videre* while connecting the site and the biblical text in a similar manner to Egeria: for example, 'We shall see (*videre*) Lazarus come forth bound with grave clothes ... We shall see (*videre*) the fountain in which the eunuch was immersed by Philip.'[47]

The variety of verbs employed to describe the act of seeing at specific holy places, and the very different interpretations of what was seen, alert us to multiple modes of perception in these pilgrimage texts and further warn us about using these reports too easily to reconstruct actual locations or even to generalize about pilgrim experience. Despite some recent valuable scholarship from the 'sensory turn', too often there is a failure to distinguish properly between physical

---

39 Jerome, *Ep.* 108.10,2 (Cain, *Jerome's Epitaph*: 55).
40 Jerome, *Ep.* 108.12,1 (Cain, *Jerome's Epitaph*: 59).
41 Jerome, *Ep.* 108.12,4 (Cain, *Jerome's Epitaph*: 61).
42 Jerome, *Ep.* 108.12,5 (Cain, *Jerome's Epitaph*: 61).
43 OLD, q.v. *cerno* 5; 6.
44 OLD, q.v. *aspicio* 1; 3; 8.
45 OLD, q.v. *intueor* 1; 6.
46 Jerome, *Ep.* 46.5 (NPNF, second series, vol. 6, 63; PL 22, 486).
47 Jerome, *Ep.* 46.13 (NPNF, second series, vol. 6, 65; PL 22, 491).

sight, perception and religious seeing, or there is a tendency to try to find physical explanations for the supposedly imaginative descriptions.[48] The pilgrims are said to see with the 'eyes of faith', or they engage in 'sacramental imagination', or have 'spiritual vision'. Such terminology, even though it may be borrowed from the ancient writers themselves, is not deployed in a manner which examines the act of seeing in conjunction with the mental processes required to identify or make sense of what has been seen. We shall turn now to examine some of the physical, philosophical and religious notions of sight which were likely to have been familiar to the writers and the pilgrims we have presented in order to reflect on the modes of cognition they imply.

Seeing in Late Antiquity

In the pilgrimage sources we have noticed that sight operates as a physical attribute, as a mode of cognition and as a religious experience, and thus we shall examine here three principal writers whose ideas on sight formed part of the cultural consensus. The theories of Galen, Plotinus and Origen are unlikely to have been at the forefront of the writers' minds, but at least we can credibly expect Cyril and Jerome, whose education would have been more systematic than the women's, to have been familiar with them. For the women writers and pilgrims, we do not find it dangerous to assume that they were familiar with these conventional ideas about sight and perception.

Physical Sight

The principal medical authority of late antiquity was Galen of Pergamon (CE 129 – c.200/c.216), he followed Hippocrates but combined experimental observations with philosophical enquiry. Jerome was familiar with his works and, in *Ep.* 54, written to the newly widowed Furia, he refers to a specific treatise and Galen's theory of humours;[49] from this one can deduce that women were familiar with Galen's works or at least his ideas. Galen describes the operation of the senses, and in particular the eyes, in his *On the Doctrines of Hippocrates and Plato*, where he presents and refutes or amends the views offered by earlier philosophers. He is particularly critical of theories which place the source of sensory perception in the heart (Aristotle) or in an unspecified soul (Chrysippus), and asserts its origin in the brain. For Galen, sight is the superior sense, followed closely by hearing, the other senses being secondary in operation and in their relation to cognition. The senses begin in the brain and are carried to the sense organs

---

48 See Cain, *Jerome's Epitaph*: 250 on what Paula saw at Bethlehem, which we shall discuss below.
49 Jerome, *Ep.* 54.9: 'Physicians and others who have written on the nature of the human body, and particularly Galen in his books entitled *On matters of health*, say that the bodies of boys and of young men and of full grown men and women glow with an interior heat . . . ' (NPNF, second series, vol. 6: 105).

78   *Juliette Day*

by sensory nerves. The optic nerve is constructed somewhat differently than the others and has a direct connection with the brain:

> The whole of the nerve itself, as much as lies between brain and eye, has an inner part that is softer and a harder outer part, as the Maker has two aims: to make the passage safe, and to preserve as far as possible the nature of the brain.[50]

This means that the *pneuma*[51] has less impeded travel between the eye and the brain.[52] He continues,

> Such is the superiority of the eye's structure over that of the other organs of sense; and it is not surprising that to the extent that its primary sense-object is more precise and more fine-particled than those of the others, to that extent it has also a greater share than they in the nature of the brain. You will not find the actual substance of the brain in any other sense organ . . . [53]

In operation it is able to discern more than the other senses, first colour and then size, shape, position, distance,[54] but the object of sight remains exactly where it is,[55] so that the luminosity of the object in conjunction with the luminous nature of the eye enables the perception of the sense object.[56] Here we can see Galen's struggle to combine the Stoic inspired idea of the *pneuma* which extends from the brain out to the sense object, and his assertion of the distinctiveness of the object in space from geometric observation.[57] Thus, he concludes that an illuminated object carries the potential for being seen, and the air between it and the eye functions as a medium:

> When something has been illuminated by the sun, it is already an instrument of vision of the same description as the *pneuma* coming to it from the brain; but until it is illuminated it does not turn into a sympathetic instrument by virtue of the change effected in it by the outflow of the *pneuma*.[58]

---

50   Galen, *De Plac. Hipp. et Plat.* VIII.5,18 (Greek and English trans. Phillip De Lacy, *Galeni: De placitis Hippocratis et Platonis, Corpus Medicorum Graecorum* V 4, 1, 2. [three vols; Berlin: Akademie-Verlag, 1978, 1980, 1984]: 457).
51   Galen understands *pneuma* as 'an instrument for the transmission of sensation and other psychological and physiological faculties' (Armelle Debru, 'Physiology', in *The Cambridge Companion to Galen*, R. J. Hankinson (ed.) [Cambridge: Cambridge University Press, 2008]: 263–82, especially 272–3). In visual perception it emanates from the brain via the optic nerve to the object of perception, and is the means by which that sensation is transmitted back to the brain.
52   Galen, *De Plac. Hipp. et Plat.* VIII.5,20.
53   Galen, *De Plac. Hipp. et Plat.* VIII.5,30 (De Lacy, *Galeni*: 459).
54   Galen, *De Plac. Hipp. et Plat.* VIII.5,33–5.
55   Galen, *On the Doctrines* VIII.5,39.
56   Galen, *On the Doctrines* VIII.5,41–2.
57   See, Rudolph E. Siegel, *Galen on Sense Perception: His Doctrines, Observations and Experiments on Vision, Hearing, Smell, Taste, Touch and Pain, and Their Historical Sources* (Basel: S. Karger, 1970).
58   Galen, *De Plac. Hipp. et Plat.* VIII.7,19 (De Lacy, *Galeni*: 475).

For our present enquiry, we note the importance in Galen's physiology of the close connection between seeing and the cognitive activity of the brain; however, for a contemporary examination of how that functions to construct identifiable objects and ideas we need to turn to Plotinus.

Sense Perception and Cognition

Patricia Cox Miller has noted how Plotinus promoted thinking in images, which brought immediacy between the perceiver and the perceived, as opposed to discursive language.[59] However, as Eyjólfur Kjalar Emilsson notes, he maintained a dualistic notion of the operation of the soul and the body in perception: external objects act upon the physical body through the sense, but the act of perception in the soul is non-physical.[60] Perception, therefore, crosses an ontological divide. Plotinus followed Plato in positing a realm of Forms (*noêta*/intelligibles), non-spatial and non-temporal, existing in the divine mind; through the Soul the intelligible realm comes into contact with the sensible, that which exists in space and requires physical apprehension.[61] In two places Plotinus discussed sight and he dismissed the idea that the object needs to touch the sense organ in order to be perceived, or that a medium was needed to effect a transmission; rather he uses the Stoic notion of *sympatheia* by which he seems to understand that perception happens because of resemblance between the object discerned by the physical sense and the intelligible Forms discerned by the soul.[62] The ubiquity of these ideas among fourth century theologians does not need establishing, although whether Egeria and Paula were familiar directly with them is difficult to discern. Of course the theory of ideal Forms needed modification in light of the story of creation and of the Incarnation, as we shall see in Philo and Origen. In relation to the focus of our investigation, though, to what extent does that which the pilgrims saw relate to physical objects and to what extent to ideal Forms? Do they see with physical eyes or, metaphorically, with their soul?

Spiritual Sight

It has been remarked by many commentators on the phenomenon of pilgrimage in the fourth century how, following Constantine (either by his patronage or by the absence of persecution), Christians became more at home in the world. Accompanied by a renewed theological focus on the Incarnation, Christian writers were more inclined to consider it possible to discern God and to experience Him in and through the material world; thus, sight, as well as touch, becomes an

---

59 Patricia Cox Miller, *The Poetry of Thought in Late Antiquity* (Aldershot; Ashgate, 2001): 6.
60 Eyjólfur Kjalar Emilsson, *Plotinus on Sense Perception: A Philosophical Study* (Cambridge: Cambridge University Press, 1988): 6.
61 Emilsson, *Plotinus*: 18–9.
62 Emilsson, *Plotinus*: 48.

extremely important aspect of religious experience, and pilgrimage to the Holy Places, like the veneration of relics, becomes a commendable spiritual activity.[63] However, the theological sources for late antique Christian writing about pilgrimage retain older ideas about the very impossibility of encountering the impassable God in matter; God is not in the world and is encountered only spiritually. Origen's concept of the spiritual senses aimed to overcome such a problem.

We can see the antecedents to Origen's view in Philo's *On the Creation*, where he makes a direct correlation between the function of the intellect and physical sight:

> Knowing that light was the most excellent of things that exist, he produced it as an instrument for the most excellent of senses, sight; for what the intellect is in the soul, this is what the eye is in the body; each of them sees, in the one case the objects of thought, in the other the objects of perception.[64]

The intellect, the 'director of the soul', is that which is made in the image of God.[65] The eye particularly enables perception of the world from which arises contemplation of God through the intellect, although that is only achieved by transcending the sense-perceptible world: the intellect 'peers beyond the whole of sense-perceptible reality and desires to attain the intelligible realm'.[66] But of more direct significance to late antique Christian writers was Origen who also shared the dominant neo-platonic philosophical background, albeit infused with Stoicism. We shall focus here on Origen because of the explicit and implicit influence he has on later fourth century writers and indeed pilgrims: of the former much has been written, of the latter we may note the report of Melania the Elder, the first Roman matron to install herself in Jerusalem, who had read three million lines of Origen not 'once only and casually, but she laboriously went through each book seven or eight times'![67]

Acknowledging the imprecision of the term '*sensus spiritualis*', which Sarah Coakley and Paul Gavrilyuk have highlighted, it principally refers to the non-physical perception of the divine, understood in relation to the particular activity of the Holy Spirit or of the Trinity.[68] For Origen in his exegetical works, it was a way to re-assign the sensual language of the biblical text in a spiritual direction, but, according to McInroy, Origen is not just speaking metaphorically, and neither does 'seeing God' simply refer to a mental act, but rather to a distinct ability

---

63 See Frank, *Memory*:112.
64 Philo, *Opif.* 53 (David T. Runia (trans.), *Philo of Alexandria: On the Creation of the Cosmos according to Moses: Intro, Translation and Commentary* [Leiden: Brill, 2001]: 59).
65 Philo, *Opif.* 69 (Runia, *Philo*, 64).
66 Philo, *Opif.* 70 (Runia, *Philo*, 64).
67 Palladius, *Hist. Laus.* 55 (W. K. Lowther Clarke (trans.), *The Lausiac History of Palladius* [London: SPCK, 1918]: 161).
68 Paul L. Gavrilyuk and Sarah Coakley (eds), *The Spiritual Senses: Perceiving God in Western Christianity* (Cambridge: Cambridge University Press, 2011): 3–4.

to perceive God through a separate set of senses or powers.[69] Thus in *Contra Celsum*, he writes:

> There are many forms of this sense: a sight which can see things superior to corporeal beings, the cherubim or seraphim being obvious instances, and a hearing which can receive impressions of sounds that have no objective existence in the air, and a taste which feeds on living bread that has come down from heaven and gives life to the world. So also there is a sense of smell which smells spiritual things, as Paul speaks of a 'sweet savour of Christ unto God' and a sense of touch in accordance with which John says that he has handled with his hands 'the Word of life'.[70]

And later on in the same work,

> We know that the holy Scriptures make mention of eyes, of ears and of hands, which have nothing but the name in common with the bodily organs; and what is more wonderful, they speak of a diviner sense, which is very different from the senses as commonly spoken of. . . . [71]

McInroy asserts that Origen is much less systematic in his treatment of the senses than modern commentators, especially Rahner, have suggested and that he does not really distinguish between metaphorical and analogical uses. For Origen, what is most important is the presence of God or other spiritual realities; it is the presence which is the precondition for perception.[72]

The ability to see spiritually is the result of removing impediments to the direct perception of divine presence; the impediments being the consequence of the Fall. In his *Commentary on the Psalms*, he says that God is present to all but not all will perceive him:

> As long as those to whom he comes are not all closed off and their ability to see clearly not impeded by their passions, God makes himself known and leads those illuminated by him to a knowledge of other spiritual things.[73]

And to Celsus he says,

> Therefore the eye of the soul of any genuine Christian is awake and that of the senses closed. And in proportion to the degree in which the superior eye

---

69 Mark McInroy, 'Origen of Alexandria', in Gavrilyuk and Coakley, *Spiritual Senses*: 20–35, especially 21.
70 Origen, *Cels.* 1.48 (Henry Chadwick (trans.), *Origen: Contra Celsum, Translated with an Introduction and Notes* [Cambridge: Cambridge University Press, 1965]: 44; quoted in McInroy, 'Origen': 23).
71 Origen, *Cels.* 7.34 (Chadwick, *Origen*, 431; quoted in McInroy, 'Origen': 29).
72 McInroy, 'Origen': 33.
73 Origen, *Hom. Ps.* 4.7. (Robert J. Daly, *Origen: Spirit and Fire. A Thematic Anthology of His Writings*, Hans Urs von Balthasar (ed.) [Edinburgh: T&T Clark, 1984]: 230–1; quoted in McInroy, 'Origen': 32).

is awake and the sight of the senses is closed, the supreme God and His Son, who is the Logos and Wisdom and the other titles, are comprehended and seen by each man.[74]

Thus Origen distinguishes physical sight which, because of the Fall, conveys imperfectly or causes imperfect perception, from spiritual sight which is available only to those advanced in the moral and ascetic life. What is seen, then, is not the material and physical, but God himself and the spiritual realm.

What Did Late Antique Pilgrims See?

Because of the close association of sense-perception and cognitive acts, the terms 'seeing' and 'sight' may refer to mental acts as well as physical ones, and so when encountering this language it is important to discern whether the direct referent is the physical location, imagination, divinely-gifted vision, or whether the author is speaking metaphorically.[75] Because our focus is on accounts of pilgrimages whose historicity does not seem in doubt and in which physical sight of actual places is recorded, the problem to be resolved is why the act of physical seeing and the subsequent mental acts differ so greatly. In short, what sort of seeing took place at the holy places?

Seeing Biblically

The objects of sight for the pilgrims were the places named in the Bible, the hierarchy being determined primarily by the theological significance of the event which took place there, but also places might be visited for more pragmatic reasons such as their proximity to a road or the presence of a monument, monastery or other edifice. These places are never seen neutrally, for what they are, but always through the text of scripture, as Maraval said of Egeria, she undertook her pilgrimage 'la Bible à la main, désireuse avant tout de voir tous les sites bibliques, sans cesse curieuse du détail scripturaire qu'elle peut vérifier sur le terrain.'[76] But as we saw earlier, in some places Egeria is 'verifying' the scriptural account in relation to the site, but in others it is scripture which verifies the place and so she questions her guides about whether they are at such and such a place which she knows only from the Bible (e.g. Salem).[77]

We need, though, to reflect on her anonymity in the physical act of seeing – only very rarely does she use *videre*, overwhelmingly she records what she was shown or what was pointed out to her by anonymous but authoritative guides.

---

74 Origen, *Cels.* 7.39 (Chadwick, *Origen*: 427).
75 See Gavrilyuk and Coakley, *Spiritual Senses*: 7.
76 Latin: Pierre Maraval, *Egérie, Journal de voyage (itinéraire)* (SCh 296, Paris: Éditions du Cerf, 1982): 120 n. 2.
77 *It. Eg.* 13.3; 15.1.

That which is to be seen has an independent existence separate from her ability to see it; she sees what is presented to her by the guides but also by the objects themselves. Might it be that she does not consider sight to be the activity of the *pneuma* passing from her brain to the illuminated object, but rather that it is the object which transmits itself to her? She only needs to put herself in the presence of the holy places in order to make the simple cognitive connection to the biblical event. In fact, it is notable how little biblical material there is in the *Itinerarium*, and indeed how little physical description: when she correlates the place and the text, she also correlates the sight and her preconception. In one place only does this fall down, in that puzzling and unique passage about the 'memorial to Lot's wife' where Egeria comments to her readers, 'We did not see it (the column) and I cannot pretend that we did.'[78] This passage is remarkable as it testifies to a complete lack of processing of what is seen – she does not employ imagination in relation to the site/sight, nor even to the biblical passage. To my mind, it is this curious episode in the pilgrimage narrative which reveals fully her approach to all the other places she visits and the way in which she travels 'la Bible à la main'.

Seeing Theologically

For Cyril, seeing enables participation in the biblical events which occurred at the location. The candidates for baptism, as viewers of the holy places, stand in a line of witnesses to salvation history – they see the holy places which witness to gospels which, in turn, witness to the salvific events of Christ's death, resurrection and ascension, events which were foretold by the prophets. He comments when what they see may not exactly correlate with the biblical text, such as in his description of the remodelled tomb; the embellishment, however, does not detract from their ability to witness to the events.[79] The viewers are not asked to assert to the accuracy of the physical appearance and location, that is the accuracy of what they see, but rather they are to assent to the truth of the events which took place there and their theological significance, namely the assertion of Jesus Christ as Messiah and Son of God.

A similar sort of theological sight is recorded in the almost contemporary mosaic at Santa Pudenziana in Rome, dated usually to the early fifth century on the basis of a lost dedicatory inscription to Pope Innocent (402–417). Here, Christ is seated on a gilded throne surrounded by some of the disciples, together with two women (identified as the patrons of the church). Behind him is a cityscape featuring a jewelled cross, and in the sky the four mystical beasts referred to in

---

78 *It. Eg.* 12.7 (Wilkinson, *Travels*: 107).
79 Cyril of Jerusalem, *Cat.* 14.9: Cyril explains that the original tomb 'is not visible now, it is true, because the outer hollowed-out rock was hewn away to make room for the present adornment. Before royal magnificence embellished the monument, there was a hollow place before the tomb' (FCh 64, 37).

Ezekiel. For James Hadley[80], following Frederick Schlatter, the image presents the eschatological vision based on Jerome's interpretation of Ezek 1:4–28, modified through Rev 4 and Ezek 40–43:[81] 'Thus the viewer of the S. Pudenziana apse sees Christ enthroned at the centre of the Temple and the cityscape of a restored Jerusalem veiled in an eschatological haze where the four beasts hover.'[82] For Hadley, the presence of the Cross is problematic. It serves to emphasize that the cityscape is indeed Jerusalem, but functions also theologically to indicate that 'it is from the cross event that Christ derives his power and lordship over life and death'.[83] But, he notes, the identification of the hill on which it stands as Golgotha is premature, given that 'close visual inspection shows that the cross is not bound to the hill', but hovers above the hill and thus above Christ, where it functions as a trophy of His victory over death. Hadley also notes how the architectural details of the mosaic are placed in continuation of the architectural features of the basilica so that the image surrounds the viewer and places them in a direct relationship to the apostles via the altar. He concludes, 'Such precise visual manipulation seems purposefully employed so that the proleptic content of the apse image is enfolded into the actual liturgical space in order to create artistically the classical liturgical Roman *hodie*.'[84]

An alternative interpretation, by Diane Apostolos-Cappadona, sees this not as an eschatological vision but as an image in which 'the historical merges with the spiritual'.[85] Christ is enthroned before the Cross of Golgotha, possibly that installed by Helena and later emperors according to tradition, with the 'identifiable outline of the city of Jerusalem' and above 'the four symbolic forms . . . which signify the Four Evangelists'.[86] Key to the image is 'the enthroned figure of Christ . . . the center of the composition and the centering point of any visual reading of this mosaic'.[87] Christ is the philosopher-teacher, but Apostolos-Cappadona also emphasizes that the image presents the divine yet incarnate Christ of the Nicene Creed.[88] As Christ is surrounded by his disciples and the two women, in a similar manner the faithful surround the bishop whose throne was placed immediately in front of the apse.[89]

This mosaic does seem to us to reflect some of themes we have explored in relation to the ways of seeing the holy places. The worshipper in Santa Pudenziana

---

80   James Hadley, 'The Apse and Cross: Ancient Precedents, Contemporary Considerations', *Anaphora* 7.2 (2013): 1–30.
81   Fredric W. Schlatter, 'The Text in the Mosaic of Santa Pudenziana', *VC* 43.2 (1989): 155–65.
82   Hadley, 'Apse and Cross': 10.
83   Hadley, 'Apse and Cross': 11.
84   Hadley, 'Apse and Cross': 13. *Hodie* (lat. 'today') refers to the ever-present mystery of Christ's incarnation, passion and resurrection which the liturgical calendar celebrates.
85   Diane Apostolos-Cappadona, '"... decorated with luminous mosaics"' Image and Liturgy in 5th/6th Century Roman Church Apse Mosaics. *StP* 71 (2014): 101.
86   Apostolos-Cappadona, '"... decorated with luminous mosaics"': 101.
87   Apostolos-Cappadona, '"... decorated with luminous mosaics"':102.
88   Apostolos-Cappadona, '"... decorated with luminous mosaics"': 104.
89   Apostolos-Cappadona, '"... decorated with luminous mosaics"': 103.

Figure 4.1 The apse mosaic at Santa Pudenziana, Rome (photograph: © Robin M. Jensen. Used with permission)

sees the physical holy places but interprets them through the theological lens of the triumphant Christ of the *eschaton*. The interpretation is conditioned by Scripture but not identical to it: the Cross is empty, and the four beasts do point to the gospels, as well as indicate an eschatological interpretation. The viewers who make these connections place themselves outside chronological time, just as they place themselves outside the ambiguously depicted physical space of historical Jerusalem; but the viewer also participates in the salvific events by means of the liturgical events which take place in front of this mosaic.

Seeing Spiritually

In the cave of the Nativity and at the Church of the Holy Sepulchre, Jerome records that Paula's seeing is of a different quality than that which we have noticed for other pilgrims or even for Paula herself at less significant locations. At Golgotha, she 'beheld the Lord hanging there', and in Bethlehem, 'I heard her swear that she could see . . . the infant wrapped in swaddling clothes crying in his crib'. At no other place does she see like this; nowhere else does she *swear* that that she really did see what she said she saw. In Jerome's account this type of seeing is reserved for the major Christological sites, and the object of seeing is not the place, but Christ himself. We note that he uses the term 'eyes of faith', but the faith required here is not belief in the veracity of the biblical text, it is about the very person of Christ.

Although what is seen is generated by being at these particular places, it is not the physical places themselves which determine what is seen. And here I part company with the most recent commentator on the *epitaphium,* Andrew Cain, who relates both these 'visions' to the physical surroundings. Cain assumes that what Paula saw at the Holy Sepulchre was 'the replica-Cross on the Rock of Calvary in the courtyard between the Anastasis and the Martyrium';[90] however, in the letter to Marcella Jerome says that they will be able to 'kiss the cross together'[91] which seems to indicate that what is visited is not the replica, but the relic of the True Cross. Paulinus has heard, presumably from Melania the Elder, that normally the True Cross is taken out only on Good Friday, as Egeria described:

> The bishop's chair is placed on Golgotha Behind the Cross . . . and he takes his seat. A table is placed before him with a cloth on it, the deacons stand round, and there is brought to him a gold and silver box containing the holy Wood of the Cross. It is opened, and the Wood of the Cross and the Title are taken out and placed on the table.[92]

But, Paulinus also tells Sulpicius Severus that,

> occasionally devout pilgrims who have come there merely for that purpose beg that it be shown them as a reward for their long journeying. It is said that this request is granted only by the kindness of the bishop, and it is likewise by his gift alone that these tiny fragments of sacred wood from the same cross are made available . . .[93]

So the size of the Cross was diminishing as the years went by; even Egeria relates how someone once bit off a piece of the Cross and stole it during the veneration ceremony on Good Friday.[94] So if, as I suggest, Paula did indeed see the relic of the True Cross, then given its dimensions, it would be very difficult to imagine Christ hanging on a Cross of such dimensions; Jerome, though, rejects the idea of Paula simply imagining things.

Cain also presumes that what Paula saw in Bethlehem is physical, and asserts that 'Paula's sensory experience would have been helped along by the visual representations of scenes relating to Christ's birth which richly decorated the walls of the Constantinian church'.[95] He continues,

> While such murals are not attested in detail for churches in Palestine until the sixth century . . . they are attested just enough . . . to confirm for us that they greatly enriched the visual landscape of the Constantinian churches and served as valuable devotional aids for pilgrims such as Paula . . .[96]

---

90 Cain, *Jerome's Epitaph*: 239.
91 Jerome, *Ep.* 46.5 (NPNF, second series, vol. 6: 62).
92 *It. Eg.*37.1 (Wilkinson, *Travels*: 137).
93 Paulinus of Nola, *Ep.* 31.6 (ACW 36: 132).
94 *It. Eg.*37.2.
95 Cain, *Jerome's Epitaph:* 18.
96 Cain, *Jerome's Epitaph*: 250.

However, it is not at all clear that the church did have wall paintings and Cain seems to have applied Crowfoot's more general reference to the decoration of church interiors to the specific case of the Church of the Nativity.[97] Although it was not unheard of for such early basilicas to have wall paintings (e.g. St Peter's and Santa Maria Maggiore in Rome, and Paulinus' church in Nola), I would maintain that there is no evidence to indicate that the Constantinian basilica in Bethlehem did at the end of the fourth century. Egeria described the interior of the Martyrium and the Church of the Nativity for the feast of the Epiphany as follows: 'the decorations are really too marvellous for words. All you can see is gold and jewels and silk; the hangings are entirely silk with gold stripes, the curtains the same . . .'[98] What was behind these wall hangings? Eusebius in the *Life of Constantine*, admittedly describing the Martyrium, said that 'Its interior was covered with slabs of varied marble, and the external aspect of the walls, gleaming with hewn stone fitted closely together at each joint, produced a supreme object of beauty by no means inferior to marble', as Constantine himself had ordered.[99] Vincent and Abel, the first achaeologists to survey the church at Bethlehem, writing in 1914, asserted the simplicity of the church there – it was elegantly built, they concluded, but was after all only an ordinary basilica.[100] Furthermore, it is clear that Paula was in the cave below the church, not in the basilica, and, as Jerome himself notes, it would have been rather difficult to imagine the infant Christ there. In his homily on the Nativity he laments,

> O, if only I were permitted to see that manger in which the Lord lay! Now, as an honor to Christ, we have taken away the manger of clay and have replaced it with crib of silver, but more precious to me is the one that has been removed. Silver and gold are appropriate for unbelievers; Christian faith is worthy of the manger that is made of clay. He who was born in that manger cared nothing for gold and silver. I do not find fault with those who made the change in the cause of honor (nor do I look with disfavor upon those in the Temple who made vessels of gold), but I marvel at the Lord, the Creator of the universe, who is born, not surrounded by gold and silver, but by mud and clay.[101]

We should note that Paula 'swore' that she saw these things in Bethlehem, and in addition to the evidence presented to indicate that she cannot possibly have physically seen these things, it is also evident that she would be unlikely to swear about something she had imagined. An interpretation of these passages is possible

---

97 John Winter Crowfoot, *Early Churches in Palestine* (London: Pub. for the British Academy, by H. Milford, Oxford University Press, 1941): 26. The assertion seems to have originated in Harvey's 1933 survey and to have been repeated without analysis ever since; even more recently by Asher Ovadiah, *Corpus of the Byzantine Churches in the Holy Land* (Bonn: P. Hanstein, 1970).
98 *It.Eg.* 25.8 (Wilkinson, *Travels*: 127).
99 Eusebius of Caesarea, *Vit. Const.* 36.1 (Averil Cameron and Stuart Hall (trans.), *Eusebius of Caesarea: Life of Constantine* [Oxford; Clarendon Press, 1999]: 136); *Vit. Const.* 31.3.
100 H. Vincent and F.-M. Abel, *Bethléem: le sanctuaire de la Nativité* (Paris: J. Gabalda, 1914): 111.
101 Jerome, *Hom.* 88 (FCh 57, 222).

if they are returned to their context in the text of the *epitaphium* which divides into two quite distinct parts, a biography leading into the travelogue and then the description of her ascetic achievements. The shift in theme is quite abrupt: Jerome writes,

> Let us thus conclude the account of her travels which she assiduously made along with many virgins and her daughter. It is now time to sketch at greater length the virtue that was innately hers. As I set out to describe it I solemnly declare, with God as my witness and judge, that I embellish nothing and in no respect exaggerate like the encomiasts do.[102]

What she saw in Jerusalem and Bethlehem was only possible because of her own holiness demonstrated by her ascetic life in which the passions had been fully controlled; Paula saw with the 'spiritual eyes' which Origen described. This is more than seeing with the 'eyes of faith': Frank defined this as 'a vivid perception of a past biblical event that is triggered by the seeing the physical holy place'[103] because although Paula does see the event, the point is that she sees Christ himself.

Conclusion

What the pilgrims saw was not simply conditioned by what they had read in the Bible, or heard in church, nor even just by what was physically there to be seen at the Holy Places; rather, what they saw was determined by how sight was considered to relate to knowing, and where truth was to be found. It has been suggested that the Christian writers, and indeed the pilgrims, were aware that seeing could be considered in terms of physiology and geometry (as Galen wrote), or in relation to ideal forms whose existence is related to but not dependent on the physical forms (Plotinus), or that the physical senses were inferior to and obscured the operation of spiritual senses which Origen proposed. Pilgrimage literature does not just tell the reader about where the pilgrims went and what they saw and did, it also tells us about the pilgrims themselves and the manner in which they interpreted what they saw. Thus we have suggested that interpretation through the lens of Scripture is only one aspect of seeing the Holy Places, but that additionally 'theological sight' is revealed by the juxtaposition of seemingly unrelated biblical passages which are filtered through theological norms about the incarnation, resurrection or the *eschaton*. The case of Paula provides a very different way of seeing, what is in focus here is the pilgrim herself and not the places or Scripture or theology: those who live piously, employing ascetic discipline to control their passions, will truly see Christ in the Holy Places.

---

102 Jerome, *Ep.* 108.14–15 (Cain, *Jerome's Epitaph*, 65).
103 Frank, *Memory*: 100.

5 Sacred Space, Virginal Consecration and Symbolic Power

A Liturgical Innovation and Its Implications in Late Ancient Christianity

David G. Hunter

Introduction

Around the year 393 Ambrose, bishop of Milan, travelled to Bologna to participate in the dedication of a new church there. The ceremonial transfer (*translatio*) of relics accompanied the event, and Ambrose contributed the relics of two martyrs to be placed under the altar – those of a master and a slave, Agricola and Vitalis.[1] As he proceeded to offer a homily in honour of the donor of the church, Ambrose described its patron, the widow Juliana, in the following terms:

> The widow of whom I speak is Juliana, who built and offered this temple to the Lord, the temple that we dedicate today. She is worthy of such an offering for she has consecrated to the Lord her own offspring to be to the Lord temples of modesty and virginity.[2]

Ambrose's appeal to the sacrality of space – a sacrality of the physical building established through its ritual dedication and a sacrality of the virgin's body established through her ritual consecration – provides the focus of this chapter. Ambrose's rhetorical interplay between the *templum* of the church and the *templa* of virginal bodies suggests that this will be a fruitful avenue of exploration.

The nature of sacred space has been a persistent issue in the study of late ancient Christianity. Post-Constantinian developments, such as large church buildings on holy sites, pilgrimage to the Holy Land, burial *ad sanctos*, and the cult of relics, have caused more than one scholar to wonder, 'How on earth could places become holy?'[3] To cite a notable example, the recent study of Ann Marie Yasin,

---

1 Ambrose, *Exh. virginit.* 1.1 (Gori (ed.): 198): '*Ego ad Bononiense inuitatus conuiuium, sub sancti martyris celebrata translatio est* . . . ' I cite from the critical edition of Franco Gori, *Verginità e vedovanza*. Sant'Ambrogio: Opere morali II/II (Milan: Biblioteca Ambrosiana; Rome: Città Nuova Editrice, 1989).
2 *Exh. virginit.* 2.10 (Gori (ed.): 206–8): '*Ea igitur vidua sancta est Juliana, quae hoc domino templum paravit atque obtulit, quod hodie dedicamus; digna tali oblatione, quae in subole sua templa iam domino pudicitiae adque integritatis sacravit.*'
3 I borrow the expression from R. A. Markus, 'How on Earth Could Places Become Holy? Origins of the Christian Idea of Holy Places', *JECS* 2 (1994): 257–71. On the history of placing relics under

Saints and Church Spaces in the Late Antique Mediterranean, has brought some much-needed clarity to the question.[4] Building on theoretical work by Jonathan Z. Smith,[5] Roy A. Rappaport,[6] and others, Yasin has argued for an understanding of 'sacred space' that emphasizes its construction through ritual and its function in establishing social hierarchy. Instead of conceiving of sacred space in a 'locative' sense – that is, as a 'place' in which the sacred is somehow resident or contained – Yasin proposes a model that stresses different degrees of holiness within a sacred space, degrees that both reflect and enforce different levels of social stratification. In this model one function of ritual is to create such a differentiated space and to generate hierarchy.[7]

Yasin was concerned primarily with the ways in which dead saints manifested their presence in the post-Constantinian church, not just in their tombs and physical remains, but in the prayers directed to them, in the mosaic representations of them, and in the commemorations of the patrons who donated their churches and shrines.[8] But her categories of analysis also provide us with a helpful way to think about the role of living saints in the production and maintenance of sacred space and social hierarchy. The 'living saints' I have in mind are the numerous women who underwent the ritual of virginal consecration in the fourth century and beyond. This ritual took the form of a *velatio* or bestowal of a veil on the consecrated virgin in a ceremony modeled after a Roman betrothal.[9] The sacred space is the church

---

the altar, see now Robin M. Jensen, 'Saints' Relics and the Consecration of Church Buildings in Rome', in *Studia Patristica, Vol. LXXI: Including papers presented at the Conferences on Early Roman Liturgy to 600 (14.11.2009 and 27.2.2010) at Blackfriars Hall, Oxford, UK*, Juliette Day and Markus Vinzent (eds) (Leuven: Peeters, 2014): 153–69.

4 Ann Marie Yasin, *Saints and Church Spaces in the Late Antique Mediterranean: Architecture, Cult, and Community* (Cambridge: Cambridge University Press, 2009).

5 In addition to Jonathan Z. Smith, *To Take Place: Toward Theory in Ritual* (Chicago: University of Chicago Press, 1987), Yasin relies especially on the following essays: 'The Wobbling Pivot' and 'Earth and Gods' in Jonathan Z. Smith, *Map is not Territory: Studies in the History of Religions* (Chicago and London: The University of Chicago Press, 1978): 88–103 and 104–28.

6 Roy A. Rappaport, *Ritual and Religion in the Making of Humanity* (Cambridge and New York: Cambridge University Press, 1999).

7 Cf. Yasin, *Saints and Church Spaces*: 27, who describes Smith's proposal thus: 'In his analysis the conceptual map of the sacred is constructed by ritual and punctuated by boundaries which separate spatial zones into areas of lesser and greater sacrality. Smith's analysis emphasizes that just as space is segregated, so is the community.'

8 As Yasin, *Saints and Church Spaces*: 285, put it: 'Saints served as instruments for the expression and construction of community identity within the space of the church while simultaneously mediating distinctions of social and sacred hierarchies.'

9 For details of the fourth-century ceremony, see Raymond d'Izarny, 'Mariage et consécration virginale au IVᵉ siècle', *La vie spirituelle: Supplément* 6/24 (1953): 92–108; René Metz, *La consécration des vierges dans l'église romaine: Étude d'histoire de la liturgie* (Paris: Press Universitaires de France, 1954): 124–38; and Nathalie Henry, 'A New Insight into the Growth of Ascetic Society in the Fourth Century AD: The Public Consecration of Virgins as a Means of Integration and Promotion of the Female Ascetic Movement', in *Studia patristica, Vol. XXXV: Ascetica, gnostica, liturgica, orientalia, Papers presented at the Thirteenth International Conference on Patristic Studies held in Oxford 1999*, M. F. Wiles and E. J. Yarnold (eds) with the assistance of P. M. Parvis (Leuven: Peeters, 2001): 102–9.

building, the site of their ritual consecration. The sacred hierarchs are the bishops or *sacerdotes*, who were specially charged (or who charged themselves) with the role of consecrating the virgins. In this chapter I first will examine how the ritual of virginal consecration unfolded within the space of a fourth century church, with special attention to the ways in which the ritual actions served to generate sacred space and to produce distinctive identities, especially that of the consecrated virgin. Then I will turn more explicitly to the theological or ideological implications of this ritual, namely to the question of how this liturgical practice provided late antique Christians, especially their bishops, with the language and images to construct a distinctive social space, namely a field in which both the consecrated virgin and the Christian bishop could acquire and exercise symbolic power.[10]

Sacred Space and the Ritual of Virginal Consecration

Communities of Christian women dedicated to perpetual virginity are known to have existed from a very early time, perhaps as early as the second century, but only in the middle to later years of the fourth century (and only in the west) do we find that a formal and public ritual of consecration was practiced.[11] At that point it was already common to celebrate the ritual in conjunction with the great liturgical feasts of the church. Ambrose says that his sister Marcellina received the veil at Rome from Pope Liberius on the feast of the Nativity.[12] 'What better day could have been chosen', Ambrose noted, 'than that on which the Virgin received her child?'[13] But an even more popular occasion for the ritual was Easter. In his *Exhortatio virginitatis*, composed in 393 or 394, Ambrose presented Pascha as the usual time both for baptism and for the consecration of virgins:

> The day of Pascha has come, all over the world the sacraments of baptism are being celebrated, and consecrated virgins are receiving the veil. Therefore in

---

10 As I will explain below, my use of the terms 'field' and 'symbolic power' owes much to the theoretical reflections of Pierre Bourdieu. I have learned most from his essays, 'Social Space and Symbolic Power', *Sociological Theory* 7 (1989): 14–25; and 'Rites as Acts of Institution', in *Honor and Grace in Anthropology*, J. G. Peristiany and Julian Pitt-Rivers (eds) (Cambridge: Cambridge University Press, 1992): 79–89. See also the helpful interpretive essay by David Swartz, 'Bridging the Study of Culture and Religion: Pierre Bourdieu's Political Economy of Symbolic Power', *Sociology of Religion* 57 (1996): 71–85.
11 Cyprian of Carthage composed a treatise, *De habitu virginum*, in the middle of the third century, but he mentioned no ritual of consecration or veiling. The same can be said of Methodius of Olympus, whose *Symposium of the Ten Virgins* assumes a recognized form of virginal life, but no public ritual of veiling.
12 As René Metz, *La consécration des vierges*: 127–8, has noted, it is unclear whether Ambrose was referring to the feast of Christmas or to Epiphany.
13 Ambrose, *Virg.* 3.1.1 (Dückers (ed.): 274): '*quo enim melius die quam quo uirgo posteritatem adquisiuit?*' I cite Ambrose, *De virginibus*, from the critical edition of Peter Dückers, *Ambrosius: De virginibus, Über die Jungfrauen*. Fontes Christiani, 81 (Turnhout: Brepols, 2009). Neil McLynn has placed the consecration of Marcellina between 353 and 356 (*Ambrose of Milan: Church and Court in a Christian Capital* [Berkeley: University of California Press, 1994]: 34 n. 122).

a single day, and without the pain of labor, the Church brings forth a multitude of sons and daughters. Aptly and truthfully it can be said of this consecrated people: 'and a nation shall be born at once' (Isa 66:8).[14]

Similarly, the contemporary treatise *De lapsu virginis* (once attributed to Ambrose, but now usually ascribed to his contemporary, Nicetas of Remesiana) reminds the fallen virgin that she had received the veil on the 'holy day of the Lord's resurrection' in 'so great and so solemn an assembly of the church of God'.[15]

The connection of virginal consecration with Easter and with the baptism of new Christians provides us with an opportunity to glimpse some of the important *visual* dimensions of the ritual. According to *De lapsu virginis* a woman who was to be consecrated as a virgin formally processed into the church along with the newly baptized who had just undergone the rites of initiation:

> Don't you remember that holy day, the day of the resurrection of the Lord, on which you offered yourself to be veiled at the divine altar? In so great and so solemn an assembly of the Church of God, you advanced amidst the shining lights of the neophytes, among the white-garbed candidates (*candidatos*) of the Kingdom of Heaven, as one about to wed a King.[16]

The 'shining lights of the neophytes', to which the text refers, were not merely metaphorical; these were candles carried by the newly baptized. Moreover, we know that after their baptismal immersion and anointing the neophytes put on white garments as a symbol of their newly cleansed state. Hence they could be referred to as *candidatos* or 'clothed in white garments'. For Ambrose, these white garments possessed theological significance: as he told the newly baptized in his post-baptismal catecheses, these garments were

> a sign that you were putting off the covering of sins, and putting on the chaste veil of innocence, of which the prophet said: "Thou shalt sprinkle me with hyssop and I shall be cleansed, Thou shalt wash me and I shall be made whiter than snow."[17]

---

14 *Exh. virginit.* 7.42 (Gori (ed.): 232): '*Venit Paschae dies, in toto orbe baptismi sacramenta celebrantur, uelantur sacrae uirgines. Vno ergo die sine aliquo dolore multos filios et filias solet ecclesia parturire. Ideoque pulchre dicitur: Et gens nata est simul, de populo consecrato.*' Raymond d'Izarny, 'Mariage et consécration virginale': 106–7, has argued that in fourth century Rome and Milan the feast of Sts Peter and Paul, 29 June, was also an occasion for the consecration of virgins.
15 *Laps. virg.* 5.19 (PL 16, 372). See the Latin text cited in the following note.
16 *Laps. virg.* 5.19 (PL 16, 372): '*Non es memorata diei sanctae Dominicae resurrectionis in quo divino altari te obtulisti velandam? In tanto, tamque solemni conventu Ecclesiae Dei, inter lumina neophytorum splendida, inter candidatos regni coelestis quasi Regi nuptura processeras*'; Maureen A. Tilley (trans.), 'An Anonymous Letter to a Woman Named Susanna', in *Religions of Late Antiquity in Practice*, Richard Valantasis (ed.) (Princeton, NJ: Princeton University Press, 2000): 222 (slightly altered).
17 Ambrose, *Myst.* 7.34 (SCh bis, 174): '*Accepisti post haec vestimenta candida, ut esse indicio, quod exueris involucrum peccatorum, indueris innocentiae casta velamina, de quibus dixit propheta:*

As liturgical scholar Edward Yarnold has observed, 'the solemn entry of the baptized, clothed in their white robes, and dispelling the darkness with the light of their baptismal candles, must have been a spectacular moment.'[18] And it was precisely at this moment that the soon-to-be-consecrated virgin made her appearance illumined by the lights of the neophytes.

The virgin's entry into the church along with the newly baptized indicates something of her unique identity within the Christian community; or, rather, it would have functioned to establish that identity. Indeed, her appearance may have actually upstaged the ordinary baptized Christian at this point in the ceremony: she would have represented the primary example of that sexual purity possessed only fleetingly by the newly baptized. Ambrose, for example, was fond of presenting the consecrated virgin as one who had recaptured the innocence of Eve in paradise, 'before she swallowed the slimy venom of the serpent, and before she was trapped by his snares, when Adam and Eve had no cause for shame.'[19] Furthermore, at Milan and elsewhere in the west, the baptism of the neophytes took place off-stage, so to speak, in a separate baptistery attached to the main church.[20] The virgin's consecration, by contrast, took place publicly in the centre of the church. One gets the impression from the descriptions of Ambrose and Nicetas that the entry of the newly baptized simply served as the prelude to the main event, the veiling and consecration of the virgin.

At this point the focus of dramatic action shifted to the altar placed in the centre of the church and to the ritual of *velatio* itself. There is no doubt that the altar played a significant role in the ritual. Ambrose frequently connected the virgin with the altar, in both a literal and a metaphorical sense.[21] In *De institutione virginis*, for example, he portrayed the virgin Ambrosia as presenting herself for consecration before the altar.[22] A striking illustration of the significance of the altar can be found in Ambrose's book, *De virginibus*, where he described an incident in which a young woman attempted actually to consecrate herself using the altar as a symbolic veil. The passage is worth quoting in full:

---

asparges me hysopo et mundabor, lavabis me et super nivem dealbabor.' He even described the moment of entry into the church with a litany of verses from the Song of Songs: *Myst.* 7.35–38 (SCh bis, 174–6), citing Song 1:4, 8:5, 4:1–3.

18 Edward Yarnold, *The Awe-Inspiring Rites of Initiation: The Origins of the RCIA*, second edition. (Collegeville, MN: The Liturgical Press, 1994): 38–9.
19 *Exh. virginit.* 6.36 (Gori (ed.): 226): '... *antequam lubricum serpentis hauriret venenum, priusquam eius supplantarentur insidiis, quando non habebant quo confunderentur*'. Cf. Peter Brown, *The Body and Society: Men, Women, and Sexual Renunciation in Early Christianity* (New York: Columbia University Press, 1988): 356: 'Though it was modeled on the veiling associated with a Roman marriage ceremony, echoes of the irrevocable and victorious transformation associated with baptism clustered around the woman's high moment of resolve.'
20 See, for example, the diagram of the church of Santa Tecla in Milan in Richard Krautheimer, *Three Christian Capitals: Topography and Politics* (Berkeley: University of California Press, 1983): 76.
21 Ambrose, *Virg.* 1.7.38; 2.2.18; *Virginit.* 5.26.
22 Ambrose, *Instit.* 17.108. Cf. *Laps. virg.* 5.19.

Not so long ago, within our memory, a young woman of distinction by the world's standards, but now more distinguished in God's sight, sought refuge at the sacred altar when she was being urged to marry by her relatives and kinsfolk. For where better for a virgin to go than where the sacrifice of virginity is offered? Nor, indeed, was this the end of her boldness. She stood by the altar of God, an offering of purity, a victim of chastity, now putting the priest's hand on her head and beseeching his prayers, now impatient at the justifiable delay and placing her head under the altar while saying: 'Could there be a better veil for me than the altar, which makes holy the veils themselves? More fitting is the bridal veil upon which Christ, the head of all things (cf. Eph. 1:10), is daily consecrated'.[23]

In the second half of this chapter I shall have occasion to comment further on the sacrificial imagery employed by Ambrose in his portrayal of the virtues of virginal consecration. Here it is enough to note that the consecration of the virgin took place in front of the altar in the centre of the church. This is where the bishop stood when he placed the veil upon the virgin's head and pronounced his benediction.[24] This location would have encouraged observers to link the virgin's consecration with the eucharistic sacrifice of Christ and would have emphasized the bishop's 'priestly duty' (*sacerdotale munus*) of consecrating virgins and offering the Eucharist.[25]

The next moment in the liturgy of consecration reveals another aspect of the ritual, this time an *aural* dimension. At some point in the service, probably immediately after the consecration, the newly consecrated virgin joined her fellow virgins in the ritual recitation (or antiphonal singing) of verses from the Song of Songs and Psalm 45. These texts contain elaborate bridal imagery and, according to the studies of Nathalie Henry, the nuptial language of these biblical texts, which appears frequently in the literature of Christian asceticism, reflects the influence of this liturgical practice.[26] Using a prayer for the consecration of virgins that is

---

23 *Virg.* 1.11.65 (Dückers (ed.): 204–6): '*Memoria nostra puella dudum nobilis saeculo, nunc nobilior deo, cum urgueretur ad nuptias a parentibus et propinquis, ad sacrosanctum altare confugit; quo enim melius virgo, quam ubi sacrificium virginitatis offertur? Ne is quidem finis audacia. Stabat ad aram dei pudoris hostia, victima castitatis, nunc capiti dexteram sacerdotis inponens, precem poscens, nunc iustae impatiens morae ac summum altari subiecta verticem: 'Num melius', inquit, 'maforte me quam altare velabit, quod sanctificat ipsa uelamina? Plus talis decet flammeus, in quo caput omnium Christus cotidie consecratur*'; Boniface Ramsey (trans.), *Ambrose* (London and New York: Routledge, 1997): 91.
24 On the basis of Ambrose, *Virg.*1.11.65 (cited in the previous note), d'Izarnay, 'Mariage et consécration virginale': 102, speculates that the veil may have been lying on top of the altar, but I think the evidence is inconclusive.
25 Cf. *Instit.* 107 (Gori (ed.): 186), where Ambrose refers to the virgin as '*quam sacerdotali munere offero*'.
26 Nathalie Henry, 'The Song of Songs and the Liturgy of the *velatio* in the Fourth Century: From Literary Metaphor to Liturgical Reality', in *Continuity and Change in Christian Worship*, R. N. Swanson (ed.) (Woodbridge, UK and Rochester, NY: The Boydell Press, 1999): 18–28. See also her essay, 'A New Insight into the Growth of Ascetic Society', cited above, n. 9.

found in the *Leonine Sacramentary*, as well as antiphons from the *Liber responsalis* of Gregory the Great, Henry plausibly argues that antiphonal singing was already practiced in the ritual of virginal consecration in Ambrose's day.[27]

Several other texts confirm Henry's argument. For example, this passage from Jerome's Letter 130 to Demetrias, celebrating that famous virgin's veiling early in the fifth century, describes the verses used in the antiphonal singing:

> I am aware that the bishop has with words of prayer covered her holy head with the virgin's bridal-veil, reciting all the while the solemn sentence of the apostle: 'I wish to present you all as a chaste virgin to Christ' (2 Cor 11:2)... Thereupon the bride herself rejoices and says: 'the king hath brought me into his bed-chamber' (Song 1:4) and the choir of her companions responds: 'the king's daughter is all glorious within' (Ps 45:14).[28]

Similarly, the author of the treatise *De lapsu virginis* berates the 'fallen' virgin with these words describing the event of her consecration:

> How is it that the virginal garment, your procession into the Church among the chorus of virgins, did not enter your mind in the course of this ignominious action? How is it that the light of vigils did not caress your eyes? How is it that the melody of spiritual songs did not penetrate your ears?[29]

If, as seems likely, the ritual of virginal consecration did include this element of antiphonal singing, then we have further evidence of its impact within the liturgical space. As Henry has noted: 'The whole ceremony was imbued with the language of love and desire.' The antiphonal singing of verses from Psalm 45 and the Song of Songs would have reinforced in ritual form the distinctive identity of the consecrated virgin as the bride of Christ.

There is one final example of the role of the ritual of virginal consecration in establishing the distinctive identity of the consecrated virgin within the sacred space of the church that I would like to note. According to *De lapsu virginis*, after

---

27 Henry's article, 'The Song of Songs and the Liturgy of the *velatio*': 24–8, contains a critical edition of the Office of Virgins from the *Liber responsalis*.

28 Jerome, *Epist.* 130.2 (CSEL 56: 176–7): '*Scio quod ad imprecationem pontificis, flammeum virginale sanctum operuerit caput; et illud apostolicae vocis insigne, celebratum sit:* Volo autem vos omnes virginem castam exhibere Christo... *Unde et ipsa sponsa laetatur ac dicit:* Introduxit me rex in cubiculum suum. *Sodaliumque respondet chorus:* Omnis gloria filiae regis intrinsicus.'

29 *Laps. virg.* 6.22 (PL 16, 373): '*Quomodo tibi in actu illo ignominioso non veniebat in mentem habitus virginalis, processus in Ecclesiam inter virgineos choros? Quomodo oculos tuos non perstringebat lux vigiliarum: aures tuas non penetrabat hymnorum spiritalium cantus: mentem tuam non ventilabat lectionum coelestium virtus?*'; Tilley (trans.), 222 (altered). Tilley translated '*habitus virginalis*' as 'virginal behavior', but in the liturgical context it most likely refers to a distinctive garment worn by the virgin as she entered the church building. Cf. Ambrose, *Virg.*, 3.1.1 (Dückers (ed.): 274), where he says that his sister Marcellina signified her virginal profession by a change of clothing: '*vestis... mutatione*'.

her consecration the virgin was accompanied to an area of the church set aside for her and her companions:

> Now you have to remember, don't you, that place where you stood in the church separated by boards and how pious and noble women earnestly ran there, seeking your kiss, women who were holier and more worthy than you? You have to remember, don't you, those precepts, which the inscribed wall itself flung at your eyes: 'The married woman and the virgin differ: the one who is not married thinks about the affairs of the Lord, how she might be holy in body and soul' (1 Cor 7:34).[30]

If this account given in *De lapsu virginis* accurately reflects the typical layout of a church building in northern Italy in the later years of the fourth century, then we have conclusive evidence in support of the argument of this chapter. The ritual of virginal consecration created a community of women set apart from the rest of the Christian community, both in physical space and in social status.

Virginal Consecration and Symbolic Power

At this point I would like to turn from a description of the physical ritual itself and consider further its symbolic or ideological dimensions. It should be apparent, even from this cursory overview of the ritual of the consecration of virgins, that the 'sacred space' of the church building also served as the context for the construction of a 'social space', that is, a field of social relations in which the various participants – clergy, laity, and consecrated virgins – each received their distinctive identities and ranks in a social hierarchy. As ritual theorist Catherine Bell has observed, rituals are capable of acting powerfully in the social world by producing 'ritualized bodies':

> A ritualized body is a body aware of a privileged contrast with respect to other bodies, that is, a body invested with schemes the deployment of which can shift a variety of sociocultural situations into ones that the ritualized body can dominate in some way ... In other words, through a series of physical movements ritual practices construct an environment structured by practical schemes of privileged contrast. The construction of this environment is simultaneously the molding of the bodies within it – a process perceived, if at all, as values and experiences impressed upon the person from without.[31]

---

30 *Laps. virg.* 6.24 (PL 16, 374): '*Nonne vel illum locum tabulis separatum, in quo in Ecclesia stabas, recordari debuisti, ad quem religiosae matronae et nobiles certatim currebant, tua oscula petentes, quae sanctiores et digniores te erant? Nonne vel illa praecepta quae oculis tuis ipse scriptus paries ingerebat, recordari debuisti:* Divisa est mulier et virgo: quae non est nupta, cogitat quae Domini sunt, quomodo sit sancta corpore et spiritu'; Tilley (trans.), 223.

31 Catherine Bell, 'The Ritual Body and the Dynamics of Ritual Power', *JRitSt* 4 (1990): 299–313, quotation at 304–5.

In the case of the ritual being considered here – the consecration of virgins – the 'privileged contrast' to which Bell refers would apply to the contrast between the veiling/marriage of an ordinary woman and the symbolic veiling/marriage of the virgin to Christ. Such ritualization, as Bell observes, 'is a way to generate privileged contrasts between the acts being performed [i.e., the veiling of the consecrated virgin] and those being contrasted or mimed' [i.e., the veiling of the normal bride].[32]

Bell's description of the process of ritualization and the formation of the 'ritualized body' provides a helpful framework for further analyzing the impact of the ritual of virginal consecration on the social construction of the virgin and of her 'consecrator', the Christian bishop. It underscores the manner in which the contrasts present in ritual action can generate the social contrasts of rank and hierarchy. As we will see below, Ambrose constantly utilized this contrast to emphasize the superiority of the virginal bride of Christ over the bride of a mere human being. But this approach can be further supplemented by insights drawn from the work of Pierre Bourdieu, especially his notions of 'social consecration' and 'symbolic power'.[33] In a pair of incisive articles Bourdieu has developed concepts that can assist us in interpreting the social role played by rituals such as the veiling of virgins in generating and maintaining social power. In his essay, 'Rites as Acts of Institution', Bourdieu describes ritual 'consecration' or 'institution' as 'an act of social magic' that establishes (i.e., 'consecrates') a boundary, that is to say, a difference, which comes thereby to be considered legitimate or 'natural':

> In this case to institute is to consecrate, that is to sanction and to sanctify, a state of affairs, an established order – which is precisely what, in the juridico-political sense of the word, a constitution does. Investiture . . . consists in sanctioning and sanctifying, in making known and recognized, a difference (preexistent or not); in making it exist as a social difference known and recognized by the agent thereby invested, and by others.[34]

Acts of consecration or institution, according to Bourdieu – whether they consist in graduation ceremonies, inauguration into political office, or the veiling of virgins – have genuine power to change reality. The 'symbolic efficacy of rites of institution', as Bourdieu puts it, consists in their ability to 'act on the real by acting on the representation of the real'.[35] Such rites genuinely transform the persons who are consecrated by transforming the way that other people perceive and treat them, as well as the way that the consecrated persons perceive and treat themselves.

---

32   Bell, 'The Ritual Body': 304.
33   Bell's essay made explicit use of Bourdieu's *Outline of a Theory of Practice* (Richard Nice (trans.), (Cambridge: Cambridge University Press, 1977), as well as the writings of Michel Foucault and Jean Camaroff, but she did not make use of the later essays of Bourdieu cited in note 10 above.
34   Bourdieu, 'Rites as Acts of Institution': 82.
35   Bourdieu, 'Rites as Acts of Institution': 82.

A second theoretical insight derived from Bourdieu that can be helpfully applied to the ritual of virginal consecration is found in his essay 'Social Space and Symbolic Power'. Here Bourdieu emphasizes the role of the consecrator as an authorized agent, that is, as one whom the community recognizes as having the authority to 'create worlds' (i.e., make groups) by speaking and defining their existence:

> Symbolic power, whose form par excellence is the power to make groups . . . rests on two conditions. Firstly, as any form of performative discourse, symbolic power has to be based on the possession of symbolic capital. The power to impose upon other minds a vision, old or new, of social divisions depends on the social authority acquired in previous struggles. Symbolic capital is a credit; it is the power granted to those who have obtained sufficient recognition to be in a position to impose recognition.[36]

In the context of our discussion of the rite of virginal consecration, it is clear that the authorized agent – the person who has been recognized as having the authority to impose recognition – is the Christian bishop. Symbolic power, which Bourdieu describes as 'the power to make things with words', is nothing other than the power of consecration or revelation that the authorized agent possesses: 'the power to consecrate or to reveal things that are already there.'[37] To put the matter another way, 'an act of social magic', such as the ritual of virginal consecration, could only be effective when conducted by an authorized agent (a 'priest' or 'magician'), who was invested by the community with the authority to act and speak on behalf of the community.

These theoretical reflections on ritual and social space by Bell and Bourdieu provide valuable tools for analyzing the discourses on virginity generated in the late fourth and early fifth centuries by the proponents of virginal consecration. As we saw in the first part of this chapter, the ritual itself produced distinctions of space and social status, especially between the consecrated virgin (and her virginal companions) and the ordinary lay members of the Christian congregation. But the making of this distinction required something more than spatial segregation; it also required the *naming* and *recognition* of this distinction by an authorized agent. This is where the discourses on consecrated virginity, which were often delivered at the ritual event by bishops such as Ambrose, played an essential role: they articulated the special status of the consecrated virgins by drawing on the symbols generated by the ritual itself. In the remainder of this chapter I would like to explore two of these symbols – the virgin as priest/sacrifice and the virgin as bride of Christ – which were mobilized by late Latin writers to legitimate and naturalize the special status of the Christian virgin.

One gains a vivid sense of the power of these two symbols from the following description given by an anonymous 'Pelagian' writer (probably Pelagius himself) of what he calls the 'special consecration' (*specialis . . . consecratio*) of the virgin.

---

36 Bourdieu, 'Social Space and Symbolic Power': 22.
37 Bourdieu, 'Social Space and Symbolic Power': 23.

First he points to the nature of consecrated virginity as a kind of sacred offering or sacrifice:

> Apart from the evidence supplied by the scriptures we are informed how great is the blessed state which holy virginity attains in heaven by the practice of the Church, from which we learn that a peculiar merit is attached to the recipients of this special form of consecration. For while the whole multitude of believers receives similar gifts of grace and all rejoice in the same blessings of the sacraments, those to whom you belong have something peculiar to themselves over and above what the rest possess: they are chosen by the Holy Spirit out of the holy and spotless flock of the Church as holier and purer offerings (*hostiae*) on account of the merits given them for their choice of vocation and are presented at God's altar by his highest priest. The offering of so precious a creature is truly worthy to be considered a sacrifice to the Lord, and there is none who will please him more than a victim in his own image, for I believe that it was especially to such an offering that the apostle referred when he said: 'I appeal to you, therefore, brethren, by the mercy of God to present your bodies as a living sacrifice, holy and acceptable to God' (Rom 12:1).[38]

After noting the specifically sacrificial element involved in the offering of the virgin's consecrated virginity, the 'Pelagian' author went on to point out another dimension of virginal consecration, namely its re-enactment of a marriage liturgy and establishment of the virgin as a 'bride of Christ':

> Ecclesiastical authority also permits us to call virgins the brides of Christ, since it veils those whom it consecrates to the Lord in the manner of brides, showing in this very special way that those who have shunned partnership of the flesh are destined to enjoy a marriage in the spirit. And, having spurned human marriage because of their love of God, they are deservedly united to him in spiritual union on the analogy of marriage. In them that saying of the apostle is especially fulfilled: 'But he who is united to the Lord becomes one spirit with him' (1 Cor 6:17).[39]

---

38 Pelagius, *Ad Claudiam sororem de uirginitate* (CSEL 1, 225): '*Quantam in caelestibus beatitudinem uirginitas sancta possideat, praeter scriptuarum testimonia ecclesiae etiam consuetudine edocemur, qua discimus peculiare illis subsistere meritum, quarum specialis est consecratio. Nam cum uniuersa turba credentium paria gratiae dona percipiat et isdem omnes sacramentorum benedictionibus glorientur, istae proprium aliquid prae ceteris habent, cum de illo sancto et inmaculato ecclesiae grege quasi sanctiores purioresque hostiae pro uoluntatis suae meritis a sancto spiritu eliguntur et per summum sacerdotem Dei offeruntur altario. Digna reuera Domino hostia tam pretiosi animalis oblatio, et nulla magis ei quam imaginis suae hostia placitura. De huiusmodi enim Apostolum praecipue dixisse reor: Obsecro autem uos, fratres, per misericordiam Dei ut exhibeatis corpora uestra hostiam uiuentem, sanctam, Deo placentem*'; B. R. Rees (trans.), *The Letters of Pelagius and his Followers* (Rochester, NY: The Boydell Press, 1991): 72.

39 Pelagius, *Ad Claudiam sororem de uirginitate* (CSEL 1, 225–6): '*Nam et Christi sponsas uirgines dicere ecclesiastica nobis permittit auctoritas, dum in sponsarum modum quas consecrat Domino uelat, ostendens eas uel maxime habituras spirituale conubium quae subterfugerint*

Here we see that the author of the epistle *Ad Claudiam sororem* has adopted both the image of the virgin as sacrifice and that of the virgin as bride of Christ, both of which were derived from and displayed in the ritual of consecration, and interpreted them as evidence of the superior status of the consecrated virgin: virgins are 'holier and purer offerings' and enjoy 'a marriage in the spirit'. It is especially noteworthy that the author has attempted to justify this higher status of the consecrated virgin by utilizing verses from the apostle Paul – Romans 12:1 and 1 Corinthians 6:17 – which Paul had originally addressed to the entire Christian community, not to an elite few. The ancient author's use of these verses to recognize the unique status of the virgin, therefore, was founded on the misrecognition of the original sense of the Pauline texts.[40]

The importance of these two symbols of consecrated virginity can also be seen in the writings of Ambrose of Milan, who did more than any other Latin writer of late antiquity to foster the practice of virginal consecration and to develop its theological underpinnings. Throughout his writings Ambrose frequently had recourse to the imagery of sacrifice and priesthood to characterize the consecrated virgin. At times the language of offering and the eucharistic imagery become so pronounced that it is not clear whether the consecrated virgin is sacrifice or priest or both. In his treatise *De virginibus*, for example, Ambrose could characterize the virgin as having the power to intercede with God on behalf of her parents and to acquire for them the forgiveness of their sins, a task he explicitly characterized as a 'priesthood' (*sacerdotium*):

> You have heard, O parents, in what virtues you ought to raise and with what discipline you ought to instruct your daughters, so that you may have ones by whose merits your own sins may be forgiven. A virgin is a gift of God, a protection for her family, a priesthood of chastity (*sacerdotium castitatis*). A virgin is an offering for her mother (*matris hostia*), by whose daily sacrifice the divine power is appeased.[41]

In a later book of the same treatise Ambrose described the consecrated virgin in a dizzying mix of metaphors that was simultaneously sacrificial, eucharistic, and (perhaps) erotic. After citing Psalm 42(43): 4 ('I shall go to the altar of my God, to the God who rejoices in my youth'), Ambrose commented:

---

carnale consortium. Et digne Deo per matrimonii comparationem spiritualiter copulantur quae eius dilectionis causa humana conubia spreuerunt. In his quam maxime illud impletur Apostoli: qui autem adhaeret Domino, unus spiritus est'; Rees (trans.): 72.

40 The notion of 'misrecognition' (*méconnaissance*) is central to Bourdieu's account of rites of institution. According to Bourdieu, 'Rites as Acts of Institution': 81, 'every rite leads towards the consecration or legitimization of an arbitrary boundary, that is to say, it attempts to misrepresent the arbitrariness and present the boundary as legitimate and natural . . .'

41 Ambrose, *Virg.* 1.7.32 (Dückers (ed.): 154): '*Virgo dei donum est, munus parentis, sacerdotium castitatis. Virgo matris hostia est, cuius cotidiano sacrificio uis divina placatur*'; Ramsey (trans.): 82.

> For I would not doubt that these altars are accessible to you whose souls I would confidently call altars of God, upon which Christ is daily sacrificed for the redemption of the body. For if a virgin's body is a temple of God, what is her soul, which, when the ashes of its members, so to speak, have been stirred by the hand of the eternal priest, exhales the warmth of the divine fire once it has been covered over again? Blessed are you virgins who breathe out with such immortal grace, as gardens do with flowers, as temples do with devotion, as altars do with a priest![42]

In this stunning passage, Ambrose has woven together several images: the body of the virgin as 'temple' (*templum*), the soul of the virgin as 'altar' (*altare*), and Christ as 'eternal priest' (*sacerdos aeternus*), who stirs the embers (or fans the flames) of the sacrificial fire, that is the virgin's heart. By portraying the consecrated virgin as both sacrifice and priest, Ambrose drew an even sharper line between the ordinary Christian believer and the woman who had undergone the ritual of consecration.[43]

Ambrose also frequently appealed to the notion of the virgin as the 'bride of Christ' in a manner that emphasized the contrast between ordinary human marriage and the 'spiritual' marriage of the consecrated virgin. Ambrose was especially fond of using the literary trope of Christ as bridegroom to draw a distinction between the (inferior) human husband wedded to an ordinary woman and the (superior) divine husband possessed by the consecrated virgin. The former may be handsome, but Christ is one to whom it is said: 'More beautiful than the sons of men, grace is poured forth on your lips' (Ps 45:2).[44] In his account of the virgin who tried to consecrate herself using the altar as a veil, which was mentioned above, Ambrose portrayed her saying these words to the family members who opposed her consecration:

> Why are you upset, my kinsfolk? Why do you trouble yourselves by continuing your matchmaking? I have already been provided for. Are you offering me a bridegroom? I have found a better one. Extol whatever riches he has, boast of his distinction, talk up his power: I have one who is without compare – rich in the world, powerful in authority, distinguished in heaven. If you have one

---

42 Ambrose, *Virg.* 2.2.18 (Dückers (ed.): 230–2): '*Neque enim dubitauerim uobis patere altaria, quarum mentes altaria dei confidenter dixerim, in quibus cotidie pro redemptione corporis Christus immolatur. Nam si corpus uirginis dei templum est, animus quid est, qui tamquam membrorum cineribus excitatis sacerdotis aeterni redopertus manu uaporem diuini ignis exhalat? Beatae uirgines, quae tam immortali spiratis gratia, ut horti floribus, ut templa religione, ut altaria sacerdote!*'; Ramsey (trans.): 95–6, slightly altered.
43 One could say much more about Ambrose's use of priestly images to characterize the consecrated virgin. Elsewhere I have argued that he adopted the notion of the virgin as 'Levite' as a way of enhancing her 'priestly' status: *Marriage, Celibacy, and Heresy in Ancient Christianity: The Jovinianist Controversy* (Oxford, 2014): 222–4, 229–30.
44 *Virg.* 1.7.36 (Dückers (ed.): 160); Ramsey (trans.), 83.

such, I will not turn him down. If you have not found him, you are not acting to my benefit, my relatives, but behaving grudgingly.[45]

Ambrose's comments make it clear that he was acting in a field that was highly competitive and that he faced strong resistance to his ascetic agenda from those Christians who had an alternative set of cultural values.[46] To put it in the terms formulated by Bourdieu, Ambrose's appeal to the status of the consecrated virgin as 'bride of Christ' was an effort to construct a sharp symbolic boundary that consecrated the difference between ordinary Christians and the women committed to perpetual virginity, thus increasing the social capital available to the virgin.

One should also note that by ritualizing the virgin's consecration in the form of a traditional Roman wedding and by characterizing that ritual in terms of a marriage to Christ in his own ritual discourses, Ambrose was demonstrating his own mastery of the ritual process. As Bell has put it (in a description of the ritual process that relies heavily on the work of Bourdieu):

> To possess this practical ritual mastery is to possess the tools for ordering and reordering the world, for perceiving and not perceiving, for evaluating, for unifying, and for differentiating – not as rules to follow, but as a flexible social instinct for what is possible and effective. As such, ritual mastery is the ability to generate culture deftly and appropriately nuanced and in a peculiar tension with other forms of cultural production.[47]

As a master of the ritual process, Ambrose instinctively recognized that the image of the virgin as 'bride of Christ' was a particularly potent cultural symbol, one that was capable of multiple variations and manipulations.[48] In his various sermons on consecrated virgins, Ambrose fully exploited marital imagery in order to establish a recognized group of women whose spiritual status placed them above the married laity.[49] If, in sociological terms, 'symbolic power' is a power of 'world-making',

---

45 *Virg.* 1.11.65 (Dückers (ed.): 206): '*Quid agitis uos, propinqui? Quid exquirendis adhuc nuptiis sollicitatis animum? Iamdudum prouisas habeo. Sponsum offertis? Meliorem repperi. Quaslibet exaggerate divitias, iactate nobilitatem, potentiam praedicate: habeo eum cui nemo se comparet, diuitem mundo, potentem imperio, nobilem caelo. Si talem habetis, non refuto optionem; si non repperitis, non prouidetis mihi, parentes, sed inuidetis*'; Ramsey (trans.): 91.
46 In his treatise, *De virginitate*, composed shortly after the three books *De virginibus*, Ambrose explicitly responded to this culture-based resistance. See my discussion in *Marriage, Celibacy, and Heresy*: 60–1.
47 Bell, 'The Ritual Body': 305–6.
48 Following earlier Christian tradition, Ambrose also spoke of the Church, as well as the Virgin Mary, as the 'bride of Christ', thus intensifying the symbolic resonances of the term when applied to the consecrated virgin. For a discussion of the place of Ambrose relative to that of other late antique commentators, especially Jerome and Augustine, see my article, 'The Virgin, the Bride and the Church: Reading Psalm 45 in Ambrose, Jerome and Augustine', *Church History* 69 (2000): 281–303.
49 Much of the history of this transfiguration of marital symbolism has been traced by Kate Cooper, *The Virgin and the Bride: Idealized Womanhood in Late Antiquity* (Cambridge, Massachusetts:

that is, of constructing groups by assigning labels and classifications, then Ambrose can be seen as seeking to establish a new world and a new vision of the social order, in which priority belonged to the sexually continent.[50]

I would like to add one final point regarding the social effect of the ritual of virginal consecration, namely its contribution to the production of the bishop's authority. Although I have focused here on the consecrated virgin, no aspect of the ritual I have described could have taken place without the approval and supervision of the bishop. It was the bishop who decided at what age a woman could undergo ritual consecration (this was a matter on which there was considerable variation);[51] it was the bishop who decided if she had the requisite virtues and if she was worthy of consecration; it was the bishop who bestowed the veil, pronounced the liturgical benediction, and customarily delivered a sermon of exhortation. There is also evidence that bishops tried to restrict the privilege of consecration to themselves to the exclusion of other clergy: for example, the council of Carthage in 390 declared that only bishops could consecrate virgins; presbyters were expressly forbidden to do so.[52] Legislation such as this suggests that the right of consecration was perceived to be an item of social capital, not to be shared even with other members of the clergy.

Ambrose's own discourses on virginal consecration often mention the privileged status of the Christian bishop as a consecrator of virgins. In *De virginitate*, for example, he urged the consecrated virgin to seek guidance on matters of doctrine and scriptural interpretation from 'the chosen and most devoted priests' (*electos et obseruantissimos sacerdotes*).[53] According to Ambrose, it had always been among the graces given to 'priests' (that is, to bishops) that they should 'sow the seeds of integrity and arouse enthusiasm for virginity'.[54] Ambrose could also speak of the consecration of virgins as part of the 'office' or 'duty' (*munus*) of his priesthood: in *De institutione virginis* he portrayed the virgin Ambrosia as one 'whom I offer in my office as priest (*sacerdotali munere*), whom I commend with

---

Harvard University Press, 1996). The language of the virgin bride created what Cooper: 58, has called 'a Christian alternative language of power and society'.

50 Cf. Bourdieu, 'Social Space and Symbolic Power': 23: 'To change the world, one has to change the ways of world-making, that is, the vision of the world and the practical operations by which groups are produced and reproduced.'

51 The council of Saragossa of 380 placed the age of veiling at 40: can. 8: '*Item lectum est: Non velandas esse virgines quae se Deo voverint, nisi XL annorum probata aetate quam sacerdos comprovaverit.*' The *Breviarium Hipponense*, which records canons from a North African council of 397, fixed the age at 25, the same as for clerics: can. 9 (CCSL 149, 33; Munier (ed.)): '*Vt ante XXV aetatis annos nec clerici ordinentur nec uirgines consecrentur.*' Ambrose does not specify an age, although he did not think it necessary for the girl to be very advanced in age: *Virginit.* 7.39 (Gori (ed.): 38): '. . . *non deest uirgini longaeua canities.*'

52 *Concilium Carthaginiense*, can. 3 (CCSL 149, 13–14; Munier (ed.)): '*Ab uniuersis episcopis dictum est: Chrismatis confectio et puellarum consecratio a presbyteris non fiat, uel reconciliare quemquam publica missa presbytero non licere, hoc omnibus placet.*'

53 *Virginit.* 4.23 (Gori (ed.): 28).

54 *Virginit.* 5.26 (Gori (ed.): 30): '. . . *quod semper spectauit ad gratiam sacerdotum, iacere semina integritatis et uirginitatis studia prouocare*'.

fatherly affection'.⁵⁵ And in the *Exhortatio virginitatis*, in the midst of a panegyric on the noble virgin Saint Soteris, he noted in a revealing aside: 'We priests have our own nobility which is greater than that of prefects and consuls; we have, I would say, the dignities of the faith which cannot perish.'⁵⁶ In so far as the consecration of virgins required an authorized agent who had 'obtained sufficient recognition to be in a position to impose recognition',⁵⁷ the act of consecrating virgins both signalled and enacted the bishop's authority as a spokesman and representative of the Christian community.

Conclusion

In her essay, 'The Ritual Body and the Dynamics of Ritual Power', Catherine Bell has articulated a description of the relation between ritual and power that is especially apt for our examination of the consecration of virgins in late antiquity:

> ritual is the social construction of a body by which 'the person' is afforded a particular sense of identity vis-à-vis other groups in which power is also localized. This is the construction of an identity that simultaneously empowers the person, by indicating his or her individuality and the basis of it, and limits or constricts the person, by defining that individuality as circumscribed by others, that is, as located within particular tensions making up the economy of power.⁵⁸

As I have argued in this chapter, the sacred space of the church was the site at which the identity of the consecrated virgin was instituted and a hierarchy of social relations was generated. In this ritual space the virgin was afforded a distinctive identity as superior to the ordinary married layperson and, simultaneously, was instituted in a role subordinate to the Christian bishop. The ritual action both empowered her and constricted her. Women who underwent formal consecration as virgins received an elevated status as 'brides of Christ', but were subsequently subject to stricter penalties if they chose later to marry a (human) husband.⁵⁹ Ambrose's treatises on virgins are filled with admonitions about the proper conduct of the consecrated virgin. Ironically, one of these stipulations was that younger virgins (*adulescentulis*) should avoid being seen in the church too often!⁶⁰

---

55   *Instit.* 17.107 (Gori (ed.): 186): '... *quam sacerdotali munere offero, affectu patrio commendo*'.
56   *Exh. virginit.* 12.82 (Gori (ed.): 262): '... *habemus enim nos sacerdotes nostram nobilitatem praefecturis et consulatibus praeferendam; habemus, inquam, fidei dignitates, quae perire non norunt*'.
57   See n.36 above.
58   'The Ritual Body': 308–9.
59   See, for example, the explicit distinction made between the penalties imposed on the *virgo velata* in contrast to those imposed on the *puella quae nondum velata est* in the decretal *Ad Gallos episcopos*, probably composed by Damasus; text in Yves-Marie Duval (ed.), *La décrétale Ad Gallos Episcopos: son text et son auteur* (Leiden: Brill, 2005): 28.
60   *Exh. virginit.* 10.71 (Gori (ed.): 256): '*Ipsa quoque ad ecclesiam progressio rarior sit adulescentulis. Considera quanta fuerit Maria, et tamen nusquam alibi, nisi in cubiculo reperitur, cum quaeritur.*'

A Liturgical Innovation and its Implications 105

And so we return to the dedication of the church at Bologna, where the widow Juliana processed into the church (or, as Ambrose puts it, 'into the temple of the Lord'),[61] accompanied by her son and daughters. As he brought his discourse to a close, Ambrose invoked a prayer that recalled his priestly task of consecrating both the church building and the bodies of the consecrated virgins:

> I beseech you, Lord, to keep a daily watch over this house of yours, over these altars, which today are dedicated to you, over these spiritual stones, each of which is consecrated as a living temple to you. May you receive in your divine mercy the prayers of your servants, which are poured out in this place. Let every sacrifice, which is offered in this temple with true faith and loving zeal, be to you as a fragrance of sanctification.[62]

In the world of Late Antiquity the task of consecrating both of these *templa* to the Lord – that is, the task of constituting the respective sacred spaces – could only have been the work of the Christian bishop. And such a task, as we have seen, also involved the consecration of his own authority.

---

61 *Exh. virginit.* 8.53 (Gori (ed.): 240): '*in templum domini deducens*'. Cf. 8.55 (Gori (ed.): 242): '*Procedit in ecclesiam filiarum uirginum septa comitatu, domesticum decus inuehens.*'
62 *Exh. virginit.* 14.94 (Gori (ed.): 270): '*Te nunc, domine, deprecor ut supra hanc domum tuam, supra haec altaria, quae hodie dedicantur, supra hos lapides spiritales, quibus sensibile tibi in singulis templum sacratur, quotidianus praesul intendas orationesque seruorum tuorum, quae in hoc funduntur loco, diuina tua suscipias misericordia. Fiat tibi in odorem sanctificationis, omne sacrificium quod in hoc templo fide integra, pia sedulitate defertur.*'

6 The City of God and the Place of Demons

City Life and Demonology in Early Christianity

Joona Salminen

This paper explores the spatial context of early Christian demonology. It is argued that during the second century, demonology was related to controlling public space: Tertullian and Clement of Alexandria serve as illuminating examples in this respect. Their views on demons are very much related to public space in the city. During the next two centuries, Christian demonology was mostly developed by authors who had decided to leave the city and move to the desert; Evagrius Ponticus serves as a good example here. However, the transition from city to the desert did not help ascetics escape from demons, but rather vice versa. In the desert, public space is transformed into inner space that needs to be controlled by the ascetic when striving for religious perfection and enacting the citizenship of heaven. As Tertullian famously asserted, demons are everywhere;[1] on another occasion he also said that 'the city is everywhere.'[2] Exploring the connection between demons and city life offers a surprising perspective on the early Christian view of urban space with all of its dark sides and temptations. Whereas urban Christians could avoid demons by following Tertullian's and Clement's instructions and thus stay away from their temptations, a disciple of Evagrius was equipped to confront his demons in the great silence of the desert. A model for this spiritual combat came from, among other things, *The Life of Antony* written by Athanasius. The story of this famous hermit was also known to Augustine, who did not favour leaving the city but emphasized that after Christ's victory, demons no longer have space in the city of God. This idea of two cities gave him an opportunity to discuss demonology in terms of Roman society, history, religious practices, and the political crisis at hand at the time.[3]

---

1 '*Deus ubique et bonitas dei ubique, daemonium ubique et maledictio daemonii ubique, iudicii diuini inuocatio ubique, mors ubique et conscientia mortis ubique et testimonium ubique.*' Tertullian, *Test.* 6.23. Elsewhere he polemically states that Satan and his Angels dwell everywhere (*totum saeculum repleverunt*), see *Spect.* 9.94.
2 Tertullian, *An.* 30.3. See also the conclusion of *Spec.* 30, where Tertullian briefly discusses things that are presented 'through faith in the imagination of the Spirit' (Glover (trans.), LCL 250, 301).
3 For the background of the political situation, see Claude Lepelley, 'The Survival and Fall of the Classical City in Late Roman Africa', in *The City in Late Antiquity*, John Rich (ed.) (London and New York: Routledge, 1992): 50–76.

In scholarship, demonology has evoked remarkable interest in recent years. *Demons and the Devil in Ancient and Medieval Christianity,* edited by Willemien Otten and Nienke Vos,[4] discusses a variety of themes regarding the topic; *Demons and the Making of the Monk: Spiritual Combat in Early Christianity* by David Brakke[5] explores especially monastic ideas on demons and asceticism combining them with some modern questions, such as gender studies; *Die Dämonen: die Dämonologie der israelitisch-jüdischen und frühchristlichen Literatur im Kontext ihrer Umwelt,* edited by Armin Lange, Herman Lichtenberger and K. F. Römheld,[6] contains important contributions to the subject at hand. In addition to these works, various articles shed light on early Christian demonology, but when it comes to demonology in early Christianity, most of the scholarly interest has been focused on such phenomena as asceticism, monasticism, exorcisms, and cosmology, and usually in the context of the New Testament and monasticism from the fourth century onward.[7] While some themes have been given much attention, other aspects have barely even been discussed.[8] In what follows demonology is seen in close contact to the public space and city life; special attention is paid to the nature of temptations in both city and desert, and how these temptations took their forms not just in certain a historical context but in a certain milieu. A careful reading of the demonological passages is combined with a comparative analysis in which the themes of space and city are related to the demonology of the first Christian centuries.

Demonological Origins

Unlike the meaning the word carries today, 'daemon' was a relatively neutral term until the second and third centuries CE. Richard Sorabji holds that it was mostly a Christian practice to treat demons as negative forces, though Plutarch and Porphyry also offer some negative cases but Plato, for example, always

---

4   Willemien Otten and Nienke Vos (eds), *Demons and the Devil in Ancient and Medieval Christianity* (Leiden: Brill, 2011).
5   David Brakke, *Demons and the Making of the Monk: Spiritual Combat in Early Christianity* (London: Harvard University Press, 2006).
6   Armin Lange, Herman Lichtenberger and K.F. Römheld (eds), *Die Dämonen: die Dämonologie der israelitisch-jüdischen und frühchristlichen Literatur im Kontext ihrer Umwelt* (Tübingen: Mohr Siebeck, 2003).
7   See for example Samuel Rubenson, 'Christian Asceticism and the Emergence of the Monastic Tradition', in *Asceticism,* V. L. Wimbush and R. Valantasis (eds) (Oxford: Oxford University Press, 1998): 49–57; Claudia Rapp, 'Desert, City, and Countryside in the Early Christian Imagination', *Church History and Religious Culture* 86/1 (2006): 93–112. In her article Rapp moves from The New Testament directly to fourth century ascetic literature whereas my intention in this chapter is to establish a link between these periods.
8   Though demons are interesting to early Christian scholars, ancient philosophical schools have not been scrutinized much in this respect; an exception is Keimpe Algra, 'Stoics on Souls and Demons: Reconstructing Stoic demonology' in *Demons and the Devil in Ancient and Medieval Christianity,* Willemien Otten and Nienke Vos (eds) (Leiden: Brill, 2011): 71–96.

described demons from a positive perspective. In Christian thinking, the distinction was made between demons that were evil and angels that were good.[9] The roots of this distinction have been discussed by Dale Martin who analyzes extensively the Hebrew vocabulary behind ancient Greek and Latin translations and shows how organically nuanced Hebrew demonology was transferred to the Greco-Roman milieu through biblical writings.[10] Altogether, early Christian demonology needs to be seen in the light of Jewish tradition to understand the thinking behind the relevant biblical texts; but it should be emphasized that not every early Christian author – for example those coming from pagan or Christian Greco-Roman families – dealing with the subject had this background in mind when composing their works and making their arguments. Rather, what they might have had in mind was probably something that was relevant to their immediate context, related to daily life problems and to the questions of members of their communities.

In scholarship the rise and function of demonology used to be related to Persian Zoroastry.[11] Recently too, the texts of Qumran and the idea of seeing Second Temple Judaism and Jewish monotheism as an inescapable context for both the New Testament and early Jewish–Christian writings have increased our understanding of the context of early Christian demonology. It has been emphasized that in both Qumranic texts and in the New Testament, the passages on demonology demonstrate 'the problem of powerlessness' when things are not under human control.[12] When it comes to vocabulary, the New Testament on many occasions speaks of 'unclean spirits' (*pneuma akatharton*, as in Matt 12:43; Mark 1:23; 5:1; 6:75; Luke 11:14), but *daimōn* is also used (e.g. Luke 11:4). Jesus and his disciples are depicted as authorized exorcists

---

9   Richard Sorabji, *The Philosophy of the Commentators, 200–600 AD: A Sourcebook*. Vol. 1, Psychology (with ethics and religion) (London: Duckworth, 2004): 403–8. See also Anders Klostergaard Petersen 'The Notion of Demon: Open Questions to a Diffuse Concept' in *Die Dämonen: die Dämonologie der israelitisch-jüdischen und frühchristlichen Literatur im Kontext ihrer Umwelt*, Armin Lange and Herman Lichtenberger (eds) (Tübingen: Mohr-Siebeck, 2003): 23–41; and Algra, 'Stoics on Souls and Demons' in *Demons and the Devil*: 88.

10 Dale Martin, 'When Did Angels Become Demons?', *JBL* 129, no. 4 (2010): 657–77. Martin has also emphasized the role of superstition (*superstitio*) concerning the relationship between Christians and pagans, see Dale Martin, *Inventing Superstition: From the Hippocratics to the Christians* (Cambridge, MA: Harvard University Press, 2004).

11 See Peter Brown, *The World of Late Antiquity: AD 150–750* (London: Thames & Hudson 1971 [reprinted 2006]): 54: 'The Christian church had inherited, through late Judaism, that most faithful legacy of Zoroastrian Persia to the western world – a belief in the absolute division of the spiritual world between good and evil powers, between angels and demons.'

12 See Hermann Lichtenberger, 'Demonology in the Dead Sea Scrolls and the New Testament', in *Text, Thought, and Practice in Qumran and Early Christianity*, Ruth A. Clements and Daniel R. Schwartz (eds) (Leiden/Boston: Brill, 2009): 267–80. Lichtenberger also discusses the theme of the space God has given for demons in this world (see pp. 270, 280, and 279 on cosmology) when they are cast out by exorcisms. Lichtenberger (276–8) also notes that some scholars consider Luke 11:20 to be an important authentic saying in relation to Jesus' self-understanding because it combines both the concept of *basileia theou* and Jesus' healing ministry, i.e. exorcisms.

who have the power to expel evil forces. Jesus' healing ministry was in many ways connected to Satan and his league (as in Matt 12:24; Luke 11:14–20).[13] In fact, some scholars have recently emphasized that exorcisms were one of the reasons that early Christianity gained followers and was considered credible in the eyes of the ancients.[14] Despite this, it is unclear what kind of exorcist Paul, for example, was. In Acts he is depicted as a miracle worker, but actual exorcisms are not mentioned. However, discerning spirits (*diakrisis pneumatōn*, mentioned in 1 Corinthians 12:10) may hint at exorcism.[15] Thus far, though we are better aware of early Christian demonology and its role in various kinds of healings, the connection between demons and public space has not been thoroughly investigated.

Demons and Public Space

Though Jesus exorcizes in public, in the gospels public space does not seem to be possessed by demons. However, when looking at texts from the next Christian generation, such as Tertullian's *De Spectaculis*, demonology becomes a way by which Christian authors describe public space to their disciples. This section explores Tertullian's account of demons especially as he presents their activity in relation to public space and spectacles; some similarities to Clement of Alexandria, another North African based author, will also be pointed out, but the main emphasis is on Tertullian's construction of the demon-possessed public space.

Regarding public life, early Christian authors usually saw their communities in relation to the society around them even though they thought that Christians were somewhat different and distinct from others.[16] For Clement and Tertullian, the city is the most ordinary place to live despite its temptations. An essential part of third century Christian city life was to avoid demons. Clement is very clear on this question. Christians should not have any contact with these powers: 'We should have no communication with demons nor should we, the living image of God, crown ourselves like dead idols.'[17] Tertullian holds a somewhat similar point of view in his discussions. In *Apologeticus* he maintains that Christians are aware of these *substantiae spirituales* that all the ancient philosophers and poets also recognize.[18] Their goal is the destruction of man (*hominis eversio*) and they strive to achieve this goal by attacking both the victim's body and the soul; violence is one of their effects. According to Tertullian, demons are very skilful and are undetectable to human senses; they are so capable that one can recognize

---

13 Heikki Räisänen, *The Rise of Christian Beliefs. The Thought World of Early Christians* (Minneapolis: Fortress Press, 2010): 205, 231, 243, 343.
14 Eric Sorensen, *Possession and Exorcism in the New Testament and Early Christianity* (WUNT 2/157; Tübingen: Mohr Siebeck, 2002): 169.
15 Sorensen, *Possession and Exorcism*: 155–7.
16 See for example Clement, *Paed.* 1.12. (cf. however *Paed.* 2.5.45.1); Tertullian, *Apol.* 42.
17 *Paed.* 2.8.73.1. (Wood (trans.)). See also *Protr.* 2.25.1 (LCL 92, 50–51).
18 Tertullian, *Apol.* 22:1.

them more easily by the consequences (*in effectu*) of their doings than in the action itself (*in actu*).[19]

Both Clement and Tertullian represent a realistic understanding of demons.[20] Christians can avoid them by avoiding certain places and events. For them demons do not seem to rise from the souls of Christians but are external powers. In this manner their view differs from the more psychologically orientated teachings of the next generation of desert fathers, such as Evagrius Ponticus (to whom we turn in the next section). Tertullian highlights the fact that corrupted angels were damned by God and thereby became *corruptior gens daemonum*, even more corrupted.[21] He also relates demons to violence and idolatry in *De spectaculis*, a work that deals with games and other spectacles. He links together the renunciation of the world that Christians declare at baptism and then extends this to apply to games as well. Scripture tells Christians that killing is wrong, which implies that it is not suitable for them to attend games.[22]

> But rather more pompous is the outfit of the games in the circus, to which the name *pomp* properly belongs. The pomp (procession) comes first and shows in itself to whom it belongs, with the long line of images, the succession of statues, the cars, chariots, carriages, the thrones, garlands, robes. What sacred rites, what sacrifices, come at the end; what guilds, what priesthoods, what offices are astir, – everybody knows in that city where the demons sit in conclave (*daemoniorum conventus consedit*).[23]

For Tertullian, the games represent the religious rites of the city in which demons are in charge. Clement too shows a similar attitude towards the games and spectacles in his work *Exhortation to the Greeks*.[24] Tertullian also mentions that good things – he uses the horse as an example – are turned from God's gifts 'into the service of demons' (*transit a dei munere ad daemoniorum officia*).[25] However, he does not seem to suggest that Christians should leave the city in spite of all this demonic activity and superstition (*superstitio*) that takes place in the name of religion (*in religionis nomine*).[26] He concludes that the spectacles were instituted by the Devil.[27] His opposition to the games is interesting both in demonological and sociological aspects because it shows a spiritual, or theological, controversy between Christians and Roman society. For Tertullian, the violent games created a city of demons.

---

19 *Apol.* 22.4–6.
20 For Clement, see his discussion in *Protr.* 2.40.1–2.41.4 (LCL 92, 87–91).
21 Tertullian, *Apol.* 22: 2–3.
22 Tertullian, *Spec.* 3–5.
23 *Spec.* 7.93. (Glover (trans.)).
24 Clement, *Protr.* 3.
25 Tertullian, *Spec.* 9.95. (Glover (trans.)).
26 *Spec.* 5.92.
27 *Spec.* 24.102.

Above we looked at what Clement and Tertullian say about demons in relation to public space. As for private space, Tertullian does not mention demons in this context very often; however, he insists that demons are everywhere (*ubique*) and warns that dreams might be sent by demons, and that Christians should be careful with traditional Roman religious practices.[28] As a warning example, he tells of two women who were possessed by demons after going to the theatre.[29] According to him, pagan spectacles ought to be hated (*odisse debemus istos conventus et coetus ethnicorum*).[30] Finally, he urges his audience to see that another kind of spectacle is coming, namely heavenly Jerusalem with its saints and angels. '*Qualis civitas*', he exclaims, '*cum alia spectacula!*'[31] He wants his audience to remember these spectacles of another kind.

It can be concluded that, in Tertullian's circle of that time, demonology becomes a rather central element of the ethics, worldview, and Christian way of life.[32] Tertullian's teaching about the possessed public space provides a background for controlling one's passions and inner life, scrutinizing one's thoughts and motives, and safeguarding oneself against the attacks of demons – the cunning and savage unseen forces that dwell in violent public spectacles. Once demons have taken public space under their control, they are on their way to possess each citizen's inner, and thus most private, space as well.[33]

To conclude, the city and demons were very much related to each other in the writings of Tertullian and Clement. Tertullian's teaching on games is an especially illuminating example of how the city and demons were related in early Christian thinking, and some of these elements are also found in Clement's writing. In the following we will look at how what I call 'the temptations of the city' are closely related to monastic life in the desert; at the same time, we are also taking a step towards the more systematic demonology of the fourth century.

Public Becomes Private: Desert as an Inner City

The connection between the city and demons can already be seen in the Gospel narratives on the temptations of Christ in the desert immediately after his baptism.

---

28 Tertullian, *Test.* 6.23; *An.* 47. For Tertullian's view of Roman religious practices, see Cecilia Ames, 'Roman Religion in the Vision of Tertullian', in *A Companion to Roman Religion*, Jörg Rüpke (ed.) (Malden, MA: Blackwell, 2007): 457–71. Tertullian also mentions exorcisms in *An.* 57. In his treatise on sleep, Clement does not mention demons (*Paed.* 3.9).
29 Tertullian, *Spec.* 26.103.
30 *Spec.* 27.103.
31 *Spec.* 30.104.
32 In other words: 'To sin was no longer merely to err: it was to allow oneself to be overcome by unseen forces', as Brown puts it in *The World of Late Antiquity*, see 53, 55–6.
33 Adopting different kinds of spiritual exercises from contemporary philosophical schools gave early Christian teachers tools with which to guide their disciples in controlling their emotions and reflecting on their everyday behaviour. By 'spiritual exercises' I refer to Pierre Hadot's remarks in *Philosophy as a Way of Life: Spiritual Exercises from Socrates to Foucault*, Arnold I. Davidson (ed.) (Michael Chase (trans.); Oxford: Blackwell Publishing, 1995): 81–9.

What the Devil does in the passages is tempt Christ with food, urge him to test his guardian angels by throwing himself off the pinnacle of the temple and, most strikingly, he shows Christ all the glorious cities and promises them to him in return for his worship (see Matt 4:5; Luke 4:5–7). It is the city, an image or illusion of it, which follows Christ into the desert. It is noteworthy that this kind of setting is apparent also in *The Life of Antony*.

There is no doubt that the *Vita* is one of the most influential pieces of early Christian desert literature.[34] However, the temptations of the demons represented in the work usually, in one way or another, refer to the city and city life. In fact, there are only rare temptations that actually have something to do with the concrete circumstances of the wilderness (e.g. wild animals, other monks, communal life).[35] This makes the demonology of the *Vita* extremely intriguing: when desert turns into a city, the ascetic must control his inner life that is filled with city-related images brought forth by demons. City life has its downsides, but leaving the city was not an easy answer to the problems ascetics had at hand. For instance, demons remind Antony of wealth, his sister and family, and comfortable city life, all of which seek to make him renounce his project of a simple life in the desert. 'The spirit of fornication' frequently appeared to him in the form of a seductive woman and aroused him in various other ways too, such as by tempting him with unclean thoughts.[36] So, then, in Athanasius' narrative, demons are interested in bringing Antony back to the city. This could imply that Athanasius himself considers the city to be a place of demons – a notion also found in Tertullian, as noted earlier. However, what is interesting in this reading is that demons seem to be in favour of what the Romans would call *pietas* and the Greeks *eusebeia* or *dikaiosynē*, taking care of one's duties regarding one's family and the *polis*. This conflict of virtues can be confusing: demons mix two spaces in order to get the ascetic back to the city he came from; the ascetic, then, needs to distinguish between these spaces. City piety is different from devotion in the desert, which creates a space for spiritual battle.

In the *Vita*, Athanasius attributes the charisma of *diakrisis pneumatōn* (1 Cor 12:10) to Antony,[37] an ability extensively elaborated on in the later monastic and ascetic literature. This charisma was central to Antony, who warns his listeners about demons who come to them saying that they are angels and admire the ascetic's discipline. According to Antony, this temptation can be overcome by making the sign of the cross and ignoring the demons. Besides discerning the spirits, this practice highlights the ascetic's independence and humility; by being aware of one's spiritual state and way of life one is able to vanquish thoughts of pride and the demons' praises. Antony says that when praising the ascetic, demons can appear in various forms that imply good intentions; however, their presence usually makes one troubled. In Antony's view it is up to God to grant the

---

34 Rapp, 'Desert, City, and Countryside': 98.
35 See *Vit. Ant.*, 9, 12, 23, 25.
36 *Vit. Ant.*, 5–6.
37 *Vit. Ant.*, 22.

ability to distinguish the presence of good from the presence of bad.[38] This is an essential part of the ascetic's battle over evil: getting to know oneself and God. In Athanasius' narrative the desert creates a more suitable space for this than the city but the conflict between these two spaces, caused by demons, breaks the solitude of the desert. However clear this conflict may seem, Athanasius' narrative does not provide the sort of nuanced analysis that we find in some of its readers.

Evagrius Ponticus was influenced by the *Vita* and made a significant contribution concerning the discernment of both spirits and thoughts in the desert.[39] When Evagrius advises his disciples to resist demons, his strategy seems to be more about analyzing and avoiding them; confronting demons is based on analyzing their methods.[40] Evagrius uses his idea of eight bad thoughts (*logismoi*) in a diagnostic manner.[41] What Evagrius offers to his readers may not be a fighting armour after all, but rather a survival kit and a diagnostic tool. Evagrius advises externalizing one's thoughts and expelling the bad ones after analyzing them.[42] His discussion on the vagabond demon (*daimōn planos*) serves as an example: according to Evagrius this is a demon who 'makes the monk's mind (*nous*) wander from village to village and from city to city and from house to house' to have conversations that look innocent, but are actually very distracting and harmful for a monk.[43] The demon of fornication can also work in this way by seducing the monk to leave his cell to go to market places and other public spaces and events to see and meet women.[44] This reminds us of what we noted earlier about Antony and his responsibilities to his sister and household. In fact, it is plausible to argue, as David Brakke has done, that some descriptions of demons in Evagrius' works were inspired by Antony's demonic encounters in the *Vita*.[45] However, in my view, instead of the language of combat we should pay more attention to the discourse of discernment when it comes to encountering demons as Evagrius presents them.

To take some examples, what makes the vagabond demon dangerous is that it destroys tranquillity and loneliness, leading the monk straight back to the city with its temptations. I argue that describing this 'battle' in militant terms and imagery, though they are also used by Evagrius himself,[46] can distract us from the actual activity, namely the discernment of spirits and thoughts. It is also illuminating to notice

---

38 *Vit. Ant.*, 35.
39 For Evagrius' writing see *Evagrius of Pontus: The Greek Ascetic Corpus* (translation and commentary by Robert E. Sinkewicz; Oxford: Oxford University Press, 2003). An excellent resource for studying Evagrius is http://evagriusponticus.net, Joel Kalvesmaki (ed.).
40 Cf. Brakke, *Demons*: 71, 76–7.
41 Evagrius' conception of this 'therapeutical process' has been discussed in detail by Simo Knuuttila, *Emotions in Ancient and Medieval Philosophy* (Oxford: Clarendon Press, 2004): 141–4.
42 Brakke, *Demons*: 71–2.
43 Evagrius, *Sur les pensées* (*De malignis cogitationibus*), 9, 1–3.
44 David Brakke puts this accurately: 'To be sure, fornication appears at times as the warm temptation to return to the world to enjoy the comforts of marriage and family.' Brakke, *Demons*: 59.
45 Brakke, *Demons*: 65.
46 See for example Evagrius, *Praktikos*, chapters 19, 42 and 54.

how Evagrius reflects, without using militant vocabulary, on the demon of anger, which he considers to be the fiercest passion of them all.[47] When it comes to resisting demons, Evagrius' instructions are more analytic than militant.[48] The critical distance to the imagery he himself uses deepens the analysis of his thought. It also seems that it is not necessary to read Evagrius' *Talking Back* or *Counter Arguments*[49] in terms of combat, but to keep in mind the methods of discernment by which monks were supposed to distance their true inner self from the thoughts and emotions that distracted them from focussing on their heavenly goal. Instead, it should be highlighted, that *diakrisis* or *discretio* is the discourse of the desert. When an ascetic first leaves the city externally, he then proceeds to the next step, namely leaving it internally.[50] In order to achieve this, he needs to practice discernment because no matter where he sets off from he will encounter the city. What is public in the city becomes private in the desert: the city is everywhere, and so are the demons.

Augustine on Public Space and the Place of Demons

Like Evagrius, Augustine, too, was impressed by what he had heard about Antony; however, moving to the desert was never a serious intention for him.[51] In this light it should be asked what made him compose a whole work about the two cities? The distinction between *civitas terrestris* and *caelestis* is usually seen as an apologetic contribution to the discussion of the role of Christians in Roman society.[52] My aim is not to question this standard view but, instead, to suggest a reading of *De Civitate Dei* in which the ascetical setting of the time is taken into account. I suggest that one goal of Augustine's work is to distance himself from the desert movement, and discussing demonology's relation to the public space was one of the strategies he applied.

Augustine opposed many ascetic extremes,[53] and from this point of view and in contrast with the desert movement, *De Civitate Dei* implies that Christians are

---

47 Evagrius, *Praktikos*, chapter 11.
48 See Evagrius, *Praktikos*, chapters 15–39.
49 William Harmless (SJ) translates the work's title as *Counter Arguments*, see *Desert Christians: An Introduction to the Literature of Early Monasticism*. (Oxford: Oxford University Press, 2004): 329. David Brakke's English translation is titled *Talking Back: A Monastic Handbook for Combating Demons*.
50 See *Praktikos*, chapter 41, where Evagrius warns that visiting cities and towns can be a challenge for monks and can put both their entire way of life and their vocation in danger. See Rapp's 'Desert as a state of mind' in her article 'Desert, City, and Countryside': 102–7.
51 See Brakke, *Demons*: 48, and James O'Donnell, *Augustine: Confessions, Commentary on Books 8–13*, vol. 3 (Oxford: Clarendon, 1992): 38.
52 See Gerard O'Daly, *Augustine's City of God. A Reader's Guide*. (Oxford: Clarendon Press, 1999): 39–52, and Johannes van Oort, *Jerusalem and Babylon: A Study into Augustine's City of God and the Sources of His Doctrine of the Two Cities* (Leiden: Brill, 1990).
53 For instance, regarding marriage and celibacy, see David G. Hunter, *Marriage, Celibacy, and Heresy in Ancient Christianity: The Jovinianist Controversy* (Oxford: Oxford University Press, 2007): 269–270, 279, 283–4.

citizens of heaven despite the fact that they do not live in the desert. In this context the city of God is not the inner space of a withdrawn ascetic striving for perfection outside the city walls and urban social structures. For Augustine the city of God is present within the concrete city, distinct from it, but at the same time intermingled with it.[54] Demons are an essential part of this idea; in fact, among Augustine's works, *De Civitate Dei* is the one that deals the most with demons.[55] Augustine's view on the essence of demons comes close to that of Tertullian, but Augustine's way of explaining what they are is more theological as he discusses demonology in relation to Christ, soteriology and God's might: he emphasizes that God has power and control over demons.[56] He thinks that demons were defeated in Christ's work of salvation and that they originally derived their power from God. For *daemones*, bad deeds by humans are a pleasure.[57] Augustine also remarks that no demon has ever denied God.[58] For Augustine, the Devil is 'the prince of demons,' whose goal is to keep humans away from God. In scholarship an interesting possibility has been discussed, namely, that Augustine might have thought that humans were created to fill the heavenly city after the fall of the bad angels.[59] This is a fascinating reflection regarding the heavenly space and the space of the city of God. It also reflects his view on public space and Roman civic religion.

Augustine finds sacrifices to demons to be vain and unnecessary.[60] In the third book of *De divinatione daemonum*, Augustine shows his concern that demons tempt people to a bad kind of *curiositas*, false happiness, and cheat them by promising worldly success.[61] Also in *De Civitate* his emphasis is on highlighting the deceptive nature of demons.[62] It seems that Augustine does not urge us either to confront demons or to avoid them. He considers them to be somewhat powerless and everything they do is under the control of God's providence.[63] Not falling for their deceptions and remembering that they have been vanquished by Christ are not Augustine's original inventions but can be found, for example, in *The Life of Antony*; however, differences can be found concerning the social setting and the context in which Christian perfection is to be strived for. Augustine does not

---

54 Augustine, *Civ.* 1.35.
55 Frederick van Fleteren, 'Demons' in *Augustine through the Ages. An Encyclopedia*, Allan D. Fitzgerald, John Cavadini, Marianne Djuth, James J. O'Donnell and Frederick van Fleteren (eds) (Michigan: Grand Rapids, 1999): 266–8. See *Civ.* 8–10 and passim. O'Daly (*Augustine's City of God*: 110) links the demonology of the work to Augustine's Platonic framework.
56 Augustine, *Civ.* 18.18; reference provided by van Fleteren, 'Demons'.
57 Augustine, *Civ.* 5.23; 6.1; *Serm.* 198; *Enchir.* 9; references provided by Fleteren, 'Demons'.
58 Augustine, *Div.* 7.11–10.14; 8.12; see Laura Holt, 'Divinatione daemonum, De', in *Augustine through the Ages. An Encyclopedia*, Allan D. Fitzgerald et al. (eds) (Michigan: Grand Rapids, 1999): 277–8.
59 Augustine, *Ennarrat. Ps.* 73.16; *Doctr. chr.* 2.23; see 'Devil' by F. van Fleteren, in *Augustine through the Ages*: 268–9.
60 O'Daly, *Augustine's City of God*: 101, 105–9.
61 Laura Holt, 'Divinatione daemonum': 277–8.
62 O'Daly, *Augustine's City of God*: 115–29, 199.
63 Augustine, *Civ.* 1.32; 2.25; 2:29; 4.32.

consider the idea of fighting demons a central aspect of Christian life because demons have already been defeated by Christ; according to him it is also useless to focus too much of one's energy in thinking about them. Possibly this view of demons affected his thinking on city life too: Augustine emphasizes that Christians can deal with demons by living in the city. Augustine seems to view demons in a realistic way, but at the same time he gives a kind of psychological explanation for the city of God. However, despite the fact that he was not a promotor of desert life, Augustine himself chose a life of celibacy and also paid positive attention to asceticism in his semi-monastic community.

In *Confessiones*, Augustine provides us with a narrative describing the transition from his ordinary city life to a more monastic kind of lifestyle.[64] Before his conversion, Augustine was familiar with the earthly pleasures that cities such as Thagaste and Carthage had to offer.[65] However, in *Confessiones* he does not find the city a place that should be rejected in order to lead a good Christian life. When presenting his plans of withdrawing from society, Augustine does not refer to the desert.[66] In fact, we cannot be sure whether Augustine had personally read the *Vita* (or, if so, which version); it is possible that he was familiar with the story of Antony only orally.[67] It is noteworthy that demons are absent from his conversion narrative and he does not fight against them, but rather presents himself and his previous way of life as major obstacles in his path to catholicism. However, comparing what he says about how he enjoyed the theatre and spectacles in his youth and how he sees the relationship between urban spectacles and the city of God later as an elderly bishop might shed some light on his demonology, too. Regarding this comparison, it should be highlighted how the two works come from different historical settings, but also differ in matters of genre: apologetic elements in *De Civitate Dei* are closely related to demonology, whereas the focus of *Confessions* is on Augustine's personal introspection in which demons are not involved.[68]

Though Augustine never wanted to move to the desert in order to imitate Antony, it is useful to note that he learns of Antony at the same time as Evagrius and others were settling themselves in the desert for a monastic life.[69] When compared to other early Christian writers, such as Clement, Tertullian, or Athanasius, Augustine's approach to city life seems to swing between the two extremes. On the one hand, second century writers do not make a distinction between two cities as he does, but their concern is that their disciples should lead a decent life among the pagans and gain their respect through their conduct. Later on the number of those who consider the desert to be a more appropriate place for those Christians

---

64   *Conf.* 6.11–15.
65   See for example *Conf.* 3.1–2; 6.1–4.
66   *Conf.* 6.12.1; 6.14.1.
67   See *Conf.* 8.6.14 and O'Donnell's commentary: 38–41.
68   A good example of this is *Conf.* 6.13–15, where Augustine has to leave his beloved concubine but needs to wait until his wife is of an age when they can start their marital life together; Augustine does not blame demons for his actions while waiting.
69   Brakke, *Demons*: 48; see also *Conf.* 8.8.19.

who want to strive towards religious perfection increases. Augustine's notion of the two cities is in the middle of these views: he does not urge his congregation to leave the city and move to the desert, nor does he say that the *civitas terrestris* is the only place for Christians. From this perspective it is important to emphasize what kind of lifestyle choices he aims to promote in his writings because his arguments are based on his idea of the city as a place of demons.

Conclusions

In this chapter it has been argued that demons are closely related to early Christian strategies for controlling public space. Unlike Augustine, Clement and Tertullian do not make a distinction between the city of God and the secular city; in their writings we come across a different way of dealing with the city as an environment for ethics and as a space for Roman or Hellenistic traditions. On the one hand, the idea of demons dwelling in the public space served the realistic demonology of Tertullian, Clement, and Augustine; on the other hand, the temptations of the city found their way into the desert, too, where teachers such as Evagrius developed psychological tools to be used in diagnosing the ascetics' spiritual progress and their inner space. It seems that monks took the city with them on their way to solitude. This implies, then, that in the actual desert it is the ascetic's own body which provides the space for demonic temptations. For those who left their cities, it soon became clear that the demons are everywhere, and so is the city – with all of its temptations, games and spectacles.

7 Preaching, Feasting and Making Space for a Meaning

Anna-Liisa Tolonen

Introduction

Feasting is a communal practice well represented in sources which date back to Late Antiquity. The homilies on the saints, in particular, provide us with varied impressions of feasting through preaching.[1] Neither the act of feasting nor that of preaching can be imagined to have taken place without people, some form of communication – and a space. Thus, even when fixed in a written form, speeches composed for feasts carry with them a sense of spatiality. As time passes, it may become increasingly difficult to verify whether those echoes ever stemmed from an actual space and yet we are left with descriptions of events, people and practices, which introduce us to the spaces of the past.[2]

One such text is the homily *On Eleazar and the Seven Boys*, ascribed to John Chrysostom (c. 347–407). Even if the text does not allow for easy historical contextualization, the homily preserves very interesting reflections concerning the spaces in which the so-called Maccabees were celebrated and preached about. In this study, I shall survey the festival space of the Maccabees by way of contextualizing it in the argumentative environment of the whole text. I will point out

---

1 See for example Johan Leemans, 'General Introduction' in *'Let Us Die That We May Live': Greek Homilies on Christian Martyrs from Asia Minor, Palestine and Syria (c. AD 350 – AD 450)*, Johan Leemans, Wendy Mayer, Pauline Allen and Boudewijn Dehandschutter (eds) (London: Routledge, 2003): 20–2, 44–7; cf. the editors' 'Preface' in the same work: viii; Jaclyn L. Maxwell, *Christianization and Communication in Late Antiquity. John Chrysostom and his Congregation in Antioch* (Cambridge: Cambridge University Press, 2006): 2–7; Christine C. Shepardson, 'Controlling Contested Places: John Chrysostom's *Adversus Iudaeos* Homilies and the Spatial Politics of Religious Controversy', *JECS* 15:4 (2007); Nathanael Andrade, 'The Processions of John Chrysostom and the Contested Spaces of Constantinople', *JECS* 18:2 (2010).
2 See for example Alexandra G. Retzleff, who has discussed the festival occasion reflected in one of John Chrysostom's famous homilies. She notes that the text in question has for a long time served as 'testimony of an unusual type of aquatic spectacle' in Late Antiquity; yet she convincingly argues for a less literal spatial reading of the text, according to which the 'swimming harlots' and the like should be understood metaphorically, rather than as real-life descriptions; Alexandra G. Retzleff, 'John Chrysostom's Sex Aquarium: Aquatic Metaphors for Theater in Homily 7 on Matthew', *JECS* 11:2 (2003): 195–6.

two different and seemingly separate descriptions of social interaction in which the homilist involves himself in the course of the homily. I argue that the homilist constructs a festival space for the Maccabees that matches his theological concerns. In other words, the feast, as represented by the homilist, provides a favourable environment for the theological agenda of his homily. The homily *On Eleazar* does not, I argue, attempt to reform a festival space; rather, it exhorts its audience to enter a spiritual state of mind. As such, the text preserves and communicates meaningfully some central theological concerns and contexts of its time, even if, as I shall point out, the historical space in which it was composed cannot be reconstructed.

On Eleazar and the Seven Boys: the Text, its Provenance and Context

Like other homilies, the homily *On Eleazar and the Seven Boys*[3] is composed in the form of a speech.[4] It includes an opening and a conclusion, in which interaction in a shared space between the homilist and his audience is implied.[5] Eleazar, the seven boys and their mother[6] are the identifiable subjects of the homily: the homilist treats these figures as a group, 'the Maccabees', and considers them to be among the Christian saints.[7] According to the homily, there is a local festival, during which (some of) the people commemorate the Maccabees.[8] Encouraging and instructing his audience to participate in it, the homilist touches upon issues related to the festival space.[9]

---

3 For a brief introduction to the text as well as the newest English translation, see Wendy Mayer, *St John Chrysostom: The Cult of the Saints* (New York: St Vladimir's Seminary Press, 2006): 119–34. The Greek text is reconstructed from Montfaucon's edition (reprinted in Migne's *Patrologia Graeca* 63: 523–530) and Wenger's corrections to and completion of it; cf. A. Wenger, 'Restauration de l'*Homélie* de Chrysostome sur Eléazar et les sept frères Macchabées (PG 63: 523–530)' in *Texte und Textkritik: Eine Aufsatzsammlung in Zusammenarbeit mit Johannes Irmscher, Franz Paschke & Kurt Treu*, J. Drummer (ed.) (Berlin: Akademie-Verlag, 1987): 599–604. In this chapter, the references to the text are made to PG as well as the passages edited by Wenger; the English quotations from the homily follow Mayer's translation, unless indicated otherwise.
4 'Homily' (ἡ ὁμιλία) translates simply as social intercourse or a communal gathering. In the early Christian context, it becomes 'an exhortation upon the text, or an application of the text to Christian living', as opposed to a mere commentary on scriptures. Moreover, from the third century onward 'the homily took a new task, that of explaining the meaning of the feast'; W. J. O'Shea and T. D. Rover, 'Homily' in *New Catholic Encyclopedia* (Detroit: Gale/Thomson Learning, Inc., 2003): 62.
5 Cf. PG 63, 524 ll. 48ff; 525 ll. 3–4, 14–15; 630 ll. 45ff; Wenger, 'Restauration de l'*Homélie*': 603–4.
6 Cf. 2 Maccabees 6:18–7 and 4 Maccabees.
7 PG 63, 525 ll. 15–16; 530 ll. 50–51.
8 The speech lacks concrete references to an actual identifiable location, such as a church or a martyrium, and it is not clear who participates in the feast, where the feast is held, and what it is like. Yet, there is nothing in the text that would suggest that there was no feast.
9 See sections PG 63, 525 ll. 31–50; 527 ll. 58–528 ll. 3; 530 ll. 45–55; and Wenger, 'Restauration de l'*Homélie*': 603–4.

The text of the homily *On Eleazar* is extant in Greek. It is included in a short collection of homilies known as *Novae homiliae*, which consists of 15 homilies and is connected with John Chrysostom's early career in Constantinople.[10] This literary context, together with the title,[11] has earned the homily a rather precise provenance: it is considered to be a speech delivered by John Chrysostom during his early years in Constantinople, one day before the feast of the Maccabees.[12]

The suggested place and date are historically possible and perhaps even likely; yet such a precise provenance should be considered with caution. First, with regard to the use of homilies as historical sources, one should remember that the surviving text is a written account which may, or may not, be identical with the original homily as it was first delivered.[13] In addition, as Wendy Mayer has pointed out, the standing proposal concerning the homily *On Eleazar* is based on several conditions which cannot be secured.[14] Finally, even if those conditions could be secured, the place and the date alone do little to reconstruct the immediate social historical circumstances in which the homily was delivered. The homilies preserved in the same collection cannot be used for reconstruction of such a historical frame; rather, they seem to be independent from one another.[15] To my knowledge, there are also no ancient references to the homily *On Eleazar*, and no other witnesses to the cult of the Maccabees in Constantinople during the time of John Chrysostom.[16] Thus, there are no external criteria against which to evaluate

---

10 Cf. Wendy Mayer, 'Les homélies des s. Jean Chrysostome en Juillet 399: A Second Look at Pargoire's Sequence and the Chronology of the *Novae Homiliae* (CPG 4441)', *Byzantinoslavica* 60 (1999): 273–5. The number is derived from codex *Stavronikita* 6. The other manuscript (ms *Ottob. gr.* 431) includes only 13 homilies. The homily *On Eleazar* is found in both manuscripts but the texts are not identical; cf. Mayer, *St John Chrysostom*: 120; Wenger, 'Restauration de l'*Homélie*': 599–601.
11 PG 63, 523 ll. 34–36.
12 The date is further narrowed down to either 398 or 399, on the basis that the day in question should have been either a Saturday or Sunday and the 31st of July; Mayer, *St John Chrysostom*: 119–20.
13 See for example Maxwell, *Christianization and Communication*: 6; Leemans, 'General Introduction': 43.
14 According to Mayer, these conditions are that (1) the homily was, as the text suggests (PG 63, 525 ll. 19–23), delivered on the proper feast day of the Maccabees but a day in advance, (2) one assumes that the Maccabees were already, at that time, celebrated in Constantinople annually on the first of August and (3) that the homily was delivered in a regular weekly service, which should have been on either a Saturday or a Sunday; Mayer, 'Les homélies des s. Jean Chrysostome': 287, 301; Mayer, *St John Chrysostom*: 119. Most scholars seem to agree with that, while some still favour Antioch as the location, e.g. Martha Vinson, 'Gregory Nazianzen's Homily 15 and the Genesis of the Christian Cult of the Maccabean Martyrs', *Byzantion* 64 (1994): 186 n. 61; Daniel Joslyn-Siemiatkoski, *Christian Memories of the Maccabean Martyrs* (New York: Palgrave MacMillan, 2009): 44; Gerhard Rouwhorst, 'The Emergence of the Cult of the Maccabean Martyrs in late Antique Christianity' in *More than a Memory: The Discourse of Martyrdom and the Construction of Christian Identity in the History of Christianity*, J. Leemans (ed.) (Leuven: Peeters, 2005): 87.
15 Mayer, 'Les homélies des s. Jean Chrysostome': 302–3.
16 See also Berger, who takes Constantinople and 398/99 as its probable provenance and notes that it is the only extant text John Chrysostom wrote on the Maccabees after he had left Antioch; Albrecht Berger, 'The Cult of the Maccabees in the Eastern Orthodox Church' in *Dying for the Faith, Killing for the Faith: Old-Testament Faith-Warriors (1 and 2 Maccabees) in Historical Perspective*, G. Signor (ed.) (Leiden: Brill, 2012): 107.

the historical accuracy or inaccuracy of the literary descriptions of the space(s), impressions of which are preserved in the text.

The homily *On Eleazar* has not been studied for the sake of its precise historical context alone but, rather, together with a vast array of other literary sources dated back to the fourth and fifth centuries, in order to give as complete as possible a view of the social historical spaces in which the Maccabees were venerated and their Christian cult formed.[17] In the context of these sources, the homily *On Eleazar* has been noted primarily for its characterization of a problematic relationship of some of the local Christians with the Maccabees. It has been read as a speech in defence of the Maccabees, as a promotion of their cult, or as an attempt to justify theologically the Christian veneration of non-Christian, Jewish martyrs.[18] Similar tendencies – defensiveness about the cult of the Maccabees – have also been detected in some other homilies on the Maccabees.[19] This has led many scholars to recognize a conflict surrounding the feasting of the Maccabees, which appears strikingly similar in sources from various places dating back to approximately the same period.[20] The contemporary state of research, therefore,

---

17 According to the general view of contemporary research, the Christian cult of the Maccabees emerged sometime during the second half of the fourth century in Antioch and, by the turn of the century, Antioch was widely recognized as a central place of their veneration; Berger, 'The Cult of the Maccabees': 105; Johannes Hahn, 'The Veneration of the Maccabean Brothers in Fourth Century Antioch: Religious Competition, Martyrdom, and Innovation' in *Dying for the Faith, Killing for the Faith: Old-Testament Faith-Warriors (1 and 2 Maccabees) in Historical Perspective*, G. Signori (ed.) (Leiden: Brill, 2012): 81–3; Joslyn-Siemiatkoski, *Christian Memories*: 42–3. It is presumed that this cult spread 'rapidly' but not without obstacles; Rouwhorst, 'The Emergence of the Cult': 81; Leonard V. Rutgers, 'The Importance of Scripture in the Conflict between Jews and Christians: The Example of Antioch' in *The Use of Sacred Books in the Antique World*, L. V. Rutgers, P. W. van der Horst, H. W. Havelaar and L. Teugels (eds) (Leuven: Peeters, 1998): 301–3. The first such historical reconstruction was published by M. Rampolla in 1897, a little more than a decade after a sarcophagus which allegedly contained the relics of the Maccabees was discovered in Rome; cf. Schatkin, 'The Maccabean Martyrs': 110–11. These historical reconstructions of the early history of the cult are based on various homilies on the Maccabees, menologies and chronicles dated to the fourth, fifth and sixth centuries and onward, which include references to the locations related to their veneration. Due to the number of sources, the analyses of specific texts are often selective (for some notable exceptions, see below n. 22).
18 For this view with references to previous research, see Raphaëlle Ziadé, *Les Martyrs Maccabées: de l'histoire juive au culte chrétien. Les homélies de Grégoire de Nazianze et de Jean Chrysostome* (Leiden: Brill, 2007): 164–74.
19 In addition to the homily *On Eleazar*, *Homily 15 In the Praise of the Maccabees* of Gregory of Nazianzus and the homilies of Augustine are most often mentioned in this connection; cf. e.g. Rouwhorst, 'The Emergence of the Cult': 93–5.
20 While the conflict situation may be commonly recognized, there remain various interpretations of what exactly it was about. To arrive at an answer, the various sources are usually combined to identify in them different aspects of what is more or less the same conflict. To give an example, Rouwhorst takes the homilies of Gregory of Nazianzus, John Chrysostom, and Augustine of Hippo as evidence for the popularity of the Maccabees as well as for the problematic character of their cult. Even a 'rapid presentation of the sermons' thus shows that 'many fourth-century Christians were aware of this difficulty'; Rouwhorst, 'The Emergence of the Cult': 93. For other examples, see references in n. 17.

takes the homily *On Eleazar* as bearing witness to some discernible but peculiar tensions in the actual, historical festival space of the Maccabees.[21]

The Homily as a Literary Composition

In most studies, the homily *On Eleazar* is taken as witness to the cult of, and the conflict about, the Maccabees. Thus the analyses of the text have mainly been focused on its references to the feast.[22] My examination of the festival space of the homily, as well as the interactions and tensions in it, is an attempt to evaluate the spatial references in light of the homily's overall purposes. I divide the literary composition into five sections,[23] all of which I consider relevant for the understanding of the rhetoric and logic of the homilist and his way of constructing and exploiting conflict(s) and related spaces. These sections consist of

1 an opening, in which there is no conflict (PG 63, 523 ll. 37–525 ll. 15);
2 a description of the feast, including both a conflict in the shared festival space and a demonstration of a correct approach to solving it (PG 63, 525 ll. 15–50);
3 a transitional[24] section from the feasting of the Maccabees to the reading of scriptures, in which the courage of the Maccabees is praised and placed in a biblical-historical continuum (PG 63, 525 ll. 50–526 ll. 30);
4 a demonstration of both a conflict connected with scriptural sources and their interpretation, in which the homilist debates with a Jew, and of a correct approach to win him over is presented (PG 63, 526 ll. 30–530 ll. 43; and Wenger, 'Restauration de l'Homélie', 601–3);
5 a conclusion, in which, again, there is no conflict (PG 63, 530 ll. 43–55 and Wenger, 'Restauration de l'Homélie': 603–4).

Each of these sections contributes to our understanding of the space(s) in which the homilist situates himself and each could be studied separately. Yet, it is not accidental that the homilist is involved in two distinct debates within one speech.

---

21 In his review of Ziadé's monograph, Rouwhorst writes: 'Whether this invention [i.e. the invention of the Christian cult of the Maccabees] had anything to do with tensions between Jews and Christians remains an intriguing question that unfortunately cannot be answered on the basis of John Chrysostom's writings or any other literary source'; Gerhard Rouwhorst, 'Raphaëlle Ziadé, Les Martyrs Maccabées: de l'histoire juive au culte chrétien. Les homélies de Grégoire de Nazianze et de Jean Chrysostome', *Reviews/VC* 66 (2012): 216.
22 Among the few exceptions, the following studies have significantly contributed to my analysis of the text as a literary piece: Rouwhorst, 'The Emergence of the Cult': 93, 95; Joslyn-Siemiatkoski, *Christian Memories of the Maccabean Martyrs*: 50; and Ziadé, *Les martyrs Maccabées*: 196ff.
23 Mayer structures the contents somewhat differently; see Mayer, *St John Chrysostom*: 120–1.
24 I consider this section transitional as it bridges the gap between two discussions. Retzleff uses the term 'transitional sentence' in a comparable way to mark a shift from a literal to a metaphorical meaning; cf. e.g. Retzleff, 'John Chrysostom's Sex Aquarium': 198. I, however, do not consider it reasonable to identify, as Retzleff does in her analysis, one of the two discussions as metaphorical and the other as literal in the analysis of the text.

My analysis begins with Sections 3 and 4, which comprise the bulk of the text typically taken as justification of the cult of the Maccabees. There (in Section 4), the homilist devotes himself to a discussion focussed on an exegesis of Jeremiah (vv. 38:31–34 in the Septuagint). This part, that is, more than a half of the whole homily, is without references to the Maccabees or their feast, either from the side of the homilist or of 'the Jew' he addresses. My analysis highlights the importance of the theological reasoning, which unfolds in Section 3 and 4, for the understanding of the problem in the festival space (Section 2; to be discussed below) as well as the whole literary composition.

'So Ask the Jew': Working Out a Debate

The theological aims of the homily start to unfold from where the homilist exhorts his audience: 'Come, then, let us demonstrate this today: that it is Christ who gave the law.'[25] The context of the feast of the Maccabees seems compelling and convenient for this demonstration. According to the homilist, the courage the Maccabees display is 'absolutely clear' to everyone; yet, because the Maccabees are known to have died for the law, he recognizes it as debatable whether they could have 'received their wounds for Christ's sake'.[26] Thus the Maccabees are associated with the more general debatable issue: is there a connection between Christ and those pre-Christian events which one may clearly deem miraculous and spectacular?

To prove to his audience that law and Christ are intimately connected, the homilist could consult 'Paul, the teacher of the world,' who, according to his evaluation, 'clearly' understood the matters of both the old and the new and knew 'it was Christ who performed . . . the miracles' of the past.[27] Yet, he determines to discuss the issue by opening a dialogue with a Jew, who, as he reckons, needs to be captured 'with his own weapons'. In this transition, the homilist distances himself from the discourse he has had so far with the audience and enters a new conflict area. He takes 'the prophets' – and no longer the story of the Maccabees – as common ground for the encounter which is to follow, showing himself as a confident debater and ready to step outside the explicitly Christian frames of discourse.[28]

---

25 *On Eleazar* 6 (Mayer (trans.), *St John Chrysostom*: 125); PG 63, 526 ll. 30–32.
26 *On Eleazar* 6 (Mayer (trans.), *St John Chrysostom*: 125); PG 63, 526 ll. 22–25. The homilist does not refer to any particular source but in both 2 and 4 Maccabees their motivation to die for the law is made clear; cf. e.g. 2 Macc 6:27–28; 7:2, 9, 23, 37; and 4 Macc 5:33–37; 6:26–27; 9:1–2.
27 *On Eleazar* 6 (Mayer (trans.), *St John Chrysostom*: 125); PG 63, 526 ll. 32–34, 42–43. I take his reference to Paul – 'the teacher of the world' who clearly understands both the old and new affairs (τά τε παλαιὰ καὶ τὰ νέα) – as a sign of transition (cf. n. 24 above), in which the old implies simultaneously both the old covenant and the law, and the new implies the new covenant and Christ.
28 *On Eleazar* 6 (Mayer (trans.), *St John Chrysostom*: 125); PG 63, 526 ll. 51–55. For a similar strategy of relying on the scriptures shared with the Jews, see Judith Lieu's analysis of Justin's approach; Judith Lieu, *Image and Reality: The Jews in the World of the Christians in the Second Century* (Edinburgh; T&T Clark, 1996): 124–5.

Yet, the homilist has not gone anywhere and it seems unlikely that there was a Jew amidst the gathering or that one had suddenly appeared there. Rather, the debate with the Jew is constructed for the argumentative purposes of the homily.[29] For even if the homilist addresses the Jew, he continues to have an interest in his observant audience and, in the course of the dialogue, the identity of the alleged Jew is mingled with that of his other opponents, the 'sick and weak' fellow Christians.[30]

Introducing the new subject (ὁ Ἰουδαῖος), the homilist turns his attention from the approaching feast to scriptures, namely, to the prophet Jeremiah.[31] This shift takes him away from the Maccabees, a topic to which he only returns at the very end of the homily.[32] By way of these associations, the homilist has constructed for himself from the festival space of the Maccabees an argumentative environment in which he can discuss scriptures with the Jew. The change of topic is notable for its impact on the construction of the spaces of the text. This new space is detached from the feast of the Maccabees and founded firmly on his chosen scriptural passages. Yet, the shift does not divert the homilist from the pressing question about the relationship between the past and the present.

'... Who Gave the New Covenant?': Reading the Present into the Past

In order to argue that Christ gave the law, the homilist exploits a biblical passage he knows from Jeremiah. He quotes: 'Behold, the days are coming, says the Lord, signifying the present time, and I shall make a new covenant with you, one unlike the covenant which I made with your fathers.'[33] Although the homilist takes these

---

29 Joslyn-Siemiatkoski has noted, in connection with this particular homily, that John Chrysostom uses a 'stereotyped' Jew, that is, 'a figure of Jews who possessed the truth of Christianity in their own Scriptures but were unwilling to embrace it', identifiable already in second century Christian polemic; Joslyn-Siemiatkoski, *Christian Memories*: 45–6. Such a Jew should be understood as a straw man who, as Maijastina Kahlos describes, is 'a caricatured or extreme version of the antagonist's arguments, simplifying and twisting the opposing views into a feeble construction that is easy to contest and ridicule. Those details that do not serve the refutation are left out and those issues that do serve one's own purposes are emphasized'; Maijastina Kahlos, *Debate and Dialogue: Christian and Pagan Cultures, c. 360–430*, Ashgate: Aldershot, 2007: 67. The method of argumentation is common in late antique rhetoric. See also Maxwell, *Christianization and Communication*: 4–5, n. 9, and Robert L. Wilken, *John Chrysostom and the Jews: Rhetoric and Reality in the Late 4th Century* (Berkeley: University of California Press, 1983): 107, 112–6.

30 See for example *On Eleazar* 7 (Mayer (trans.), *St John Chrysostom*: 126); PG 63, 527 ll. 15–17. In addition, the Jew gets to speak so few words in the alleged encounter that it is not even possible to reconstruct his reasoning.

31 The references to scriptures are specified throughout the homily as references to specific writers who have the authority to represent the homilist's scriptural sources; cf. e.g. *On Eleazar* 6–7 (Mayer (trans.), *St John Chrysostom*: 125); PG 63, 526 ll. 53–55, 59. Therefore, I use 'scriptures' in this chapter as a general term and write it without capitalization. Consequently, 'the scriptures', if used, imply nothing more than the text(s) the homilist discusses.

32 Even when he returns to the Maccabees, the link is hardly explicit; PG 63, 530 ll. 36ff.

33 He mentions Jeremiah by name; *On Eleazar* 7 (Mayer (trans.), *St John Chrysostom*: 125–6); PG 63, 526 ll. 57–59. The Greek text, Ἰδοὺ ἡμέραι ἔρχονται, λέγει Κύριος, τὸν παρόντα καιρὸν δηλῶν,

verses to serve as commonly accepted ground for the discussion in which the Jew is also involved,[34] he is soon to establish a line of argumentation in which it is presumed that everyone should acknowledge the new covenant as Christ-given.[35] The homilist does not invest in arguing for this premise; instead, he goes on with his final and thoroughly Christian claim, according to which Christ not only gave the new but also the old covenant. He identifies the Lord, whose words Jeremiah repeated, as Christ: 'in saying "I shall make a new covenant, one unlike the covenant that I have", he [Christ] showed that he himself made that [old] covenant too.'[36] This straightforward line of argumentation and the lack of more thorough reasoning or any credible counter-argument from the Jew, indicate that his partner in the dialogue is not what truly seems to challenge the homilist. The Jew is there not to demonstrate the hard labour of such debates but, rather, to point to the easiness of the solution.

The main concern of the homilist is the nature of the new covenant and, more precisely, not its contents, but its recipients. He continues with the words of the prophet: 'This is the covenant which I shall make with you, says the Lord. I shall place my laws in their mind and engrave them on their heart.'[37] According to his quotation, it is his audience, 'you' (ὑμῖν), whom the prophet addresses.[38] He has hinted at this reading earlier, having explained that the 'coming days' which Jeremiah prophesied were meant as a reference to the present ('Ἰδοὺ ἡμέραι ἔρχονται... τὸν παρόντα καιρὸν δηλῶν).[39] With such minor, but significant, changes in the words of the prophet, the homilist contextualizes the ancient promises in his contemporary time and (re)directs them to his audience.[40]

καὶ διαθήσομαι *ὑμῖν* διαθήκην καινήν, οὐ κατὰ τὴν διαθήκην ἣν διεθέμην τοῖς πατράσιν *ὑμῶν* (PG 63, 527 ll. 12–15), corresponds with Jeremiah 38:31–32 (text according to Ziegler's edition, 1957) but the two are not identical. The main differences are marked in italics (mine). For more, see the discussions below in n. 37 and n. 38.

34 Cf. above n. 28.
35 *On Eleazar* 7 (Mayer (trans.), *St John Chrysostom*: 126); PG 63, 527 ll. 15–17.
36 *On Eleazar* 7 (Mayer (trans.), *St John Chrysostom*: 126); PG 63, 527 ll. 18–20.
37 *On Eleazar* 8 (Mayer (trans.), *St John Chrysostom*: 127). Ὅτι αὕτη ἡ διαθήκη, ἣν διαθήσομαι *ὑμῖν*, λέγει Κύριος· διδοὺς νόμους μου εἰς διάνοιαν *αὐτῶν*, καὶ ἐπὶ καρδίας *αὐτῶν* ἐπιγράψω *αὐτούς*; PG 63, 528 ll. 5–8. Again, the italics (mine) indicate where the text digresses from the text of the Septuagint (Ziegler's edition, 1857).
38 All in all, if compared with the text (variants) of the Septuagint (Jer 38:31–34; cf. n. 33 and 37), the quote appears slightly but significantly modified: the people of Israel (v. 31) are replaced with a direct addressee (ὑμῖν) and 'their fathers' (v. 32) likewise with 'your fathers'; 'their mind and ... their heart' which follow (v. 33) are not replaced with the second person plural. As it is not the purpose of this paper to consider any further what scriptures the homilist may have known and used, or how accidentally or intentionally he may have memorized the passage in question, let it suffice to say that all the notable differences between the texts indicate that the version of the homilist suits his purposes better. For a discussion on the use of the quote, see Joslyn-Siemiatkoski, *Christian Memories*: 46; Ziadé, *Les martyrs Maccabées*: 171–4.
39 *On Eleazar* 7 (Mayer (trans.), *St John Chrysostom*: 126); PG 63, 527 ll. 12–13.
40 His practice resembles one of the many (early) Christian responses to the question of the relationship between the pre-Christian scriptures, or the 'Jewish past', and Christianity. In Christian discourse, the old and the new covenants, or 'testaments', are often used to denote the two. This

What seems significant in these new promises and their reception is the increased involvement of the mind (εἰς διάνοιαν αὐτῶν) and heart (ἐπὶ καρδίας αὐτῶν). The recipients of the new covenant can be recognized from their inner perception, as the laws are embodied in their spirituality. Thus, the distinguished features of the new covenant result in the recipients' capacity to 'learn the harmony of the heralds of both the new and the old [covenants]'.[41] This teaching – and this capacity – brings him back to Paul, who in his own time 'was doing battle with the Jews' and whom he has already declared to be the universal teacher.[42] The homilist seems content with this rather circular reasoning. He has demonstrated his capacity to deal with the old and new matters like Paul and argued clearly what he wanted the Jew to realize, which is 'that while the facts are on his side, the meaning is on ours.'[43]

'We Shall Correct the Weaker': Striving for a Meaning amidst the Feasting

The most notable references to the Maccabees and their feast are found in the part of the homily (Section 2) which precedes the exegesis discussed above (Section 4). Introducing the Maccabees, the homilist expresses his unreserved enthusiasm about them and describes vividly the effect they have on him: 'But what can I do? The chorus of the Maccabees stands before my eyes and, illuminating my mind with the splendour of their familiar wounds, summons our tongue towards their familiar beauty.'[44] Thereafter he apologizes for the 'odd timing' of his speech;

---

discourse was an essential part of Christian identity formation as it shaped the understanding of the scriptural intellectual background of Christianity. Yet these matters were not only abstract but were often also reflected in terms of more contemporary conflicts between the church and the synagogue or in debates over who represents the true Israel. In this latter sense, the discourse does not only have an intra-Christian function but also indicates actual – and complex – Jewish–Christian relations and rivalry. Marcel Simon's *Verus Israel. A Study of the Relations between Christians and Jews in the Roman Empire (135–425)* (New York: Oxford University Press, 1986), originally published in French in 1964, remains a classic study of the conflict. For some of the most influential early Christian authors and their dealings with scriptures, past Judaism and contemporary Jews, see also Lieu, *Image and Reality*: 35–9, 124–9, 136–40, 178–80, as well as her contribution on the early Christians' dealings with both Judaism and Jews; Judith Lieu, 'History and Theology in Christian Views of Judaism' in *Jews among Pagans and Christians*, Judith Lieu, John North and Tessa Rajak (eds) (London: Routledge, 1992): 81–2. The conflict over the Maccabees is often also discussed in a similar context; cf. e.g. Joslyn–Siemiatkoski, who reads their Christian reception in Late Antiquity not so much as an example of Jewish–Christian relations but, rather, of Christian appropriation – or, as he says, colonialization – of something that was originally Jewish for the sake of 'creating useable pasts in the process of creating a Christian imperial culture', Joslyn-Siemiatkoski, *Christian Memories*: 4.

41 *On Eleazar* 14 (Mayer (trans.), *St John Chrysostom*: 131); Wenger, 'Restauration de l'Homélie': 603 l. 70.
42 *On Eleazar* 14 (Mayer (trans.), *St John Chrysostom*: 132); PG 63, 529 ll. 49. Cf. above n. 27.
43 *On Eleazar* 6 (Mayer (trans.), *St John Chrysostom*: 125); PG 63, 526 ll. 55–56.
44 *On Eleazar* 4 (Mayer (trans.), *St John Chrysostom*: 123, slightly modified); PG 63, 525 ll. 15–19.

'although the day of their wrestling matches is tomorrow, we are . . . proclaiming the trophy in advance of the time of battle.'[45]

The homilist is well aware of the short temporal distance between the present occasion and the feast and returns to it so often that it appears almost like a *topos*.[46] Indeed, the allegedly untimely timing is not accidental but, rather, carefully crafted. First, it gives the speech a preparatory character. Secondly, it implies not only the homilist's anticipation but some kind of foreknowledge of the feast: tomorrow's winners can already be recognized today. Finally, with the help of the distance, the homilist may postpone the praises and set off to address a more pressing, contemporary issue.[47]

Having paved the way, the homilist then turns to the issue which keeps him from praising the Maccabees immediately. It unfolds as follows: '. . . many of the more naïve, due to a mental incapacity, are being swept along by the Church's enemies [and] do not hold the appropriate opinion of these saints, nor, in the same way, do they number them in the rest of the chorus of the martyrs.'[48] By this time, the audience is already familiar with the homilist's own opinion, his eagerness to praise the Maccabees and to recognize them as martyrs of Christ.[49] Introducing this second opinion about these martyrs, the homilist thus situates himself in a confrontational situation. The tensions of the opinions about the Maccabees set him off on a mission: '. . . today', he declares in reference to those who are of the wrong opinion, 'we shall correct the weaker among our brothers and sisters. . . . Come, then, let us correct their way of thinking.'[50]

According to the text, the feast is characterized by 'everyone's mutual enjoyment'.[51] It could be equated with wrestling matches, featuring crowns, trophies and combatants, and the homilist is fascinated by the spectacle.[52] The issue at hand is a deep strife which splits the festival crowds. The homilist sees the festival crowd as divided into two groups: those who feast 'in ignorance' and those who are aware of 'the festival's basis.'[53] The homilist is concerned about the strife and wants to fix it by way of correcting the ignorant ones. The proposed cure for their weakness is that they, too, should be made to 'grasp the combatants with a

---

45 *On Eleazar* 4 (Mayer (trans.), *St John Chrysostom*: 123); PG 63, 525 ll. 19–23.
46 The temporal transition is repeated three times (PG 63, 525 ll. 15–21, 31–34, 44–50); Mayer, 'Les homélies des s. Jean Chrysostome': 278–9 n. 44. Notably, all the three instances are found in the same section of the homily.
47 *On Eleazar* 4 (Mayer (trans.), *St John Chrysostom*: 123); PG 63, 525 ll. 31–34.
48 *On Eleazar* 4 (Mayer (trans.), *St John Chrysostom*: 123); PG 63, 525 ll. 34–38.
49 To affirm it, he later adds that 'I don't hesitate to count them (sc. the Maccabees) with the other martyrs, to the extent that I declare that they are even more brilliant'; *On Eleazar* 5 (Mayer (trans.), *St John Chrysostom*: 124); PG 63, 525 ll. 50–52.
50 *On Eleazar* 4 (Mayer (trans.), *St John Chrysostom*: 123); PG 63, 525 ll. 33–34, 41–42.
51 *On Eleazar* 5 (Mayer (trans.), *St John Chrysostom*: 124); PG 63, 525 ll. 44.
52 See for example PG 63, 525 ll. 13–14, 20–23. On the commonly used metaphors related to the stadium, see Leemans, 'General Introduction': 29.
53 *On Eleazar* 4 (Mayer (trans.), *St John Chrysostom*: 123); PG 63, 525 ll. 42–43.

pure mind (καθαρᾷ τῇ διανοίᾳ) and see them with clear eyes'.[54] He sees it as his task, and as the task of his audience, to prepare them to perceive the approaching communal and enjoyable feast as spiritual.[55] There is no question about whether the Maccabees were feasted or not; moreover, it is noteworthy that there seems to be nothing wrong with the feast. Rather, the issue boils down to how the spectacles are perceived: the conflict in the festival space has mostly to do with clear and correct perception.

The conflict in the festival space appears to be scriptural. After having rebuked the 'weaker' brothers and sisters, the homilist tells how their weakness can be recognized: they argue for their opinion about the Maccabees by 'saying that they did not shed their blood for Christ but for the law and the edicts that were in the law, in that they were killed over pig's flesh.'[56] In the view of the homilist, this hits right at the core of the issue: his opponents simply repeat what is known about the Maccabees factually, while they fail to see the true meaning of their suffering; it is as if they admired the wrestlers without acknowledging their strength and courage. The reason for the suffering of the Maccabees, as everyone knew, was their obedience to the law and everyone who knew them knew that 'they displayed considerable courage by competing in those times'. This – that is, what he considers factual – does not divide the festival crowds but, rather, places them on common ground. How they perceive what is factual, that is, what they are able to recognize in what they see, is what matters. The conflict in the festival space is a conflict over correct interpretation.

'While the Facts Are on His Side . . . ': What the Two Conflicts Have in Common

In the course of the homily, the homilist places himself in two separate conflict areas. In one of them, he debates with a Jew about the true meaning of the law and, more correctly, about the relationship between the past and the present, the old and new covenants. The confrontation features two opposing views on how to understand some scriptural passages and, not surprisingly, it is his own view which the homilist deems to make more sense: it is clearer, purer, and more insightful. As a result of the drama the Jew is stifled, having been taught, to quote the homilist, that 'while the facts are on his side, the meaning is on ours' (τὰ πράγματα παρ' αὐτῷ δὲ νοήματα παρ' ἡμῖν).[57]

The debate with the Jew is preceded by another confrontation in which the homilist also enters a conflict area, that is, the festival space of the Maccabees, to correct a controversial and incomplete opinion. The confrontation is crystallized in two distinct and seemingly opposite views about what the Maccabees really

---

54 On Eleazar 5 (Mayer (trans.), St John Chrysostom: 124); PG 63, 525 ll. 46–47.
55 On Eleazar 5 (Mayer (trans.), St John Chrysostom: 124); PG 63, 525 ll. 44–50.
56 On Eleazar 4 (Mayer (trans.), St John Chrysostom: 123); PG 63, 525 ll. 39–41.
57 On Eleazar 6 (Mayer (trans.), St John Chrysostom: 125); PG 63, 526 ll. 55–56.

died for. The 'weaker brothers and sisters' know the story of the Maccabees as a story of heroes who died for the sake of the law as they bravely refused to eat polluted meat.[58] The perceptive, preferable view is to recognize them, through their deeds, as martyrs. This is the meaning of the feast, as explained by the homilist. One should not be content with what is actually known about the Maccabees but recognize, 'with pure understanding and clear eyes',[59] what they (must) have anticipated with their exceptional courage: the coming of Christ.[60] As a result of this understanding, the Law and Christ are no longer opposites; Christ is recognized as the law-giver.[61]

These two confrontations make sense as independent cases; yet, it should be noted that they have much in common. For one, they are both carefully designed as binary opposites. Pedagogically, this makes it easy to learn right from wrong. With regard to the contents, both are concerned with the relevance of pre-Christ matters to Christians. Both constructions work according to the same principle: be they historical, scriptural, or both, the known facts need to be accompanied with the true meaning. This way of thinking characterizes the entire homily. What is more, it brings about a tension and a division between the people which is not shown in the opening or conclusion of the homily. Before introducing the issue(s), the homilist praises his audience for their 'enthusiasm and keen and precise attention' (cf. Section 1).[62] Having closed the case, he exhorts his audience: 'So then, so that we may enjoy this lovely sight, let us go off with considerable enthusiasm . . .'[63] No mention of ignorant participants or warning about their detrimental influence is included in the conclusion (Section 5).[64] It is as if the wrong perception has been diagnosed and overcome, as if mutual enjoyment has been restored and guaranteed, during the delivery of the homily.

Spectacles and Rivalry

Thus far, I have analysed the dispute over scriptures as well as the conflict-torn festival space of the homily *On Eleazar and the Seven Boys* in order to illuminate resemblances in the way in which the homilist describes and deals with the two

---

58 *On Eleazar* 4 (Mayer (trans.), *St John Chrysostom*: 123); PG 63, 525 ll. 39–41. No scriptural source is referred to in the homily *On Eleazar*. For references to these martyrs and pork/polluted meat in the Books of the Maccabees, see for example 2 Maccabees 6:18–20; 7:1–2; 4 Maccabees 5:1–3; 8:2–3; 10:1.
59 *On Eleazar* 5 (Mayer (trans.), *St John Chrysostom*: 124); PG 63, 525 ll. 44–50.
60 *On Eleazar* 5 (Mayer (trans.), *St John Chrysostom*: 124); PG 63, 526 ll. 19–21.
61 PG 63, 526 ll. 27–31; see also PG 63, 530 ll. 44–45.
62 *On Eleazar* 2 (Mayer (trans.), *St John Chrysostom*: 122–3); PG 63, 525 ll. 4–7.
63 *On Eleazar* 16 (Mayer (trans.), *St John Chrysostom*: 134); PG 63, 630 ll. 45–47; Wenger, 'Restauration de l'Homélie': 604 ll. 7–9.
64 There is one passing remark in the middle of the homily, in which the homilist cautions his audience about the 'ill-timed gatherings and mindless frivolity in these intervening days'; *On Eleazar* 8 (Mayer (trans.), *St John Chrysostom*: 127); PG 63, 527 ll. 59; 528 ll. 1–2. Even there, his criticism is not aimed at the feast itself but at what he considers to be the immoral aspects of feasting.

confrontations which characterize the homily. In what follows, through a comparison between the homily *On Eleazar* and two homilies *On the Maccabees* also ascribed to John Chrysostom, I shall suggest that, despite its title, the subjects of the homily *On Eleazar* are not the Maccabees. Finally, I shall attempt to outline what is the point at issue in the homily *On Eleazar* and contextualize the work in a theological environment known from John Chrysostom's writings.

The two homilies *On the Maccabees* are mutually connected and sequential. According to the information they provide, they were delivered during the days of the feast of the Maccabees and possibly even in a place devoted to their cult in proximity to the relics of the martyrs.[65] In them, just as in the homily *On Eleazar*, the dominant imagery applied to the descriptions of the feast is that of the games.[66] Now, in the homily *On Eleazar*, the feast is referred to as 'the day of the wrestling matches' and the crowns and trophies resemble the victories of the martyrs.[67] The design, represented by these images, gives the feast a positive and attractive character and the comparisons applied also provide positive correlations: the approaching feast is compared to other spectacles in order to point to their common beautiful and communal qualities, not to disparage one over the other. There is no sense of rivalry between the feast of the Maccabees and other feasts in the homily *On Eleazar*, but the non-Christian spectacles are reflected upon somewhat differently in the homilies *On the Maccabees*. There, the games serve to create a contrast of quality between the spectacles provided by the martyrs and those of the worldly sportsmen: '[I]n the outside world when the presidents of games set up contests they think it extremely showy when they escort into the arena and into the contests young and vigorous athletes, such that, prior to the display in the wrestling matches, they provide a source of wonder for the spectators from the prime condition of their physique; here it isn't like this, but entirely the opposite.'[68] The homilies suggest that to admire the martyrs is not rational by any logical worldly

---

65 There are three homilies *On the Maccabees* attributed to John Chrysostom; cf. PG 50, 617–628. According to the contemporary scholarly consensus, the third (PG 50, 627–628) is not authentic; cf. the appendix in Ziadé, *Les martyrs Maccabées*: 345–50. The first and the second were most probably composed in Antioch; Mayer, *St John Chrysostom*: 135–6, 147; Berger, 'The Cult of the Maccabees': 107.

66 In applying the imagery of the stadium to his speech, the homilist does nothing exceptional, nor is the practice of rhetoric in any way particular to the Maccabees. Quite the contrary, such comparisons had already been used in the earliest Christian martyr narratives and were frequently reproduced in homilies on the saints; a number of John Chrysostom's homilies attest to that; Wilken, *John Chrysostom and the Jews*: 110; cf. also n. 52 above. The stadium and its games were also public institutions present in Greek and Roman cultural, political and communal life, and were popular among the people, which is probably where the power of expression of the imagery lay; cf. Andrade, 'The Processions of John Chrysostom and the Contested Spaces of Constantinople': 165–6.

67 *On Eleazar* 3 (Mayer (trans.), *St John Chrysostom*: 123); PG 63, 525 ll. 20–21. Likewise, in the second homily *On the Maccabees*, the brothers are compared to the judges of the Olympic Games, as they sit crowned, 'not judging the wrestling matches, but urging on the victor'; *Hom. 2 On the Maccabees* 2 (Mayer (trans.), *St John Chrysostom*: 149); PG 50, 624 ll. 21–24.

68 *Hom. 1 On the Maccabees* 2 (Mayer (trans.), *St John Chrysostom*: 138); PG 50, 618 ll. 38–44.

standards; rather, their admiration reflects the paradoxical logic of strength in weakness, also known from Christian writings such the Epistles of Paul.[69]

The feast of the Maccabees is the implied calendric context of all the three homilies, but the homily *On Eleazar* stands out because of the homilist's defensive attitude toward their veneration.[70] Even if the homilist acknowledges that the feast was enjoyable to all, the alleged confrontation in the festival space indicates that the Maccabees were less popular than the rest of the martyrs, or that they were altogether unpopular among some people, whereas the homilist appreciated them even more than other martyrs.[71] In contrast, the two homilies *On the Maccabees* imply the undisputed popularity of these martyrs and their feast among the people.[72] Unlike the homily *On Eleazar*, these homilies do not to defend or justify the recognition of the Maccabees as martyrs.

These differences could be explained in many ways. In her analysis of John Chrysostom's homilies delivered in Antioch,[73] Jaclyn L. Maxwell sketches out the historical context of the preacher. She writes that 'the diversity of the population ... intensified the danger, from the preacher's point of view, of blurring the lines between Christian and non-Christian' and, as a result, 'the urban preacher was faced with the job of explaining to his fellow Christians why they were not allowed to attend horse races with the pagans or celebrate Passover with the Jews', that is, his duty was to provide 'basic guidelines'.[74] The characterization implies that the homilist was faced with actual social powers while preaching.[75]

The two homilies *On the Maccabees* read along Maxwell's lines: they show awareness of the attractive traditional feasts and attempts by the homilist to compete for the people's attention. The popularity of the martyrs also appears as

---

69 Cf. e.g. 2 Corinthians 12:9. Ziadé notes this as a typically 'Chrysostomian' emphasis; Ziadé, *Les martyrs Maccabées*: 347.
70 See the section of this chapter titled 'On Eleazar and the Seven Boys: the Text, its Provenance and Context' above.
71 *On Eleazar* 4–5 (Mayer (trans.), *St John Chrysostom*: 123–4); PG 63, 525 ll. 36–38, 50–52.
72 The first of the two homilies is explicitly focused on the mother, who is considered the best example of their power in weakness; *Homily 1 On the Maccabees* 5 (Mayer (trans.), *St John Chrysostom*: 139); PG 50, 619 ll. 50–54. In the second, the homilist needs almost to apologize for not continuing with the mother. He promises that 'certainly the mother will come into [the sermon] for us today too, even if we don't touch [on her*] here. For the progress of the sermon will attract her for sure and she won't be able to leave her children. ... But he [the youngest of the brothers] had a more august theater than his brothers – the eyes of the mother. Didn't I say to you that even without our trying their mother would certainly come into it too? Look, then; the sermon's progress has introduced her' (Mayer (trans.), *St John Chrysostom*: 148–9); PG 50, 624 ll. 43–48. (*Indicates my own insertion.)
73 For Maxwell, Antioch appears as a more suitable example of 'Christianization' than Constantinople; Maxwell, *Christianization and Communication*: 3. Yet both destinations were urban settings in which a preacher would encounter various forms of Christianity, as well as other religions. On Antioch and Constantinople, see also Mayer, *St John Chrysostom*: 20–9.
74 Maxwell, *Christianization and Communication*: 4.
75 For analyses of such encounters, see Andrade, 'The Processions of John Chrysostom', and Shepardson, 'Controlling Contested Places'.

something which was – at least partly – beyond the homilist's control. The homily *On Eleazar* does not seem to stem from a similar setting. In it, one place is not contrasted with another one. Instead, two different approaches to the same feast are constructed, and the homilist urges his audience to perceive in a spiritual way what is factually known to all.[76] If the homilist provides some instructions, in the case of the homily *On Eleazar* they are on questions related to perception and interpretation, and accordingly value judgments.[77]

'So That We May See . . . ': Instructions on the Imitation of Virtue

In the homilies *On the Maccabees*, the martyrs are examples which the audience is supposed to imitate. In the first, the orator exhorts his audience to be mindful of the examples provided, '. . . so that by imitating the virtue of these saints here, we may be able to share their crowns too there, with us displaying as much endurance in the irrational passions . . . '[78] The mother's example of endurance is characterized as the 'contests and wrestling matches', and her tortures are identified with contemporary passions the audience needs to struggle with.[79] In the second, the homilist encourages everyone to 'pray together . . . that through invoking the same bold speech as her we can be considered worthy of the same race as her . . . We'll be able [to achieve this], . . . by conquering the passions in us . . . If God who loves humankind decides to affect the same contest for us, we shall come to the wrestling matches prepared and shall attain the heavenly blessings.'[80] In these cases, imitation of either acts or words is taken as a way to identify with the martyrs and to lead to a better life. Despite the differences, the two homilies share the same basic idea, that is, that the martyrs are the subjects to focus on and to learn from. The homilist points toward their exemplarity.

Although the homilist shows great admiration for the Maccabees and their courage, it is not easy to define the example the martyrs provide in the homily *On Eleazar*. In fact, the homilist arrives at their examples only in his concluding remarks where he notes that Eleazar, the old mother, and the chorus of the young

---

76 *On Eleazar* 5 (Mayer (trans.), *St John Chrysostom*: 124); PG 63, 525 ll. 48–50.
77 As the feasts were communal in nature, the festival spaces were often civic spaces and as such contested; see for example the contribution of Maijastina Kahlos in this volume. Even if this may often be the case, not all the polemic homilies necessarily address actual historical communal conflicts in those spaces. Rather, each source needs to be studied carefully in order to understand the nature of the conflict. This is the more important in cases in which homilies are an essential, if not sole witness to the festival practices or conflicts surrounding feasts; see also Retzleff's argument, presented above in n. 2.
78 *Hom. 1 On the Maccabees* 11 (Mayer (trans.), *St John Chrysostom*: 145); PG 50, 622 ll. 56–58.
79 *Hom. 1 On the Maccabees* 11 (Mayer (trans.), *St John Chrysostom*: 145); PG 50, 622 ll. 52–53, 60–63.
80 *Hom. 2 On the Maccabees* 6 (Mayer (trans.), *St John Chrysostom*: 153); PG 50, ll. 30–31, 35–36, 41–46. Mayer remarks that this concluding paragraph could also be a later addition; cf. Mayer, *St John Chrysostom*: 152–3 n. 5.

men are suitable examples to each gender and all age groups (ἑκατέρα τῇ φύσει καὶ ἡλικίᾳ πάσῃ ὑποδείγματα). The relation between the audience and the examples is defined through vision (ἔστιν ἰδεῖν): these wrestlers – that is, the winners, the ones crowned and heralded – are to be seen and be amazed at (θεάσωνται; ἴδωσι; ἐκπλαγῶσι).[81] The homilist is eager to direct the attention of his audience to the deeper and truer understanding of the martyrdom of the Maccabees. This, however, is not achieved by turning away from the visible heroic acts, but rather, a purer mental impression is created through careful contemplation of the physical. The emphasis on the act of contemplation invites the audience to relate to the homilist, to admire the martyrs and to grasp the true meaning of their suffering just like he does. Thus, although the Maccabees were surely also exemplary in his mind, the primary example to be imitated in the homily *On Eleazar* is, in fact, the homilist.

With regard to the Maccabees, one learns from the homily *On Eleazar* that they were exceptionally courageous in their own time. One cannot miss the homilist's emphasis that they died just before the coming of Christ.[82] The alleged and important claim that they died on account of the law is repeated twice, but both times by somebody else; it does not come from the homilist's mouth.[83] The courage of the martyrs could serve as an example; yet, the homilist exhorts admiration, rather than imitation, of their virtue. All the specifics, according to which the agency of the martyrs is construed, give grounds for the theological reasoning constitutive of the homily.

When the homilist is understood to be the primary example of the homily and the one to be imitated, the whole homily – and not just the sections about the martyrs – can be read as promoting that example. The homilist shows how to act properly in the festival space: how to be excited about the Maccabees and how to recognize them as martyrs equal to Christian martyrs. Likewise, he exemplifies how one can identify the law-giver in the given laws/promises and how, in fact, to view scriptures in the correct light. In the concluding exhortations, he puts his soul into everyone who attends the approaching festival, showing how great the benefit of such a beautiful sight is when one perceives it correctly. The main purpose of the martyrs is to provide historical examples which suit the theological worldview of the homilist. He recognizes the historical – over the ethical – meaning of their example as a means by which to identify Christ with the law and to connect the present with the past. The homilist's ability to grasp the meaning of these spectacles, as well as of the scriptures, is sovereign; it is his example the audience should learn from and imitate.

---

81 *On Eleazar* 16 (Mayer (trans.), *St John Chrysostom*: 133–4); Wenger, 'Restauration de l'Homélie': 603–4 ll. 1–6.
82 *On Eleazar* 5–6 (Mayer (trans.), *St John Chrysostom*: 124–5); PG 63, 525 ll. 57–526 ll. 1; 526 ll. 9 – 11, 22–24.
83 *On Eleazar* 4, 6 (Mayer (trans.), *St John Chrysostom*: 123, 125); PG 63, 525 ll. 39–41; 526 ll. 25–27.

A Harmonious Space and the Making of a Thoroughly Christian World

The homily *On Eleazar* does not allow for easy historical contextualization. The debate between the homilist and the Jew over the contemporary identification of the recipients of God's promises could be found in many other Christian texts, and similar arguments about the relationship between the law and Christ, or the old and the new covenants, were in circulation.[84] My analysis of the homily *On Eleazar* encourages us to look at the festival space in which the homilist operates as a theologically constructed space, much in the same way as one should look at the space in which the homilist reads scriptures with the Jew. As a result, and perhaps as a response to previous research, my analysis suggests that the homily *On Eleazar* is a rather erudite treatise on and about the meaning of (the feast of) the Maccabees, which elaborates on the correct recognition of the Maccabees in order to reconcile contemporary Christianity with its pre-Christian past and argue for the intellectual superiority of the Christian (that is, the homilist's) worldview.

The two conflict areas in which the homilist places himself appear with some notable similarities which have to do with reasoning. The spaces of the homily are characterized by the agency of the mind (ἡ διάνοια).[85] In his reasoning, the homilist relies on this alleged intellectual capacity, attributing to it an active role in the perception of the spectacles and other – and less visual – intellectual matters. The homilist does not provide an explicit definition of this agency; however, the scriptural sources he refers to explain its authority. In his exegesis of Jeremiah (vv. 38:31–34), the homilist connects the agency of the mind with God as well as with Christ: the new covenant, identified as the covenant of Christ, implies that Christ has carved the laws on the mind of the people (εἰς διάνοιαν αὐτῶν).[86] This

---

[84] Cf. above n. 28. Likewise, the debate about the recognition of the Maccabees emerges from various Christian texts in different historical contexts; cf. above n. 17, 18, 19 and 20. A homily on the Maccabees ascribed to Augustine is of particular interest, as it discusses Christ and law and is likewise partly composed as a dialogue with 'a Jew', who is involved in order to be intellectually defeated by the homilist (cf. *Sermo CCC: In solemnitate martyrum Machabaeorum*; PL 38, 1376–1380). Despite the many elements that text has in common with the homily *On Eleazar*, its general tone differs. In Augustine's homily, the Christian (homilist) treats the Jew from a distance, as a representative of a particular collective. The Jew has a role to fulfil in the history of revelation. In the homily *On Eleazar*, the Jew – even if he is a rhetorical construct – is comparable to ignorant Christians. They all have in common a failure to understand the scriptures properly, that is, in agreement with the homilist. I discuss these sources and the different strategies for dealing with the Maccabees in my forthcoming dissertation. In this connection, Retzleff's article is again noteworthy, as she observes that the metaphorical constructs, which she identifies in the homily she analyzes, can be identified in various other sources. She suggests that they may have circulated among the Christian writers of the time, possibly even in manuals or sourcebooks; cf. Retzleff, 'John Chrysostom's Sex Aquarium': 200, 202–5.

[85] With respect to the intelligence of the implied audience, see PG 63, 525 ll. 5–6, 10. The right mind-set is likewise emphasized in the instructions to correct the weaker ones, see PG 63, 525 ll. 34–35, 41–4. It is also found in the words of Jeremiah, quoted in PG 63, 528 ll. 21–22, 38, and emphasized in the explanation of their meaning, PG 63, 528 ll. 39–42.

[86] *On Eleazar* 9 (Mayer (trans.), *St John Chrysostom*: 127); PG 63, 528 ll. 6–7.

intellectual capacity does not only affect people internally, so that they perceive things in a certain way, but it also has an impact on the reality around them, because clear and pure perception is accompanied by correct behaviour.

Characterizing the nature of the covenant(s), the homilist tries to reconcile his contemporary Christian time with biblical times. He wants to appreciate both the old and the new matters, and does so by establishing a harmonious continuum between the past and the present: he claims the new to be different from and better than, but not opposed to, the old covenant. Rather, the new completes the old and, when correctly perceived, both should be embraced.[87] The Maccabees provided him with a useful reference because they died for the sake of the law and, yet, their past courage and vision connects seamlessly with the present glory of the martyrs. The dialogue with 'the Jew' is also useful: the incomplete understanding of scriptures, allegedly typical of the Jews, highlights the homilist's comprehensive and harmonious capacity to interpret them.

According to Maxwell, John Chrysostom is a preacher devoted to an overarching vision of a united – Christian – world, in which all the pieces fall into place in harmony. Consequently, he

> 'envisioned a "*homo Christianus*", whose disposition (*habitus*) would be the result of a Christian environment of mutually reinforcing beliefs and practice. [. . . his] goal was not social change (or control) as an end in itself, but to encourage a lifestyle conductive to collective salvation, which would include his own. With knowledge of sins and virtues being automatic, that is, embedded in their *habitus*, people would reflexively withdraw from sin and temptation.'[88]

Maxwell's illuminating characterization defines what she perceives to be 'Christianization', in the context of John Chrysostom's homilies. The instructions to 'Christianize' should not be seen merely as a politics of practices but – and perhaps fundamentally – as an attempt to transform the whole mentality of the people. Consequently, we may imagine the practices related to 'Christianization' less as efforts to convert (Jewish/pagan) feasts into Christian and more as attempts to claim feasting as properly Christian, when correctly perceived and acted out.[89]

---

87 *On Eleazar* 9 (Mayer (trans.), *St John Chrysostom*: 127–8); PG 63, 528 ll. 13–20; *On Eleazar* 14 (Mayer (trans.), *St John Chrysostom*: 131); Wenger, 'Restauration de l'Homélie': 603 ll. 69–70.
88 Maxwell, *Christianization and Communication*: 147. The distinction between habits and *habitus*, which she takes from the sociologist Pierre Bourdieu, is significant for her argument: while the Christian preachers may have tried to teach their audience to reject 'bad habits' and to offer Christian habits instead, such 'specific customs and everyday actions' should be understood in connection with habitus, that is 'the core of ideas that underlies the choices and attitudes'; Maxwell 2006: 147.
89 Discussing philology and Christianization, Christian Glinka notes that the church fathers connected with the cultures preceding them by both theological and historical means. The theological principle was that God's power and divine nature could be seen through the creation (cf. e.g. Rom 1:20–21), and the historical principle aimed at showing how all the ancient – and contemporary – wisdom could in fact be found already in old scriptures; Christian Glinka, *Chrêsis*:

According to the composer of the homily *On Eleazar*, it follows from the 'substantial grace' that instructions are no longer needed (cf. Jer. 38:34, Ziegler's ed.); '... the successful outcome of the new covenant [... is] the easy digestibility of the knowledge and the swiftness of the proclamation'.[90] To conclude his exegesis, the homilist connects the prophetic vision of a community which knows God 'from the smallest to the greatest' with Paul, the one apostle who could proclaim the good news in such a short time to such a wide space and audience.[91] By the time the homilist preaches, then, the good news was (seemingly) within everyone's reach and the universal truth easy for the mind to grasp; it was, the homilist quotes Paul, 'proclaimed in all of the creation'.[92] Nevertheless, when observing the festival space, the homilist distinguishes between right and wrong perceptions which give the agency of the mind a missionary character: one who has a clear and pure mind could, and in fact should, go off to persuade the minds of others, that is, to carry on the mission and to draw the entire world into the net of the Gospel.[93] The Jew, but presumably not only the Jew, is addressed 'so that he might learn that while the facts are on his side the meaning is on ours'.[94]

The homily *On Eleazar* participates in the making of a thoroughly Christian world. The claim that the feast of the Maccabees is already fundamentally Christian, even if it may not appear as such, is constitutive of the reality constructed throughout the homily *On Eleazar*. The wrestlers embody triumphs and glory and, embracing them, one should be led to contemplate the triumph and glory of Christ. The same is true about the promises of scriptures which unfold as Christ-given when they are read with the right insight. Seeing things clearly and purely, one is able not only to join the mutual unity and solidarity of all people, but also to recognize the connection between the present and the past. Thus, viewing the spectacular earthly sights, one also reflects on what spiritual good is and

---

Die Methode der Kirchenväter im Umgang mit der antiken Kultur. (I) Der Begriff des 'rechten Gebrauchs' (Basel/Stuttgart: Schwabe & Co Ag, 1984): 12–16. Also Joslyn-Siemiatkoski considers 'Christianization' in terms of transformation of the cultural discourses of the late Roman Empire. To him it is evident in the capacity of the Christian authors to 'articulate a totalizing identity for their own Christian communities while also ideologically colonizing Jewish narratives', of which the Maccabees provide an example; Joslyn-Siemiatkoski, *Christian Memories*: 79. Cf. also Shephardson, who notes 'spatial rhetoric' as a powerful means by which Christians, such as John Chrysostom, 'shaped their world'; Shephardson, 'Controlling Contested Places': 486. On the other hand, Jason Moralee approaches 'Christianization' in much more concrete terms, focusing on material culture; Jason Moralee, 'The stones of St. Theodore: Disfiguring the Pagan Past in Christian Gerasa', *JECS* 14:2 (2006): 192.

90 *On Eleazar* 11 (Mayer (trans.), *St John Chrysostom*: 129); Wenger, 'Restauration de l'Homélie': 602 ll. 19–21.
91 *On Eleazar* 15 (Mayer (trans.), *St John Chrysostom*: 133); PG 63, 530 ll. 36–43.
92 *On Eleazar* 15 (Mayer (trans.), *St John Chrysostom*: 133); PG 63, 530 ll. 39–40.
93 *On Eleazar* 15 (Mayer (trans.), *St John Chrysostom*: 133); PG 63, 530 ll. 38–39. Also Andrade writes about John Chrysostom's idea of 'harmony of mind' in connection with mutual inspiration and piety; Andrade, 'The Processions of John Chrysostom': 180–1. Cf. Ch. 6 above.
94 *On Eleazar* 6 (Mayer (trans.), *St John Chrysostom*: 125); PG 63, 526 ll. 55–56.

becomes part of the harmony of souls together with the angels.[95] These aspects – the superior intellectual capacity of the (true, contemporary) Christians, their harmonious relationship with the past and the present, and the universal agreeability and spreadability of their worldview – are constitutive of the argumentation and worldview of the homilist. The homily is not concerned with the reform of a feast, as much as it is concerned with transformation of the human mind to better suit a thoroughly Christian world. A universalizing and harmonizing tendency can best explain the reasoning of the whole homily, including its conflict-solving method.

Conquering the Space by Perception: '. . . the Meaning Is Ours'

According to the homilist, the spectacles of the feast of the Maccabees can be perceived with or without correct understanding. In a similar way, the promises of scripture can be interpreted correctly (his way) or incorrectly (the way of the Jew). Thus, the festival space, as it is constructed in the homily, appears as a space which can be invested with different meanings. It is possible, of course, that the homilist would have wanted to interfere in the festival space more concretely but was simply short of power to do so. What we have is his emphasis on perception and the inner aspects which is why he shows little, if any, interest in changing anything about the feast or the festival space. Instead, he was most motivated to reform and educate the minds of the people who took part in the feasting and, in this endeavour, he set himself as an example of how to view spectacles. Much in the same way, he also took himself as an example of how to understand scriptures.

In my analysis, I have demonstrated that it is enlightening to observe the festival space in the homily *On Eleazar and the Seven Boys* as a theological space. I have argued that it is constructed according to the ideological objectives of the homilist. Now, even if the conflict identified in that space should primarily reflect theological concerns, one cannot exclude the option that the homilist was also inspired by an actual, spatial conflict. However, to prove it wrong or right should require a more solid historical contextualization of the source than has so far been possible. My conclusion highlights that the homily reflects some more general theological tensions and reasoning of its time, concerning which the feast of the Maccabees could serve as a meaningful point of discussion. This argument goes beyond the distinction between what can be identified as historical or ideological in the text.

The homily *On Eleazar* shows that the martyrdom of the Maccabees was not only considered historically pre-Christian but, more importantly, it connected with Christ's coming in ways which made sense to its composer. As he could recognize Christian martyrdom in the acts performed by the Maccabees, he used these figures to bridge the gap between pre- and post-Christ events. John Chrysostom, or any other Christian, who wished to underline the universal nature of faith, as well as continuity from pre-Christian to his Christian times, should indeed have found the 'untimely' martyrdoms of the Maccabees most topical.

---

95 *On Eleazar* 14 (Mayer (trans.), *St John Chrysostom*: 131); Wenger, 'Restauration de l'Homélie': 603 ll. 69–70.

Part III
Archaeological Perspectives

8 Galilean Jews and Christians in Context

Spaces Shared and Contested in the Eastern Galilee in Late Antiquity

Raimo Hakola

Introduction

In this chapter, I discuss Jewish and Christian groups in eastern rural Galilee particularly in relation to synagogues that recent archaeological excavations have firmly dated to Late Antiquity. In earlier scholarship, many previously discovered Galilean synagogues were dated to the second and third centuries CE, but there is now mounting archaeological evidence that demonstrates how synagogues were built, renovated and in use in the region from the late fourth to the seventh centuries. Not only are the synagogues in, for example, Capernaum and Chorazin now generally dated to the fifth century or even later, but the evidence for the newly found synagogues at Horvat Kur and Huqoq clearly demonstrates that rural Jewish communities continued to establish these public buildings well into the period when the influence of Christianity became more and more visible in the region.

In the area discussed in this chapter, just north of the plain of Ginosar, the synagogues of Chorazin, Horvat Kur and Huqoq are situated quite close to Tabgha, where a Christian pilgrim church was established during the fifth century, and Capernaum, where the Byzantine church and the synagogue are located next to each other. Günter Stemberger has emphasized the relevance of this area for the study of Jewish–Christian relations in Late Antiquity because 'Jews and Christians lived side by side in a plainly Jewish territory'.[1] The co-existence of these different communities in a rather small area raises questions concerning their mutual relationships; however, it is difficult to reconstruct these relations in any more detail because direct literary and archaeological evidence that could shed light on them is limited at best. In circumstances like this, it is evident that our imaginative reconstructions of the situation in Galilee are shaped to a great extent by models and patterns put forward on the basis of the evidence connected to Jewish–Christian relations elsewhere in the ancient world.

---

1 Günter Stemberger, 'Christians and Jews in Byzantine Palestine', in *Christians and Christianity in the Holy Land: From the Origins to the Latin Kingdoms*, Ora Limor and Guy G. Stroumsa (eds) (Cultural encounters in Late Antiquity and the Middle Ages 5; Turnhout, Belgium: Brepols, 2006): 300.

I argue here that recent changes in how the relations between Jews and Christians in Late Antiquity are understood should become more fully incorporated into Galilean studies. For this reason, the first part of the chapter sets up a broader context for evaluating the relations between Jewish and Christian communities in Galilee. While many older historical reviews have replicated polemical accounts found in many Christian and Jewish literary sources, several scholars have concluded that the portraits advocating separation and antagonism need to be balanced by evidence – literary and archaeological – demonstrating parallel developments and social and cultural interaction between different communities. I suggest that Galilean synagogues and pilgrim churches may be taken as spaces that gave a sense of distinct and secure identity for local Jewish and Christian communities but, at the same time, the shared Galilean rural landscape enabled various interactions between the members of these communities.

Jews and Christians in Context

Blurred Boundaries

Averil Cameron has remarked that 'the mutual relations between Christians and Jews in Late Antiquity ... cannot be taken out of the wider context of the development of early Christianity'.[2] In earlier scholarship, the development of Christianity in the first centuries CE has often been seen in light of the so-called 'parting of the ways' model.[3] However, this model has increasingly been criticized in recent scholarship.[4] One of the main criticisms against the model has been that it does not match the evidence showing an intense intellectual and social interaction, continuing well into Late Antiquity, between various Jewish and Christian communities. There is evidence beginning from some New Testament writings for the so-called 'Gentile Christian Judaizing', a term that, using Michele

---

2 Averil Cameron, 'Jews and Heretics – A Category Error?', in *The Ways that Never Parted: Jews and Christians in Late Antiquity and the Early Middle Ages*, Adam H. Becker and Annette Yoshiko Reed (eds) (Minneapolis: Fortress Press, 2007): 345.

3 For the 'parting of the ways' -model and its ideological underpinnings, see Raimo Hakola, 'Erik H. Erikson's Identity Theory and the Formation of Early Christianity', *JBV* 30 (2009): 5–15. The following events have been presented either as one singular event or as successive moments that brought about separation between Christianity and Judaism: the ministry of Jesus, the division between Hebrews and Hellenists in the early church in Jerusalem, the mission of Paul to the Gentiles, the first Jewish War (CE 66–74), the tensions between early Christians and synagogues reflected in the Gospels of Matthew and John, the Bar Kokhba revolt (CE 132–135). See Edwin K. Broadhead, *Jewish Ways of Following Jesus: Redrawing the Religious Map of Antiquity* (WUNT 266; Tübingen: Mohr Siebeck, 2010): 354.

4 For critical reviews of the 'parting of the ways' -model , see Judith M. Lieu, *Neither Jew Nor Christian: Constructing Early Christianity* (London and New York: T & T Clark, 2002): 11–29; Annette Y. Reed and Adam H. Becker, 'Introduction: Traditional Models and New Directions', in Becker and Reed, *The Ways That Never Parted*: 1–33; Andrew S. Jacobs, 'Jews and Christians', in *The Oxford Handbook of Early Christian Studies*, Susan Ashbrook Harvey and David G. Hunter (eds) (Oxford: Oxford University Press, 2008): 169–85; Broadhead, *Jewish Ways*: 354–74.

Murray's definition, refers to Christians who were Gentiles and 'combined a commitment to Christianity with adherence in varying degrees to Jewish practices without viewing such behavior as contradictory.' As Murray continues, from the perspective of certain Christian leaders these community members dangerously blurred boundaries between Christian and Jewish communities, which aroused their fierce denunciation in some sources.[5]

The same kind of boundary crossing is well attested in various Christian literary sources stemming from the second to early fifth centuries.[6] As Petri Luomanen has remarked, 'the intensity of admonitions' directed against those who attended both Jewish and Christian community gatherings shows that this was an acute problem and a serious challenge for those Christian writers who wanted to keep the boundaries of their communities intact.[7] The discontent caused by blurred boundaries between Jewish and Christian communities is also expressed in the decisions of many ecclesiastical councils that tried to prohibit the interaction of Christians – even clergy – with their neighbouring Jewish communities.[8] The same concern is visible in an imperial edict issued in 383 dealing with Christians who had taken part in pagan, Jewish and Manichean cults.[9] While the participation of some Christians in Jewish gatherings and rituals is much more common in the surviving records, limited evidence can also

---

5 Michele Murray, *Playing a Jewish Game: Gentile Christian Judaizing in the First and Second Century* CE (SCJ 13; Waterloo, Ont.: Wilfrid Laurier University Press, 2004): 2. Murray finds evidence for this phenomenon, for example, in Paul's Epistle to the Galatians, the Epistles of Ignatius, *Epistle of Barnabas*, The *Didache*, Pseudo-Clementine Literature and Revelation. I have recently argued that the Fourth Evangelist uses various dualistic images in order to create a secure social identity in a diverse social environment where some of those who believed in Jesus still kept ties with local Jewish synagogue communities. See Raimo Hakola, *Reconsidering Johannine Christianity: A Social Identity Approach* (New York and London: Routledge, 2015): 118–31 and *passim*.
6 For the evidence, see for example Reuven Kimelman, 'Identifying Jews and Christians in Roman-Syria Palestine', in *Galilee through the Centuries: Confluence of Cultures*, Eric M. Meyers (ed.) (Winona Lake, IN: Eisenbraums. 1999): 301–33. For Christians following Jewish practices and visiting synagogues, see for example Justin the Martyr, *Dial.*46.1–2; 47; Irenaeus *Haer.* 1.26.29; Origen *Cels.* 2.1; 5.61; *Comm. ser. Matt* 79; *Hom. Lev.* 5.8; *Hom. Jer.* 12.13; *Sel. Exod.* 12.46; *Didascalia Apostolorum* 26; Johannes Chrysostom *Adv. Jud.* 1.3.3–4 and *passim*.
7 Petri Luomanen, *Recovering Jewish–Christian Sects and Gospels* (VCSup 110; Brill: Leiden, 2012): 30. In a similar way, such Christian writers as Augustine of Hippo and Petrus Chrysologus tried to prevent the participation of their audiences in feasts and gatherings that they regarded as pagan. See Maijastina Kahlos' chapter in this volume.
8 Kimelman, 'Identifying': 317. For example, the council of Laodicea (363–364) prohibited resting on the Sabbath (Canon 29) and the participation in Jewish feasts and ceremonies (Canons 37 and 38). Other church orders forbade the clergy from participating in Jewish festivals or entering synagogues to pray or to feast (*Apostolic Constitutions* 8.47, 62, 65, 70, and 71).
9 *CTh* 16.7.3. For the text, its translation and interpretation see Amnon Linder, *The Jews in Roman Imperial Legislation* (Detroit and Jerusalem: Wayne State University Press and The Israel Academy of Sciences and Humanities, 1988): 168–73. It is a debated question how imperial edicts were enforced and how widely they were followed. The need to reissue the same prohibitions time and again already indicates the limited effectiveness of these edicts. I return to this question later when I discuss the edicts prohibiting the building of new synagogues.

be found of Jews visiting Christian churches and services.[10] In the light of this evidence, Paula Fredriksen has aptly concluded that 'the threats, complaints, and laments' by various Christian writers, together with decisions in church canons and imperial legislation, 'suggest that these efforts at separation met with frustration much more routinely than with success'.[11]

As is the case of Christian sources, scholars have reconsidered those rare rabbinic passages that seem to encourage the strict separation between Jews and Christians.[12] The most famous and often cited example is the story of rabbi Eliezer ben Hyrcanus' arrest and later release: rabbi Eliezer was suspected of heresy, which in this case most probably meant contacts with some sort of Christians. The meeting between Eliezer and a heretic is placed in a Galilean context in late first or early second century Sepphoris but, as often is the case with rabbinic stories, the historical context and the details of the story remain elusive.[13] Particularly in previous scholarship of early Christianity, passages like this were taken quite unproblematically as evidence of how rabbinic Jews were able to regulate interactions between emergent Christian communities and other Jews.[14] However, the power and influence of the rabbinic movement during the first centuries CE have been significantly reconsidered in recent rabbinic scholarship (cf. below) and, accordingly, passages advocating separation are no longer taken as direct

---

10 Cf. Paula Fredriksen, *Augustine and the Jews: A Christian Defence of Jews and Judaism* (New York: Doubleday, 2008): 399 n. 24. Fredriksen refers to the decision of the Fourth Council in Carthage in 436 (canon 84) according to which a bishop may not prohibit a pagan, a heretic or a Jew from entering into the church and hearing the word of God; however, these persons should leave together with the catechumens before the Eucharist is celebrated.

11 Fredriksen, *Augustine*, 99. Thus also Lieu, *Neither Jew Nor Christian*: 206: 'The Christian polemic against the Jews seeks to construct an identity of separation and alienation, to build impermeable boundaries, but ... there is much, even within the pages of polemic, which denies that, witnessing to intersecting lives, a shared identity of monotheistic worship, ethical code and textual interpretation'.

12 As Kimelman ('Identifying': 302) remarks, Christians sources are 'so full of references to Jews and Judaism that the phrase *obsessed with* may be in order' while 'the data on Christianity in rabbinic literature is comparably sparse' (italics original). For a discussion of rabbinic passages possibly referring to Christians, see Günter Stemberger, 'Rabbinic Reactions to the Christianization of Roman Palestine: A Survey of Recent Research', in *Encounters of the Children of Abraham from Ancient to Modern Times*, Antti Laato and Pekka Lindqvist (eds) (Studies on the Children of Abraham 1: Leiden: Brill, 2010): 141–63. In addition, many scholars have recently argued that Christian theological concepts have been assumed and addressed to in a number of rabbinic writings. Cf. Daniel Boyarin, *Border Lines: The Partition of Judaeo-Christianity* (Philadelphia: The University of Pennsylvania Press, 2004); Peter Schäfer, *The Jewish Jesus: How Judaism and Christianity Shaped Each Other* (Princeton: Princeton University Press, 2012).

13 For the earliest version of the story, see *t. Ḥul.* 2:24; other versions appear in *b. 'Abod. Zar.* 16b–17a and *Qoh. Rab.* 1:24. See Daniel Boyarin, *Dying for God: Martyrdom and the Making of Christianity and Judaism* (Stanford, CA; Stanford University Press, 1999): 26–41; Pekka Lindqvist, 'Less Antagonistic Nuances in the Early Jewish Attitude towards Christianity', in *Encounters of the Children of Abraham*, Antti Laato and Pekka Lindqvist (eds): 175–7.

14 For references, see Raimo Hakola, *Identity Matters: John, the Jews and Jewishness* (NovTSup118; Brill: Leiden, 2005): 43–4.

reflections of historical reality but as attempts to clarify distinct identities. Daniel Boyarin has suggested that the Eliezer story shows how the rabbis are

> both recognizing and denying at one and the same time that Christians are us, marking out the virtual identity between themselves and the Christians in their world at the same time that they are very actively seeking to establish difference.[15]

This story and other rabbinic passages (e.g. *t. Ḥul.* 2:20–21) that try to limit interaction among Jews actually testify that rabbis could not avoid constant contacts with those they regarded as heretics, *minim*.[16] It thus seems that although many Christian theologians and rabbis tried to shape particular ideological beliefs and behavioural patterns in their respective audiences, the social reality was much more complicated and unpredictable than these attempts to construct clearly defined identities would imply.

There is evidence of other kinds of mixing between Jews and Christians. Mixed marriages and sexual relations between Christians and Jews were prohibited already in the synod of Elvira in 306 (canons 16 and 78)[17] but the reappearance of this theme in later imperial legislation shows the persistence of these relationships despite increasing public pressure against them.[18] Legislators also tried to regulate conversions among Christians and Jews: for example, Christian emperors prohibited the circumcision of non-Jewish slaves by their Jewish owners, thus following some precedents in Roman law.[19] The general prohibition against Christian conversions to Judaism appears in a number of edicts which suggests that this phenomenon continued to haunt the Christian establishment for a long time.[20] Many of the laws regulating Jewish–Christian relations in the *Codex Theodosianus* were later reissued as such or with minor revisions in the *Codex Justinianus* which also speaks for their continued relevance.

---

15 Boyarin, *Dying for God*: 32.
16 Thus Stuart S. Miller, 'The Minim of Sepphoris Reconsidered', *HTR* 86 (1993): 401; Claudia Setzer, *Jewish Responses to Early Christians: History and Polemics 30–150 C.E.* (Minneapolis: Fortress Press, 1994): 161; Martin Goodman, 'The Function of Minim in Early Rabbinic Judaism', in *Geschichte–Tradition–Reflexion: FS für Martin Hengel zum 70. Geburtstag. Band I: Judentum*, H. Cancik, H. Lichtenberger and P. Schäfer (eds) (Tübingen: Mohr-Siebeck, 1996): 505; Richard Kalmin, *The Sage in Jewish Society in Late Antiquity* (New York: Routledge, 1999): 72; Boyarin, *Dying for God*: 101; Hakola, *Identity Matters*: 43–4; Lindqvist, 'Less Antagonistic': 180.
17 Paula Fredriksen, 'What Parting of the Ways; Jews, Gentiles, and the Ancient Mediterranean City,' in Becker and Reed, *The Ways That Never Parted*: 60 n. 79.
18 For the interdiction against marriages between Christians and Jews, see *CTh* 3.7.2 = *CTh* 9.7.5 (in 388) in Linder, *Jews*: 178–80. Fredriksen ('What Parting', 60 n. 79) remarks that the legislation up to Visigothic period attests to continuing mixed marriages between Jews and Christians.
19 For the laws against circumcision of non-Jewish slaves by Jewish owners, see *CTh* 16.8.5 and 16.9.1 (in 335), *CTh* 16.8.6 and 16.9.2. (in 339) and *CTh* 3.1.5 (in 384) in Linder, *Jews*: 82–4, 138–51, 174–7. For Roman precedents for these laws, see Linder, *Jews*: 117–20.
20 *CTh* 16.8.1 (in 329), *CTh* 16.8.19 (in 409), *CTh* 16.8.22 (in 415), *CTh* 16.8.26 (in 423) and Theodosius II, *Novella* 3 (in 438) in Linder, *Jews*: 124–32, 256–62, 267–71, 289–91, and 323–36.

In the case of Jewish converts to Christianity, the main concerns were the harassment of these converts by other Jews, the right of Jewish converts to inherit from their Jewish parents and cases where it was suspected that some Jews converted because they wanted to avoid their debts or escape judicial proceedings.[21] While other laws clearly try to encourage and make the conversion of Jews to Christianity easier, the last mentioned cases are interesting, as they are based on encouraging those who have joined Christian communities, but allegedly for the wrong reasons, to return to their Jewish communities.[22] It is also noteworthy that these laws deal with the practical, everyday consequences of conversions, which suggests that they reflect a real-life phenomenon even though it is difficult, if not impossible, to estimate the prevalence of such conversions.

It is significant that one of the best-known Jews who is said to have converted to Christianity is from late antique Galilee: Epiphanius of Salamis tells of Joseph of Tiberias whom he is said to have met in Scythopolis (presumably in the 350s or 360s). According to Epiphanius, Joseph had been a close assistant to the Jewish patriarch in Tiberias and was, after his conversion, authorized by Constantine to build churches in Tiberias, Sepphoris, Capernaum and Nazareth.[23] Epiphanius repeatedly asserts that he has heard Joseph's story directly from the man himself, but many aspects in Epiphanius' long and colourful story invite doubt.[24] Andrew Jacobs has analyzed the story of Joseph's conversion together with other corresponding conversion stories told by Epiphanius and he has shown that these stories resonate with Epiphanius' theological agenda as they help him portray Christianity as able to absorb true and authentic Judaism at its core.[25] We should, therefore, be cautious in drawing far-reaching historical conclusions from Epiphanius' story; for example, it may not help in assessing how common or uncommon conversions of Jews to Christianity were. What the story does show is that it made perfect sense for a Christian writer in the 370s to imagine that such

---

21 The protection of Jewish converts to Christianity from harassment *CTh* 16.8.1 (in 329), *CTh* 16.8.5 and 16.9.1 (in 335) in Linder, *Jews*: 79, 124–32, 138–51; the prohibition preventing the disinheritance of Jewish converts to Christianity *CTh* 16.8.28 and 16.7.7. (in 426), *CJ* 1.5.13 (in 527 or 528) in Linder, *Jews*: 313–19, 368–9; the prohibition against receiving Jewish converts who seek asylum from creditors or to escape judicial proceedings, *CTh* 9.45.2 (in 397), *CTh* 16.8.23 (in 416) in Linder, *Jews*: 199–201, 275–6.

22 Feigned conversions to Christianity are often addressed by Christian writers, see Maijastina Kahlos, *Debate and Dialogue: Christian and Pagan Cultures C. 360-430* (Aldershot: Ashgate, 2007): 26–48; *Forbearance and Compulsion: The Rhetoric of Religious Tolerance and Intolerance in Late Antiquity* (London: Duckworth, 2009): 114–16.

23 Epiphanius, *Pan.* 30.4.1–12.9. For the translation, see *The Panarion of Epiphanius of Salamis, Book I (Sects 1–46)*, Frank Williams (trans.) (second edition; NHMS 63; Brill: Leiden, 2009): 133–41. See further, Stephen Goranson, 'Joseph of Tiberias Revisited: Orthodoxies and Heresies in Fourth-Century Galilee', in *Galilee through the Centuries*, Eric M. Meyers (ed.): 335–43; Andrew S. Jacobs, 'Matters (Un-)Becoming: Conversions in Epiphanius of Salamis', *Church History* 81 (2012): 27–47.

24 For historical problems in Epiphanius' story, see Günter Stemberger, *Jews and Christians in the Holy Land* (Ruth Tuschling (trans.), Edinburgh: T& T Clark, 2000): 71–81.

25 Jacobs, 'Matters': 44.

conversions took place among high-ranking Jews even in such a renowned centre of Jewish learning as Tiberias.[26] Such a possibility of Palestinian Jews converting to Christianity appears also in later Christian sources.[27]

The Ways that Never Parted?

The evidence presented above has caused many scholars to question whether the 'parting of the ways' model aptly describes the varied relations among Christians and Jews. Daniel Boyarin has suggested that we should think of Christianity and Judaism in Late Antiquity as 'points on a continuum' so that

> on one end were the Marcionites ... and on the other the many Jews for whom Jesus meant nothing. In the middle, however, were many gradations that provided social and cultural mobility from one end of this spectrum to the other.[28]

In the book *The Ways That Never Parted*, Annette Yoshiko Reed and Adam Becker summarize the emerging new thinking by saying that 'Jews and Christians (or at least the elites among them) may have been engaged in the task of "parting" throughout Late Antiquity and the early Middle Ages, *precisely because* the two never really "parted"'.[29]

It is perhaps predictable that this new perspective has also received criticism. Peter Schäfer admits that 'the old model of the "parting of the ways" of Judaism and Christianity needs to be abandoned in favour of a much more differentiated and sophisticated model, taking into consideration a long process of mutual demarcation *and* absorption'. However, Schäfer refers to Daniel Boyarin's claim that '"Christianity" is simply a part and parcel of ancient Judaism'[30] and says that

---

26 The final redaction of the Palestinian Talmud is usually located in Tiberias in the early fifth century, which shows the importance of the city for the rabbinic movement. Cf. Herman L. Strack and Günter Stemberger, *Introduction to the Talmud and Midrash* (Markus Bockmuehl (trans.); second edition; Minneapolis: Fortress Press, 1996): 171. For the urban character of the rabbinic movement, see below.
27 John Moschos, *Pratum spiritual*: 176 and 227 in John Moschos, *The Spiritual Meadow (Pratum Spirituale)*, John Wortley (trans.) (Kalamazoo, MI: Cistercian Publications, 1992): 144–6, 205–10. I thank Dr Ulla Tervahauta for bringing these passages to my attention.
28 Boyarin, *Dying for God*: 8. Cf. also Daniel Boyarin, 'Semantic Difference; or, "Judaism"/ "Christianity"', in Becker and Reed, *The Ways That Never Parted*: 66–85, especially 83–4; *Border Lines*: 1–33.
29 Reed and Becker, 'Introduction': 23 (italics original).
30 Daniel Boyarin, 'The Parables of Enoch and the Foundation of the Rabbinic Sect: A Hypothesis', in *"The Words of a Wise Man's Mouth are Gracious" (Qoh 10,12): Festschrift for Günter Stemberger on the Occasion of His 65th Birthday*, Mauro Perani (ed.) (Berlin and New York: De Gruyter, 2005): 53–72, especially 64. It should be remarked that while Boyarin's continuum model (cf. above) can be used to describe variations among Jews and Christian, the claim that 'Christianity is simply part and parcel of Judaism' is clearly an overstatement which does not take seriously enough the point that many Jewish and Christian groups not only presented themselves as separated but actually did not have much in common.

this statement 'means to replace one evil with another'. According to Schäfer, the debates between Jews and Christians should not always be taken as 'inner-Jewish debates' because this would represent a 'misguided attempt to harmonize the historical dissonances'.[31] In a more direct way, Shaye Cohen has argued that various discussions between Jews and Christians in antiquity could not be used as evidence against the parting of the ways. According to Cohen, the actions of the Roman authorities from the early second century onward coincide with the sense of separate communities reflected in various Jewish and Christian writings. This evidence suggests that 'the mutual demarcation had been achieved by the early decades of the second century CE'.[32] Cohen's argumentation could be supplemented with references to second and third century Roman philosophers who already assessed Christians as a group separated from Jews.[33]

These critical comments are important because they remind us that separation, and quite often antagonism, were not merely literary or rhetorical constructions but a living reality for many Jews and Christians. In Palestine, one of the most notorious examples is the rampage instigated by the Syrian monk Barsauma who, together with his supporters, attacked and destroyed several synagogues in the early fifth century.[34] Furthermore, tense relations between some local Christian and Jewish communities are reflected in recurring imperial edicts that forbade attacks against Jews and the destruction of their synagogues.[35]

While I think that there is much to recommend in recent criticisms against the 'parting of the ways' model, it also seems that some criticisms may have gone too far in the opposite direction by playing down the evidence for separation between many Jewish and Christian groups. Given the evidence for local and temporal varieties and complexities among different Jewish and Christian communities, both dictums, 'the ways that never parted' or 'the ways that parted', may be considered unrepresentative as general descriptions of Jewish–Christian relations in the ancient world. The 'parting of the ways' model one-sidedly emphasizes separation between Christian and Jewish communities, but it is likewise misleading to claim that 'the ways never parted' because many Jews, Christians and even Romans were well capable of making a distinction between Jewish and Christian

---

31 Schäfer, *The Jewish Jesus*: 84–85.
32 Shaye J. D. Cohen, 'In Between: Jewish–Christians and the Curse of the Heretics', in *Partings: How Judaism and Christianity Became Two*, Hershel Shanks (ed.) (Washington D.C.: Biblical Archaeology Society, 2014): 350 n. 4.
33 Cf. Niko Huttunen, 'In the Category of Philosophy? Christians in Early Pagan Accounts', in *Others and the Construction of Early Christian Identities*, Raimo Hakola, Nina Nikki and Ulla Tervahauta (eds) (PFES 106; Helsinki: Finnish Exegetical Society, 2013): 239–81. Huttunen argues that some quite negative portraits of early Christians in the works of Tacitus, Suetonius and Pliny the Younger should be complemented by more positive accounts in the works of Epictetus, Marcus Aurelius, Lucian and Galen.
34 For Barsauma, see Hagith Sivan, *Palestine in Late Antiquity* (Oxford: Oxford University Press, 2008): 176–84.
35 *CTh* 16.8. 9. (in 393), *CTh* 16.8.12 (in 397), *CTh* 16.8.20 (in 412), *CTh* 16.8.21 (in 420), *CTh* 16.8.25 (in 423) in Linder, *Jews*: 189–91, 197–8, 262–7 and 283–9.

communities and already from the second century onwards most – but not all – Jewish and Christian groups followed their own religious authorities, beliefs, rituals and festival calendars.[36] As Stuart Miller has rightly concluded, rabbis and Christian theologians may have used similar kinds of theological arguments, as for example Daniel Boyarin has concluded, but they were clearly not similar 'as Jews who lived and practiced in many of the same ways'.[37]

Diverse Jewish and Christian Communities

The preceding discussion has demonstrated that our reconstructions of Jewish and Christian communities in Late Antiquity should not be based on a simple model that presents these communities as separate with fixed and stable boundaries.[38] Most of our literary sources are written from the perspective of religious elites who wanted to secure the boundaries of their communities. The difference between religious rhetoric and a more diverse social reality has been repeatedly demonstrated by Judith Lieu who has remarked that the 'emphasis on internal rhetoric inevitably leads to a strong sense of self-identity, often at odds with other evidence that early Christian groups were more amorphous'. Furthermore, 'the moment of separation provokes much more vigorous rhetoric, enhancing this sense of otherness, which may be less visible to outsiders'.[39] Lieu's conclusion can be supported by various social psychological studies that explain those cognitive, emotional and motivational factors relevant in the formation of distinct group identities. The so-called social identity approach has recently become common in the study of early Judaism and Christianity and, from this perspective, it is only natural that members of a group try to maximize the differences between their own group and other groups when building a secure and distinct social

---

36 It is noteworthy that Annette Yoshiko Reed and Adam Becker make it clear that, despite the provocative title of their collection, *The Ways That Never Parted*, they are not suggesting that their book sets up a new paradigm for the study of Jewish–Christian relations. Cf. Reed and Becker, 'Introduction': 23: 'Even as the "Parting" model still remains regnant, a new understanding of how late antique Jews and Christians related and interrelated with one another is slowly yet steadily developing. It is, however, neither the right time nor the right place to propose a new model to replace the older.'
37 Stuart S. Miller, 'Review Essay. Roman Imperialism, Jewish Self-Definition, and Rabbinic Society: Belayche's *Iudaea-Palaestina*, Schwartz's *Imperialism and Jewish Society*, and Boyarin's *Border Lines* Reconsidered', *AJSR* 31 (2007): 360.
38 The new understandings of ancient Jewish–Christian relations have clear parallels in how the relationship between Christians and pagans in Late Antiquity is nowadays increasingly understood. Cf. Kahlos, *Debate and Dialogue*: 26: 'Scholars before the 1970s for the most part took the division between pagans and Christians for granted and regarded them as mutually exclusive categories and even as opposed and hostile to each other. Several modern scholars nonetheless have recently questioned the clear borderlines and investigated the late antique persons who do not fit into the category of the rigid Christian–pagan dichotomy.'
39 Lieu, *Neither Jew Nor Christian*: 176. See also Judith M. Lieu, *Image and Reality: The Jews in the World of the Christians in the Second Century* (London: T & T Clark, 1996); *Christian Identity in the Jewish and Graeco-Roman World* (Oxford: Oxford University Press, 2004).

identity.[40] However, the evidence reviewed above cautions us to bear in mind that the actual positions of such groups as Jews and Christians in society are not necessarily identical with how their members imagine their position in relation to the outside world.[41]

The more dynamic view that allows for various interactions and exchanges between Jewish and Christian communities is in line with the recent focus on religion as 'lived' in the field of sociology of religion. As Meredith McGuire has remarked, this focus does not consider religions as stable and single entities but as 'made up of diverse, complex, and ever-changing mixtures of beliefs and practices, as well as relationships, experiences and commitments'.[42] From this perspective, the borders of religious identity and commitment are always potentially 'contested, shifting and malleable'.[43] The tension between lived religion and attempts to stabilize and authenticate a particular form of religious identity as the only accepted alternative is clearly seen in in the writings of both Christian theologians and rabbis. Judith Lieu has expressed this by saying that it is never straightforward 'to explain theological data with historical categories' because 'theological boundaries and social boundaries are not necessarily coterminous'.[44] For this reason, Andrew Jacobs is right in remarking that various literary representations of relations between Jews and Christians in Late Antiquity never reflect the reality in an innocent and transparent way, but rather show how 'that reality was produced, scripted, and resisted through linguistic representations' and how 'Christians and Jews constructed their world'.[45]

The emphasis on the dynamic nature of lived religion reflects changes in how the formation of identity is currently understood. While sameness and continuity

---

40 For the application of the social identity approach with relevant references, see Hakola, *Reconsidering*: 24–6.
41 The discrepancy between the rhetoric of separation and social reality is also clearly seen in how various Christian writers positioned themselves in relation to polytheistic cults and their adherents. Kahlos has shown that, despite all the polemic and the dismissal of these cults by Christian theologians, 'ordinary people often continued in peaceful coexistence throughout the fourth and fifth centuries', Maijastina Kahlos, *Forbearance and Compulsion: Rhetoric of Tolerance and Intolerance in Late Antiquity*. (London: Duckworth, 2009): 138.
42 Meredith B. McGuire, *Lived Religion: Faith and Practice in Everyday Life* (Oxford: Oxford University Press, 2008): 185.
43 McGuire, *Lived Religion*: 187. For a similar kind of view regarding the practical realizations of ethnic and religious categories in the field of archaeological theory, see Siân Jones, 'Identities in Practice: Towards an Archaeological Perspective on Jewish Identity in Antiquity', in *Jewish Local Patriotism and Self-Identification in the Graeco-Roman Period*, Siân Jones and Sarah Pearce (eds) (JSPSup, 31; Sheffield: Sheffield Academic Press, 1998): 45: 'Indeed, it is possible to question the very existence of bounded, homogeneous ethnic entities except on an abstract level . . . In contrast, the praxis of ethnicity results in multiple transient realizations of ethnic difference in particular contexts. These practical realizations of ethnicity, in many instances, involve the repeated production and consumption of distinctive styles of material culture.'
44 Lieu, *Neither Jew Nor Christian*: 19.
45 Andrew S. Jacobs, 'The Lion and the Lamb: Reconsidering Jewish–Christian Relations in Antiquity', in Becker and Reed, *The Ways That Never Parted*: 118.

were earlier seen as characteristic of successful identity formation, it has recently become increasingly common to take various individual and group identities as socially constructed and potentially always in need of renegotiation.[46] In light of the social identity approach, social categories are not fixed but always dependent on the specific social environment so that 'people who are categorized and perceived as different in one context . . . can be recategorized and perceived as similar in another context'.[47] This approach can explain why some early Christian writers are sometimes more unbiased or even favourable in their attitudes to Jews, and in other contexts disparage them and their religion. Origen, for example, may at some points be very critical of Jews and their religion but when he is disputing with Celsus he acknowledges that the worship of the Jews is superior to all other forms of worship and that Jewish wisdom is superior to the wisdom of the Greek philosophers.[48] Similarly, it has often been noticed that Augustine, particularly influenced in his views of Jews and Judaism by Romans 9–11, was rather moderate and not polemical when compared to other early Christian writers.[49] Given this thrust in some of Augustine's writings, his attacks against Jews in his *Tractatus in Ioannis Evangelium* are surprisingly harsh and hard to understand.[50] Paula Fredriksen even says that Augustine's Johannine Jews in his *Tractatus* 'seem a different tribe from the one encountered in [his] *Against Faustus*.'[51]

In light of the variations in how even Christian intellectuals assessed Jews and their religion, we can conjecture that attitudes on the ground were much more diverse than regular occasions of mistrust and even open hostility in the written record would imply. From the social identity point of view, it is only to be expected

---

46 Cf. Hakola, 'Identity Theory': 5–15; *Reconsidering*: 21–4.
47 Penelope J. Oakes, S. Alexander Haslam and John C. Turner, *Stereotyping and Social Reality* (Oxford: Blackwell, 1994): 98.
48 *Cels.* 5.42–43. For this passage, see Robert Louis Wilken, 'Something Greater than Temple', in *Anti-Judaism and the Gospels*, William R. Farmer (ed.) (Harrisburg, Pennsylvania: Trinity Press, 1999): 198–199. Wilken concludes that 'even as he [Origen] draws a contrast between the Jews and the Christians, he steadfastly maintains that the Jews are not to be placed in the same category as the idolaters, the pagans'. Cf. also Nicholas de Lange, *Origen and the Jews: Studies in Jewish–Christian relations in Third-Century Palestine* (University of Cambridge Oriental Publications 25; Cambridge: Cambridge University Press, 1976). De Lange argues that even though Origen is at times critical of Jews, for example because of their literal interpretation of the Scriptures, his writings also imply that he had contact with Jewish teachers and was familiar with the Jewish thought of his time.
49 For the discussion, see Jeremy Cohen, '"Slay Them Not:" Augustine and the Jews in Modern Scholarship', *Medieval Encounters* 4 (1998): 78–92; Franklin T. Harkins, 'Nuancing Augustine's Hermeneutical Jews: Allegory and Actual Jews in the Bishop's Sermons,' *JSJ* 36 (2005): 41–64; Paula Fredriksen, *Augustine*: 213–352.
50 Cf. David P. Efroymson, 'Whose Jews? Augustine's Tractate on John', in *A Multiform Heritage: Studies on Early Judaism and Christianity in Honor of Robert A. Kraft*, B.G. Wright (ed.) (Atlanta: Scholars Press, 1999): 211: 'The Augustine of these homilies on John seems more implacable than the author of *C. Faust*. So I would only add that he seems to grow angrier as he reads John, believing, as he did, that the Johannine "Jews" actually said and did to Jesus what John ascribes to them.'
51 Fredriksen, *Augustine*: 305.

that writings that aim at creating a common group emphasize the distinctiveness of the writer's group and minimize or even completely ignore similarities between this group and other groups in its surroundings.[52] A more diverse social reality is reflected, however, in practically oriented sources that speak about mundane relations among Jews and Christians. The letters of two Gazan ascetics, Barsanuphius and John, respond to many everyday concerns among their Christian lay audience who are seemingly interacting with their Jewish and pagan neighbours in a variety of ways. The topics addressed include invitations to shared meals or the use of shared winepresses, themes that illustrate what kind of peaceful interactions took place between Palestinian Christians and Jews in the first part of the sixth century.[53] Another source from the late sixth/early seventh century presents a scene where Christian and Jewish children are playing together in an unnamed village somewhere in Palestine.[54]

The incongruity between religious rhetoric and more diverse social reality has led many scholars to re-evaluate the scope of influence of Christian and Jewish religious expert groups. In the field of early Christian studies, the discovery of the Nag Hammadi library has challenged earlier notions of 'orthodoxy' and 'heresy' among various early Christian groups and shown that it is too simplistic to approach diverse historical sources in terms of doctrinal disputes between heretical and orthodox positions.[55] This has been one of the main reasons why the concepts of 'heresy' and 'orthodoxy' are now increasingly understood, not as accurate descriptions of diverse early Christian groups, but as instruments in the process of self-definition that is always achieved in relation to those experienced, and excluded, as others.[56]

In a similar way, scholars have been reassessing the power and influence of the rabbinic movement that has been repeatedly described in recent studies as a relatively powerless group concerned with issues of purity. This view emerges from the stratigraphic study of the rabbinic laws as well as from the study of legal case histories connected to rabbis of different eras. Many scholars have concluded that the rabbis were neither representative of Judaism at the time, nor were they in any position to enforce their views on those Jews who did not belong to their

---

52 Cf. Hakola, *Reconsidering*: 25–6, 118–29.
53 For the question of whether a Christian can accept an invitation to a meal by a Jew or a pagan during their festivals, see *Letters* 775–776, in *Barsanuphius and John Letters, Volume 2*, John Chryssavgis (trans.) (FCh 114; Washington, DC: Catholic University of America Press, 2007): 281. For the question of whether Christians and Jews may use a shared wine press, see *Letter* 686 on p. 242.
54 John Moschos, *Pratum spiritual*: 227 (John Moschos, *The Spiritual Meadow*: 205–10). I thank Dr Ulla Tervahauta for bringing this passage and the passages mentioned in the previous footnote to my attention.
55 See Raimo Hakola, Nina Nikki and Ulla Tervahauta, 'Introduction', in Hakola et al., *Others*: 16–19.
56 Karen L. King, *What is Gnosticism* (Cambridge, MA: The Belknap Press of Harvard University, 2003): 20–54; Boyarin, *Border Lines*: 22–7; Ismo Dunderberg, *Gnostic Morality Revisited* (WUNT 347; Mohr Siebeck, 2015): 3–10.

circles.[57] Several specific rabbinic regulations, such as those connected to food and dietary practices, separated those Jews who observed these regulations not only from non-Jews but also from other, non-rabbinic Jews.[58] Joshua Ezra Burns summarizes the recent mainstream view among rabbinic scholars when he says that 'the rabbis' legal authority over the Jewish community extended only to those who voluntarily placed themselves under their jurisdiction'.[59]

The diversity of Jewish groups is evident in the use of the term *minim* to refer to different individuals and groups that the rabbis regarded as heretical. In earlier scholarship, it was common to connect these references with clearly defined historical groups such as Christians in general or Jewish Christians in particular; however, it has become all the more evident that references to the *minim* are far too miscellaneous and scattered for us to reconstruct, in detail, the groups that the rabbis are opposing. In fact, many scholars have pointed out that the rabbinic sources describe the *minim* in quite general terms and blur distinctions between different groups.[60] Stuart Miller has remarked that attempts to identify the *minim* with clearly defined groups of Jews (or 'Jewish Christians') have 'obfuscated our understanding of the facts on the ground. The *min* was in many ways indistinguishable from other Jews, not only in the eyes of the rabbis but also in reality.'[61] In the same vein, Peter Schäfer says that rabbinic references to the *minim* do not reflect 'the controversy of firmly established "religions" – "Jewish," "pagan," "Christian," "gnostic," or other – but allow for still

---

57 Martin Goodman, *State and Society in Roman Galilee, AD 132–212* (Totowa NJ: Rowman & Allanheld, 1983): 93–118; Jacob Neusner, *Judaism: The Evidence of the Mishnah* (second edition; BJS 129; Atlanta, GA: Scholars Press, 1988): 76–121; Catherine Hezser, *The Social Structure of the Rabbinic Movement in Roman Palestine* (TSAJ 66; Tübingen: Mohr-Siebeck, 1997): 360–68; Shaye J. D. Cohen, 'The Rabbi in Second Century Jewish Society', in *The Cambridge History of Judaism, Volume Three: The Early Roman Period*, W. Horbury, W. D. Davies and J. Sturdy (eds) (Cambridge: Cambridge University Press, 1999): 961–90; Günter Stemberger: 'Die Umformung des palästinischen Judentums nach 70: Der Aufstieg der Rabbinen', in *Jüdische Geschichte in hellenistisch-römischer Zeit. Wege der Forschung: Vom alten zum neuen Schürer*, Aharon Oppenheimer (Schriften des Historischen Kollegs: Kolloquien 44; München: R. Oldenbourg Verlag, 1999): 85–99. For discussions with further references, see Hakola, *Identity Matters*: 55–65; Stuart S. Miller, *Sages and Commoners in Late Antique 'Erez Israel: A Philological Inquiry into Local Traditions in Talmud Yerushalmi* (TSAJ 111; Tübingen: Mohr Siebeck, 2006): 7–16.
58 David Kraemer, 'Food, Eating, and Meals', in *The Oxford Handbook of Jewish Daily Life in Roman Palestine*, Catherine Hezser (ed.) (Oxford: Oxford University Press, 2010): 409–11; Jordan D. Rosenblum, *Food and Identity in Early Rabbinic Judaism* (Cambridge: Cambridge University Press, 2010): 185–92.
59 Joshua Ezra Burns, 'The Archaeology of Rabbinic Literature and the Study of Jewish–Christian Relations in Late Antiquity', in *Religion, Ethnicity, and Identity in Ancient Galilee*, Jürgen K. Zangenberg, Harold W. Attridge and Dale B. Martin (eds) (WUNT 210; Tübingen: Mohr Siebeck, 2007): 406 n. 13.
60 Miller, 'The Minim': 401; 'Review Essay': 357; Richard Kalmin, 'Christians and Heretics in Rabbinic Literature of Late Antiquity', *HTR* 87 (1994): 169; Goodman, 'The Function': 506–7; Hakola, *Identity Matters*: 47–8.
61 Miller, 'Review Essay': 351.

fluid boundaries within (and beyond) which a variety of groups were competing with each other in shaping their identities'.[62]

Interestingly, the rabbinic policy of ignoring the detailed characteristics of their opponents and blending them all together has clear parallels in Christian sources. Maijastina Kahlos has shown how various Christian authors grouped together those groups they regarded as dissident – pagans, Jews, and heretics – and saw them all as adherents of the same error.[63] The tendency of religious ideologues – both Jewish and Christian – to lump their opponents together can be seen as an attempt to reduce a diverse and sometimes even threatening social reality into controllable categories, a tendency well-attested in research dealing with intergroup relations.[64]

It also seems that the involvement and influence of the rabbis in the development of synagogues was considerably more limited than was earlier thought.[65] This view is especially relevant in the study of Jewish communities in Galilee because a great deal of what we know of these communities is based on the archaeological excavations of Galilean synagogues. While late antique synagogues could be taken as spaces that gave expression to a distinct Jewish identity, many scholars have actually recognized how, for example, synagogue art developed alongside Roman and Christian art in its various parallel themes and patterns.[66] This means that synagogues were not only tokens of separate identities, but spaces

---

62 Schäfer, *The Jewish Jesus*: 5–6.
63 Maijastina Kahlos, *Debate and Dialogue*: 68; 'The Shadow of the Shadow: Examining Fourth- and Fifth-Century Christian Depictions of Pagans', in *The Faces of the Other: Religious Rivalry and Ethnic Encounters in the Later Roman World*, Maijastina Kahlos (ed.) (Cursor Mundi 10; Turnhout, Belgium: Brepols, 2011): 190–92. Thus also Cameron, 'Jews and Heretics': 345–60.
64 In social psychological literature, this tendency is called the outgroup homogeneity effect which refers to the inclination of groups to present other groups as homogenous. See Hakola, *Reconsidering*: 28–9. I suggest that a crucial part of the invention of distinct early Christian identity was the creation of the portrait of the Jews as united in their opposition to Christians.
65 Cf. Shaye J. D. Cohen, 'Were Pharisees and Rabbis the Leaders of Communal Prayer and Torah Study in Antiquity: The Evidence of the New Testament, Josephus, and the Church Fathers,' in *The Echoes of Many Texts: Reflections on Jewish and Christian Traditions. Essays in Honor of Lou H. Silberman*, W. G. Dever and J. E. Wright (eds) (BJS 313; Atlanta, GA: Scholars Press, 1997): 99–114; Lee I. Levine, *The Ancient Synagogue; The First Thousand Years* (second edition; New Haven, CT: Yale University Press, 2005): 466–98; Hakola, *Identity Matters*: 61–5. Cf. also Stuart S. Miller, '"Epigraphical Rabbis, Helios and Psalm 19: Were the Synagogues of Archaeology and the Synagogues of the Sages One and the Same', *JQR* 94 (2004): 27–76. Miller emphasizes that 'the synagogue should not be seen as an institution whose form and function were monolithic'. This means that 'in some synagogues rabbis could have had a say where the liturgy and ritual were concerned without necessarily controlling or running the institution' (p. 37). Miller concludes that 'the synagogues of archaeology and the synagogues of the sages need not have been identical, but they were not altogether distinct either' (p. 76).
66 Cf. B. Kühnel, 'The Synagogue Floor Mosaic in Sepphoris: Between Paganism and Christianity': 31–43, and Herbert L. Kessler, 'The Sepphoris Mosaic and Christian Art': 64–72 both in *From Dura to Sepphoris: Studies in Jewish Art and Society in Late Antiquity*, Lee. I. Levine and Zeev Weiss (eds) (JRASup 40; Portsmouth, RI: Journal of Roman Archaeology, 2000).

that allowed various negotiations between local Jewish communities and their surroundings. Hagith Sivan has described late antique Sepphoris 'as a space with a Jewish identity that allowed for acceptance of other discourses'. Sivan continues that 'a sense of citizenship' in this Galilean urban landscape was nurtured by 'a shared appreciation of aesthetics, intellectual and artistic, that espoused an astonishing breadth of Judaism in the Galilee of late antiquity. Public spaces ... reinforced the impression of a collectivity poised between textual strictures and civic culture.'[67] This view of Galilean synagogues as participating in various ways in wider late antique culture provides a promising point of departure for the discussion of the evidence related to Galilean rural synagogues.

Galilean Synagogues in Late Antiquity

The discussion above suggests that we should examine the evidence connected to Galilean rural synagogues bearing in mind the diversity that characterized Jewish communities in Late Antiquity. As a matter of fact, the study of Galilean synagogues in recent decades has revealed a great amount of diversity in their layout and decoration. In earlier scholarship, it was usual to think that different types of synagogues in Galilee followed each other chronologically so that the earliest Galilean or basilical type of synagogue (second and third centuries) was followed by transitional or broadhouse synagogues (fourth century) and finally by Byzantine synagogues with a basilical plan including an apsis for the Torah ark in the Jerusalem-oriented wall and rich floor mosaics.[68] In this scenario, the monumental limestone synagogue in Capernaum was taken as the best example of an early, third century, Galilean-type synagogue, a conclusion that was based mainly on alleged stylistic similarities between this synagogue and some Roman temples in the Syria of the second and third centuries. In the excavations of the Capernaum synagogue in the late 1960s and early 70s, however, the synagogue was dated to the early fifth century on the basis of pottery and coins found underneath its floors.[69] The later dating of the Capernaum synagogue resulted in a reconsideration

---

67 Sivan, *Palestine*: 320.
68 This view was developed gradually in such studies as Heinrich Kohl and Carl Watzinger, *Antike Synagogen in Galiläa* (Leipzig: Hinrichs, 1916); Eleazar Sukenik, *Ancient Synagogues in Palestine and Greece* (London: British Academy, 1934); Michael Avi-Yonah, 'Synagogue Architecture in the Late Classical Period', *Jewish Art: An Illustrated History* (C. Roth (ed.); London: Valentine Mitchell, 1961): 157–89. For histories of research of Galilean synagogues, see Rachel Hachlili, *Ancient Synagogues – Archaeology and Art: New Discoveries and Current Research* (HO, Section One 105; Leiden: Brill, 2013): 600–603; Rick Bonnie, *Galilee During the Second Century: Archaeological Examination of a Period of Socio-Cultural Change* (PhD Dissertation: KU Leuven, 2014): 293–6.
69 Cf. Stanislao Loffreda, 'The Late Chronology of the Synagogue of Capernaum', *IEJ* 23 (1973): 37–42.; Hachlili, *Ancient Synagogues*: 63. Jodi Magness has proposed an even later, sixth century date for the Capernaum synagogue, see Jodi Magness, 'The Pottery from the Village of Capernaum and the Chronology of Galilean Synagogues', *Tel Aviv* 39 (2012): 238–50.

of the dating of other Galilean synagogues.[70] In addition, Eric Meyers conducted excavations at several sites in Upper Galilee in the 1970s and early 80s and the results of these excavations revealed that synagogues representing different types dated to approximately the same period.[71] Meyers proposes also that the diversity of synagogues may be taken as a reflection of diversity among rural Galilean Jewish communities: 'The great diversity in synagogue types as well as in decoration suggests variety within Talmudic Judaism even though each divergence still belongs very much to a common culture.'[72]

In recent years, there has been an intense debate on the dating of Galilean synagogues.[73] Even if the evidence for the earliest phase of the synagogue in Nabratein, for example, remains contested, there is no doubt that these buildings were used and renovated well into Late Antiquity. The situation with newly found synagogues at Huqoq and Horvat Kur is different because, even though only preliminary reports of these buildings are available, it is quite clear that they could not have been constructed before the late fourth or early fifth centuries.[74] These

---

70 For example, Jodi Magness has suggested, on the basis of numismatic and ceramic evidence, that the synagogue in Chorazin should be dated to the fifth century. Jodi Magness, 'Did Galilee Decline in the Fifth Century? The Synagogue at Chorazin Reconsidered', in *Religion, Ethnicity, and Identity in Ancient Galilee*, Jürgen K. Zangenberg et al (eds): 259–74.

71 Eric M. Meyers, A. Thomas Kraabel and James F. Strange, *Ancient Synagogue Excavations at Khirbet Shema', Upper Galilee, Israel 1970–72* (MEPR 1; Durham, NC: Duke University Press, 1976); Eric M. Meyers, James F. Strange and Carol L Meyers, *Excavations in Ancient Meiron, Upper Galilee, Israel 1971–1972, 1974–1975, 1977* (MEPR 3; Cambridge, MA: ASOR, 1981); Eric M. Meyers, Carol L Meyers and James F. Strange, *Excavations at the Ancient Synagogue of Gush Halav* (MEPR 5; Winona Lake, IN: Eisenbrauns, 1990); Eric M. Meyers and Carol L Meyers, *Excavations at Ancient Nabratein: Synagogue and Environs* (MEPR 6; Winona Lake, IN: Eisenbrauns, 2009).

72 Eric M. Meyers, 'Recent Archaeology in Palestine: Achievements and Future Goals', in *The Cambridge History of Judaism, Volume Three: The Early Roman Period*, W. Horbury, W. D. Davies, and J. Sturdy (eds) (Cambridge: Cambridge University Press, 1999): 59–74, especially 68. However, it may not be accurate to describe rural Galilean communities as 'Talmudic', see below.

73 Jodi Magness in particular has challenged the evidence presented by Eric Meyers and his colleagues for the early layers of the synagogues in Khirbet Shema', Meiron and Nabratein. See *Judaism in Late Antiquity, Part Three, Where We Stand: Issues and Debates in Ancient Judaism. Volume Four: The Special Problem of the Synagogue*, Alan J. Avery-Peck and Jacob Neusner (eds) (HO, Section One 55; Leiden: Brill, 2001). See the following articles: Jodi Magness, 'The Question of the Synagogue: The Problem of Typology': 1–48; 'A Response to Eric. M. Meyers and James F. Strange': 93–120; Eric M. Meyers, 'The Dating of the Gush Halav Synagogue: A Response to Jodi Magness' in *Judaism in Late Antiquity, Part Three, Where We Stand: Issues and Debates in Ancient Judaism. Volume Four: The Special Problem of the Synagogue*, Alan J. Avery-Peck and Jacob Neusner (eds) HO, Section One 55; Leiden: Brill, 2001: 49–70; James F. Strange, 'Synagogue Typology and Khirbet Shema'': 71–8. See further, Jodi Magness, 'The Ancient Synagogue at Nabratein' *BASOR* 358 (2010): 61–8; Eric M. Meyers and Carol L Meyers, 'A Response to Jodi Magness's Review of the Final Publication of Nabratein', *BASOR* 359 (2011): 67–76.

74 The excavators state that the construction of the Huqoq synagogue cannot be dated earlier than the late fourth century, see Jodi Magness, Shua Kisilevitz, Karen Britt, Matthew J. Grey and Chad Spigel, 'Huqoq (Lower Galilee) and Its Synagogue Mosaics: Preliminary Report on the Excavations of 2011–2013', *JRA* 27 (2014): 327–55. The Horvat Kur synagogue seems to have

two buildings endorse the view that synagogues were built and used in the region long after Christianity had gained ground across the Empire.

The late dating of Galilean synagogues, together with the evidence for other Byzantine synagogues in Palestine, has challenged the older view according to which Judaism in Palestine was in decline and under attack and, therefore, increasingly defensive and inward looking after the Constantinian turn.[75] Lee Levine has concluded that this view has been re-evaluated because 'Jews throughout the Byzantine era were building synagogues everywhere [in Palestine], often on a grand and imposing scale.'[76] The evidence for late antique synagogues is at odds with several imperial edicts that tried to restrict or prohibit the building of synagogues from the early fifth century onwards.[77] In earlier scholarship, the imperial legislation was seen as one of the most important factors in the alleged decline of Jewish communities in Late Antiquity and these laws are still often used to explain certain features of Galilean synagogues.[78] However, imperial laws

---

been established in the early fifth century and the building went through one or two rebuilding phases in the late sixth or early seventh century before it was finally abandoned sometime in the second half of the seventh century. See Jürgen K. Zangenberg, Stefan Münger, Raimo Hakola and Byron R. McCane, 'The Kinneret Regional Project Excavations of a Byzantine Synagogue at Horvat Kur, Galilee, 2010–2013: A Preliminary Report', *HeBAI* 2 (2013): 557–76. For further references, see Jürgen K. Zangenberg's chapter in this volume.

75 For the view that Judaism was in decline from the fourth century onwards, see Michael Avi-Yonah, *The Jews of Palestine: A Political History from the Bar Kokhba War to the Arab Conquest* (Blackwell's Classical Studies; Oxford: Blackwell, 1976); Ze'ev Safrai, *The Missing Century, Palestine in the Fifth Century: Growth and Decline* (Palestina Antiqua 9: Leuven, Peeters, 1998).

76 Levine, *The Ancient Synagogue*: 212. The view that Jewish settlements in Galilee went through a severe crisis in the fourth century as a result of which the number of these settlements remained scanty in the fifth through to the seventh centuries, has recently been revived by Uzi Leibner, 'Settlement Patterns in the Eastern Galilee: Implications Regarding the Transformation of Rabbinic Culture in Late Antiquity', in *Jewish Identities in Antiquity: Studies in Memory of Menahem Stern*, Lee I. Levine and Daniel R. Schwartz (eds) (TSAJ 130; Tübingen: Mohr-Siebeck, 2009): 269–95. Leibner acknowledges that there are in his survey material examples of settlements that 'evidently remained in existence throughout most or all of the Byzantine period' (p. 277). It now seems that the settlements at Huqoq and Horvat Kur should be counted among those sites that continued to flourish in Late Antiquity.

77 *CTh* 16.8.22 (in 415) prohibits the foundation of new synagogues and orders that synagogues in deserted places should be destroyed, see Linder, *Jews*: 267–72. *CTh* 16.6.25 (in 423) says that the Jews should be granted places for the construction of synagogues to replace those seized from them but, at the same time, forbids the construction of new synagogues and states that the existing synagogues should be preserved as they are, see Linder, *Jews*: 287–9; Theodosius II, *Novella*, 3 (in 438) prohibits the construction of new synagogues but allows the renovation of old synagogues, see Linder, *Jews*: 323–37. For the prohibition against building new synagogues, see also Justinian, *Novellae*, 131 (in 545) in Linder, *Jews*: 398–402.

78 Cf. Anders Runesson, 'Architecture, Conflict, and Identity Formation: Jews and Christians in Capernaum from the First to the Sixth Century', in *Religion, Ethnicity, and Identity*, Jürgen K. Zangenberg *et al.* (eds), 252, n. 80. Runesson remarks that the prohibition against building new synagogues could 'explain why synagogues were built on the same spot on which earlier synagogues had stood'. See also Mordechai Aviam, 'The Ancient Synagogues at Bar'am', in *Judaism in Late Antiquity*, Avery-Peck and Neusner (eds): 171. Aviam speculates whether the use of *spolia*

and their enforcement should be seen in the larger context of imperial power politics. The situation with the edicts dealing with Jews is not different from the laws that were directed against pagans or groups regarded as heretics. In both cases, imperial enactments had to be renewed again and again, which suggests that these rulings were quite often ignored at the local level and that they had only a limited effect in different parts of the Empire.[79] Hagith Sivan has concluded that this was clearly the case in Galilee where 'the scale of the synagogues and their decoration reflected considerable means and a sense of security'.[80]

I have demonstrated above how recent scholarship has underlined diversity among late antique Jewish communities. This emphasis is well-founded in the case of Jewish communities in rural Galilee. The excavations of two Galilean synagogues at Khirbet Wadi Hamam and Huqoq have revealed floor mosaics that have been interpreted as representing scenes from the story of Samson as it is told in the Hebrew Bible.[81] Matthew Grey has remarked that the rarity of Samson in ancient Jewish art as well as Samson's lack of historical ties to Galilee raises the question of why these village communities had such an interest in the exploits of this biblical character that they wanted to have him depicted in their community centres.[82] Rabbinic traditions regarding Samson do not answer this question because they portray Samson mostly in a negative light.[83] Grey turns to Jewish liturgical and targumic texts that depicted Samson as an example of how God delivered Israel in the past and which attached future messianic hopes to him. What is remarkable here is that the portrait of Samson as a messianic prototype in the Targums does not correspond to how Samson is depicted in rabbinic literature.[84] Grey aptly concludes that these sources and their depictions of Samson may 'provide valuable insight into the practices and worldviews of

---

    in the building of some Galilean late antique synagogues could be regarded as 'a trick' to avoid imperial laws against the building of new synagogues. According to our present knowledge, the newly found synagogues at Huqoq and Horvat Kur do not support either suggestion because these buildings were genuinely new constructions located where there is no evidence yet for earlier public structures.

79 See David Hunt, 'Christianising the Roman Empire: the Evidence of the Code', in *The Theodosian Code: Studies in the Imperial Law of Late Antiquity*, Jill Harries and Ian Wood (eds) (London: Duckworth, 1993): 143–58; Kahlos, *Forbearance and Compulsion*: 90–92.

80 Sivan, *Palestine*: 46. Sivan is speaking here mainly of Galilean urban synagogues in Sepphoris and in Tiberias but recent evidence suggests that her conclusions could be applied to the late antique Galilean rural synagogues at Huqoq and Horvat Kur as well.

81 For the Wadi Hamam mosaic, see Uzi Leibner and Shulamit Miller, 'A Figural Mosaic in the Synagogue at Khirbet Wadi Hamam', *JRA* 23 (2010): 238–64. On the basis of the pottery found under the mosaic's plaster bedding, the excavators date the floor to the late third or early fourth centuries. Jodi Magness has contested this dating and suggests that the floor dates to the mid to late fourth-century, see Magness, 'The Pottery': 110–22. For the mosaic in the synagogue of Huqoq, see Jodi Magness, *et al.* 'Huqoq': 327–55.

82 Matthew J. Grey, '"The Redeemer to Arise from the House of Dan": Samson, Apocalypticism, and Messianic Hopes in Late Antique Galilee', *JSJ* 44 (2013): 553–89.

83 Grey, 'The Redeemer': 557.

84 Grey, 'The Redeemer': 578.The targumic sources referred to by Grey have increasingly been understood in recent scholarship to represent popular liturgical practices that were not in the control of the rabbis.

synagogue congregations in the late antique Galilean villages, including Huqoq and Wadi Hamam'.[85] Grey's conclusions are in line with recent reappraisals of the rabbinic movement and show that these revisions should be taken seriously in the Galilean studies.

The above conclusion can be complemented by Stuart Miller's discussion of the predominantly urban character of the rabbinic movement in the fourth century.[86] Miller notes that even though a limited number of rural sages are mentioned in the Palestinian Talmudic sources, 'there are very few sayings attributed to these sages'.[87] Miller concludes that the traditions in the Palestinian Talmud clearly reflect the concerns of urban teachers in centres such as Tiberias, Sepphoris or Caesarea but less the interests of more remote village rabbis. According to Miller, the Palestinian Talmud's 'depiction of rural rabbis is a world that, on the one hand, was dependent upon big city rabbis, but on the other hand had a vitality of its own that enabled it to contribute to the larger movement'.[88] This view implies that while there self-evidently were local, religious leaders with prestige in Galilean rural communities, it is unproblematic to identify these leaders with authorities known from rabbinic sources.[89]

The building and renovation of rural Galilean synagogues in Late Antiquity speaks for the vitality of various village settlements in the region. Following Lee Levine, these buildings can be described as communal centres whose nature was determined by the needs and resources of local communities that also bore the responsibility for their construction, maintenance and repairs and whose chosen representatives had authority over running these institutions.[90] Each of the recently found synagogues has remarkable features of its own. The synagogue at Huqoq had a magnificent mosaic floor that, up until now, is only partially exposed and the Horvat Kur synagogue originally had a mosaic floor, frescoed walls and at some point a decorated *bemah*, a platform which supported a chest holding Torah scrolls; while the rest of the building was made of black basalt, the *bemah* was made of carefully dressed high-quality limestone.[91] The closest parallel to this *bemah* is known from the contemporary synagogue at Umm el-Qanatir on the

---

85 Grey, 'The Redeemer': 573.
86 Miller, *Sages and Commoners*: 17. Miller says that he takes the urbanization of the rabbinic movement for granted and considers some of the ramifications of this phenomenon. Other scholars have noticed the increasing urbanization of the rabbinic movement from the third century on, cf. Cohen, 'The Rabbi': 941; Hezser, *The Social Structure*: 31; Hayim Lapin, 'Rabbis and Cities in Later Roman Palestine: The Literary Evidence', *JJS* 50 (1999): 187–207.
87 Miller, *Sages and Commoners*: 11.
88 Miller, *Sages and Commoners*: 458.
89 The stone seat found in the Horvat Kur synagogue gives evidence for a person who had an exceptional and authoritative position in this community, as Jürgen K. Zangenberg shows in his chapter elsewhere in this volume.
90 Cf. Levine, *The Ancient Synagogue*: 381–90.
91 Cf. Zangenberg, *et al.*, 'The Kinneret Regional Project': 557–76. For the function of the *bemah* inside the synagogue, see Zangenberg's chapter in this volume. For the Horvat Kur Mosaic, see also *Bible History Daily*, available at http://www.biblicalarchaeology.org/daily/ancient-cultures/ancient-israel/magnificent-menorah-mosaic-found-in-galilee/, accessed 22 January 2016.

Golan Heights.[92] This parallel is not the only connection between synagogues in Galilee and on the Golan; as Hagith Sivan says, architectural fragments throughout the Golan Heights 'display striking similarities with the art of the Galilean synagogues'. The new dating of the Galilean synagogues to the fifth if not sixth century is in agreement with the dating of synagogues on the Golan. On the basis of this evidence, Sivan speaks of 'a building "boom" in both the Golan and the Galilee' which 'indicates that Jews ignored imperial restrictions on the construction of new synagogues'.[93]

The synagogues at Horvat Kur and Huqoq complement the repertoire of imposing late antique synagogues in the region represented earlier by the synagogues of Capernaum and Chorazin. This new evidence suggests that the Capernaum synagogue should not be taken as a special case whose construction needs to be explained by exceptional circumstances. Such a view has been expressed by Anders Runesson – and he, of course, was not aware of the synagogues in Horvat Kur and Huqoq – who has argued that the construction of the Capernaum synagogue is 'a defiant act of defence against [Byzantine Christian] colonizers'. Furthermore, 'the building was not financed by the local population, but rather by politically and economically more powerful Jews in Tiberias'. According to Runesson, the Capernaum synagogue provides 'us with an example of how and why the rabbis could assert themselves as the leaders of the Jews'.[94] More recently, Benjamin Arubas and Rina Talgam have revived the view that the building of the Capernaum synagogue was at least partly sponsored by Christian ecclesiastical authorities who wanted to foster Christian pilgrimage to the site where the octagonal church was built, approximately at the same time, on the alleged spot of the House of St. Peter.[95] Both of these views treat the building of the Capernaum

---

92 Zangenberg, *et al.*, 'The Kinneret Regional Project': 571.
93 Sivan, *Palestine*: 101. See also Eric M. Meyers, 'Living Side by Side in Galilee', in *Partings*, Hershel Shanks (ed.): 146. Meyers speaks of 'a kind of floruit of Jewish life in Galilee in the early Byzantine period', which is most clearly attested in the building and rebuilding of various synagogues. Meyers dates 'a similar burst in synagogue building' on the Golan to the fifth and sixth centuries.
94 Runesson, 'Architecture': 252–3. Runesson agrees to a great extent with Seth Schwartz who has said that the Christianized state played a decisive role in the formation of rabbinic Judaism, see Seth Schwartz, *Imperialism and Jewish Society: 200 B.C.E. to 640 C.E.* (Princeton: Princeton University Press, 2001). For a critical review of Schwartz's thesis, see Miller, 'Review Essay': 334–50. The Palestinian rabbinic sources do not necessarily support the view that the rabbis saw Christianity as a threat, see Burns, 'The Archaeology': 404: 'The rabbis do not appear to have seen themselves as facing an insurmountable threat; the Jews continued to proliferate throughout the Galilee region and would only begin to feel the invasive brunt of the new Christian empire later in the Byzantine era.'
95 Benjamin Y. Arubas and Rina Talgam, 'Jews, Christians and "*Minim*": Who really Built and Used the Synagogue at Capernaum – a Stirring Appraisal', in *Knowledge and Wisdom: Archaeological and Historical Essays in Honour of Leah Di Segni*, Giovanni C. Bottini, L. Daniel Chrupcala and Joseph Patrich (eds) (SBFCM 54; Milano: Edizioni Terra Santa, 2014): 237–74. This view revises an earlier proposition by Z. U. Ma'oz, 'The Synagogue at Capernaum: A Radical Solution', in *The Roman and Byzantine Near East, Volume 2. Some Recent Archaeological Research,*

synagogue as a special case. However, the synagogues at Horvat Kur and Huqoq now provide more material to examine these impressive rural buildings as manifestations of the resources and aspirations of *local* communities, rather than as examples of centralized building projects controlled from afar. Lee Levine may be right when he observes that local synagogues may have been 'a cause of rivalry between neighbouring communities, and at times envy motivated one to imitate and even outdo the achievements of the other'.[96]

Christians in Galilee in Late Antiquity

Our direct evidence of Christians in Galilee in Late Antiquity is even more meagre than the fragmentary evidence related to Jewish communities. According to a once influential view, supported by many Franciscan scholars, Jewish Christian communities survived throughout Palestine from the late first century CE to the third and fourth centuries and these communities cherished the memory of Christian holy places in Nazareth, Capernaum and elsewhere.[97] However, the archaeological shortcomings of this so-called Bagatti-Testa hypothesis have repeatedly been exposed.[98] It has become all the more evident that references to the *minim* in Capernaum in a late rabbinic source,[99] or discussions of Jewish Christian groups by various Christian theologians, do not provide solid evidence for the presence

---

J. H. Humphrey (ed.) (JRASup 31: Portsmouth, RI: JRA, 1999): 137–148. For the shortcomings of this view, see Hachlili, *Ancient Synagogues*: 62.

96 Levine (*The Ancient Synagogue*: 384) with a reference to *Seder Eliyahu Rabbah* 11.

97 Bellarmino Bagatti, *The Church from the Circumcision: History and Archaeology of the Judaeo-Christians* (E Hoade (trans.): second edition; SBFCM; Jerusalem: Franciscan Printing Press, 1984); Emmanuele Testa, *The Faith of the Mother Church: An Essay on the Theology of the Judeo-Christians* (SBFCM; Jerusalem: Franciscan Printing Press, 1992).

98 Joan E. Taylor, *Christians and the Holy Places: The Myth of Jewish-Christian Origins* (Oxford: Clarendon, 1993); 'Parting in Palestine', in *Partings*, Hershel Shanks (ed.): 102; Broadhead, *Jewish Ways*: 301–51; Jürgen K. Zangenberg, 'From the Galilean Jesus to the Galilean Silence: Earliest Christianity in the Galilee until the Fourth Century CE', in *The Rise and Expansion of Christianity in the Three Centuries of the Common Era*, Clare K. Rothschild and Jens Schröter (eds) (WUNT 301; Tübingen: Mohr Siebeck, 2013): 101–7.

99 The two passages in *Midrash Qohelet Rabbah* 1:8 and 7:26 refer to the *minim* in Capernaum and these references have often been taken as evidence for a Jewish Christian community at the site already in the second century, cf. Stanislao Loffreda, *Recovering Capernaum* (Jerusalem: Franciscan Printing Press, 1993): 30–31. Benjamin Y. Arubas and Rina Talgam, 'Jews, Christians and *"Minim"*: Who really Built and Used the Synagogue at Capernaum – a Stirring Appraisal,' in *Knowledge and Wisdom: Archaeological and Historical Essays in Honour of Leah Di Segni*, Giovanni C. Bottini, L. Daniel Chrupcala and Joseph Patrich (eds), SBFCM 54. Milano: Edizioni Terra Santa, 2014: 245–6, 269, take these references as a direct reflection of the position of the Jews in Capernaum in the fifth century; in their scenario, the Capernaum Jews had constant contacts with Christian pilgrims which blurred their Jewish identity and resulted in them being accused of heresy. However, we cannot know how widespread and representative views expressed in this seventh or even eighth century source were (for the dating, see Strack and Stemberger, *Introduction*: 318). In addition, the discussion above has suggested that we should be cautious in arriving at far-reaching historical conclusions on the basis of rabbinic references to *minim*.

of Jewish Christian communities in Galilee before the fourth century.[100] After a nuanced discussion, Jürgen K. Zangenberg has concluded that the oft-repeated view of specific Jewish Christian sects in Galilee prior to the Constantinian turn needs to be revised. The scant archaeological traces, for example some graffiti in Capernaum, speak for a growing interest during the late second through to the fourth centuries but it is probable that those visitors who left these traces represented a 'mainstream' or 'international' type of Christianity, while the evidence for earlier, local Jewish Christian sects remains inconclusive.[101]

We are on the safe side if we assume that the appearance of Christians in the late antique Galilean landscape should be connected to the beginning of Christian pilgrimage. While there are some examples of second or third century pilgrims to Palestine, mostly male Christian intellectuals, pilgrimage to the Holy Land as a popular movement started after the Constantinian turn in the fourth century.[102] These visitors soon reported what they had seen on their travels; for example, Egeria told her readers that during her visit to Galilee in the 380s she saw churches in Capernaum, Tabgha, Tiberias and Nazareth.[103] Yet, pilgrim accounts rarely reveal any specifics of local circumstances because this literature 'is marked by a deep religious aura, a lack of interest in the present, and carelessness about space and time, view, and landscape'.[104] Blake Leyerle has described how for Egeria, 'the value of the land depends on its biblical past' which explains her 'blindness to contemporary Jewish life' in Galilee. On the basis of the gospels, she attaches special significance to simple geographic features like hills and fields, which marks 'the beginning of the process of social framing through which terrain becomes infused with meaning'.[105] Andrew Jacobs has examined how Christians found ways to cope with contemporary Jewish communities in their pilgrim accounts so

---

100 References to Ναζαρηνοί or Ναζωραῖοι in various Christian sources have figured prominently in discussions of alleged Jewish Christian groups in Galilee. Luomanen (*Recovering*: 241–2) has shown how Epiphanius created the well-defined, heretical group of Nazarenes from some scattered earlier references. Luomanen concludes that the 'heresy' of the Nazarenes never existed but real, historical Nazarenes were Syriac-speaking Christians with a Jewish background who had a clear Christian identity and were openly pro-Pauline. Cf. Zangenberg ('Galilean Jesus': 89) who says that 'there appears no genuine connection between Ebionites and Nazoreans with the Galilee as such'.

101 Zangenberg, 'Galilean Jesus': 107.

102 Cf. Pierre Maraval, 'The Earliest Phase of Christian Pilgrimage in the Near East (before the 7th Century)', *DOP* 56 (2002): 63–74; Ora Limor, '"Holy Journey", Pilgrimage and Christian Sacred Landscape', in *Christians and Christianity*, Limor and Stroumsa (eds): 321–53.

103 For Egeria's references to these churches, see Taylor, *Christians*: 226, 276 and 289; Stefano De Luca, 'Vorgeschichte, Ursprung und Funktion der byzantinischen Klöster von Kafarnaum/Tabgha in der Region um den See Gennesaret', in *Tabgha 2012: Festschrift zur Einweihung des neuen Klostergebäudes am 17. Mai 2012*, Abtei Dormitio and Kloster Tabgha (eds) (Jerusalem: Emerezian est., 2012): 35–7.

104 Limor, '"Holy Journey"', 347. For the concept of seeing in pilgrim accounts, see Juliette Day's chapter in this volume.

105 Blake Leyerle, 'Early Christian Perceptions of the Galilee', in *Galilee through the Centuries*, Eric M. Meyers (ed.): 351–2.

that they were able to incorporate 'the "local" experience of Jews into the universality of sacred Christian time and space'.[106]

Christian pilgrimage to the holy sites soon became tightly connected with the emergence of monasticism in the Holy Land.[107] The first pilgrim centres in Galilee were located in close proximity to the synagogues discussed above. In Capernaum, earlier structures were transformed into a *domus ecclesia*, a house church, in the late fourth century and finally an octagonal church was built near the synagogue in the fifth century.[108] In Tabgha, a small chapel was built in the late fourth century to commemorate the place where Jesus allegedly fed five thousand men with five loaves and two fish. A larger building with magnificent mosaics was built in the vicinity in the fifth century. Stefano De Luca has recently emphasized that the church buildings at the site were closely connected to the adjacent structures and that the building complex as a whole is the first attestation of monastic life in Galilee.[109] The circumstances in this part of eastern Galilee were different from many neighbouring areas because Capernaum and Tabgha seem to have been the only rural Christian settlements in this still predominantly Jewish region throughout Late Antiquity.[110] The evidence that we have for this area by the Sea of Galilee speaks of a gradual and limited spread of Christianity that took place, to the best of our knowledge, peacefully.[111]

We do not have any direct evidence, literary or archaeological, that could clarify how emergent Christian communities in Tabgha and in Capernaum interacted with their surrounding Jewish communities. The archaeological evidence speaks for the relative prosperity of these sites, evidenced for instance by the churches in Capernaum and in Tabgha and their richly decorated mosaic floors.[112]

---

106 Andrew S. Jacobs, 'Visible Ghosts and Invisible Demons: The Place of Jews in Early Christian Terra Sancta', in *Galilee through the Centuries*, Eric M. Meyers (ed.): 375.
107 Cf. Limor, '"Holy Journey"': 332; Yizhar Hirschfeld, 'The Monasteries of Palestine in the Byzantine Period', in *Christians and Christianity*, Limor and Stroumsa (eds): 410.
108 Virgilio C. Corbo, *Cafarnao I: Gli Edifici Della Città* (Jerusalem: Franciscan Printing Press, 1975): 26–111; Runesson, 'Architecture': 240–4.
109 De Luca, 'Vorgeschichte': 38–44. As De Luca mentions, other examples of early monasteries in the region include the complex in Magdala (fifth/sixth centuries to eighth century) and at Kursi on the eastern side of the Sea of Galilee (sixth century). An urban monastery was built in Tiberias during the reign of Justinian I (527–567), see Hirschfeld, 'The Monasteries': 406.
110 For the distribution of Christian sites in Galilee, see Mordechai Aviam, *Jews, Pagans and Christians in the Galilee: 25 Years of Archaeological Excavations and Surveys, Hellenistic to Byzantine Periods* (Rochester, NY: University of Rochester Press and Institute for Galilean Archaeology, 2004): 9–21. The landscape in the surroundings of Capernaum and Tabgha was totally different from the rural western Galilee, where there is abundant evidence of Christian churches and monasteries in Late Antiquity (ibid: 181–204). See also Jacob Ashkenazi and Mordechai Aviam, 'Monasteries, Monks, and Villages in Western Galilee in Late Antiquity', *JLA* 5 (2013): 293–331.
111 For example, we do not have any examples in Galilee of the violent conversion of synagogues into churches. This policy is attested archaeologically in places such as Stobi, Gerasa and Apamea, see Levine, *The Ancient Synagogue*: 211.
112 For Capernaum, see Corbo, *Cafarnao*: 43–5; for Tabgha, De Luca, 'Vorgeschichte': 41–2.

164 *Raimo Hakola*

The similarities between Byzantine church and synagogue mosaics have often been noticed, and scholars have asked whether the artisans representing the same workshops or using similar pattern books could have been used both by Jewish and Christian communities.[113]

The sources of wealth generation for these remote Galilean Christian pilgrim sites are still unclear and can be assessed only in light of relevant parallel material. Stefano De Luca has suggested that there are signs in Tabgha that members of this monastic community were involved in small-scale agricultural production, evidenced in other monastic sites in Palestine, even though the main source of income was most probably connected to Christian pilgrimage.[114] Yizhar Hirschfeld has described how the monasteries provided pilgrims with physical and spiritual services and, at the same time, often benefited directly from the pilgrims' work contributions and donations.[115] Many Christian pilgrims belonged to the wealthy upper class, and it is fully possible that the economic boost brought by the influx of these pilgrims was not limited to the monasteries but benefited the local population on a larger scale.[116] Hagith Sivan, referring to the co-existence of the synagogue and the Christian pilgrimage church in Capernaum, suggests that 'in the first half of the sixth century a general state of prosperity was pre-eminently responsible for moments of conciliation . . . [and] pilgrimage assumed a conciliatory function'.[117] The large body of rabbinic evidence refers to permanent and periodic markets, merchants, various craftsmen and so forth in both urban and rural contexts, and these references suggest that Galilean villages were well integrated into larger Byzantine trade networks.[118] It is also likely that local Christian pilgrim communities participated in these networks which provided a venue for the interaction between these communities and their larger, predominantly Jewish, surroundings.

---

113 Levine, *The Ancient Synagogue*: 230. Cf. also Zeev Weiss, *The Sepphoris Synagogue: Deciphering an Ancient Message through Its Archaeological and Socio-Historical Contexts* (Jerusalem: IES, 2005): 170: 'It seems that the figural style of the Sepphoris [synagogue] mosaic bore some of the stylistic trends prevailing in the Byzantine mosaics, such as those from Khirbet el-Murrassas, the Leontis House, and Tabgha which are dated to the second half of the fifth and early sixth centuries CE.' For artists and their workshops, see Hachlili, *Ancient Synagogues*: 473–515.
114 De Luca, 'Vorgeschichte': 43–4. De Luca draws on parallel material for agricultural practices in monastic settings in Palestine from Nina Heiska, 'The Economy and Livelihoods of the Early Christian Monasteries in Palestine' (Master Thesis, University of Helsinki, Institute for Cultural Research, Archaeology, 2003): 37–48.
115 Hirschfeld, 'The Monasteries': 410.
116 Taylor, *Christians*: 338.
117 Sivan, Palestine: 47.
118 Thus Sharon Lea Mattila, 'Inner Village Life in Galilee: A Diverse and Complex Phenomenon', in *Galilee in the Late Second Temple and Mishnaic Periods, Volume 1: Life, Culture and Society*, David A. Fiensy and James R. Strange (eds) (Minneapolis: Fortress Press, 2014): 312–45. See also Ben-Zion Rosenfeld and Joseph Menirav, *Markets and Marketing in Roman Palestine* (JSJSup 99. Leiden: Brill, 2005).

Conclusion

As I remarked at the beginning of this chapter, we must rest our reconstructions of Jewish and Christian communities in late antique Galilee on limited and mostly indirect literary and archaeological evidence. There have emerged two quite opposite ways to envision Jewish–Christian relations in Galilee. Mordechai Aviam emphasizes the strict boundaries between Jewish and Christian areas of settlements and interprets the available evidence in light of 'Jewish-Christian conflict' or 'Jewish–Christian antagonism'.[119] My review of recent scholarship dealing with Jewish–Christian relations in the ancient world suggests, however, that these relations were not only characterized by conflict and mutual hostility. This recent scholarly trend lends support to Eric Meyers, who sees Jewish and Christian communities in Galilee as living side by side with each other and remarks that 'we would be making a great mistake if we were to think of Jews and Christians only as enemies'.[120]

In light of this discussion, I would like to nuance the view that emphasizes the coexistence of Jewish and Christian communities in Galilee. My conclusion is that despite the rhetoric of separation evident in many written sources, various kinds of interactions took place between Jewish and Christian communities. Recent theoretical discussions emphasize how both individual and group identities are flexible and adaptable to changing circumstances. The members of one group that in some contexts defines itself as completely distinct from other groups, may in different contexts interact with members of their rival groups in many ways. I suggest that local Jewish and Christian communities in late antique Galilee cherished their particular traditions by constructing for themselves specific spaces that set them apart from the rest of the society and in this way reinforced their collective identity. These buildings, synagogues and pilgrim churches, may share much in the details of their art and architecture, but they also epitomize the need of these communities to present themselves as different from one another. Just as literary sources echo the rhetoric of separation and one-sidedly give voice to antagonism and separation, distinct Christian and Jewish holy places probably draw an incomplete portrait of relations between Jews and Christians in Galilee. Members of these communities may have felt unthreatened when they gathered in their sanctuaries, but as soon as they stepped outside of their own communities' buildings, they were exposed to a more diverse social reality where they interacted with their neighbours in a variety of ways.

---

119 Cf. Mordechai Aviam, 'Christian Galilee in the Byzantine Period', in *Galilee through the Centuries*, Eric M. Meyers (ed.): 281–300; *Jews, Pagans and Christians*: 316–17. For example, Aviam suggests that the octagonal church in Capernaum and the monastery in Kursi were surrounded by walls to 'guard' these sites in predominantly Jewish surroundings ('Christian Galilee': 282, 298).

120 Meyers, 'Living Side by Side': 150.

9 Performing the Sacred in a Community Building

Observations from the 2010–2015 Kinneret Regional Project Excavations in the Byzantine Synagogue of Horvat Kur (Galilee)[1]

Jürgen K. Zangenberg

Making the Sacred Concrete

'The Sacred' – a Difficult Category

Ever since Rudolf Otto declared 'the sacred' a central category in Religious Studies and defined it as *fascinosum tremens*, as pious awe in the face of the overwhelming experience of the numinous, 'the sacred' has remained a category that proves very difficult to grasp – especially as far as material culture studies are concerned. How could something 'totally different', an emotional experience 'wholly of its own kind', as Otto put it, in the end be detected, described and compared without losing its very essence?[2]

And yet, we all know that there is hardly any human expression independent of material aspects. Prayers may be uttered in private without any fellow-human listening, but they can be engraved onto stone and become tangible; liturgy is celebrated in a moment of time, but the room housing the liturgical performances reflects their pragmatic and intellectual implications and remains 'real' even after active celebration is over. In that respect, the 'sacred' has an irresistible tendency to become 'material' by using objects and spaces from the material world as a means of expression. Religion as a set of convictions, values and rituals through which humans relate to 'the sacred' cannot exist without objects and spaces created and shaped by and according to these convictions, values or rituals.

---

1 I thank my many colleagues and students (and students who became colleagues) from Kinneret Regional Project who excavated and discussed the fascinating finds from 'the small village on a hill'. I am especially grateful to my friends from Helsinki University for inviting me to the fruitful and stimulating conference at quiet and peaceful Tvärminne. Needless to say that stratigraphic assumptions in particular are still preliminary, as analysis is still underway.
2 Rudolf Otto, *Das Heilige: Über das Irrationale in der Idee des Göttlichen und sein Verhältnis zum Rationalen* (Breslau: Trewendt & Granier, 1917; reprint München, 2004).

Fortunately enough, modern sociology, archaeology and religious studies have long realized the importance of the 'material' for performing the 'sacred' and reconstructing past expressions of it. Even if we might not be able to grasp 'the Holy itself' in Otto's sense, we might nevertheless detect its traces in the material and historical world – which I would like to call 'the sacred'. The 'sacred' might keep a distance from the material world by its aspirations to transcend it, but it is never separated from it. In myriads of ways, 'the sacred' remains connected with 'the profane'. It needs the world in order to be revealed.

Some time ago, Jonathan Z. Smith correctly emphasized the social context of relating to 'the sacred' in the world of the profane. Steven Fine picks that up and writes: '(T)he sacrality of a place is not static and metahistorical, but rather is determined by the society that construes it to be holy.'[3] Holiness is communication with and about a reality that is connected but not identical to the visible world, but this 'world' is not something theoretical or general, it is performed by and within specific groups of people. In addition to that, Lawrence Hoffman has shown that 'liturgy' is much more than following a textually prescribed and interpreted performance. The space that surrounds 'liturgy' is equally important, i.e. the way it is structured, decorated and used bears significance and carries meaning and therefore needs our attention.[4]

In his magisterial study Peter Brown has described how actions and objects can create an aura of 'sanctity' when they are joined together in a meaningful way:

> In a Late Antique church, the processional movements, the heavy silver of the sacred vessels and the binding of the gospel books as they flashed by on their way to the altar, the mysterious opacity of the curtains shrouding the entrance ... these things themselves were the visual 'triggers' of a Late Antique worshipper's sense of majesty. Indeed, it is in such terms that Late Antique sources describe their churches ... They are *ho topos*, the 'place' where it was possible to share for a moment in the eternal repose of the saints in paradise.[5]

Steve Fine and many others have shown how synagogues were construed as holy places in a similar way to churches, creating a sort of *heiliges Gesamtkunstwerk*. Instead of relics and saints, however, the Torah and the gathering of the community represented 'the Holy's presence', which in turn also made the synagogue a

---

3 Steven Fine, *This Holy Place: On the Sanctity of the Synagogue during the Greco-Roman Period* (Notre Dame: University Press, 1997): 9–10 on Jonathan Z. Smith, *Map Is Not Territory: Studies in the History of Religion* (Leiden: Brill, 1978): 291–3.
4 Lawrence A. Hoffman, *Beyond the Text: A Holistic Approach to Liturgy* (Bloomington and Indianapolis: University of Indiana Press, 1989); Chad S. Spigel, *Ancient Synagogue Seating Capacities: Methodology, Analysis and Limits* (TSAJ 149; Tübingen: Mohr Siebeck, 2012): 27–8.
5 Peter Brown, *Art and Society in Late Antiquity* (Berkeley and Los Angeles: University of California Press, 1982): 25.

'holy place'.[6] Synagogues, too, demonstrate that 'the sacred' is not a given, but that it is perceived and performed by human agents in space and time.[7]

To describe how that worked and what it looked like in one particular instance is the purpose of this chapter. The basis for my considerations is recent results from the excavations conducted by Kinneret Regional Project in the Byzantine-period synagogue at Horvat Kur, roughly 2 km northwest of the Lake of Galilee.[8] The synagogue was excavated in four subsequent campaigns between 2010 and 2013, and a study season in 2014 allowed us to start the first analyses and interpretations. Although the synagogue was not found to be as well preserved as many others in the region, like Capernaum or Chorazin, several objects, as well as architectural and decorative features, provided us with valuable information about how the building was constructed and functioned as a 'holy space' in its village context.

The Synagogue at Horvat Kur, Galilee: Location of the Site and History of Research

Horvat Kur is located *c.* 2 km northwest of the Lake of Galilee, in an area apparently dotted with villages and synagogues in antiquity. It can be assumed that the area was predominately inhabited by Jews during the period relevant to our site. The ancient name of the village located on Horvat Kur is not known, aerial photographs revealed that the ancient village might have covered an area of about 3 ha during its most prosperous period. So far, only a few sherds in later fills were found that dated to the Bronze Age, Iron Age I and II or Late Hellenistic periods, suggesting that there was some habitation of unknown character on the hill. A substantial pocket of fill in a natural crack in the bedrock adjacent to the southern synagogue comes from the Early Roman period, possibly indicating the time when the village was founded.

According to the current state of architectural analysis carried out during the 2014 Kinneret Regional Project study season, the synagogue at Horvat Kur had five phases. After a pre-synagogue occupation, probably comprising several

---

6 Fine, *Holy Place*: 59: 'The Tannaim considered whatever sanctity was ascribed to synagogues to derive from the sacred books that were stored and studied in synagogues. . . . The Tannaim were careful that synagogues not become replacements for the Temple. While sanctity within the synagogue was an established fact, this holiness was to be "ordinary" in comparison to that of the Temple.' As Fine is able to show in the course of his study, the process of sanctification of the synagogue was later intensified.

7 See also Lee I. Levine, *Visual Judaism in Late Antiquity: Historical Contexts of Jewish Art* (New Haven and London: Yale University Press, 2012): 354–9.

8 On the synagogue at Horvat Kur see the latest reports by Jürgen K. Zangenberg, 'Ein Dorf auf dem Hügel: Neue Entdeckungen des Kinneret Regional Project in der Synagoge von Horvat Kur, Galiläa', in *Bauern, Fischer und Propheten: Galiläa zur Zeit Jesu*, Jürgen K. Zangenberg and Jens Schröter (eds) (Mainz: Von Zabern, 2012): 131–44 (on the site see p. 132, Fig. 2) and Jürgen K. Zangenberg, Stefan Münger, Raimo Hakola and Byron R. McCane, 'The Kinneret Regional Project Excavations of a Byzantine Synagogue at Horvat Kur, Galilee, 2010–2013: A Preliminary Report', *HeBAI* 2 (2013): 557–76. The preliminary stratigraphy presented here was worked out by project architect Annalize Rheeder with the help of Tine Rassalle, Rick Bonnie, Lise den Hertog, Byron McCane and Raimo Hakola. For regular updates see www.kinneret-excavations.org (accessed 22 January 2016).

Figure 9.1 Aerial photograph of synagogue at the end of the 2013 campaign (© Skyview Ltd. and Kinneret Regional Project)

sub-phases (pre-synagogue Phase 1), the first synagogue was built shortly before 400 CE (Phase 2). After severe damage, probably caused by an earthquake, a new synagogue was built (Phase 3). During this first phase of the basilical-broadhouse synagogue built ca. 450 CE a portico was added west of the western wall, benches were built along the interior faces of the walls and the large *bemah* attached to the southern wall. Very shortly after CE 600 the building was rebuilt again and more low benches were inserted between the columns to increase seating capacity (Phase 4). All following a basilical broadhouse type, synagogue Phases 2–4 are closely connected to each other and provide the subject of this chapter. The synagogue apparently went out of use and was abandoned sometime in the second half of the seventh century CE. There are indications that the area was used later by very low-scale habitation, but this is very difficult to date (post-synagogue Phase 5). Only very few remains in unsealed fills close to the topsoil securely date to the Umayyad period. The synagogue was intensively robbed sometime during the Ayyubid / Crusader period.[9]

The following observations will demonstrate *how* the local community created and organized the 'sacred space' at Horvat Kur by reconstructing functions and hierarchies that community members apparently wished to see expressed during liturgical service.

---

9 I am hereby correcting previous publications.

The Synagogue

An Exceptional Place

At least since Phase 2, the synagogue at Horvat Kur could be distinguished as an exceptional building in various ways.

a   Like many, but not all, contemporary synagogues, the one at Horvat Kur was erected in a particularly prominent location.[10] Though very little is known yet about the structure of the surrounding village,[11] the synagogue is located close to the hill's steep slopes to the north and east, making the building easily visible from almost all directions. On the south a piazza and to the west a portico further emphasized the building's monumentality. In that regard, the location of the Horvat Kur synagogue is nicely in line with Tannaitic tradition (*Midrash Tanhuma* 3:475)[12].

b   The fact that the Horvat Kur synagogue had a tiled roof and probably was higher than the domestic units around it, further underlines the synagogue's prominence. No other buildings have so far been identified on Horvat Kur as having been covered by a tiled roof.

c   The layout of the Horvat Kur synagogue is quite remarkable. During building Phases 2–4, the synagogue measured *c.* 16.5 m east–west and *c.* 11 m north–south. Internally it is divided up into a nave and two aisles by two rows of columns running north–south. The main entrance apparently opened to the west; there was a smaller door to the south. At least in Phases 2–4, the synagogue at Horvat Kur, therefore, shows a rather rare combination of a basilica-like layout with a 'broadhouse type' – like, for example, the synagogues at Khirbet Shema' or Nabratein I in the Galilee, Horvat Rimmon I in the Shephelah or Eshtemoa and Khirbet Susya in Judaea.[13]

The long southern wall was clearly the liturgically significant part of the synagogue.[14] Like the vast majority of the northern synagogues in Byzantine period Israel, the one at Horvat Kur was oriented south towards Jerusalem and not

---

10 Cf. e.g. the synagogues at Khirbet Shema' or Meron. On preferred locations for synagogues see Lee I. Levine, *The Ancient Synagogue: The First Thousand Years* (second edition; New Haven and London: Yale University Press, 2005): 314–16.

11 Only a very small amount of domestic architecture was excavated at Horvat Kur in 2010, see Jürgen K. Zangenberg and Stefan Münger, 'Horbat Kur: Preliminary Report', in *HA/ESI* 123 (2011). Available online at http://www.hadashot-esi.org.il/report_detail_eng.aspx?id=1746&mag_id=118, accessed 25 January 2016.

12 Fine, *Holy Place*: 93.

13 Fine, *Holy Place*: 107–8, Rachel Hachlili, *Ancient Synagogues – Archaeology and Art: New Discoveries and Current Research* (Handbook of Oriental Studies 1/105; Leiden and Boston: Brill, 2013): 58 (on Horvat Rimmon I): 73 (on Khirbet Shema') and 117–18 (on Eshtemoa and Khirbet Susya).

14 See Hachlili, *Ancient Synagogues*: 205–6.

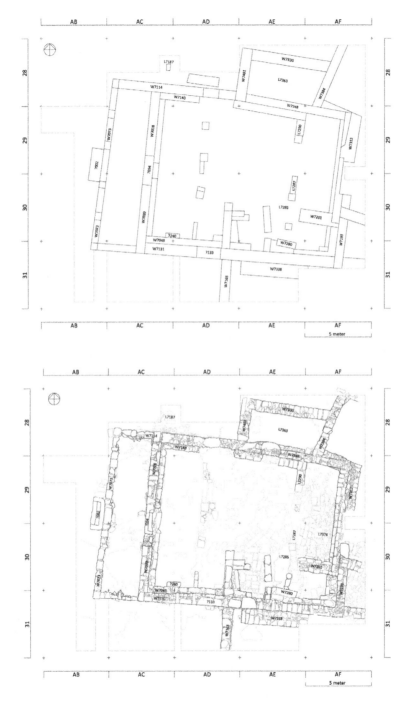

Figure 9.2 a and b Plan of synagogue (drawing by A. Rheeder: © Kinneret Regional Project) – a) schematic plan b) stone plan

eastwards towards the rising sun like many pagan temples or churches. That by itself was a 'powerful statement of its religious and ethnic distinctiveness'.[15] But unlike elsewhere,[16] only a single, remarkably narrow, single-winged entrance is located in the southern wall.[17] It is supplemented by another, wider double-winged entrance in the western wall. The latter entrance, not the one in the southern wall, seems to have provided the main access to the synagogue, perhaps directly connecting it to the centre of the village on the flat hilltop further west. With such an arrangement, the synagogue at Horvat Kur is quite unique among the synagogues in Galilee or the Golan. It again demonstrates that synagogue architecture never followed any 'standard' models, but was to a very large extent dependent upon the given topography and local needs and means.[18]

Architecture and Decoration

In addition to location, size and layout, the synagogue at Horvat Kur (Phases 2–4) significantly differs from 'normal' domestic buildings in its architectural and decorative elements. Unfortunately, only very few parts of the original decoration have been found reasonably well preserved at Horvat Kur; much was found *ex situ*, contained in fills.[19]

A most obvious testimony of the public character of the building in Horvat Kur Area A are numerous dressed and decorated building stones. Not only were the exteriors of the walls nicely cut and smoothed out (especially on the western and southern sides), many more architectural pieces featuring cornices and other forms of Hellenistic decorative masonry were found in fills.[20]

Mosaics belonged to the standard decoration of many Galilean synagogues, some of them displaying patterns imitating floor textiles, others showing figurative scenes, symbols or inscriptions.[21] At Horvat Kur, a small patch of a mosaic was discovered *in situ* in the south-eastern corner of the synagogue at the end of the 2013 campaign. Closer examination of that patch during the 2014 study season revealed the edge of a wavy line embedded in a white area, perhaps marking

---

15 Levine, *Visual Judaism*: 355–6 (355).
16 The synagogues at Khorazim and Capernaum, for example, feature three monumental entrances in the southern wall, and the side entrance is considerably less prominent.
17 See Hachlili, *Ancient Synagogues*: 133–6 on the monumental entrances in the respective liturgically significant walls at most other synagogues.
18 Hachlili, *Ancient Synagogues*: 205–6.
19 Jürgen K. Zangenberg, Stefan Münger, Raimo Hakola, Rick Bonnie and Patrick Wyssmann, 'Horvat Kur. Kinneret Regional Project – The 2011 Season', *HA /ESI* 125 (2013). Available online at http://www.hadashot-esi.org.il/report_detail_eng.aspx?id=2230&mag_id=120, accessed 25 January 2016; Zangenberg, Münger, Hakola and McCane, 'Excavations': 565–7.
20 These fragments are currently being studied by KRP team members Ulla Tervahauta and Annalize Rheeder.
21 See in general Hachlili, *Ancient Synagogues*: 251–73; Rina Talgam, *Mosaics of Faith: Floors of Pagans, Jews, Samaritans, Christians and Muslims in the Holy Land* (Jerusalem: Yad Ben-Zvi and University Park: Pennsylvania State University Press, 2014): especially 257–332.

the fringe of a *tesserae* carpet ('guilloche'). Apart from this single patch *in situ*, over 70,000 mostly single *tesserae* in white, black, grey, brown or buff had been found in fills in or around the synagogue in various amounts during the previous seasons. The vast majority of them came from layers that created the secondary floor of the veranda in Phase 3, running along the synagogue's western wall.[22] Finally, during the 2015 campaign this mosaic patch *in situ* was systematically cleaned and a large fragment of a mosaic panel appeared, showing the upper part of a menorah and an Aramaic inscription above it.[23] Since the mosaic was pierced by a column belonging to Phase 2, it must belong to one of the earlier phases currently combined under the label 'Phase 1' and can therefore be ignored in this chapter. Neither the exact architectural context of the mosaic, nor its absolute date (*c.* CE 400?) can be established with any confidence at the moment.

Finally, small pieces of painted wall plaster showing red, green and possibly also yellow hues indicate that the synagogue's interior was not only (at least partly) whitewashed.[24]

Ritual Separation Between Outside and Inside: Two Basins

That a synagogue is not a place like any other, of course, becomes evident when we look at the behaviour required from people who wish to enter it or are already *in* it (see, for example, *t. Meg.* 2:18). An especially sensitive place, of course, is the entrance, the place where the demarcation line between inside and outside can be crossed.[25]

During excavations in 2010, two fragmented water basins were found at Horvat Kur, both, however, unfortunately *ex situ*. Both basins were made of a single piece of bright local limestone and consisted of a straight, round, stumpy foot and a flat water receptacle surrounded by a curved lip; neither of the basins had ears, handles or ledges. One of them (registration number 15830/1; KRP data base photographs 1010751 and 1010752) came to light as part of a late fill including many other architectural fragments just outside the north-western corner of the veranda in Area A (square B29: probably a dump of architectural pieces piled

---

22 See the veranda on Fig. 7 in Zangenberg, 'Dorf': 135.
23 On the situation up to 2014 see Zangenberg, Münger, Hakola and McCane, 'Excavations': 560–62 and 570–71. A brief report on the 2015 discovery can be found at http://kinneret-excavations.org/?p=1788, accessed 22 January 2016; see also *Bible History Daily* at http://www.biblicalarchaeology.org/daily/ancient-cultures/ancient-israel/magnificent-menorah-mosaic-found-in-galilee/, accessed 22 January 2016. A preliminary publication on the mosaic is currently in preparation. Kinneret Regional Project wishes to thank Orna Cohen for her careful work to expose the mosaic, and appreciates the support from Gideon Avni and his colleagues (IAA), as well as David Mevorakh and his team (IMJ) during excavation, transport and conservation. The mosaic is now being cleaned and restored in the Israel Museum, Jerusalem.
24 See the painted plaster fragments in Fig. 11 in Zangenberg, Münger, Hakola, Bonnie and Wyssmann, 'The 2011 Season'; on wall paintings in synagogues in general see Hachlili, *Ancient Synagogues*: 249–50.
25 Levine, *Synagogue*: 335–7 on synagogue entrances as areas of demarcation.

up by the stone robbers and covered by loose fill). The basin's foot was nearly undamaged and measured 74 cm from the bottom of the foot to the inner surface of the basin's water receptacle. The sides of the receptacle, however, were almost totally broken off and only preserved to a width of 40 cm.

The other basin was found reused as an installation in the courtyard of the larger house in Area C (registration number 16364/1; KRP data base photographs 1010776 and 1010777).[26] Like the specimen from Area A, basin 16364/1 was heavily damaged and preserved to a depth of 40 cm, a width of 59 cm and a height of 54 cm. Both basins have a very characteristic shape consisting of a flat, circular laver with a lip/edge around it (*labrum*) and a mushroom-like foot with round diameter – all hewn from one single block of stone and roughly dressed.

Interestingly enough, a similar object comes from the neighbouring synagogue at Wadi Hamam some 15 km to the south of Horvat Kur.[27] It was found approximately 10 m southeast of the main entrance and may originally have been set up at the synagogue entrance to serve worshippers for purification before entering the synagogue.[28] Though the two specimens from Horvat Kur were found in less clear contexts than the one from Wadi Hamam, their physical similarity (shape, material) suggests they all fulfilled a very similar function.

Installations for purification are already known from late Second Temple period synagogues. Next to the much better known *miqva'ot* for full immersion,[29] small basins of various shapes and locations (*gornah*) were used for washing hands, feet and perhaps also the face. Rachel Hachlili has mentioned such basins from Gamla and Jericho,[30] but they were built up of stones and plaster. The single-piece lavers

---

26 See the basin from Area C *in situ* on Fig. 7 in Jürgen K. Zangenberg and Stefan Münger, 'Preliminary Report'.
27 On the synagogue at Wadi Hamam see, for the time being, Uzi Leibner, 'Excavations at Khirbet Wadi Hamam (Lower Galilee): The Synagogue and the Settlement,' *JRA* 23 (2010): 220–37. Leibner dates the Hamam synagogue to the third century CE, considerably earlier than the first Phase of the Kur synagogue.
28 Kinneret Regional Project and the author of the present chapter wish to thank Uzi Leibner who discussed many aspects of the Horvat Kur synagogue with us and supplied valuable information on the basins at Hamam and Kur. Uzi Leibner will shortly publish on the basin from Wadi Hamam. See also Levine, *Synagogue*: 331f on the location of water basins in general.
29 On *miqva'ot* see for example Jürgen K. Zangenberg, 'Pure Stone: Archaeological Evidence for Jewish Purity Practices in Late Second Temple Judaism (Miqwa'ot, Stone Vessels)', in *Purity and the Forming of Religious Traditions in the Ancient Mediterranean World and Ancient Judaism*, Christian Frevel and Christophe Nihan (eds); (DHR 3; Leiden and Boston: Brill, 2013): 537–72 (541–5) with ample references.
30 Hachlili, *Ancient Synagogues*: 27 and 42–4; see the discussion in Danny Syon and Zvi Yavor, *Gamla II: The Architecture. The Shmarya Gutmann Excavations, 1976–1989* (IAA Reports 44; Jerusalem: Israel Antiquities Authority, 2010): 53–4; Yuval Yannai, 'The Gorna – A Basin from Beth She'an', in *The 12th World Congress of Jewish Studies: Division B: The History of the Jewish People*, Ron Margolin (ed.) (Jerusalem: Magness Press, 1999): 61–9 (Hebrew). A similar plastered, but probably later basin was found in En-Gedi. Zvi Safrai, 'The Communal Function of the Synagogue in the Land of the Israel in the Rabbinic Period', in *Ancient Synagogues: Historical*

Figure 9.3 Stone basin found in secondary use as installation in Area C (© Kinneret Regional Project, reg. nr. 16364/1, database photo nr. 1010777)

from Horvat Kur and Wadi Hamam, however, look quite different and can be dated to a much later period (fifth century at least regarding Horvat Kur). Written sources suggest that washing hands and feet was already common practice among Jews before the rise of Islam. According to a tradition from the Byzantine or early Muslim period, ablutions before entering the synagogue safeguard its holiness: 'The ancients decreed in all synagogue courtyards that lavers of living water for the sanctification of hands and feet (be set up).'[31]

Analysis and Archaeological Discovery, Dan Urman and Paul Virgil McCracken Flesher (eds) (StPB 47; Leiden, Boston and Köln: Brill, 1998): 181–204 (184 and n. 14) supplies additional information.

31 Fine, *Holy Place*: 82–3 (quoting *Hilkhot Eretz-Israel*). Various types of *labra* are discussed in Levine, *Synagogue*: 330–37; P. Sanders (ed.) *Judaism: Practice and Belief 63 B.C.E.–66 C.E.* (London: SCM; Philadelphia: Trinity Press International, 1992): 222–30 illuminates the theological background. A passage in *y. Meg.* 3,4 74a mentions a basin in a synagogue at Bet-Shean for washing hands and legs; see also Meir Bar Ilan, 'Washing Feet Before Prayer: Moslem Influence or an Ancient Jewish Custom', *Mahanaim* 1 (1991): 162–9 (Hebrew).

But water basins are no Jewish invention and were not infrequent in other ancient religious or profane contexts.[32] Large, footed basins similar to the ones at Horvat Kur or Wadi Hamam were, for example, set up in an *atrium* or forecourt as decoration in baths or private houses; others allowed visitors to wash their hands and feet when coming from the street and before entering a house.[33] A famous example for a large stone *labrum* consisting of a wide, circular basin and a short round foot is still visible in the men's *caldarium* in the Forum Baths at Pompeii. In public as well as private spaces, *labra* were made of precious materials such as marble or bronze and were much more than solely functional objects.[34] On the basis of these observations, it seems possible that the *labra* from Horvat Kur were once set up in front of each entrance, or perhaps both were in the veranda on the western side of the synagogue which might have served as a kind of *atrium*.

Hierarchical Seating

In a world that was so profoundly guided by rituals and manifestations of status as the ancient Mediterranean, seating is a highly symbolic act. How and where people sat conveyed a significant message; it made relationships among groups and people visible to insiders as well as to outsiders. That, however, has not always received necessary attention. In his dissertation *Ancient Synagogue Seating Capacities*, Chad S. Spigel rightly criticizes the 'unhistorical nature of viewing the archaeological remains of synagogue buildings as empty spaces: What is empty today was once filled with furniture and people.'[35]

It is therefore highly significant, and a fortunate gift of archaeology, that several forms of seating were preserved in Horvat Kur synagogue Phases 2–4. With its broad, spacious interior, the synagogue offered room not only for religious celebrations, but also for many other occasions that required the presence of as many villagers as possible. Three different areas for seating are offered: the floor,

---

32 Levine, *Synagogue*: 333.
33 The most famous is perhaps the large basin in the *atrium* at Sardeis; see Levine, *Synagogue*: 331–2.
34 See for example Garrett G. Fagan, *Bathing in Public in the Roman World* (Ann Arbor: University of Michigan Press, 1999): 174–7 with Fig. 10–12; A. Trevor Hodge, *Roman Aqueducts and Water Supply* (London: Duckworth, 1999): 330 on private, garden contexts. A good example for a basin quite similar to the ones from Horvat Kur and Wadi Hamam is the fourth century *mithraeum* in Saarburg (Lorraine, France): 'a stone vase, height 45 cm, with narrow base and broad belly, its rim, diameter 18 cm, carrying two ears' was found directly in front of the Cautopates figure flanking the large cult relief showing Mithras slaying the bull, see Vivienne J. Walters, *The Cult of Mithras in the Roman Provinces of Gaul* (EPRO 81; Leiden: Brill, 1974): 19; on the Mithraeum see Friedrich von Fisenne, 'Das Mithräum zu Saarburg in Lothringen: Bericht über die Ausgrabungen im Sommer 1895', *JGLGA* 8 (1896): 119–75, available online at via https://archive.org/stream/jahrbuchdergesel08gese/jahrbuchdergesel08gese_djvu.txt, accessed September 2014.
35 Spigel, *Synagogue Seating*: 11–12 taking up observations from Steven Fine, *Art and Judaism in the Greco-Roman World: Toward a New Jewish Archaeology* (Cambridge: University Press, 2005): 167; Levine, *Synagogue*: 337–41. Steven Fine, 'Furnishing God's Study House: An Exercise in Rabbinic Imagination', in id., *Art, History and the Historiography of Judaism in Roman Antiquity* (BRLJ 34; Leiden: Brill, 2014): 139–59.

the benches and a single stone seat. According to the current state of analysis, the synagogue did not yet have any benches in Phase 2; they were only added when the synagogue had to be rebuilt (Phase 3). More low benches were inserted in the course of subsequent repairs (Phase 4).

The Floor

The floor certainly is the most obvious, but perhaps also the most frequently overlooked, 'space' in a synagogue[36] – unless it carries a mosaic. But art-historical considerations alone are not enough to understand the role of a synagogue floor. At least equally important is the functional aspect, namely the fact that the floor constitutes the largest interior space available to accommodate (parts of) the congregation. Even if there were benches along the walls, most worshippers in a synagogue simply gathered on the floor, resting on mats, rugs or carpets spread out on the surface. Theoretically, worshippers could also have sat on wooden benches set up across the interior space of the synagogue,[37] but no marks, dents or other traces of the use of such benches were identified on the floor at Horvat Kur.

Several layers of grey plaster covered the floor in Phases 2–4. Plaster floors are quite rare in Galilean synagogues. Though Nabratein I is not the only other example with a plaster pavement next to Horvat Kur,[38] mosaic or stone slab / cobble stone floors are much more common. Patches and areas of repair show that the plaster floor at Horvat Kur was used over a considerable time until the synagogue's final destruction.

The Benches

As in many other contemporaneous synagogues,[39] benches ran along the interior face of the western, northern and southern walls at Horvat Kur from Phase 3

---

36 Spigel, *Synagogue Seating*: 38–42. In a forthcoming article I will apply Spigel's methodology to the seating facilities at Horvat Kur and present a calculation of their capacity.
37 Levine, *Synagogue*: 337–8.
38 So Hachlili, *Ancient Synagogues*: 250–51; apart from Nabratein I, which Hachlili mentions, Nabratein II (Eric M. Meyers and Carol L. Meyers, *Excavations at Ancient Nabratein: Synagogue and Environs* [Meiron Excavation Project Reports 6; Winona Lake: Eisenbrauns, 2009]: 35–8 and 48) and Khirbet Shema' patches of plaster floor from Synagogue I were found in front of the benches (Eric M. Meyers, A. Thomas Kraabel and James F. Strange, *Ancient Synagogue Excavations at Khirbet Shema', Upper Galilee, Israel 1970–1972* (AASOR 42; Durham: Duke University Press, 1976): 36–7, traces of a plaster floor on top of irregularly laid out pavers (bedding?) were also found at Gush Halav, see Eric M. Meyers, Carol L. Meyers and James F. Strange, *Excavations at the Ancient Synagogue of Gush Halav* (Meiron Excavation Project Reports 5; Winona Lake: Eisenbrauns, 1990): 79 and also the synagogue at Meiron may have been paved with a plaster floor but this is uncertain (Eric M. Meyers, James F. Strange and Carol L. Meyers, *Excavations at Ancient Meiron, Upper Galilee, Israel 1971–72, 1974–75, 1977* (Meiron Excavation Project Reports 3; Cambridge: ASOR, 1981): 10. This topic will be further elaborated in the forthcoming Final Report on the synagogue at Horvat Kur.
39 Spigel, *Synagogue Seating*: 38–42; Hachlili, *Ancient Synagogues*: 149–51.

onwards, only to be interrupted at both entrances, in the centre of the northern wall and where the *bemah* was attached to the southern wall.[40] Usually, the bench was one course high (on average c. 30–50 cm from the floor) and c. 30–40 cm deep. On the eastern wall, however, two rows of seats above each other were provided, but with some reduced depth of c. 25–30 cm. Only to the east of the *bemah*, the depth of the bench was doubled to c. 80 cm by laying a column flat down on the floor along the edge of the bench, creating some sort of platform which may or may not have been used for seating.

During Phase 4, the benches lining the interior wall remained and were supplemented by low building blocks (mostly *spolia*) inserted between the column bases supporting the roof between nave and aisles. Since none of these two lines was preserved above a single course, there are good reasons to assume that these structures did not serve as 'stylobate walls' closing off the aisles from the nave (as initially thought),[41] but indeed functioned as low benches that provided additional seating capacity for the congregation. The insertion of more benches clearly demonstrates an increase in demand for seating space. Does that indicate a rise of population in the village, or a change in function for the synagogue? In any case, the benches between the columns were very badly preserved, the western line especially was only recognizable as robber trenches, created when parts of the bench were broken out from the floor.

For the sages, apparently, different areas and levels of sanctity existed in a synagogue. Rabbinical texts mention benches (*safsal*) and couches (*qaltara*) in synagogues (*b. Meg.* 26b) and distinguish their 'holiness' from, for example, that of the ark.[42] Other traditions may indicate that not everybody was allowed to sit on a bench, but that they were reserved for elders, but that is not entirely clear.[43] Given the fact that in Horvat Kur the available benches offered much less seating space than the floor, and taking into consideration that whoever sat on a bench enjoyed a more prominent position, it does seem likely that only privileged people might have been permitted to use the bench. What kind of people exactly were allowed to sit on benches, however, remains open to speculation: was it heads of families, people with special positions in a synagogue, or both?

It is significant that benches were installed on all sides at Horvat Kur, not just on a particular wall (e.g. the one facing the *bemah* or next to it). The builders of the Horvat Kur synagogue apparently chose to create several visual directions for the people sitting on the benches. If they all looked straight ahead, they focussed

---

40 See Figs. 4, 5 and 6 in Zangenberg, 'Dorf', 134f for aerial pictures showing benches at Horvat Kur.

41 This term is still used in Zangenberg, Münger, Hakola and McCane, 'Excavations', e.g. p. 573. If compared with, for example, the real stylobate walls in Khirbet Shema' II, the difference to the stone structures between the columns at Horvat Kur becomes evident, see Meyers, Kraabel and Strange, *Khirbet Shema'*: 65–7.

42 Fine, *Holy Place*: 70; Samuel Krauss, *Synagogale Altertümer* (Berlin: Harz, 1922; reprint Hildesheim: Olms, 1966): 379–92.

43 Fine, *Holy Place*: 73.

on the centre of the building. If they all wanted to see the *bemah* (i.e. Jerusalem), a large part of the congregation had to turn their heads.[44] It is, of course, also possible that both directions played a role at various moments during a gathering or a religious service. In Phase 4, the situation was not much different, although people sitting on the benches between the columns might partly have obstructed the view of the ones on the benches around the walls.

In any case, it is likely that the different seating facilities implied some sort of hierarchical differentiation among 'floor sitters' and 'bench sitters'. At what occasions / events in the synagogue such a differentiation really mattered, we do not know, but the more people gathered in the building, the more manifest the hierarchization became. The concept of 'hierarchical seating' becomes even more significant if we look at a third seating installation found in Horvat Kur in 2012.

A Stone Seat

Excavations along the south wall of the synagogue in the summer of 2012 added significantly to our understanding of the local synagogue hierarchy at Horvat Kur. After a balk running north–south across the interior parallel to the western wall had been removed, a single stone seat came to light that apparently had survived, *in situ*, west of the small entrance in the southern wall. The western side of the seat had already been visible from 2010, but the rest and with it its architectural context and significance remained hidden in the balk until 2012.[45]

The seat was directly plastered onto the bench, and two stones were fixed onto the plaster floor in front of it, either forming a step to provide access, or a footstool. Since the steps rest on the plaster floor which is currently dated to the mid to late sixth century CE (Phase 4) and because the seat makes no sense without the step, both features belong to Phase 4 at the earliest and are therefore contemporaneous with the *bemah* (see below).

Unlike the synagogue walls and most parts of the interior benches that were mainly made of basalt, the seat was cut from a single block of the same bright local limestone that was also used for the *bemah*. When the seat was discovered, large parts of the backrest and both armrests were broken off. No traces of decoration were identified on the seat, all sides were flat and the faces carefully smoothed out. The broken edge of the backrest rose 40 cm above the highest preserved course of the southern wall. At this point, the seat extended from its supporting bench to only 10 cm below the topsoil, making it truly remarkable that the seat was preserved in its proper spot at all.

So far, the stone seat from Horvat Kur is the only such object ever found either in the Galilee or the Golan *in situ*. Two similar specimens had been discovered in Galilee before. One was found by Nahum Slouschz in 1921 in a synagogue *c.*

---

44 Hachlili, *Ancient Synagogues*: 206.
45 Zangenberg, 'Dorf': 136–8; Zangenberg, Münger, Hakola and McCane, 'Excavations': 571–3, both with illustrations.

Figure 9.4 Stone seat and benches in southwestern corner of synagogue, situation at the end of the 2012 campaign (© Skyview Ltd. and Kinneret Regional Project)

500 m north of the southern wall of Hammat Tiberias ('Hammat Tiberias A'); its present location is unknown. This seat was hewn from a single block of limestone and is tentatively dated by Rachel Hachlili to the fourth century.[46] The other, by far more famous stone seat, was excavated by Jacob Ory in 1926 at Chorazin, c. 15 km northeast of Horvat Kur.[47] This piece is elaborately decorated and carries a four-line Aramaic dedicatory inscription. The Chorazin seat was not found *in situ*, but '3 m north of the south-eastern corner' of the synagogue.[48] Though it is very likely that the seat was originally set up with its back against the southern wall, its exact location inside the synagogue, of course, is a matter of reconstruction and debate, just like its date (most likely not before the fourth century CE)[49].

---

46 According to Moshe Dothan, 'Hammath-Tiberias', *NEAEHL* 2 (1993): 574 Nahum Slouschz found a basilical type synagogue oriented south c. 500 m north of the city's southern wall: 'In the eastern aisle stood the "seat of Moses".' A drawing can be found in, for example, Hachlili, *Ancient Synagogues*: 219 Figs. IV–68. This synagogue is not identical with the one still visible at the hot springs excavated by Moshe Dothan.

47 Zeev Yeivin, *The Synagogue at Korazim: The 1962–1964, 1980–1987 Excavations* (IAA Reports 10; Jerusalem: Israel Antiquities Authority, 2000): 54 and 22*–23*, Fig. 130 and pl. 26:1 no. 71; Hachlili, *Ancient Synagogues*: 217–19; Zangenberg, 'Dorf': 137 with Fig. 11.

48 Lacking access to Ory's original files at the IAA, I am quoting his remarks from Hachlili, *Ancient Synagogues*: 217.

49 Hachlili, *Ancient Synagogues*: 217.

The original is now displayed in the Israel Museum; a replica was set up against the southern wall in the course of restoration work. So far, no comparable seats are known from the Golan.

Apart from the two northern parallels, a third seat was found in the south at En-Gedi. The general arrangement in the En-Gedi synagogue is quite similar to the one in Horvat Kur. Here, the synagogue's interior was divided up into an aisle, nave, aisle-arrangement in the course of a major refurbishment during which a niche was added to the northern wall (the one facing Jerusalem) sometime between the end of the third and the beginning of the fourth centuries CE, just as columns were added and three entrances built in the western wall.[50] 'Between the entrance next to the northeast corner and the Torah ark a stepped seat ("Seat of Moses")' was constructed.[51] Furthermore, a basin (*kiyor*) was found next to the southern entrance of the corridor-narthex 'for washing the feet of worshipers, with a clay jar used to store the water found nearby, in situ. A stone basin, also found nearby, may have been used for washing hands.'[52] Contrary to the Hammat Tiberias A, Chorazin and Horvat Kur seats, the seat at En-Gedi was made of plastered building stones and not hewn from a single block. In that respect, it resembles the arrangement at Dura Europos.[53]

What was the purpose of these seats?[54] Very obviously, the stone seat offered space for only one person at a time, underlining the unique importance of the person who rested on it. Apart from that, it is very likely that this person's importance had something to do with his function during the synagogue service. It would therefore make sense to interpret the function of the seat in conjunction with other liturgical installations in the synagogue as part of a much more complex performance. That, however, is not easy since the written sources name various 'highly significant persons' (such as a priest, a teacher, an elder) and are notoriously difficult to systematize. In addition to that, Hammat Tiberias A and Chorazin should not be used as the basis for any detailed argumentation because the original place of the stone seat is unknown (Chorazin) or not documented sufficiently (Hammat Tiberias A). The only site in the north of Israel that can help solve these questions is Horvat Kur, because only here a stone seat was found and documented *in situ*. On the other hand, the question arises if and in what way the situation at Horvat Kur was representative of other synagogues. So far, the sequence of (from the east) bench, *bemah*, entrance, bench, stone seat and bench is unique to Horvat Kur.

An example might illustrate the dilemma when reconstructing how the seat might have been used. On the basis of two partly reconstructed (!) podia at the southern wall of the synagogue, Zeev Yeivin postulates that the stone seat at Chorazin was once placed on top of a second podium (*iztaba*) built for

---

50 See Dan Barag, 'En Gedi. The Synagogue', *NEAEHL* 2 (1993): 405–9 (407).
51 Barag, 'En Gedi': 407.
52 Barag, 'En Gedi': 408.
53 Hachlili, *Ancient Synagogues*: 219–20.
54 See the debates in Fine, *Holy Place*: 72–3; Levine, *Synagogue*: 347–51; Hachlili, *Ancient Synagogues*: 217–20.

reading the Torah, next to the one for housing the scroll in the Torah shrine.[55] Interpreting *t. Meg.* 4(3) 21, Yeivin further hypothesizes that such an arrangement would imply three different active functionaries: one reading from the scroll, one standing and holding it up, and a third person translating the passage read. Yeivin assumes that all these activities were performed on the *iztaba* platform. No matter how convincing this scenario is regarding Chorazin, the architecture precludes it working in Horvat Kur, since the synagogue here only has one platform. In fact, Lee I. Levine amply demonstrates that there was no uniform regulation for how many persons should read the Torah during service and from where.[56] Moreover, the Horvat Kur seat clearly did not stand on an extra podium as at Chorazin, but on the 'normal' bench, on the opposite side of the *bemah* relative to the southern entrance. Furthermore, there would be no space for an extra person holding a Torah scroll next to the one seated on the stone seat, unless that person stood on the bench next to the seat which is possible but cannot be demonstrated on the basis of the archaeological remains. Consequently, in Horvat Kur, one might hypothesize, the Torah was either read from in front of the seat, or the person on the seat had to leave his place and go to the *bemah*, climb the stairs to the platform, turn around towards the congregation and perform his task from here. Another option is that the person on the seat did not read the Torah at all, but somebody else did, while the person from the seat interpreted it either standing or seated. Movement patterns in Horvat Kur, therefore, were certainly not identical to what Yeivin supposes for Chorazin. In any case, more research is necessary to discuss the liturgical implications of the arrangement with bench, *bemah*, entrance and seat along the southern wall of the Horvat Kur synagogue.

One more aspect deserves attention. To explain the function and significance of stone seats in synagogues, many scholars refer to Matt 23:2, the famous antipharisaic Jesus logion mentioning the 'seat of Moses' on which the scribes and Pharisees would take their place to emphasize their authority. Though the starting point for interpreting the Horvat Kur stone seat should not be the Matthean passage, but the possible liturgical function of the person occupying it, Matt 23:2 – in conjunction with later rabbinic passages – adds a significant aspect to the 'meaning' of this object. Regardless of all Matthean polemical hyperbole, a number of later rabbinic texts do indeed mention a 'cathedra', on which rabbis and nobles sat down to teach their congregations during service or apart from it. A reference to Moses is not always explicit, but would not be far-fetched, as Moses had brought the law to his people and was considered the founder of the synagogue in antiquity. In this context, Lee I. Levine refers to a late-antique rabbinic tradition according to which Rabbi Joshua, after the passing of famed Rabbi Eliezer, came into his academy and kissed the seat on which the deceased had sat. When Rabbi Joshua did that, he said: 'This stone is like Sinai, and whoever sat on it, was like

---

55 Yeivin, *Korazin*, 27*, 29*–30*.
56 On the 'worship setting' in a synagogue see, for example, Levine, *Synagogue*: 375–80.

the Ark of the holy Covenant.'[57] Passages like this emphasize that reputation is connected to function and is made visible through architectural objects.

Be that as it may, the elevated position of the person occupying the stone seat had, of course, very practical implications and consequences. Whoever sat on such a seat was able to oversee the entire congregation and could be seen by everybody else. In Horvat Kur, this person was facing the congregation, had the *bemah* with the Torah shrine to his right and Jerusalem at his back. This arrangement created a very powerful visual message: When the congregation flocked into the synagogue, sat down on floor and benches and turned south to look towards the *bemah* and Jerusalem, they would all face the person on the seat. This person, in turn, would have been regarded as speaking 'from the direction of Jerusalem' to the entire assembly. So, while the floor and the benches emphasized the communal character of the congregation and its leadership assembled in the synagogue, the single stone seat adds to the hierarchy and gave the person occupying it an exceptional position and authority that nobody else enjoyed in the synagogue.[58]

Taking all these observations together, the Horvat Kur stone seat can be considered the honorary seat of the leader of the local congregation whose authority derived from his association with Moses.

Displaying the Sacred: The Torah Shrine or Bemah

The clear focal point of the Horvat Kur synagogue interior is a large podium measuring *c.* 3 x 3 m on the southern wall just to the east of the southern entrance, which we, for the sake of convenience, here call the *bemah.*[59] The *bemah* should not be confused with the Torah shrine (the structure on top of the *bemah*), or the Torah ark (*aron*), a chest inside the Torah shrine in which the scrolls were kept.[60] In Horvat Kur, only a few possible fragments of the Torah shrine have been found, and no traces of the Torah ark. In any case, the presence of the *bemah* indicates the 'permanent presence of the Torah' in the synagogue at Horvat Kur just like in any other synagogue.[61]

Since the entire southern wall has been excavated, it is clear that Horvat Kur only had a single platform just east (left, if seen from inside the synagogue) of the southern entrance. The Horvat Kur synagogue shares this feature with, for

---

57 Levine, *Synagogue*: 348.
58 This person should, therefore, not be identified with one of the 'elders' who, according to a late tradition, sat with their faces toward the holy ark: 'The sons of Babylonia turn their faces toward the congregation and their backs toward the holy ark. The sons of the Land of Israel turn their faces toward the holy ark' (Fine, *Holy Place*: 73).
59 In general see Spigel, *Synagogue Seating*: 42–4; Levine, *Synagogue*: 343–7 on 'Bimot, Tables, and Platforms'; Hachlili, *Ancient Synagogues*: 163–98; Levine, *Visual Judaism*: 356–7. On Horvat Kur cf. for the moment Zangenberg, Münger, Hakola and McCane, 'Excavations': 562 and 570–71.
60 I follow the definition offered by Hachlili, *Ancient Synagogues*: 163–4, Horvat Kur belongs to Hachlili's type c (*bemah* next to single entrance) (ibid: 168).
61 Levine, *Visual Judaism*: 356.

184 *Jürgen K. Zangenberg*

Figure 9.5 The *bemah* from the air (© Skyview Ltd. and Kinneret Regional Project)

example, the Galilean/Golani synagogues at 'Ammudim or En Nashut, while others have the platform on the opposite side, to the right of the entrance, as for example at Gush Halav, Meiron, Dabbiye or Umm el-Qanatir. All these synagogues belong to the longhouse type, only Hirbet Shema' is a broadhouse synagogue and has a single *bemah*, but the entire arrangement of entrances is different to that in Horvat Kur.[62]

The fact that the walls of the *bemah* at Horvat Kur cover the continuation of the bench on the southern wall clearly suggests that it post-dates Phase 3 and was very likely added in Phase 4 sometime during the sixth century CE. A similar secondary date is also known from the platform at Khirbet Shema'.[63] Traces of a possible earlier pavement, however, might suggest that the large *bemah* excavated by Kinneret Regional Project between 2011 and 2013 at Horvat Kur had a smaller

62 See the overview in Hachlili, *Ancient Synagogues*: 177–9.
63 On Khirbet Shema' see Fine, *Holy Place*: 107: 'A torah shrine on a stone platform that rose nearly 70 cm, was built sometime after the synagogue's initial construction on the southern (Jerusalem) wall, partially covering the bench.' Uzi Leibner informs us that the *bemah* in the synagogue at Wadi Hamam also was added in a later phase (phase IIb), see Leibner, 'Excavations': 230 and 232.

predecessor which was completely removed on the construction of its successor, but this certainly needs further clarification.[64]

With each wall measuring *c.* 3.4 m, the Horvat Kur platform is particularly prominent relative to the size of the interior space. It was built like a cubus using nicely dressed limestone ashlars with smooth exteriors and pilasters that were elaborately set upon each other, similar to the larger *aedicula* at Meroth.[65] Usually the space created by the platform walls was filled with sand or rubble. Unlike all other *bamot* except Umm el-Qanatir, however, the platform at Horvat Kur had an interior room that was accessible through a low and narrow entrance with a dressed threshold. Since the *bemah* walls at Horvat Kur are often not preserved higher than two courses due to extensive theft, it is difficult to determine clearly how high the platform may originally have risen above the synagogue floor. An overall height of *c.* 60–70 cm between synagogue floor and the upper edge of the platform would not have been impossible. In any case, it must have been high enough to allow somebody to crawl into the interior chamber. The interior of the platform was carefully paved with large slabs. The Torah shrine, and with it the platform, was regarded as a place of particular power, for example an ideal place to store amulets and spells.[66] In Horvat Kur, however, apart from several bronze coins and a second century CE Roman type bronze lamp in a robbers' pit under the stone pavement, nothing was found inside the *bemah.*[67]

The floor on the platform was probably made of wood and – as indentations on the inner sides of some ashlars still demonstrate – rested on wooden beams connected to the walls. On the northern side of the platform only a large gap was found, no access up to its top was discovered *in situ*, but three fragments of white limestone can be reassembled into a narrow staircase with handrails leading up to the *bemah* from the north, i.e. the main hall of the synagogue.[68]

Such a platform usually provided the base for an elaborate superstructure, erected often in the form of an *aedicula* and consisting of columns and on top a roof with various decorated elements (Torah shrine). Though no remains of the original superstructure were found *in situ*, various fragments of finely carved limestone columns and decorated architectural pieces of limestone or basalt were excavated in soil located just to the east, west and above all to the north of the *bemah*. They indicate that the platform once carried some sort of arched superstructure.

---

64 On the *bemah* at Horvat Kur see Zangenberg, 'Dorf': 138–40; Zangenberg, Münger, Hakola and McCane, 'Excavations': 562 Fig. 2. The remains of the *bemah* and of the Torah shrine are currently being analyzed by Ulla Tervahauta.
65 On the masonry of the Horvat Kur *bemah* see Fig. 14 in Zangenberg, 'Dorf': 139; on Meroth see Fig. IV–33a in Hachlili, *Ancient Synagogues*: 175.
66 Fine, *Holy Place*: 73.
67 See the bronze lamp in Zangenberg, 'Dorf': 140, Fig. 16 and Zangenberg, Münger, Hakola and McCane, 'Excavations': 572, Fig. 9. Since the few bronze coins from the *bemah* were scattered across several loci, it seems unlikely that they were (part of) an intentional deposit, but further analysis is required; on coins placed in the Torah shrine area see Hachlili, *Ancient Synagogues*: 562.
68 See the aerial picture in Zangenberg, Münger, Hakola and McCane, 'Excavations': 560, Fig. 1.

Especially interesting are two limestone fragments from a relief of a prancing lion similar to, but simpler than, the one from Nabratein.[69] Regarding the form, the *bemah* at Horvat Kur has only one really close parallel as far as we can see now: the *bemah* at Umm el-Qanatir.[70]

Such platforms with superstructure are no Jewish invention, but common elements of Greco-Roman architectural decoration. They were used as an elaborate architectural feature framing or housing a statue, books or other sacred objects. In the case of Jewish synagogues, the precious object encapsulated by the architectural elements rising from the *bemah*-platform was the Torah ark. Outside the Jewish world, however, similar combinations of platform and decorated top can be found in Roman houses (*lararia*) or in Nabatean temples as their cultic centre.[71] Further research, of course, is required to examine these questions.

'Holiness' and Money

There can be no doubt that a synagogue in many ways was the centre of a local community, not only in religious matters. Every synagogue fulfilled political and economic purposes. The exceptionality of the synagogue has, therefore, many facets that all add up to what we call 'sanctity'. One last aspect that needs to be mentioned in this respect has to do with money that, of course, played an important role in any community, be it religious or not. Money in a synagogue is nothing exceptional. We know from several written sources that synagogues (especially in the diaspora) housed donations before they were sent to the Temple and that local synagogues held collections for the poor. Significant numbers of coins in various assemblages have been found in 27 synagogues in the Land of Israel. They indicate that 'at the very least money was collected and stored in synagogues.'[72] We are fortunate to have found evidence for that aspect of synagogue life in Horvat Kur,

---

69 The pieces have been analyzed by Ben de Groot and will be fully discussed in the forthcoming final report. For the moment see Zangenberg, 'Dorf': 139, Fig. 15. On lions as part of synagogue decorations see in general Hachlili, *Ancient Synagogues*: 436–47 and Levine, *Visual Judaism*, passim. On the ark pediment from synagogue IIa at Nabratein see John G. Younger, 'Architectural Elements and Sculptures' in Meyers and Meyers, *Nabratein*: 78–92 (84–6 with Photo 26 and Fig. 27).

70 I am grateful to Yeshu Dray for many helpful discussions about the synagogues at Umm el-Qanatir and Horvat Kur. Work at Umm el-Qanatir is continuing. For the lack of a final publication I refer to Hachlili, *Ancient Synagogues*: 178–80 and 196–7, as well as Dafna Meir and Eran Meir, *Ancient Synagogues in the Golan Heights* (Jerusalem: Yad Yitzhak Ben-Zvi, 2013): 90–109.

71 On platforms in Nabatean sanctuaries such as Khirbet et-Tannur or Khirbet edh-Dharih, see Judith S. McKenzie, Joseph A. Greene et al. (see Bibliography for full list), *The Nabatean Temple at Khirbet et-Tannur, Jordan. Volume 1: Architecture and Religion. Final Report on Nelson Glueck's 1937 Excavation* (AASOR 67; Boston: ASOR, 2013): 39–159.

72 Spigel, *Synagogue Seating*: 36; Levine, *Synagogue*: 356 (on 'community chest') and 396–8 (on charity in synagogues in general); on coins in synagogues see now the detailed discussion Hachlili, *Ancient Synagogues*: 539–65 (with chart XII–3 on pp. 553–5) and the brief survey in Nili Ahipaz, 'Floor Foundation Deposits in Byzantine-Period Synagogues', in *Hoards and Genizot as Chapters in History*, Deborah Stern (ed.) (Haifa: Hecht Museum, 2013): 63*–9*.

too. Interestingly enough, we encountered money in two very different archaeological contexts.

Minimi under the Floor or 'Fontana di Trevi' in the Galilee?

Apart from the usual amount of coins found here and there across the excavated areas inside and outside the synagogue, a very dense concentration of more than 1,000 small bronze denominations was excavated in layers on top of bedrock in the porch area west of the synagogue right in front of the western entrance. Despite the large number of coins, their actual value in the sixth century was not great, and so they were discarded and not retrieved.[73] How did these coins end up where they were found? Two scenarios are being discussed at the moment:[74]

a   The concentration could have accumulated when visitors kept dropping coins before they entered the synagogue (or when they left it) as some sort of magical or apotropaic offering. Though evidence is scant, there are examples of that practice from other cultic contexts.[75] No coins, however, were found near the southern entrance, which would at least raise the question of why visitors made such a distinction, or if both entrances served the same purposes.
b   The second option is that these coins originally constituted some sort of foundation offering that had been buried under the mosaic floor of the synagogue's Phase 2.[76] When this floor was removed sometime late in the sixth century (beginning Phase 3), the debris, including coins and tesserae, was dumped outside the western entrance to create a new floor in the veranda. Though this scenario would explain why the coins were found mixed together with so many tesserae, there are stratigraphic problems that require closer examination in the future.

A Bank Under the Bench?

A very different assemblage, more resembling a hoard spread out in later times,[77] came to light when final excavations were carried out below and around the decorated basalt stone table (B21200/1)[78] in 2013 and a large limestone

---

73   Following Hachlili, *Ancient Synagogues*: 557 (based on Bijovsky) we can calculate the approximately 1,000 minimi from the veranda area to be worth 25 *folles* which equals about 3–4 daily wages or 12 loaves of bread.
74   The coins are currently being analyzed by project numismatist Patrick Wyssman.
75   See, for example, Eberhard Sauer, 'Not Just Small Change. Coins in *Mithraea*', in *Roman Mithraism: The Evidence of the Small Finds. Papers of the international conference / Bijdragen van het internationaal congres, Tienen 7/8 November 2001*, Guy De Boe and Marleen Martens (eds) (AIVM 4; Brussels: I.A.P., 2004): 327–53.
76   Ahipaz, 'Floor Foundation Deposits': (63*).
77   On hoards see Hachlili, *Ancient Synagogues*: 559; Ahipaz, 'Floor Foundation Deposits': 63*.
78   For a first presentation see Zangenberg, 'Dorf': 140–43; after initial analysis by Lise den Hertog, the decorated basalt stone table from Horvat Kur is now presented and discussed in Jürgen

block (B21207/1) was lifted. As under the stone table next to it, a soft soil layer was encountered under B21207/1. In this soil a lead vessel was found without a lid (B22464/1), along with two gold coins very close-by in the sediment (B22465/1 and B22466/1). These coins had apparently slid out of the lead vessel together with the two others found just a few inches further north (B21597/1, B21610/1). The latest of the coins was struck under emperor Maurikios (CE 582–602). Further research must show if these gold coins (eight altogether: six *solidi* and two *tremisses*) originally belonged together with the ones found in the fill further inside square AE 29 in 2012 and once formed a hoard that had been scattered only when the area was later robbed. In any case, it is noteworthy that the lead vessel and parts of the coin deposit were found under the only decorated components of bench W7290/7287. No matter what its original context was, the hoard is of a very different character compared to the scattered *minimi* in the porch area. Unlike the hundreds of bronze coins, the gold coins from under and around the decorated stones inside the synagogue constituted a considerable value[79] and perhaps constitute the community treasury – at least what was left of it.[80] The fact that it was hidden in the synagogue resembles a habit that we also know from pagan temples. Like a local temple, a synagogue also served as a bank.

Conclusions and Outlook

The synagogues of the Land of Israel were not built according to any stereotyped plan, nor were they designed according to an authoritative law. The important basic architectural imperative was the provision of space for the assembly of people, for a community, for a congregation.[81]

Just like the late Second Temple-synagogue, the synagogue of the Byzantine period first and foremost was a community building. But at the same time, the synagogue has a religious status and function, in the Byzantine period perhaps more than its earlier predecessors.

Lee I. Levine rightly states that '(t)he sacred dimension of the synagogue found a variety of expressions.'[82] In the case of the Horvat Kur synagogue, the

---

K. Zangenberg, 'A Basalt Stone Table from the Byzantine Synagogue at Horvat Kur, Galilee. Publication and First Interpretation', in print for *Yizhar Hirschfeld Memorial Volume*, Yosef Patrich, Lea DiSegni, Orit Peleg-Barkat and Erez Ben-Yosef (eds) (Jerusalem: Israel Exploration Society, 2015).

79 Gold coins were rarely used for everyday business transactions, see Daniel Sperber, *Roman Palestine 200–400: Money and Prices* (second edition; Ramat Gan: Bar Ilan University Press, 1991): 89–90 with a reference to Sifre Dtn 32,2. According to Hachlili, *Ancient Synagogues*: 557 'a worker earned about one solidus a month'.
80 On 'charity boxes' and 'community or private savings deposits' see Ahipaz, 'Floor Foundation Deposits', 63*. The topic will be further analyzed in the course of preparing the Final Report.
81 Hachlili, *Ancient Synagogues*: 220.
82 Levine, *Visual Judaism*: 354.

location, architectural elements such as benches and the stone seat, the *bemah*, the mosaic floor with an inscription and a depiction of the *menorah*, and the fact that the building was used to safeguard a large amount of money demonstrate that the synagogue was perceived to be and used as a special building that fulfilled a unique function in and for the village. Further research will explore more deeply how the synagogue 'worked' in its ritual and spatial context as a witness to the *Heilsgeschichte* between God and Israel, thereby sometimes using, it would seem to us, very 'profane' means.

10 Thrown into Limekilns
The Reuse of Statuary and Architecture in Galilee from Late Antiquity onwards

Rick Bonnie

Introduction[1]

In any city of the Roman Empire, inhabitants were surrounded by statuary as they visited theatres, baths, fountains, sanctuaries, and other public spaces. [It] was part of the expected armature of the Roman city, and comprised portraits of emperors and local notables, as well as ... statues of divinities and mythological figures.[2]

The pervasiveness of statuary in Roman cities, as described here by Lea Stirling, is an often-used opening when discussing the social role and meaning of sculpture in the Roman Empire.[3] The region of Galilee, however, located in modern-day northern Israel, has usually been considered atypical to the representation of ancient life described above. This is because Galilee's population was, during the first centuries of our era, largely Jewish and, therefore, in light of the Biblical prohibition, hesitant about conforming easily to a behaviour of displaying (potentially) idolatrous images.[4] To be sure, evidence of figurative depictions on civic coinage from Sepphoris and Tiberias, the region's two major centres, and on mosaics found in some of the peristyle houses and synagogues, as well as on a variety of other materials, has in recent years received much renewed attention.

---

1 All dates are CE unless otherwise indicated.
2 Lea M. Stirling, 'Collections, Canons, and Context: The Afterlife of Greek Masterpieces in Late Antiquity', in *Using Images in Late Antiquity*, Stine Birk, Troels M. Kristensen and Birte Poulsen (eds) (Oxford: Oxbow, 2014): 96.
3 For similar statements, see Yaron Z. Eliav, 'Viewing the Sculptural Environment: Shaping the Second Commandment', in *The Talmud Yerushalmi and Graeco-Roman Culture III*, Peter Schäfer (ed.) (TSAJ 93; Tübingen: Mohr Siebeck, 2002): 413–4; Peter Stewart, *Statues in Roman Society: Representation and Response* (Oxford: Oxford University Press, 2003): 6; Mark A. Chancey, *Greco-Roman Culture and the Galilee of Jesus* (SNTS 134; Cambridge: Cambridge University Press, 2005): 204; Ine Jacobs 'Production to Destruction? Pagan and Mythological Statuary in Asia Minor', *AJA* 114 (2010): 267.
4 Exod 20:2–5; Deut 5:6–9. For discussion of the Biblical prohibition and the later rabbinic attitudes, see also Steven Fine, 'Iconoclasm and the Art of Late-Antique Palestinian Synagogues', in *From Dura to Sepphoris: Studies in Jewish Art and Society in Late Antiquity*, Lee I. Levine and Zeev Weiss (eds) (JRASup 14; Portsmouth: JRA, 2000): 186–7; Eliav, 'Viewing the Sculptural Environment': 417–19.

It has also revised, to some extent, our ideas about Jewish attitudes towards the visual.[5] The acknowledgement that figurative art was present and known within Jewish society in Galilee has so far, however, not been widely claimed for the field of statuary. In fact, the existence of statuary in Galilee's urban centres is often considered to be minimal at best. As Mark Chancey wrote: '[s]tatues appear to have been rare there . . . for the entire Roman era.'[6] This and other statements rest upon the little – but clearly not absent[7] – evidence of sculptural decoration that has been found in excavations across Galilee.

The idea of Galilee being a region that during the second to third centuries – the prime period of marble import into Palestine[8] – was principally vacant of

---

[5] For example: Eliav 'Viewing the Sculptural Environment'; Steven Fine, *Art and Judaism in the Greco-Roman World: Toward a New Jewish Archaeology* (Cambridge: Cambridge University Press, 2005); Lee I. Levine, *Visual Judaism in Late Antiquity: Historical Contexts of Jewish Art* (New Haven: Yale University Press, 2012).

[6] Chancey, *Greco-Roman Culture*: 210. For a broadly identical statement, see also Zeev Weiss, 'Greco-Roman Influences on the Art and Architecture of the Jewish City in Roman Palestine', in *Religious and Ethnic Communities in Later Roman Palestine*, Hayim Lapin (ed.) (STJHC 5; Bethesda: University Press of Maryland, 1998): 244–5; 'Sculptures and Sculptural Images in Urban Galilee', in *The Sculptural Environment of the Roman Near East: Reflections on Culture, Ideology, and Power*, Yaron Z. Eliav, Elise A. Friedland and Sharon C. Herbert (eds) (ISACR 9; Leuven: Peeters, 2008): 573. On the other hand, Eliav ('Viewing the Sculptural Environment': 414–15) claims that, rather than as a result of socio-religious concerns, the number of statues in Palestine was substantially more modest than in other provinces because of the region's political and economic inferiority.

[7] For evidence of freestanding statuary at Sepphoris (including fragments of six individual, marble statues and statuettes) and Tiberias, see Weiss, 'Greco-Roman Influences': 244–5; 'Sculptures and Sculptural Images'. In addition to the evidence reported by Weiss, an unknown number of marble sculptural fragments were found in the area of the 'Eastern Basilical Building' (James F. Strange, Thomas R. W. Longstaff and Dennis E. Groh, 'Zippori – 1991', *ESI* 13 [1994]: 30). Note, in addition, the evidence of a bronze statuette of a winged-male figure, identified as Cupid, at Tiberias (Moshe Hartal, 'Tiberias, Galei Kinneret', *HA/ESI* 120 [2008], available online at http://www.hadashot-esi.org.il/report_detail_eng.asp?id=773&mag_id=114), accessed 28 September 2015. Finally, a marble and a limestone foot were found in a cistern in Nazareth dating to the Crusader period (Bellarmino Bagatti, *Gli Scavi di Nazaret, Volume I: Dalle Origini al Secolo XII* [SBF 17; Jerusalem: Franciscan printing press, 1967): 305–306. The excavator supposes that the two life-size statues to which the feet belonged were originally set up in Tiberias or Caesarea Maritima, but Sepphoris is equally possible. A building inscription from Sepphoris, dated to 517–18, mentions the existence of imperial statues in a civic basilica there (*SEG* XX 417; XXVI 1667; XLVI 1931). For evidence of a marble head of a female figure originally said to have come from Beth She'arim, see below, n. 50. Furthermore, an unidentified statue was found at Khilf-Tabash (Ariel Berman, 'Lower Galilee and Jezreel Valley – Reports', *ESI* 7–8 [1988]: 200) and the reused bust of a soldier with a cap of Phrygian-type at Magdala (Virgilio Corbo, 'Piazza e Villa Urbana a Magdala', *Liber Annuus* 28, 1978): 235. In Rome, a statue of a female figure, possibly a personification of Tiberias (Hygieia?), was dedicated by a Tiberian named Ismenos, son of Ienos, to the Tiberian *statio* there (*IGUR* 1.83). Cf. Chancey, *Greco-Roman Culture*: 205, who erroneously describes Tiberias as this statue's findspot.

[8] See Moshe L. Fischer, *Marble Studies: Roman Palestine and the Marble Trade* (Xenia 40; Konstanz: Universitätsverlag Konstanz, 1998): 40–41, 233; Lorenzo Lazzarini, 'La determinazione della provenienza delle pietre decorative usate dai Romani', in *I marmi colorati della Roma Imperiale*, Marilda De Nuccio and Lucrezia Ungaro (eds) (Venice: Marsilio, 2002): 246; 'La diffusione e il riuso dei più importanti marmi Romani nelle province Imperiali', in *Pietre e Marmi Antichi: natura, caratterizzazione, origine, storia d'uso, diffusione, collezionismo*, Lorenzo Lazzarini (ed.) (Padua: CEDAM, 2004): 108.

freestanding statues should, however, be reconsidered. The absence of statuary in Galilee dating to that period, as will be argued in this chapter, could to some extent be a result of the reuse of marble fragments in later limekilns. That much, if not most, of the marble sculpture and architectural elements that once adorned the cities of the Roman East was thrown into such limekilns is generally viewed by scholars as the main reason why so little of this material has survived.[9] As evidenced by their location at such sites as Bosra, Gerasa, Scythopolis and Sardis, these limekilns were usually installed in the ruins of, or set up nearby, the monumental buildings of those cities.[10] That the marble sculpture and architecture of

9 For example: Niels Hannestad, *Tradition in Late Antique Sculpture: Conservation – Modernization – Production* (Aarhus: Aarhus University Press, 1994): 151; Stewart, *Statues in Roman Society*: 175; Jacobs, 'Production to Destruction?': 291. But limekilns were, of course, not the only devices destroying ancient statues. Sculpture made of precious metals, such as bronze, was probably more common, but was also more easily melted down for other uses because of the higher scrap value. See Jakob M. Højte, *Roman Imperial Statue Bases: From Augustus to Commodus* (ASMA 7; Aarhus: Aarhus University Press, 2005): 14, 47–8.
10 Bosra, East Cathedral: Pierre-Marie Blanc, Jean-Marie Dentzer and Jean-Pierre Sodini, 'La Grande Église à Plan Centré (ou "Cathédrale de l'Est")', in *Bosra: Aux Portes de l'Arabie*, Jacqueline Dentzer-Feydy, Michèle Vallerin, Thibaud Fournet, Ryad Mukdad and Anas Mukdad (eds) (Beirut: Presses de l'institut français du Proche-Orient, 2007): 146; Gerasa, macellum: Alexandra Uscatescu and Manuel Martín-Bueno, 'The Macellum of Gerasa (Jerash, Jordan): From a Market Place to an Industrial Area', *BASOR* 307 (1997): 78, 81; Hippodrome: Antoni A. Ostrasz, 'The Hippodrome of Gerasa: A Report on Excavations and Research 1982–1987', *Syria* 66 (1989): 55, 75 n. 29; Scythopolis, West Bathhouse: Gabriel Mazor, 'Beth She'an Project: City Center of Ancient Beth She'an (South)', *ESI* 6 (1988): 11; 'Beth She'an Project 1988: Department of Antiquities Expedition', *ESI* 7–8 (1989): 22; Sardis, bath-gymnasium: George M. A. Hanfmann and Nancy H. Ramage, *Sculpture From Sardis: The Finds through 1975* (AES 2; Cambridge, MA: Harvard University Press, 1978): 81; Fikret Yegül, *The Bath-Gymnasium Complex at Sardis* (AES 3; Cambridge, MA: Harvard University Press, 1986): 15–16, 89–93, Fig. 262; Temple of Artemis: Howard C. Butler, *Sardis, Vol. I: The Excavations, pt. 1: 1910–1914* (Leiden: Brill, 1922): 28, 74; *Sardis, Vol. II: Architecture, pt. 1: the Temple of Artemis* (Leiden: Brill, 1925): 10, 13. For limekilns in other cities in the East, see Caesarea Maritima, Vaults below Temple Platform/Warehouses in Area CC: Yosef Porath, 'The Caesarea Excavation Project – March 1992–June 1994: Expedition of the Antiquities Authority', *ESI* 17 (1998): 47; Gadara, Five-aisled Basilica: Thomas Weber and Ulrich Hübner, 'Gadara 1998: The Excavation of the Five-aisled Basilica at Umm Qays: A Preliminary Report', *ADAJ* 42 (1998): 449; Philadelphia, Temple of Hercules: Ignacio Arce, 'Early Islamic Lime Kilns from the Near East: The Cases from Amman Citadel', in *Proceedings of the First International Congress on Construction History, Madrid, 20th–24th January 2003*, S. Huerta (ed.) (Madrid: I. Juan de Herrera, 2003): 214–18, 221–2; Palmyra, Sanctuary of Allat: Michal Gawlikowski, 'Excavations in the Allat Sanctuary, 2005–2006', *PAM* 18 (2008): 535–6; Apamea, Long Hall/Agora: Clive Foss, 'Syria in Transition, A.D. 550–750: An Archaeological Approach', *DOP* 51 (1997): 209–10; Baths: Hannestad, *Tradition in Late Antique Sculpture*: 151, n. 254; Antioch, Bath C: George W. Elderkin (ed.), *Antioch-on-the-Orontes I. The Excavations of 1932* (Princeton: Princeton University Press, 1934): 19–31; House of the Calendar: Princeton University, *Research Photographs: Antioch Photo Archive*, no. 1977, available online at http://www.princeton.edu/researchphotographs/archaeological-archives/antioch/, accessed 28 September 2015; Ephesus, Temple of Artemis: Clive Foss, *Ephesus after Antiquity* (Cambridge: Cambridge University Press, 1979): 87; Byzantine Palace: Andreas Pülz, 'Ephesos in Spätantiker und

these former monuments was used to feed these limekilns is suggested both by the discovery of marble near these kilns[11] and by numerous travel accounts attesting to such practices among the local population during the nineteenth century.[12] Indeed, there is abundant evidence suggesting that much of the marble of the cities of the Roman Levant eventually ended up in limekilns to be reused in the later building industry.[13] Therefore, the contrast between urban Galilee and other areas of the Levant was not necessarily as great as some scholars tend to suggest, and the habit of setting up statuary in Galilee may not be so different to that in surrounding regions.[14] In any case, evidence for reusing marble sculpture and architectural elements in Galilean limekilns requires us, at least, to nuance the idea that the region was devoid of freestanding statues.

Ancient limekilns, however, have remained at the margins of scholarship in general. Not only is the evidence for limekilns at archaeological sites across the Roman Empire often poorly reported, but their place and role within the society of that time is also something that is not generally discussed.[15] Indeed, scholars only show a faint interest in the societal and economic motives behind the appearance of urban limekilns during Late Antiquity and later, but instead view them as ferocious villains that

Byzantinischer Zeit', *FA* 53/XII (2009), available online at http://farch.net, accessed 25 January 2016; Pergamon, City Excavations: Wolfgang Radt, 'Pergamon, 1986', *AS* 37 (1987): 212–13. For discussion of limekilns that is more focused on the Western provinces, see Beth Munro, 'Sculptural Deposition and Lime Kilns at Roman Villas in Italy and the Western Provinces in Late Antiquity', in *The Afterlife of Greek and Roman Sculpture: Late Antique Responses and Practices*, Troels M. Kristensen and Lea M. Stirling (eds) (Ann Arbor: University of Michigan Press, forthcoming).

11 For example, Pergamon (Radt, 'Pergamon': 213), Ptolemais (in Cyrenaica) (Karl H. Kraeling, *Ptolemais: City of The Libyan Pentapolis* (Chicago: The University of Chicago Press, 1962): 148, 163, 168, 170), Sardis (Hanfmann and Ramage, *Sculpture from Sardis*: 81). At all three sites a substantial number of partly burned sculptural fragments were found near the limekilns.
12 For such travel accounts, see Michael Greenhalgh, *Constantinople to Córdoba: Dismantling Ancient Architecture in the East, North Africa and Islamic Spain* (Leiden: Brill, 2012): 56–60; *From the Romans to the Railways: The Fate of Antiquities in Asia Minor* (Technology and Change in History 13; Leiden: Brill, 2013): 134–6. One salient example forms the account of the German civil engineer Carl Humann, who in the mid-1860s alarmingly observed how the local population was feeding the remnants of the Great Altar of Pergamon to the limekilns.
13 For a similar observation, see Hannestad, *Tradition in Late Antique Sculpture*: 151 and n. 254.
14 As suggested by some recent datasets, when compared to neighbouring regions of the Empire (North Africa, Asia Minor), the Levant in general seems to have remained rather devoid of statues – at least those of life-size. Cf. Højte, *Roman Imperial Statue Bases*, especially p. 629 for statue bases from the first and second centuries and University of Oxford, *Last Statues of Antiquity Database*, available online at http://laststatues.classics.ox.ac.uk/, accessed 28 September 2015, for evidence of statues set up after 284. Note, however, that this observation remains tentative as both datasets, for obvious reasons, remain incomplete.
15 Brigitte Demierre, 'Les Fours à Chaux en Grèce', *JRA* 15 (2002): 283; Anna Leone, *The End of the Pagan City: Religion, Economy, and Urbanism in Late Antique North Africa* (Oxford: Oxford University Press, 2013): 153; Munro, 'Sculptural Deposition'. A case in point is the recent, three-volume work *The Economic History of Byzantium* (Angeliki E. Laiou (ed.), DOP 39; Washington, DC: Dumbarton Oaks, 2002) that, aside from two rare instances at Anemourion and Sardis, leaves the topic of limekilns completely undiscussed.

are partly to blame for the ruinous and incomplete state of the classical landscape we have inherited. With the rise of scholarly interest in late antique society in general, however, changes in the attitude towards limekilns are becoming more apparent.[16] This chapter is in part an attempt to contribute to this growing movement which seeks to understand the role of urban limekilns in Late Antiquity and later.

Limekilns and the Production of Lime

While in earlier times lime was produced and used only on a limited scale, from the Roman period onwards it became a highly desired product.[17] The main reason for this is the importance of lime for the construction industry, for the production of such bonding material as mortar and concrete, as well as of plaster and stucco.[18]

In order to produce lime, limestone blocks first had to be heated in a kiln specifically built for this purpose to a temperature of 900–1100°C, depending on which stone-type was used, for a prolonged period of time. This process is called calcination. The duration of heating and subsequent cooling of a full limekiln could in antiquity easily take up to as long as one to two weeks. Also taking into account time for loading and unloading, the entire production process would have taken as long as two to three weeks.[19] The resulting product after the limestone blocks have been heated in the kiln is calcium oxide, or 'quicklime'.[20] After calcination, the limestone blocks retained their original shape but became more crumbly and lost half their weight.[21]

For its use in the construction industry, however, the crumbly quicklime still needed to be decomposed by hydration, or slaking, to become a bonding agent, or 'slaked lime'. The resulting lime putty would then form the base to which sand and other materials (e.g. crushed tiles and potsherds) were added to create mortar and plaster. The slaking process of the lime was usually done in a pit dug close to the limekiln, from where it was eventually transported to the construction site, or at the construction site itself.[22]

---

16 See Demierre, 'Les Fours à Chaux en Grèce'; Anna Leone, *Changing Townscapes in North Africa From Late Antiquity to the Arab Conquest* (Bari: Edipuglia, 2007): 213–17; Munro, 'Sculptural Deposition'.
17 Brian Dix, 'The Manufacture of Lime and Its Uses in the Western Roman Provinces', *OJA* 1 (1982): 339–40; Jean-Pierre Adam, *Roman Building: Materials and Techniques* (London: Routledge, 1994): 116.
18 See Dix, 'The Manufacture of Lime': 341–2 with further references to ancient sources. Lime was also used as a fertilizer in agriculture, as well as for other purposes (for example, tanning and medicine).
19 Dix, 'The Manufacture of Lime': 335–6. For the duration of the heating process of some modern limekilns, see Adam, *Roman Building*: 123–4.
20 Dix, 'The Manufacture of Lime': 331; Adam, *Roman Building*: 116–17.
21 Dix, 'The Manufacture of Lime': 336. Cf. Vitruvius, *Arch.*, 2, 5.3.
22 Roger Ling, 'Stuccowork', in *Roman Crafts*, Donald Strong and David Brown (eds) (London: Duckworth, 1976): 210–12; Dix, 'The Manufacture of Lime': 337–9; Adam, *Roman Building*: 127–9.

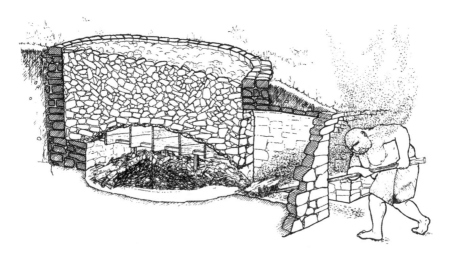

Figure 10.1 Reconstruction of a limekiln ready for firing (after Dix, 'The Manufacture of Lime', Fig. 2, courtesy of Brian F. Dix)

As described already by Cato the Elder around 160 BCE, for the calcination of lime the ancients used mainly periodic, or 'flare' kilns, in which lime was produced by radiant heat (Fig. 10.1).[23] These kilns were circular in shape and measured 2–7 m in diameter, while their height would usually have been a little less.[24] The upper part of these kilns resembled a truncated cone. It would be set either in a specially quarried pit or into a hillside slope. The latter position was favoured because it produced a more constant temperature and provided easy access to the kiln's lower part for the fire and its upper part for the loading and unloading of the limestone blocks.[25] Finally, limekilns usually had one or two stokeholes for fuelling and ventilation purposes.

For the production of lime, ancient craftsmen appear to have favoured white limestone and marble above other types of stone, mainly because of the few impurities that these stones have.[26] For instance, in Late Republican times, Cato the Elder pointed out that a white, uniform stone is the best material for such purpose.[27] The fifth century author Palladius also acknowledged the use of marble,

---

23 Cato, *Agr.*, 38. See also Dix, 'The Manufacture of Lime': 332–3.
24 Dix, 'The Manufacture of Lime': 333; Adam, *Roman Building*: 119.
25 Adam, *Roman Building*: 119.
26 Ling, 'Stuccowork': 210; Dix, 'The Manufacture of Lime': 334; Michael Greenhalgh, *The Survival of Roman Antiquities in the Middle Ages* (London: Duckworth, 1989): 206; *Constantinople to Córdoba*: 59; Munro, 'Sculptural Deposition'.
27 Cato, *Agr.*, 38. See also Pliny the Elder, *Hist. nat.*, 36, 53, who repeats Cato the Elder's statement.

among other stones, as a suitable material for lime production.[28] Vitruvius provided a further functional distinction between limestones of a harder texture and the more porous ones; the former being more suited as a mortar for wall construction, while the latter was better for plastering.[29]

Because of the weight of the stone, the proximity to its source material was a key factor in the location of limekilns. Another factor determining their location was the availability of sufficient fuel. For these reasons limekilns were, in antiquity, usually situated as near as possible to limestone quarries, at some distance from the settlements where the large building projects took place.[30] However, in certain instances, limekilns were set up within settlements because of the nearness of sufficient building material that could be reused as well as the proximity of the construction site. For example, a limekiln that was exposed in the House of the Iliac Chapel in Pompeii was apparently used to rebuild this neighbourhood after the earthquake of 62.[31] With more and more limestone and marble material of gradually abandoned monuments lying around in urban contexts and available for recycling, the placement of limekilns in such contexts became a relatively common phenomenon from Late Antiquity onwards. This holds true both for the western and the eastern provinces of the Empire, including the region of Galilee.

Table 10.1 Limekilns and associated evidence in Galilee, alphabetically ordered

No.	Site	Type of evidence	Location	Date
1	Beth She'arim[32]	Deposit of broken marble sarcophagi	Catacomb no. 20, mainly in its central hall	Late Byzantine/ Early Islamic(?)
2	Beth She'arim[33]	Deposit of broken marble revetment and lime	Near one of the exterior walls of a basilical building	–
3	Beth She'arim[34]	Deposit of broken marble revetment and inscribed slabs	Spread around the synagogue and adjoining buildings	–

28 Palladius, *Op. agr.*, 1, 10.3.
29 Vitruvius, *Arch.*, 2, 5.1.
30 Dix, 'The Manufacture of Lime': 337; Adam, *Roman Building*: 126; Munro, 'Sculptural Deposition'.
31 Adam, *Roman Building*: 127–8.
32 Nahman Avigad, *Beth She'arim III: Report on the Excavations during 1953–1958: Catacombs 12–23* (Brunswick: Rutgers University Press, 1976): 93–115, 164–5.
33 Benjamin Mazar, 'Beth She'arim', *IEJ* 6 (1956): 261; Nahman Avigad, 'Excavations at Beth She'arim, 1955: Preliminary Report', *IEJ* 7 (1957): 75.
34 Benjamin Mazar, 'Excavations in Palestine and Trans-Jordan – Esh Sheikh Ibreiq', QDAP (1941): 213; *Beth She'arim I: Report on the Excavations during 1936–1940: Catacombs 1–4* (Brunswick: Rutgers University Press, 1973): 18; Moshe Schwabe and Baruch Lifshitz, *Beth She'arim II: The Greek Inscriptions* (Brunswick: Rutgers University Press, 1974): 189–98, pl. VII, 2–5.

4	H. 'Ammudim[35]	Limekiln(?)	–	–
5	Kh. en-Nabrah[36]	Limekiln + deposit of architectural fragments	–	Modern(?)
6	Kh. Shifat[37]	Limekiln(?)	North of the settlement	–
7	Meiron[38]	Limekiln	North of a terrace wall, c. 40 m northeast of synagogue	11th–14th century
8	Meiron[39]	Deposit of slaked lime	Unidentified structure, c. 40 m west of synagogue	Mameluke
9	Nabratein[40]	Limekiln	Several metres east of synagogue	Modern(?)
10	Sepphoris[41]	Limekiln + deposit of marble fragments	Near the *Cardo*, north of the 'Eastern Basilical Building'	≥ Byzantine

(continued)

35 Eliot Braun, 'Soundings at Horbat 'Ammudim, Lower Galilee', *'Atiqot* 42 (2001): 238; Uzi Leibner, *Settlement and History in Hellenistic, Roman and Byzantine Galilee: An Archaeological Survey of the Eastern Galilee* (TSAJ 127; Tübingen: Mohr Siebeck, 2009): 243. Leibner probably identified the circular structure that was earlier exposed by Braun as a limekiln. Yet, while the shape and size of this feature indeed match those of a limekiln, it should be noted that Braun did not at the time of his discovery identify it as such.

36 Victor M. Guérin, *Description Géographique, Historique et Archéologique de la Palestine, III – Galilée* (Paris: L'Imprimerie Nationale, 1880): 441; Claude R. Conder and Horatio H. Kitchener, *The Survey of Western Palestine. Memoirs of the Topography, Orography, Hydrography, and Archaeology: Volume I, Sheets I–VI, Galilee* (London: Palestine Exploration Fund, 1881): 243; Ernest W. G. Masterman, *Studies in Galilee* (Chicago: The University of Chicago Press, 1909): 121; Eric M. Meyers, James F. Strange, Carol L. Meyers and Joyce Raynor, 'Preliminary Report on the 1980 Excavations at en-Nabratein, Israel', *BASOR* 244 (1981): 3; Eric M. Meyers and Carol L. Meyers, *Excavations at Ancient Nabratein: Synagogue and Environs* (MEPR 6; Winona Lake: American Schools of Oriental Research, 2009): 2, 15.

37 Rafer Abu Raya and Anastasia Shapiro, 'Yodefat, Survey', *HA/ESI* 123 (2011), 2015, available online at http://www.hadashot-esi.org.il/report_detail_eng.aspx?id=1838&mag_id=118, accessed 28 September.

38 Meyers et al., *Excavations at Ancient Meiron*: 20–22; James F. Strange, pers. comm.

39 Eric M. Meyers and Dan Barag, 'Meiron', in *Encyclopedia of Archaeological Excavations in the Holy Land III*, Michael Avi-Yonah (ed.) (Oxford: Oxford University Press, 1977): 860 (terrace wall mistakenly described as a fortification tower, and the limekiln's dimensions are mistaken); Eric M. Meyers, James F. Strange and Carol L. Meyers, *Excavations at Ancient Meiron, Upper Galilee, Israel, 1971–72, 1974–75, 1977* (MEPR 3; Cambridge, MA: American Schools of Oriental Research, 1981): 87, Figs 4.8 and 4.10.

40 Eric M. Meyers, James F. Strange and Dennis E. Groh, 'The Meiron Excavation Project: Archaeological Survey in Galilee and Golan, 1976', *BASOR* 230 (1978): Fig. 2 (mistakenly described as a 'pool'); Meyers et al., 'Preliminary Report on the 1980 Excavations at en-Nabratein, Israel': 5, 7; Meyers and Meyers, *Excavations at Ancient Nabratein*: 23.

41 Zeev Weiss and Ehud Netzer, 'Zippori – 1992/1993', *ESI* 14 (1995): 45; 'Zippori – 1994–1995', *ESI* 18 (1998): 24; Zeev Weiss, pers. comm.

Table 10.1 (continued)

No.	Site	Type of evidence	Location	Date
11	Sepphoris[42]	Two limekilns + deposit of marble fragments	East side of the 'Eastern Basilical Building'	≥ Byzantine
12	Sepphoris[43]	Limekiln + deposit of architectural fragments, incl. marble	Southern row of shops along the *Decumanus*	≥ Late Byzantine
13	Sepphoris[44]	Limekiln	South side of the House of Dionysos	≥ Byzantine
14	Sepphoris[45]	Limekiln + deposit of architectural (marble?) fragments	East of the theatre's stage area	Byzantine(?)
15	Sepphoris[46]	Limekiln	Northwest corner of 'Unit VII'	≥ Late Byzantine; excavators assume a Crusader date
16	Sepphoris[47]	Deposit of broken marble revetment	Southwest area of 'The Villa'	≥ 4th century
17	Tarshiha[48]	Limekiln	North of modern village	–

The Lime Industry in Galilee

At least thirteen limekilns and ten associated deposits have been discovered so far in Galilee (Table 10.1). The period in which these limekilns were in use ranges from the Byzantine period up to early modern times.

42 Strange et al., 'Zippori – 1991': 30; C. Thomas McCollough, 'Monumental Changes: Architecture and Culture in Late Roman and Early Byzantine Sepphoris', in *The Archaeology of Difference: Gender, Ethnicity, Class and the 'Other' in Antiquity: Studies in Honor of Eric M. Meyers*, Douglas R. Edwards and C. Thomas McCollough (eds) (AASOR 60/61; Boston: American Schools of Oriental Research, 2007): 273; James F. Strange, pers. comm.
43 Zeev Weiss, 'Sepphoris (Sippori): 2005', *IEJ* 55 (2005): Figs 1–2 and 224; 'Sepphoris (Sippori): 2007', *IEJ* 57 (2007): Fig. 5; 'From Roman Temple to Byzantine Church: A Preliminary Report on Sepphoris in Transition', *JRA* 23 (2010): 214.
44 Weiss and Netzer, 'Zippori – 1992/1993': 41; Zeev Weiss, pers. comm.
45 Leroy Waterman (ed.), *Preliminary Report of the University of Michigan Excavations at Sepphoris, Palestine, in 1931* (Ann Arbor: University of Michigan Press, 1937): 11 and pl. XVIII, Fig. 2; Zeev Weiss and Ehud Netzer, 'Sepphoris during the Byzantine Period', in *Sepphoris in Galilee: Crosscurrents of Culture*, Rebecca M. Nagy, Carol L. Meyers, Eric M. Meyers and Zeev Weiss (eds) (Winona Lake: Eisenbrauns, 1996): 82; Alysia Fischer, *Hot Pursuit: Integrating Anthropology in Search of Ancient Glass-Blowers* (Lanham: Lexington Books, 2008): 48–9.
46 Byron R. McCane, pers. comm.
47 James F. Strange, Thomas R. W. Longstaff and Dennis E. Groh, *Excavations at Sepphoris, Volume I: University of South Florida Probes in the Citadel and Villa* (BRLJ 22; Leiden: Brill, 2006): 87.
48 Yoav Lerer, 'Tarshiha, Survey', *HA/ESI* 123 (2011), http://www.hadashot-esi.org.il/report_detail_eng.aspx?id=1689&mag_id=118, accessed 28 September 2015.

A first point to be noted is that no date is known for those circular features exposed in rural Galilee of which the identification as a limekiln remains uncertain, such as Horvat 'Ammudim, Khirbet Shifat and Tarshiha (Table 10.1:4, 6, 17). On the other hand, the securely identified circular limekilns from rural Galilee were all constructed relatively late, around the Late Islamic period or later. For example, in the second half of the nineteenth century, the French explorer V. Guérin noticed a limekiln at the small hilltop site of Khirbet en-Nabrah (Table 10.1:5), located *c.* 250 m south of Nabratein, around which a considerable number of architectural fragments were gathered for burning. Whether it was still in use at the time of Guérin's visit is not entirely clear from his description, but it remains a possibility. The best-dated limekiln is found at Meiron, in northern Galilee, and is located to the southeast of the late-antique synagogue (Table 10.1:7). It was dated on the basis of stratigraphic finds to the Late Islamic period. To the southwest of this limekiln, *c.* 60 m uphill, a deposit of slaked lime was discovered in an unidentified structure from the Mameluke period (Table 10.1:8). Considering their proximity in location and date, it is very possible that the two features are related to one another.

Besides the relatively late date of the limekilns in rural Galilee, another notable feature is that only local limestone appears to have been used for the production of lime. This supports Moshe Fischer's earlier argument that the population living in the more remote, rural areas of Palestine chiefly relied on local limestone for producing lime, despite its inferiority to marble as a source.[49] The reason for this preference was purely practical. The limestone construction material from former local buildings was more easily available to them than the marble remains lying around the relatively distant, former urban settlements.

Beth She'arim, in southwestern Galilee, is an exception to this however. Although this site was not a major urban centre in antiquity, archaeological explorations at this settlement and its extensive necropolis have exposed a considerable number of fragmentary marble sarcophagi, wall revetment, floor slabs, inscriptions and even a statue (Table 10.1:1–3).[50] The reason for the abundance of marble there seems to be related to the social importance of its large necropolis, with at least 27 extensive catacombs and several mausolea, to the Jewish community in the region (and, perhaps, even far beyond) during antiquity.[51] Another reason,

---

49 Moshe L. Fischer, 'The Fate of Holy Land Marble: Remarks on Recycling in the Past', in *Archéomatériaux: Marbres et Autres Roches – Actes de la IVe Conférence Internationale ASMOSIA IV, France, Bordeaux-Talence, 9–13 Octobre 1995*, Max Schvoerer (ed.) (Bordeaux: Centre de Recherche en Physique Appliquée à l'Archéologie, 1999): 283.
50 In 1872, C. R. Conder and H. H. Kitchener were shown in Nazareth a *c.* 18 cm high female head, carved in white marble, that was said to have originated from Beth She'arim. See Conder and Kitchener, *The Survey of Western Palestine*: 350–51.
51 Inscriptions that were found there demonstrate the burial of certain individuals who were referred to as 'rabbi', as well as of certain individuals who originated from regions beyond Galilee. Based upon this epigraphic evidence in particular, the excavators have argued that after certain members of the rabbinic family were buried there during the third century, Beth She'arim promptly became a central burial site for Jews throughout Palestine and the Diaspora. In more recent years, however, certain scholars have expressed doubts regarding the excavator's original narrative of Beth She'arim's necropolis as a rabbinic centre where Diaspora Jews wanted to be buried.

however, was probably its location along an Imperial road leading from the coastal city of Ptolemais, where imported marble would first arrive, to the inland cities of Scythopolis, Gadara, Bosra and Gerasa. While no limekiln has been found so far at Beth She'arim, the particular circumstance in which the marble fragments at the site were found suggests that its marble was reused for the production of lime. For example, in the central hall of Catacomb 20, near its entrance, marble fragments of at least 20 sarcophagi, some decorated with mythological scenes, were found (Table 10.1:1). According to the excavator, people began splitting the marble sarcophagi into pieces after the catacombs had gone out of use in order to make the marble suitable for a limekiln and stored the fragments near the catacomb's entrance. From there, these marble fragments were most probably transported to a limekiln.[52] The excavator suggested that this occurred in the Early Islamic period or somewhat later. Yet, more recently, Fanny Vitto has argued, based on a re-dating of certain finds associated with the thick layer of debris in Catacomb 20, that the splitting of the marble sarcophagi may already have happened as early as the Late Byzantine period.[53] Other marble deposits at Beth She'arim were found in the settlement on top of the hill. A considerable deposit of broken marble slabs and ornaments was found, for instance, near one of the exterior walls of a basilical building, while other marble fragments, including 14 epitaphs that probably derived from the necropolis, were found spread around the settlement's synagogue (Table 10.1:2–3).

Feeding white marble to the limekilns occurred, however, primarily in urban settlements, including those of Galilee, because the structures here were, during

For discussion, see Tessa Rajak 'The Rabbinic Dead and the Diaspora Dead at Beth She'arim', in *The Talmud Yerushalmi and Graeco-Roman Culture I*, Peter Schäfer (ed.) (TSAJ 73; Tübingen: Mohr Siebeck, 1998); Lee I. Levine, 'Bet Še'arim in Its Patriarchal Context', in *'The Words of a Wise Man's Mouth are Gracious' (Qoh 10,12): Festschrift for Günter Stemberger on the Occasion of his 65th Birthday*, Mauro Perani (ed.) (SJ 32; Berlin: De Gruyter, 2005).

52 The marble fragments in the central hall were found upon a 20–50 cm layer of debris (Avigad, *Beth She'arim III*: 93). As suggested from the remains of ash, wood, cloth and animal bones in the layer of debris, it is possible that the people who reused the marble sarcophagi also lived there for some time. It is, furthermore, important to note that only the marble was of significance to these later intruders, as they left the approximately 125 limestone sarcophagi in Catacomb 20 intact.

53 Avigad, *Beth She'arim III*; Fanny Vitto, 'Byzantine Mosaics at Beth She'arim: New Evidence for the History of the Site', *'Atiqot* 28 (1996). Based on the high lime content of a large glass slab that was also found at Beth She'arim, Vitto ('Byzantine Mosaics': 140–41) suggested furthermore that the lime obtained from the marble sarcophagi was possibly used for the production of ancient glass. However, analysis of the glass slab's composition has determined that its high lime content was a result of mixing plant ash and shell-bearing sand, two lime-rich materials. See Ian C. Freestone and Yael Gorin-Rosen, 'The Great Glass Slab of Bet Shearim: An Early Islamic Glass-Making Experiment?', *JGS* 41 (1999): 115. Subsequent studies have shown, furthermore, that it was chiefly the shell-bearing sand of the Levantine coastal area that produced the relatively high lime content in the Roman-Byzantine glass produced there. See Ian C. Freestone, K. A. Leslie, M. Thirlwall and Yael Gorin-Rosen, 'Strontium Isotopes in the Investigation of Early Glass Production: Byzantine and Early Islamic Glass from the Near East', *Archaeometry* 45 (2003): 29–30; Patrick Degryse and Jens Schneider, 'Pliny the Elder and Sr–Nd Isotopes: Tracing the Provenance of Raw Materials for Roman Glass Production', *JAS* 35 (2008): 1997.

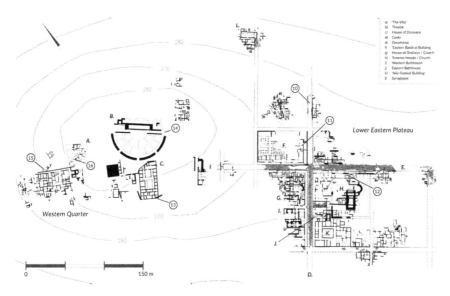

Figure 10.2 Ground plan of Sepphoris. The limekilns are numbered as in Table 10.1 (after Weiss, 'From Roman Temple to Byzantine Church', Fig. 1, courtesy of Zeev Weiss, The Sepphoris Expedition, The Hebrew University of Jerusalem; drawings by Anna Iamim)

antiquity, more richly decorated with marble sculpture and architectural elements. That being said, there is, to my knowledge, no evidence related to a lime industry exposed so far in any excavation in Tiberias. This is probably because of Tiberias' continuous occupation history from its early first century foundation onwards, since this has obliterated much of the earlier remains and hinders systematic archaeological investigations of the city's previous histories. That limekilns were used in Tiberias during Late Antiquity is, however, suggested by the fourth-century Church Father Epiphanius of Salamis. Epiphanius provides the story of how the Jewish-convert Joseph of Tiberias built a small church in Tiberias upon the ruins of a former temple, the 'Hadrianeion'.[54] Josephus first required lime in order to build this church and, therefore, constructed seven limekilns along the borders of the city. Considering the fact that material from the former 'Hadrianeion' was being reused, it is reasonable to suggest that these kilns were stacked with marble building elements and statuary belonging to that structure.

For Sepphoris, on the other hand, there is ample archaeological evidence for a late-antique lime industry due to the large-scale excavations at this site.[55]

---

54 Epiphanius of Salamis, *Pan.* 30.12, especially 30.12.4.
55 For an overview of the excavations, see Zeev Weiss, 'Sepphoris', in *NEAHL 4*, Ephraim Stern (ed.) (Jerusalem: Israel Exploration Society, 1993); 'Sepphoris', in *NEAHL 5*, Ephraim Stern (ed.) (Jerusalem: Israel Exploration Society, 2008).

So far at least seven limekilns have been exposed (Fig. 10.2), though none is reported in considerable detail. On the Lower Eastern Plateau, one limekiln was exposed to the north of the so-called 'Eastern Basilical Building', near the *Cardo* (Table 10.1:10).[56] Nearby, lay a substantial number of marble fragments, including part of a statue that, presumably, was moved there before throwing it into the limekiln. Further southwest, on the eastern grounds of the former 'Eastern Basilical Building', two other limekilns have been found (Table 10.1:11).[57] Furthermore, related to these limekilns, 'hundreds of marble fragments, including pieces of a screen, Corinthian capitals, [and] statues' were found piled over a corner of the former building.[58] Another limekiln was found above one of the southern shops aligning the *Decumanus*, directly north of a fifth century church that was built over the remains of a second century temple complex (Table 10.1:12). Immediately south of this limekiln, and associated with it, lay a large number of architectural fragments, including pieces of broken marble that derived from the church.

Moving west to the hilltop area, in close association to an east–west running, broad wall there, a limekiln was dug into the ruins of the House of Dionysos, which was abandoned by the late fourth century (Table 10.1:13). Another circular limekiln, exposed in 1931 by Leroy Waterman, sat directly east of the stage area of the former theatre (Table 10.1:14; Fig. 10.3). Decorative architecture from the former theatre, either of limestone or marble, lay around next to it. The theatre area 'was [during the Byzantine period] a quarry for stones and raw materials for the lime industry'.[59] The final limekiln exposed so far at Sepphoris sits in the so-called Western Quarter, built into the ruins of a domestic building (named 'Unit VII') that was in use from the first to the fifth century (Table 10.1:15). Relatively nearby, *c.* 40 m to the east, a heap of broken marble revetment was found piled in one of the rooms of a former peristyle house (named 'The Villa') after it had fallen in ruins during the fourth century (Table 10.1:16). It is possible that people intended to store the marble here temporarily before it was thrown into the nearest limekiln.

The evidence from Sepphoris (but note also Beth She'arim) makes it particularly clear that the availability of sufficient marble in Galilee's urban areas played an important role when deciding where to set up limekilns. This is evident from the fact that in at least three cases there, possibly four, a heap of broken marble was found very near to some limekilns. Though the reports do not provide much detail, there is explicit evidence at Sepphoris of marble statuary being broken up for reuse in these limekilns, as in the cases of Pergamon, Ptolemais and Sardis.[60]

---

56 The precise identification of this building is still debated (civic basilica, forum or macellum). For discussion, see Rick Bonnie, 'Galilee during the Second Century AD: An Archaeological Examination of a Period of Socio-Cultural Development', (PhD dissertation; KU Leuven, 2014): 110–20.
57 Only one limekiln was reported in excavation reports of this area (McCollough, 'Monumental Changes': 273). However, in a personal communication, James F. Strange, the director of the excavations, noted a second limekiln there.
58 Strange et al., 'Zippori – 1991': 30.
59 Weiss, 'Sepphoris', *NEAEHL* 4, 1327.
60 See above, n. 11.

Figure 10.3 Sepphoris, circular limekiln found at the east end of the theatre's stage area (Waterman, *Preliminary Report*, pl. XVIII, Fig. 2, courtesy of the Kelsey Museum of Archaeology)

Second, the limekilns were mainly found in or around former public monuments (temples, churches, theatres) and peristyle houses. This location corresponds with that of the majority of limekilns found in the urban centres of the Roman East,[61] and represents those buildings most likely to have been adorned with marble decoration and statuary.

One important matter that remains to be discussed is when these limekilns appeared in the urban context of Sepphoris. This remains an issue because, as mentioned above, excavations and scholarship in general have been little interested in limekilns. The unfortunate result is that the period when these limekilns were constructed and used – two critical aspects for understanding their role within society – often remains obscure at best. In those cases at Sepphoris where a construction date is mentioned, the excavators tend to remain rather vague about it.[62] While the *terminus post quem* for all the limekilns at Sepphoris lies in the

---

61 See above, n. 10.
62 For example, the limekiln found north of the 'Eastern Basilical Building' (Table 10.1:10) is considered to date 'probably after the Byzantine period' (Weiss and Netzer, 'Zippori – 1994–1995': 24). Another example is the two limekilns found on the eastern grounds of the 'Eastern Basilical Building', which are sometimes dated to the Byzantine period (McCollough, 'Monumental

Byzantine period, there is in two cases some evidence that may provide a more specific construction date. If the chancel screen fragments found in two marble deposits were meant for the nearby limekilns (Table 10.1:11–12), then presumably these limekilns considerably post-date the construction of the nearby fifth century churches. Yet, we should also keep in mind that probably not all limekilns were used at the same time, but that what now is observed represents a long history of reuse of the building material and statuary of ancient Sepphoris. Furthermore, the fact that all limekilns date no earlier than the Byzantine period at least suggests that this was probably the initial period when limekilns were being introduced into Galilee's urban space. This observation is supported by the fourth century account of Epiphanius of Salamis describing the construction of limekilns at Tiberias.

Obviously, this attempt to locate and discuss the limekilns in Galilee remains incomplete. Certain exposed limekilns have probably remained unreported in publication, while many remain invisible to traditional excavations due to their remote, extra-urban location near ancient quarries.[63] Nonetheless, this discussion shows that, as in other cities of the Roman East, from Late Antiquity onwards limekilns were relatively commonplace within the urban centres of Galilee. Their place within the city limits suggests, furthermore, that the reuse of marble building material and statuary for lime used in building construction played an important role within the society of that time. In the following, I reflect upon the societal motivations behind these changes.

Feeding Marble to the Kilns

Why did the population begin feeding the sculptural and architectural elements made of marble, which, as elsewhere, once decorated the public monuments and élite mansions in Galilee, to nearby limekilns? The main cause given by scholars for this kind of marble reuse is that it happened for economic reasons.[64] As mentioned earlier, marble is superior to limestone when it comes to the production of lime. While that is the case, for most of antiquity marble was considered too rare and valuable a commodity to be used for this purpose and was, instead, used primarily for purposes of decoration and lavish display. When, by Late Antiquity, limekilns began to be built within the city limits, scholars reasoned that this was because, by that time, marble was amply available there in the form of architectural decoration and sculpture. Aside from marble's superior quality, reusing this stone from former urban structures nearby also probably saved considerable transportation costs. According to these scholars then, the burning of sculptural and architectural marble in limekilns set up within cities during Late Antiquity

---

Changes': 273) and at other times attributed to the Early Islamic period (James F. Strange, pers. comm.). For a Byzantine/Early Islamic date, see (Strange et al. 'Zippori – 1991': 30). For some limekilns no construction date is explicitly given. See, for example, Table 10.1:13–14.

63 This last argument was raised by Demierre, 'Les Fours à Chaux en Grèce': 286–7 in the case of Greece.
64 See Peter Stewart, 'The Destruction of Statues in Late Antiquity', in *Constructing Identities in Late Antiquity*, Richard Miles (ed.) (London: Routledge, 1999): 183–4; Jacobs, 'Production to Destruction?': 291; Greenhalgh, *Constantinople to Córdoba*: 57; Munro, 'Sculptural Deposition'.

was primarily chosen for its productive efficiency: the product was superior and transportation more cost-efficient.

Inherent in this argument about why the late antique population began to reuse urban marble for lime production is that by then this stone came to be valued primarily for its material properties, no matter what the style, representation or context of that marble would have been. Peter Stewart describes the situation of statuary in sixth century Rome thus: 'Divorced from the social and religious circumstances of their creation, the city's statues were at risk: the balance between intrinsic and symbolic value had tipped in favour of the lime-kilns and furnaces.'[65] Ine Jacobs, more recently, has repeated this idea for the eastern empire as a whole: 'The need for raw materials may indeed be the main reason why on the whole we have recovered so little statuary . . . of the Late Antique cities of the eastern empire.'[66]

But was 'the need for raw material' really the sole incentive for these people to have stripped the ruins of their marble decoration and to have broken the statuary of the cities into piecemeal fragments ready to be reused as mortar or plaster? Granted, economic incentives would have certainly been in play when deciding on throwing marble into the limekilns. Yet, recent scholarship has highlighted it as the only deciding factor and has, to my opinion, not sufficiently evaluated other possible incentives. The issue with earlier suggestions is that they implicitly assume that throughout the Roman Empire marble's exotic, aesthetic and symbolic qualities had more or less faded by Late Antiquity and, hence, its market value had diminished markedly. This stone-type would otherwise not have been turned into lime, a relatively cheap material that was widely used in building construction.

There is no evidence, however, to indicate that by Late Antiquity the market value of marble would have dropped to such a low that it was more favourable to turn it into lime than to use it as marble. The labour that was put into the quarrying and shaping of the marble into the respective architectural elements, wall veneer and statuary added a considerable value that should not be underestimated.[67] To this should be added that the admiration for and value of marble would have been higher in regions located further from its source.[68] A point especially worth considering in the case of Palestine, a region with no marble sources but sufficient local limestone for filling the limekilns. Recent overviews of marble usage in the Roman Empire during Late Antiquity and later sketch a picture of a region in which marble continued to be valued by society for its aesthetic and symbolic qualities.[69] This

---

65 Stewart, 'The Destruction of Statues': 183–4.
66 Jacobs, 'Production to Destruction?': 291.
67 For discussion on the demand for and cost of marble, see Ben Russell, *The Economics of the Roman Stone Trade* (Oxford Studies on the Roman Economy; Oxford: Oxford University Press, 2013): 8–35.
68 Russell, *The Economics of the Roman Stone Trade*: 14. See Pliny the Elder, *Nat.*, 36.5. Note also how the fifth century Mark the Deacon (*Vit. Porph.*, 84) describes the awe and excitement of Gaza's local population when a cargo of marble intended for the decoration of a church there entered its harbour.
69 Marc Waelkens, 'Marble', in *Late Antiquity: A Guide to the Postclassical World*, Glen W. Bowersock, Peter R.L. Brown and Oleg Grabar (eds) (Cambridge, MA: Harvard University Press,

was also shown by the fact that the reuse of marble to decorate public buildings still comprised a substantial industry.[70] After the marble quarries in the eastern Mediterranean went out of use around the seventh century, the marble reused in new constructions evidently had to come from the former buildings that, at the time, lay in ruins.[71] Such a reduction in the production of marble would also imply a higher exotic value for this good.

Thus, during Late Antiquity the population still seems to have valued marble as a decorative stone. The columns, statuary, wall veneer and floor slabs made of this material adorning civic spaces were still appreciated, even to such an extent that it was being ripped off on a considerable scale from older structures to be reused in new ones. Questions still remain, however, about why limekilns began to appear in urban areas during Late Antiquity and why these limekilns apparently transformed the highly-appreciated marble into a relatively cheap construction material? What has not been afforded much significance in this regard is the potential symbolic value such limekilns may have had during this period, as well as later on. It is indeed interesting that, where scholars often acknowledge that the use of *spolia* bore a specific political, religious or cultural message,[72] such a possibility is disregarded when discussing the purpose of limekilns. While the destructive act of these devices is often cited as a reason why so little marble decoration and statuary from antiquity has been preserved, the reasons for this particular destructive act usually remain undiscussed.

A look at the broader, socio-historical context in which limekilns were first introduced into urban areas, however, provides us with possible indications for their significance. There appear to have been parts of the cities' urban space in which, during Late Antiquity, marble was under substantial threat; that is, when it was used as a decorative stone in pagan monuments and for statuary. During the fourth and

---

1999): 559–62; Jean-Pierre Sodini, 'Marble and Stoneworking in Byzantium, Seventh–Fifteenth Centuries', in *The Economic History of Byzantium*, Angeliki E. Laiou (ed.) (DOS 39; Washington: Dumbarton Oaks, 2002): 129–46.

70 For Byzantine sources mentioning the use of marble in the decoration of public buildings, chiefly churches, see Cyril Mango, *The Art of the Byzantine Empire, 312–1453: Sources and Documents* (Toronto: University of Toronto Press, 1986), s.v. 'marble'.

71 Waelkens, 'Marble': 561–2; Sodini, 'Marble and Stoneworking': 135–45.

72 For example: Beat Brenk, 'Spolia from Constantine to Charlemagne: Aesthetics Versus Ideology', *DOP* 41 (1987); Helen G. Saradi-Mendelovici, 'Christian Attitudes toward Pagan Monuments in Late Antiquity and Their Legacy in Later Byzantine Centuries', *DOP* 44 (1990); John Curran, 'Moving Statues in Late Antique Rome: Problems of Perspective', *Art History* 17 (1994); Helen G. Saradi, 'The Use of Ancient Spolia in Byzantine Monuments: The Archaeological and Literary Evidence', *IJCT* 3 (1997); *The Byzantine City in the Sixth Century: Literary Images and Historical Reality* (Athens: Society of Messenian Archaeological Studies, 2006): 366; Sodini, 'Marble and Stoneworking': 145; Robert Coates-Stephens, 'Attitudes to *Spolia* in Some Late Antique Texts', in *Theory and Practice in Late Antique Archaeology*, Luke Lavan and William Bowden (eds) (LAA 1; Leiden: Brill, 2003); Jacobs, 'Production to Destruction?'; Troels M. Kristensen, 'The Display of Statues in the Late Antique Cities of the Eastern Mediterranean: Reflections on Memory, Meaning, and Aesthetics', in *Debating Urbanism Within and Beyond the Walls A.D. 300–700: Proceedings of a Conference Held at the University of Leicester, 15th November 2008*, Denis Sami and Gavin Speed (eds) (Leicester: School of Archaeology and Ancient History, 2010).

fifth centuries especially, the Christian community launched an offensive against any resilient pagan population and, in their pursuit, physically attacked those physical elements associated with that population, especially statuary and temples.[73] It should be highlighted, however, that alongside these negative acts of religious violence against the pagan population and culture (so dominant in earlier scholarship), at certain times the Christian community also used more peaceful methods of conversion and held positive attitudes towards the pagan material culture.[74]

What could have been regarded as such a positive response are the numerous Imperial edicts from the mid-fourth to early-fifth century in the *Codex Theodosianus* that prohibit the removal of statuary or decorative marble from public buildings and spaces.[75] However, the substantial number of these edicts does suggest that they were issued in response to an act that frequently occurred in the towns and cities of that time. Hence, they should be seen as a testimony that, in reality, the Christian destruction was a severe threat to earlier marble decoration and statuary. Marble was apparently too valuable to the Christian community to be considered appropriate as a decorative stone for buildings and statuary associated with the pagan past.

'All Reduced to Powder': Limekilns and the Destruction of Paganism

If we take this socio-historical context of a dominant Christian community into account and observe that marble was actually still appreciated in Late Antiquity and later on, it becomes apparent that marble destruction may have been a religiously

---

73 The scholarly literature on this particular topic is extensive. For some modern discussions, see Cyril Mango, 'Antique Statuary and the Byzantine Beholder', *DOP* 17 (1963); Liz James, '"Pray Not to Fall into Temptation and Be on Your Guard": Pagan Statues in Christian Constantinople', *Gesta* 35 (1996); Stewart, 'The Destruction of Statues'; Johannes Hahn, Stephen Emmel and Ulrich Gotter (eds), *From Temple to Church: Destruction and Renewal of Local Cultic Topography in Late Antiquity* (RGRW 163; Leiden: Brill, 2008); Jacobs, 'Production to Destruction?': 267–8, 282–92. For Palestine in particular, see Yoram Tsafrir 'The Classical Heritage in Late Antique Palestine: The Fate of Freestanding Sculptures', in *The Sculptural Environment of the Roman Near East: Reflections on Culture, Ideology, and Power*, Yaron Z. Eliav, Elise A. Friedland and Sharon C. Herbert (eds) (ISACR 9; Leuven: Peeters, 2008).

74 For example: Saradi-Mendelovici, 'Christian Attitudes Toward Pagan Monuments'; Michele Salzman, 'Rethinking Pagan-Christian Violence', in *Violence in Late Antiquity: Perceptions and Practices*, H. A. Drake (ed.) (Aldershot: Ashgate, 2006); Jacobs, 'Production to Destruction?'

75 For example: *CTh.* 9.17.2 (in 349); 9.17.4 (in 356); 15.1.1 (in 357); 16.10.8 (in 382); 15.1.25 (in 389); 16.10.15 (in 399); 15.1.43 (in 405). For an extensive list, see Waelkens, 'Marble': 562. Later, under Theodoric, an official was appointed specifically to prevent such destruction. Similar orders were made during the Renaissance. In 1534, Pope Paul III issued a directive ordering punishment for plunderers of marble (David A. Levine, 'The Roman Limekilns of the Bambocchianti', *The Art Bulletin* 70 (1988): 579). See also Cassiodorus' heartfelt plea (*Variae* 7.13 and 15) in the 530s to preserve Rome's sculptural heritage. A few imperial edicts in the *CTh.* (16.10.18 [in 399]; 16.10.19.1 (in 407)) actually ordered the destruction of idols. The same happened during the eighth century, when Popes Sisinnius and Gregory II officially sanctioned the use of ancient statuary and ruins to produce lime for the restoration of Rome's city walls (Levine, 'The Roman Limekilns': 579).

(and politically) meaningful act associated with the destruction of paganism. As will be argued, urban limekilns may have played a vital role in this destructive act.

A substantial amount of archaeological and textual evidence documents how the Christian community during Late Antiquity mutilated pagan statuary, dragged it around in a dismembered state, and then ridiculed it.[76] As the Syriac bishop Jacob of Sarug describes it in the early sixth century, pagan statues became a pile of fragments 'made to arouse laughter and scorn'.[77] In certain instances, reference is even made to the burning of these statues, as noted for example by Eusebius in the fourth century: 'whatever part of the material [of the statuary] appeared valuable they scraped off and melted in the fire to prove its worth.'[78] To be fair, Eusebius might have meant here statues made out of gold, silver and brass, because of their higher intrinsic value. However, other late antique authors do not make a distinction between precious metals and marble when describing the destruction of statues in late antique towns and cities.[79] In fact, Jacob of Sarug even explicitly refers to the state of idols and deities as being 'all reduced to powder', an almost direct reference to quicklime.[80]

Important in this regard was the location where the marble was burned. As Peter Stewart notes, 'iconoclasm was not that violence should be done, but that violence should be *seen* to be done'.[81] It was not so much the erasure of sculptural imagery that was important, but the visibility of this act of erasing. In this respect, the central location of many of the urban limekilns, providing current inhabitants with a visual reference to the destruction of a once dominant culture, appears striking. Thus, the reuse of marble in limekilns located within the cities was not only effective for lime production that could be used within the building industry, but also seems to have stood as a symbol of revenge on paganism. While in earlier times the pagan population had ridiculed the Christian community, now the latter appears to have effectively 'displayed' the end of paganism. The fact that the process of turning marble into quicklime in a limekiln is a slow one that extends over several weeks and is continuous day and night (see above), makes the destruction an obvious and highly visual performance.

Interestingly, it would not have been the last time in history that such a metaphor related to urban limekilns was used. In seventeenth-century Rome, the Dutch painter Pieter van Laer and some of his followers – later to be known as

---

76 For examples and discussions of these destructive acts, see Greenhalgh, *Survival of Roman Antiquities*: 203–10; Stewart, 'The Destruction of Statues': 175–80; Saradi, *The Byzantine City*: 372–4; Tsafrir, 'The Classical Heritage'; Jacobs, 'Production to Destruction?': 282–92; Kristensen, 'The Display of Statues'.
77 Jacob of Sarug, *Homily on the Fall of the Idols*: 185. See also M. l'Abbé Martin, 'Discours de Jacques De Saroug sur la Chute des Idoles', *ZDMG* 29 (1875): 135; Stewart, 'The Destruction of Statues': 179–80.
78 Eusebius, *Vit. Const.*, 3.54. See also Eusebius, *Tr. or.*, 9.6.
79 Jerome, *Epist.*, 107.2; Zacharias Scholasticus, *Vit. Sev.* (*PO* 2.1, M.-A. Kugener (ed. and trans.) 1907): 27–35, especially 33.
80 Jacob of Sarug, *Homily*: 375–80. See also Martin, 'Discours de Jacques De Saroug': 140.
81 Stewart, 'The Destruction of Statues': 167.

Figure 10.4 Cornelis Visscher, after Pieter van Laer, *The Large Limekiln*, engraving (RP-P-1904-723; Rijksmuseum, Amsterdam). Van Laer's original painting has been lost; this engraving is probably a mirror-image of it

the '*Bamboccianti*'[82] – depicted in at least 15 distinct compositions the theme of limekilns in Roman settings.[83] The best-known of these is a painting by Van Laer himself, named *The Large Limekiln*, which shows an apparently fictional scene of a large limekiln, surrounded by animals, workers and tramps, situated on the banks of the River Tiber (Fig. 10.4). As David Levine has rightly argued, the limekiln's ruinous nature in this painting highlights the critical role of this structure in the eradication of Rome's past.[84] More importantly, aside from displaying destruction, Levine has argued that Van Laer's limekiln would also have been understood as an allegory for the processes of purification and renewal – 'a metaphor for the regenerative power' of a society.[85] This reminds us to a certain extent of the triumph of

---

82 The name 'Bamboccianti' derived from *il Bamboccio*, a nickname given to Van Laer because of his awkward proportions (Levine, 'The Roman Limekilns': 569–70).
83 For a list of these compositions, see Levine, 'The Roman Limekilns': 588–9.
84 Levine, 'The Roman Limekilns': 580.
85 Levine, 'The Roman Limekilns': 580–81.

the Christian present over the pagan past, as the melting of marble statuary and architectural elements provided a direct economic contribution to contemporaneous society. The limekiln, thus, served as an actor in the societal renewing process.

It has been argued, thus, that the urban limekiln not only provided society with lime, but also provided a deeper meaning embedded in the sociohistorical context of that time. It was a small part of the symbolism surrounding the triumph of Christianity and later Islam over the Classical past. As mentioned, to reduce marble into lime was a process of several weeks' duration. During this process, sculptural marble fragments that were once part of 'animated representations worthy of worship' now, at the hands of Christians and Muslims, became 'lifeless and manmade'.[86] As Michael Greenhalgh has noted, the limekiln highlighted the mortality of both marble and what it represented.[87] At the same time, however, the substance produced from this marble was of central importance in making the new monuments displaying the triumph of Christianity and, later, Islam.

Conclusions

This chapter has aimed to reconsider the idea that during the second and third centuries Galilee's built environment was largely vacant of freestanding statues. While most inhabitants of the Roman Empire usually expected to be surrounded by statuary wherever they went within a city, the small amount of preserved remains of especially figurative stone sculpture in Galilee's urban centres has led to the suggestion that Galilee and its population was somehow different. Most of its population, according to some scholars, followed the Biblical and rabbinic prohibition on displaying idolatrous images. Hence, the built environment of its cities was largely devoid of statuary.

With regard to the above argument, however, the evidence of later limekilns in Galilee has usually gone completely unnoticed. Limekilns are nevertheless worthy of consideration, since their presence in urban settings has important repercussions for our understanding of the earlier sculptural and architectural environment there. Indeed, in any discussion on Roman statuary, scholars hasten to add that, from Late Antiquity onwards, unfortunately much of the material that adorned the urban environment – precisely how much remains unknown – disappeared into limekilns.

This chapter, therefore, has examined the evidence of limekilns and associated marble deposits in Galilee from Late Antiquity onwards, with a special emphasis on its urban regions. In particular, the extensive excavations at Sepphoris indicate that limekilns were commonplace devices to be found in the urban built environment of Galilee during the Byzantine and Early Islamic periods. Moreover, the evidence of marble statuary fragments near to some limekilns shows that at, a certain time,

---

86 Kristensen, 'The Display of Statues': 272.
87 Greenhalgh, *Constantinople to Córdoba*: 57.

statues would indeed have adorned the built environment of Sepphoris. However, almost all traces of them within the cities have disappeared due to the reuse of these statues for the later construction industry. Indeed, the evidence of limekilns, in urban Galilee especially, suggests that stone statuary was a more common phenomenon than has hitherto been suggested.[88]

What these statues would have represented, who ordered them, and for what reasons remains unknown and requires further study. Nor is it suggested that statuary in Galilee was as common as anywhere else. Obviously, as implied for instance by the considerably larger number of preserved statues in Asia Minor when compared to the Levant, there were regional differences at play with regard to the 'sculptural habit' of a population.[89] It is, however, suggested that we should nuance our view concerning the practice of setting up statuary in the urban settings of Galilee and show more caution concerning the alleged absence of evidence.

Acknowledgements

The research for this chapter was supported by the Research Foundation – Flanders (FWO) and by the Academy of Finland Centre of Excellence in Changes in Sacred Texts and Traditions. Furthermore, I gratefully wish to thank Professors Byron McCane, James Strange and Zeev Weiss for clarifying matters regarding the limekilns at Sepphoris, as well as Professor Patrick Degryse for discussing Byzantine and Early Islamic glass production in the Levant. I am also thankful to Dr Beth Munro, who kindly provided me with a copy of her forthcoming article on late antique limekilns in the Roman West. Brian Dix, Zeev Weiss, and the Kelsey Museum of Archaeology generously granted me permission to reproduce images. Finally, I wish to thank the editors and the anonymous reviewer for their useful comments and suggestions.

---

88 A more or less similar explanation has been given for Roman Britain. See Stewart, *Statues in Roman Society*: 175.
89 On regional differences, see above, n. 14. In light of presumed regional differences, the fact that no statue bases have been found so far in Galilee remains an important aspect to consider, as these were not usually thrown into limekilns. They may, however, have been reused in other ways.

Bibliography

Abu Raya, Rafeh, and Anastasia Shapiro. 'Yodefat, Survey.' *HA/ESI* (2011). Available online at http://www.hadashot-esi.org.il/report_detail_eng.aspx?id=1838&mag_id=118, accessed 28 September 2015.

Adam, Jean-Pierre. *Roman Building: Materials and Techniques*. London: Routledge, 1994.

Ahipaz, Nili. 'Floor Foundation Deposits in Byzantine-Period Synagogues.' In *Hoards and Genizot as Chapters in History*, edited by Deborah Stern: 63–9. Haifa: Hecht Museum, 2013.

Aist, Rodney. *The Christian Topography of Early Islamic Jerusalem: The Evidence of Willibald of Eichstätt (700–787 CE)*. Turnhout: Brepols, 2009.

Algra, Keimpe. 'Stoics on Souls and Demons: Reconstructing Stoic Demonology.' In *Demons and the Devil in Ancient and Medieval Christianity*, edited by Willemien Otten and Nienke Vos: 71–96. Leiden: Brill, 2011.

Ames, Cecilia. 'Roman Religion in the Vision of Tertullian.' In *A Companion to Roman Religion*, edited by Jörg Rüpke: 457–71. Malden: Blackwell, 2007.

Andrade, Nathanael. 'The Processions of John Chrysostom and the Contested Spaces of Constantinople.' *JECS* 18:2 (2010): 161–89.

Apostolos-Cappadona, Diane. '"... decorated with luminous mosaics."' Image and Liturgy in 5th/6th Century Roman Church Apse Mosaics.' *StP* 71 (2014): 93–110.

Arce, Ignacio. 'Early Islamic Lime Kilns From the Near East. The Cases From Amman Citadel.' In *Proceedings of the First International Congress on Construction History, Madrid, 20th–24th January 2003*, edited by S. Huerta: 213–24. Madrid: I. Juan de Herrera, 2003.

Arubas, Benjamin Y. and Rina Talgam. 'Jews, Christians and "*Minim*": Who Really Built and Used the Synagogue at Capernaum – a Stirring Appraisal.' In *Knowledge and Wisdom: Archaeological and Historical Essays in Honour of Leah Di Segni*, edited by Giovanni C. Bottini, L. Daniel Chrupcala and Joseph Patrich: 237–274. SBFCM 54. Milano: Edizioni Terra Santa, 2014.

Ashbrook Harvey, Susan. *Asceticism and Society in Crisis: John of Ephesus and the Lives of the Eastern Saints*. Berkeley: University of California Press, 1990.

Ashkenazi, Jacob and Mordechai Aviam. 'Monasteries, Monks, and Villages in Western Galilee in Late Antiquity.' *JLA* 5 (2013): 293–331.

Aubreton, Robert. *Anthologie Grecque, Tome X. Anthologie Palatine, Livre XI*. Paris: Les Belles Lettres, 1972 (reprinted 2002).

Aubreton, Robert and Félix Buffière (eds). *Anthologie Grecque, Tome XIII. Anthologie de Planude*. Paris: Les Belles Lettres, 1980 (reprinted 2002).

Aviam, Mordechai. 'Christian Galilee in the Byzantine Period.' In *Galilee through the Centuries: Confluence of Cultures*, edited by Eric M. Meyers: 281–300. Winona Lake, IN: Eisenbrauns, 1999.

——. 'The Ancient Synagogues at Bar'am.' In *Judaism in Late Antiquity, Part Three, Where We Stand: Issues and Debates in Ancient Judaism. Volume Four: The Special Problem of the Synagogue*, edited by Alan J. Avery-Peck and Jacob Neusner: 155–171. HO, Section One 55; Leiden: Brill, 2001.

——. *Jews, Pagans and Christians in the Galilee: 25 Years of Archaeological Excavations and Surveys, Hellenistic to Byzantine Periods*. Rochester, NY: University of Rochester Press and Institute for Galilean Archaeology, 2004.

Avigad, Nahman. 'Excavations at Beth She'arim: Preliminary Report.' *IEJ* 7 (1957):1–37, 239–55.

——. *Beth She'arim III. Report on the Excavations During 1953–1958: Catacombs 12–23*. Brunswick: Rutgers University Press, 1976.

Avi-Yonah, Michael. 'Synagogue Architecture in the Late Classical Period.' In *Jewish Art: An Illustrated History*, edited by C. Roth: 157–89. London: Valentine Mitchell, 1961.

——. *The Jews of Palestine: A Political History from the Bar Kokdba War to the Arab Conquest*. Blackwell's Classical Studies. Oxford: Blackwell, 1976.

Bagatti, Bellarmino. *Gli Scavi Di Nazaret, Volume I: Dalle Origini al Secolo XII*. SBF 17. Jerusalem: Franciscan printing press, 1967.

——. *The Church from the Circumcision: History and Archaeology of the Judaeo-Christians*, translated by E. Hoade; second edition. SBFCM. Jerusalem: Franciscan Printing Press, 1984.

Bal, Mieke. *Narratology: Introduction to the Theory of Narrative*. Third edition. Toronto: University of Toronto Press, 2009.

Baldwin, Barry 'Four Problems in Agathias.' *ByzZ* 70 (1970): 295–305.

——. 'The Date of the *Cycle* of Agathias.' *ByzZ* 73 (1980): 334–40.

Bar Ilan, Meir. 'Washing Feet Before Prayer: Moslem Influence or an Ancient Jewish Custom.' *Mahanaim* 1 (1991): 162–9.

Barag, Dan. 'En Gedi. The Synagogue.' *NEAEHL* 2 (1993): 399–409.

Barnes, Timothy D. 'Christians and the Theater.' In *Roman Theater and Society*, edited by William J. Slater: 161–80. Ann Arbor Michigan: University of Michigan Press, 1996.

Bassett, Sarah. *The Urban Image of Late Antique Constantinople*. Cambridge and New York: Cambridge University Press, 2004.

Belayche, Nicole. 'Des lieux pour le "profane" dans l'Empire tardo-antique? Les fêtes entre koinônia sociale et espaces de rivalités religieuses.' *AntTard* 15 (2007): 35–46.

Bell, Catherine. 'The Ritual Body and the Dynamics of Ritual Power.' *JRitSt* 4 (1990): 299–313.

Bell, Peter N. *Three Political Voices from the Age of Justinian*. Liverpool: Liverpool University Press, 2009.

——. *Social Conflict in the Age of Justinian: Its Nature, Management, and Mediation*. Oxford and New York: Oxford University Press, 2013.

Berger, Albrecht. 'The Cult of the Maccabees in Eastern Orthodox Church.' In *Dying for the Faith, Killing for the Faith: Old-Testament Faith-Warriors (1 and 2 Maccabees) in Historical Perspective*, edited by Gabriela Signori: 105–23. Brill's Studies in Intellectual History, vol. 206. Leiden: Brill, 2012.

Berman, Ariel. 1988. 'Lower Galilee and Jezreel Valley – Reports.' *ESI* 7–8 (1988): 200.

Blanc, Pierre-Marie, Jean-Marie Dentzer and Jean-Pierre Sodini. 'La Grande Église à Plan Centré (ou "Cathédrale de l'Est").' In *Bosra. Aux Portes de l'Arabie*, edited by

214 Bibliography

Jacqueline Dentzer-Feydy, Michèle Vallerin, Thibaud Fournet, Ryad Mukdad, and Anas Mukdad: 137–46. Beirut: Presses de l'institut français du Proche-Orient, 2007.

Bonnie, Rick. *Galilee During the Second Century AD: An Archaeological Examination of a Period of Socio-Cultural Development*. PhD dissertation, KU Leuven, 2014.

Bourdieu, Pierre. *Outline of a Theory of Practice*, translated by Richard Nice. Cambridge: Cambridge University Press, 1977.

———. 'Social Space and Symbolic Power.' *Sociological Theory* 7 (1989): 14–25.

———. 'Rites as Acts of Institution.' In *Honor and Grace in Anthropology*, edited by J. G. Peristiany and Julian Pitt-Rivers: 79–89. Cambridge: Cambridge University Press, 1992.

Bowersock, G. W. *Hellenism in Late Antiquity*. Ann Arbor: The University of Michigan Press, 1990.

Boyarin, Daniel. *Dying for God: Martyrdom and the Making of Christianity and Judaism*. Stanford, California; Stanford University Press, 1999.

———. *Border Lines: The Partition of Judaeo-Christianity*. Philadelphia: The University of Pennsylvania Press, 2004.

———. 'The Parables of Enoch and the Foundation of the Rabbinic Sect: A Hypothesis', in *'The Words of a Wise Man's Mouth are Gracious' (Qoh 10,12): Festschrift for Günter Stemberger on the Occasion of His 65th Birthday*, edited by Mauro Perani: 53–72. Berlin and New York: De Gruyter, 2005.

———. 'Semantic Difference; or, "Judaism"/"Christianity"', in *The Ways that Never Parted: Jews and Christians in Late Antiquity and the Early Middle Ages*, edited by Adam H. Becker and Annette Yoshiko Reed: 65–85. Minneapolis: Fortress Press, 2007.

Brakke, David. *Demons and the Making of the Monk: Spiritual Combat in Early Christianity*. London: Harvard University Press, 2006.

Braun, Eliot. 'Soundings at Horbat 'Ammudim, Lower Galilee.' *'Atiqot* 42 (2001): 237–42.

Brenk, Beat. 'Spolia From Constantine to Charlemagne: Aesthetics Versus Ideology.' *DOP* 41 (1987): 103–9.

Broadhead, Edwin K. *Jewish Ways of Following Jesus: Redrawing the Religious Map of Antiquity*. WUNT 266. Tübingen: Mohr Siebeck, 2010.

Brooks, Ernest Walter, (ed.). *Iohannis Ephesini Historiae Ecclesiasticae Pars Tertia*. Leuven: Peeters, 1935.

———. (trans.). *Iohannis Ephesini Historiae Ecclesiasticae Pars Tertia*. Leuven: Peeters, 1964.

Brown, Peter. *The World of Late Antiquity: AD 150–750*. London: Thames & Hudson, 1971 (reprinted 2006).

———. 'St. Augustine's Attitude to Religious Coercion.' *JRS* 54 (1964): 107–16, reprinted in Brown, Peter. *Religion and Society in the Age of Saint Augustine*, 260–78. London: Faber & Faber 1972.

———. *Art and Society in Late Antiquity*. Berkeley and Los Angeles: University of California Press, 1982.

———. *The Body and Society: Men, Women, and Sexual Renunciation in Early Christianity*. New York: Columbia University Press, 1988.

———. 'Aspects of the Christianisation of the Roman World.' The Tanner Lecture on Human Values, Delivered at Cambridge University, November 22, 23, and 24, 1993. Available online at tannerlectures.utah.edu/_documents/a-to-z/b/Brown95.pdf. accessed 13 October, 2014.

———. 'The Problem of Christianization.' *PBA* 82 (1993): 89–106.

——. *Authority and the Sacred: Aspects of the Christianization of the Roman World.* Cambridge: Cambridge University Press, 1995.
——. 'Christianization and Religious Conflict.' In *The Late Empire, A.D. 337–425*, edited by Averil Cameron and Peter Garnsey: 632–64. *The Cambridge Ancient History*, vol. 13. Cambridge: Cambridge University Press, 1998.
Brubaker, Rogers. *Ethnicity without Groups.* Cambridge MA: Harvard University Press, 2004.
Burns, Joshua Ezra. 'The Archaeology of Rabbinic Literature and the Study of Jewish–Christian relations in Late Antiquity.' In *Religion, Ethnicity, and Identity in Ancient Galilee*, edited by Jürgen K. Zangenberg, Harold W. Attridge and Dale B. Martin: 403–24. WUNT 210. Tübingen: Mohr Siebeck, 2007.
Burns, Thomas S. and John W. Eadie (eds). *Urban Centers and Rural Contexts in Late Antiquity.* East Lansing, MI: Michigan State University Press, 2001.
Busch, Stephan. *Versus Balnearum: die antike Dichtung über Bäder und Baden im römischen Reich.* Stuttgart: Teubner, 1999.
Butler, Howard C. *Sardis, Vol. I: The Excavations, pt. 1: 1910–1914.* Leiden: Brill, 1922.
——. *Sardis, Vol. II: Architecture, pt. 1: the Temple of Artemis.* Leiden: Brill, 1925.
Buxton, Richard. 'Imaginary Greek Mountains.' *Journal of Hellenic Studies* 112 (1992): 1–15.
Cain, Andrew. *Jerome's Epitaph on Paula: A Commentary on the Epitaphium Sanctae Paulae, edited with an introduction and translation.* Oxford; Oxford University Press, 2013.
Cameron, Alan. *The Last Pagans of Rome.* Oxford: Oxford University Press, 2011.
Cameron, Alan and Averil Cameron. 'The *Cycle* of Agathias.' *JHS* 86 (1966): 6–25.
Cameron, Averil. *Agathias.* Oxford: Clarendon Press, 1970.
——. 'Jews and Heretics – A Category Error?' In *The Ways that Never Parted: Jews and Christians in Late Antiquity and the Early Middle Ages*, edited by Adam H. Becker and Annette Yoshiko Reed: 345–60. Minneapolis: Fortress Press, 2007.
Canivet, Pierre. *Le monachisme syrien selon Théodoret de Cyr.* ThH 42. Paris: Beauchesne, 1977.
Caseau, Beatrice. 'POLEMEIN LITHOIS: La désacralisation des espaces et des objects religieux païens durant l'antiquité tardive.' In *Le sacré et son inscription dans l'espace à Byzance et en occident*, edited by Michel Kaplan: 61–123. Paris: Publications de la Sorbonne, 2001.
Cecconi, G. A. 'Il rescritto di Spello: Prospettive recenti.' In *Costantino prima e dopo Costantino: Constantine before and after Constantine*, edited by Giorgio Bonamente, Noel Lenski and Rita Lizzi Testa: 273–90. Bari: Edipuglia, 2012.
Chancey, Mark A. *Greco-Roman Culture and the Galilee of Jesus.* SNTS 134. Cambridge: Cambridge University Press, 2005.
Coates-Stephens, Robert. 'Attitudes to *Spolia* In Some Late Antique Texts.' In *Theory and Practice in Late Antique Archaeology*, edited by Luke Lavan and William Bowden: 341–58. LAA 1. Leiden: Brill, 2003.
Cohen, Jeremy. '"Slay Them Not:" Augustine and the Jews in Modern Scholarship.' *Medieval Encounters* 4 (1998): 78–92.
Cohen, Shaye J. D. 'Were Pharisees and Rabbis the Leaders of Communal Prayer and Torah Study in Antiquity: The Evidence of the New Testament, Josephus, and the Church Fathers.' In *The Echoes of Many Texts: Reflections on Jewish and Christian Traditions. Essays in Honor of Lou H. Silberman*, edited by W. G. Dever and J. E. Wright: 99–114. BJS 313. Atlanta, Georgia: Scholars Press, 1997.
——. 'The Rabbi in Second Century Jewish Society.' In *The Cambridge History of Judaism, Volume Three: The Early Roman Period*, edited by W. Horbury, W. D. Davies and J. Sturdy: 922–90. Cambridge: Cambridge University Press, 1999.

——. 'The Ways That Parted: Jews, Christians, and Jewish–Christians ca. 100–150 .' In *Near Eastern Languages and Civilizations, Harvard University*. Digital Access to Scholarship at Harvard, available online at http://dash.harvard.edu/handle/1/10861143?show=full, 2013, accessed 25 January 2016.

——. 'In Between: Jewish–Christians and the Curse of the Heretics.' In *Partings: How Judaism and Christianity Became Two*, edited by Hershel Shanks: 207–36. Washington D.C.: Biblical Archaeology Society, 2014.

Conder, Claude R. and Horatio H. Kitchener. *The Survey of Western Palestine. Memoirs of the Topography, Orography, Hydrography, and Archaeology: Volume I, Sheets I–VI, Galilee*. London: Palestine Exploration Fund, 1881.

Cooper, Kate. *The Virgin and the Bride: Idealized Womanhood in Late Antiquity*. Cambridge, MA: Harvard University Press, 1996.

Corbo, Virgilio C. *Cafarnao I: Gli Edifici Della Città*. Jerusalem: Franciscan Printing Press, 1975.

——. 'Piazza e Villa Urbana a Magdala.' *Liber Annuus* 28 (1978): 232–40.

Cox Miller, Patricia. *Dreams in Late Antiquity: Studies in the Imagination of a Culture*. Princeton: Princeton University Press, 1994.

——. *The Poetry of Thought in Late Antiquity*. Aldershot; Ashgate, 2001.

——. *Corporeal Imagination: Signifying the Holy in Late Ancient Christianity*. Philadelphia: University of Pennsylvania Press, 2009.

Cresswell, Tim. *In Place/Out of Place: Geography, Ideology, and Transgression*. Minneapolis: University of Minnesota Press, 1996.

——. *Place: A Short Introduction*. Oxford: Blackwell, 2004.

Crowfoot, John Winter. *Early Churches in Palestine*. London: published for the British Academy by H. Milford, Oxford University Press, 1941.

Curran, John. 'Moving Statues in Late Antique Rome: Problems of Perspective.' *AH* 17 (1994): 46–58.

——. *Pagan City and Christian Capital: Rome in the Fourth Century*. Oxford: Clarendon, 2000.

d'Izarny, Raymond. 'Mariage et consécration virginale au IVe siècle.' *La vie spirituelle: Supplément* 6/24 (1953): 92–108.

Daly, Lawrence J. 'Themistius' Plea for Religious Tolerance.' In *GRBS* 12 (1971): 65–79.

de Lange, Nicholas. *Origen and the Jews: Studies in Jewish–Christian relations in Third-Century Palestine*. University of Cambridge Oriental Publications 25. Cambridge: Cambridge University Press, 1976.

De Luca, Stefano. 'Vorgeschichte, Ursprung und Funktion der byzantinischen Klöster von Kafarnaum/Tabgha in der Region um den See Gennesaret.' In *Tabgha 2012: Festschrift zur Einweihung des neuen Klostergebäudes am 17. Mai 2012*, edited by Abtei Dormitio and Kloster Tabgha: 24–59. Jerusalem: Emerezian est., 2012.

Debru, Armelle. 'Physiology.' In *The Cambridge Companion to Galen*, edited by R. J. Hankinson: 263–82. Cambridge: Cambridge University Press, 2008.

Degryse, Patrick and Jens Schneider. 'Pliny the Elder and Sr–Nd Isotopes: Tracing the Provenance of Raw Materials for Roman Glass Production.' *JAS* 35 (2008): 1993–2000.

Demierre, Brigitte. 'Les Fours À Chaux en Grèce.' *JRA* 15 (2002): 282–96.

Devos, Paul. 'La date du voyage d'Égérie.' *AnBoll* 85 (1967): 165–84.

Dix, Brian. 'The Manufacture of Lime and Its Uses in the Western Roman Provinces.' *OJA* 1 (1982): 331–46.

Dothan, Moshe. 'Hammath-Tiberias.' *NEAEHL* 2 (1993): 573–7.

Drake, H. A. 'Constantinian Echoes in Themistius.' *StPatr* 34 (2001): 44–50.
Dunderberg, Ismo. *Beyond Gnosticism: Myth, Lifestyle and Society in the School of Valentinus*. New York: Columbia University Press, 2008.
———. *Gnostic Morality Revisited.* WUNT 347. Tübingen: Mohr Siebeck, 2015.
Duval, Yves-Marie (ed.), *La décrétale Ad Gallos Episcopos: son text et son auteur*. Leiden: Brill, 2005.
Efroymson, David P. 'Whose Jews? Augustine's Tractate on John.' In *A Multiform Heritage: Studies on Early Judaism and Christianity in Honor of Robert A. Kraft*, edited by B. G. Wright: 197–211. Atlanta: Scholars Press, 1999.
Elderkin, George W. (ed.), *Antioch-on-the-Orontes I: the Excavations of 1932*. Princeton: Princeton University Press, 1934.
Eliav, Yaron Z. 'Viewing the Sculptural Environment: Shaping the Second Commandment.' In *The Talmud Yerushalmi and Graeco-Roman Culture III*, edited by Peter Schäfer: 411–33. TSAJ 93. Tübingen: Mohr Siebeck, 2002.
Emilsson, Eyjólfur Kjalar. *Plotinus on Sense Perception: A Philosophical Study.* Cambridge: Cambridge University Press, 1988.
Errington, R. Malcolm. *Roman Imperial Policy from Julian to Theodosius*. Chapel Hill: The University of North Carolina Press, 2006.
Fagan, Garrett G. *Bathing in Public in the Roman World*. Ann Arbor: University of Michigan Press, 1999.
Festugière, André-Jean. *Antioche païenne et chrétienne: Libanius, Chrysostome et les moines de Syrie*. Paris: E. de Boccard, 1959.
Fine, Steven. *This Holy Place: On the Sanctity of the Synagogue during the Greco-Roman Period*. Notre Dame: University Press, 1997.
———. 'Iconoclasm and the Art of Late-Antique Palestinian Synagogues.' In *From Dura to Sepphoris: Studies in Jewish Art and Society in Late Antiquity*, edited by Lee I. Levine and Zeev Weiss: 183–94. JRASup 14. Portsmouth, RI: JRA, 2000.
———. *Art and Judaism in the Greco-Roman World. Toward a New Jewish Archaeology.* Cambridge: Cambridge University Press, 2005.
———. 'Furnishing God's Study House: An Exercise in Rabbinic Imagination.' In Steven Fine, *Art, History and the Historiography of Judaism in Roman Antiquity*: 139–59. BRLJ 34. Leiden: Brill 2014.
Fischer, Alysia A. *Hot Pursuit: Integrating Anthropology in Search of Ancient Glass-Blowers*. Lanham, MD: Lexington Books, 2008.
Fischer, Moshe L. *Marble Studies: Roman Palestine and the Marble Trade*. Xenia 40. Konstanz: Universitätsverlag Konstanz, 1998.
———. 'The Fate of Holy Land Marble: Remarks on Recycling in the Past.' In *Archéomatériaux: Marbres Et Autres Roches – Actes De La IVe Conférence Internationale ASMOSIA IV, France, Bordeaux-Talence, 9–13 Octobre 1995*, edited by Max Schvoerer: 281–84. Bordeaux: Centre de Recherche en Physique Appliquée à l'Archéologie, 1999.
Foss, Clive. *Ephesus after Antiquity*. Cambridge: Cambridge University Press, 1979.
———. 'Syria in Transition, A.D. 550–750: An Archaeological Approach.' *DOP* 51 (1997): 189–269.
Frank, Georgia. *The Memory of the Eyes: Pilgrims to Living Saints in Christian Late Antiquity*, Berkeley: University of California Press, 2000.
———. 'The Pilgrim's Gaze in the Age before Icons.' In *Visuality Before and Beyond the Renaissance. Seeing as Others Saw*, edited by Robert S. Nelson: 98–115. Cambridge; Cambridge University Press, 2000.
Fredriksen, Paula. 'What Parting of the Ways; Jews, Gentiles, and the Ancient Mediterranean City.' In *The Ways that Never Parted: Jews and Christians in Late Antiquity and the*

Early Middle Ages, edited by Adam H. Becker and Annette Yoshiko Reed: 35–63. Minneapolis: Fortress Press, 2007.

———. *Augustine and the Jews: A Christian Defence of Jews and Judaism*. New York, Doubleday, 2008.

Freestone, Ian C. and Yael Gorin-Rosen. 'The Great Glass Slab of Bet Shearim – an Early Islamic Glass-Making Experiment?' *JGS* 41 (1999): 105–16.

Freestone, Ian C., K. A. Leslie, M. Thirlwall and Yael Gorin-Rosen. 'Strontium Isotopes in the Investigation of Early Glass Production: Byzantine and Early Islamic Glass From the Near East.' *Archaeometry* 45 (2003): 19–32.

Funke, Hermann. 'Majestäts- und Magieprozesse bei Ammianus Marcellinus.' *JAC* 10 (1967): 145–75.

Garland, Lynda. 'Public Lavatories, Mosquito Nets and Agathias' Cat: The Sixth-Century Epigram in its Justinianic Context.' In *Basileia: Essays on Imperium and Culture in Honour of E. M. and M. J. Jeffreys*, edited by Geoffrey Nathan and Lynda Garland: 141–58. Byzantina Australiensia 17. Virginia, Queensland, Australia: Centre for Early Christian Studies, Australian Catholic University, 2011.

Garnsey, Peter, and Caroline Humfress. *The Evolution of the Late Antique World*. Cambridge: Orchard Academic, 2001.

Gaşpar, Cristian-Nicolae. *In Praise of Unlikely Holy Men: Elite Hagiography, Monastic Panegyric, and Cultural Translation in the Philotheos Historia of Theodoret, Bishop of Cyrrhus*. PhD dissertation, Central European University, 2006.

———. 'An Oriental in Greek Dress: The Making of a Perfect Philosopher in the *Philotheos Historia* of Theodoret of Cyrrhus.' *AMSCEU* 14 (2008): 193–229.

Gavrilyuk, Paul L. and Sarah Coakley (eds). *The Spiritual Senses: Perceiving God in Western Christianity*. Cambridge; Cambridge University Press, 2011.

Gawlikowski, Michal. 'Excavations in the Allat Sanctuary, 2005–2006.' *PAM* 18 (2008): 531–41.

Glinka, Christian. *Chrêsis: Die Methode der Kirchenväter im Umgang mit der antiken Kultur. (I) Der Begriff des 'rechten Gebrauchs.'* Basel/Stuttgart: Schwabe & Co Ag, 1984.

Goehring, James E. 'The Encroaching Desert: Literary Production and Ascetic Space in Early Christian Egypt.' *JECS* 1 (1993): 281–96.

Goldhill, Simon. *Foucault's Virginity: Ancient Erotic Fiction and the History of Sexuality*. Cambridge and New York: Cambridge University Press, 1995.

Goodman, Martin. *State and Society in Roman Galilee, AD 132–212*. Totowa, NJ: Rowman & Allanheld, 1983.

———. 'The Function of Minim in Early Rabbinic Judaism.' In *Geschichte–Tradition–Reflexion: FS für Martin Hengel zum 70. Geburtstag. Band I: Judentum*, edited by H. Cancik, H. Lichtenberger and P. Schäfer: 501–10. Tübingen: Mohr-Siebeck, 1996.

Goranson, Stephen. 'Joseph of Tiberias Revisited: Orthodoxies and Heresies in Fourth-Century Galilee.' In *Galilee through the Centuries: Confluence of Cultures*, edited by Eric M. Meyers: 335–43. Winona Lake, IN: Eisenbrauns, 1999.

Greenhalgh, Michael. *The Survival of Roman Antiquities in the Middle Ages*. London: Duckworth, 1989.

———. *Constantinople to Córdoba: Dismantling Ancient Architecture in the East, North Africa and Islamic Spain*. Leiden: Brill, 2012.

———. *From the Romans to the Railways. The Fate of Antiquities in Asia Minor*. Technology and Change in History 13. Leiden: Brill, 2013.

Grey, Matthew J. '"The Redeemer to Arise from the House of Dan": Samson, Apocalypticism, and Messianic Hopes in Late Antique Galilee.' *JSJ* 44 (2013): 553–89.

Grig, Lucy. 'Interpreting the Kalends of January: A Case Study for Understanding Late Antique Popular Culture?' In *Popular Culture in the Ancient World*, edited by Lucy Grig. Cambridge: Cambridge University Press, forthcoming.

Gruenwald, Ithamar. 'The Other Self: Introductory Notes.' In *Concepts of the Other in Near Eastern Religions*, edited by Ilai Athon, Ithamar Gruenwald and Itamar Singer: 7–16. IOS 14. Leiden: Brill, 1994.

Guérin, M. Victor. *Description Géographique, Historique et Archéologique de la Palestine, III – Galilée*. Paris: L'Imprimerie Nationale, 1880.

Gutzwiller, Kathryn. 'Art's Echo: The Tradition of Hellenistic Ecphrastic Epigram.' In *Hellenistic Epigrams*, edited by M. Annette Harder, Remco F. Regtuit, and G. C. Wakker: 85–112. Leuven, Belgium; Sterling, VA: Peeters, 2002.

Hachlili, Rachel. *Ancient Synagogues – Archaeology and Art: New Discoveries and Current Research*. Handbook of Oriental Studies 1/105. Leiden and Boston: Brill, 2013.

Hadley, James. 'The Apse and Cross: Ancient Precedents, Contemporary Considerations.' *Anaphora* 7.2 (2013): 1–30.

Hadot, Pierre. *Philosophy as a Way of Life: Spiritual Exercises from Socrates to Foucault*. Edited with an Introduction by Arnold I. Davidson, Translated by Michael Chase. Oxford: Blackwell Publishing, 1995.

Hahn, Johannes. 'The Veneration of the Maccabean Brothers in Fourth Century Antioch: Religious Competition, Martyrdom, and Innovation.' In *Dying for the Faith, Killing for the Faith: Old-Testament Faith-Warriors (1 and 2 Maccabees) in Historical Perspective*, edited by Gabriela Signori: 79–104. Brill's Studies in Intellectual History, vol. 206. Leiden: Brill, 2012.

Hahn, Johannes, Stephen Emmel and Ulrich Gotter (eds). *From Temple to Church: Destruction and Renewal of Local Cultic Topography in Late Antiquity*. RGRW 163. Leiden: Brill, 2008.

Hakola, Raimo. *Identity Matters: John, the Jews and Jewishness*. NovTSup 118. Brill: Leiden, 2005.

——. 'Erik H. Erikson's Identity Theory and the Formation of Early Christianity.' *JBV* 30 (2009): 5–15.

——. *Reconsidering Johannine Christianity: A Social Identity Approach*. New York and London: Routledge, 2015.

Hakola, Raimo, Nina Nikki and Ulla Tervahauta. 'Introduction.' In *Others and the Construction of Early Christian Identities*, edited by Raimo Hakola, Nina Nikki and Ulla Tervahauta: 9–30. PFES 106. Helsinki: The Finnish Exegetical Society.

Hanfmann, George M. A. and Nancy H. Ramage. *Sculpture From Sardis: The Finds through 1975*. AES 2. Cambridge, MA: Harvard University Press, 1978.

Hannestad, Niels. *Tradition in Late Antique Sculpture: Conservation–Modernization–Production*. Aarhus: Aarhus University Press, 1994.

Harkins, Franklin T. 'Nuancing Augustine's Hermeneutical Jews: Allegory and Actual Jews in the Bishop's Sermons,' *JSJ* 36 (2005): 41–64.

Harl, Marguerite. 'La dénonciation des festivités profanes dans le discours épiscopal et monastique en Orient chrétien à la fin du Ive siècle.' In *La Fête, pratique et discours*: 123–47. AUB 262. Paris 1981.

Harmless, William (SJ). *Desert Christians: An Introduction to the Literature of Early Monasticism*. Oxford: Oxford University Press, 2004.

Hartal, Moshe. 'Tiberias, Galei Kinneret.' *HA/ESI* 120 (2008). Available online at http://www.hadashot-esi.org.il/report_detail_eng.asp?id=773&mag_id=114, accessed 28 September 2015.

Heather, Peter J., and David Moncur. *Politics, Philosophy, and Empire in the Fourth Century: Select Orations of Themistius.* Translated Texts for Historians, vol. 36. Liverpool: Liverpool University Press, 2001.

Heiska, Nina. 'The Economy and Livelihoods of the Early Christian Monasteries in Palestine.' Masters Thesis, University of Helsinki, Institute for Cultural Research, Archaeology, 2003.

Henderson, Jeffrey. *The Maculate Muse: Obscene Language in Attic Comedy*, second edition. Oxford and New York: Oxford University Press, 1991 (originally published 1975).

Henry, Nathalie. 'The Song of Songs and the Liturgy of the *velatio* in the Fourth Century: From Literary Metaphor to Liturgical Reality.' In *Continuity and Change in Christian Worship*, edited by R. N. Swanson: 18–28. Woodbridge, UK and Rochester, NY: The Boydell Press, 1999.

——. 'A New Insight into the Growth of Ascetic Society in the Fourth Century AD: The Public Consecration of Virgins as a Means of Integration and Promotion of the Female Ascetic Movement.' In *Studia Patristica, Vol. XXXV: Ascetica, Gnostica, Liturgica, Orientalia, Papers Presented at the Thirteenth International Conference on Patristic Studies Held in Oxford 1999*, edited by M. F. Wiles and E. J. Yarnold with the assistance of P. M. Parvis: 102–9. Leuven: Peeters, 2001.

Hernández de la Fuente, David. 'Parallels Between Dionysos and Christ in Late Antiquity: Miraculous Healings in Nonnus *Dionysiaca*.' In *Redefining Dionysos*, edited by Alberto Bernabé, Miguel Herrero de Jáuregui, Ana Isabel Jiménez San Cristóbal, and R. Martín Hernández: 464–87. Berlin: De Gruyter, 2013.

Hezser, Catherine. *The Social Structure of the Rabbinic Movement in Roman Palestine*. TSAJ 66. Tübingen: Mohr-Siebeck, 1997.

Hirschfeld, Yizhar. 'The Monasteries of Palestine in the Byzantine Period.' In *Christians and Christianity in the Holy Land: From the Origins to the Latin Kingdoms*, edited by Ora Limor and Gay G. Stroumsa: 401–19. Cultural Encounters in Late Antiquity and the Middle Ages 5. Turnhout, Belgium: Brepols, 2006.

Hodge, A. Trevor. *Roman Aqueducts and Water Supply*. London: Duckworth, 1999.

Hoffman, Lawrence A. *Beyond the Text: A Holistic Approach to Liturgy*. Bloomington and Indianapolis: University of Indiana Press, 1989.

Højte, Jakob M. *Roman Imperial Statue Bases: From Augustus to Commodus*. ASMA 7. Aarhus: Aarhus University Press, 2005.

Holt, Laura. 'Divinatione daemonum, De.' In *Augustine through the Ages: An Encyclopedia*, edited by Allan D. Fitzgerald and John C. Cavadini: 277–8. Grand Rapids MI: W. B. Eerdmans, 1999.

Holum, Kenneth G. 'Hadrian and St. Helena: Imperial Travel and the Origins of Christian Holy Land Pilgrimage.' In *The Blessings of Pilgrimage*, edited by Robert Ousterhout: 66–81. Urbana: University of Illinois Press, 1990.

Humphries, Mark. '*Nec metu nec adulandi foeditate constricta:* The Image of Valentinian I from Symmachus to Ammianus.' In *The Late Roman World and its Historian*, edited by J. W. Drijvers and D. Hunt: 117–26. London: Routledge, 1999.

Hunt, David. 'Christianising the Roman Empire: the Evidence of the Code.' In *The Theodosian Code: Studies in the Imperial Law of Late Antiquity*, edited by Jill Harries and Ian Wood: 143–58. London: Duckworth, 1993.

Hunter, David G. 'The Virgin, the Bride and the Church: Reading Psalm 45 in Ambrose, Jerome and Augustine.' *Church History* 69 (2000): 281–303.

———. *Marriage, Celibacy, and Heresy in Ancient Christianity: The Jovinianist Controversy.* Oxford: Oxford University Press, 2007.
Huttunen, Niko. 'In the Category of Philosophy? Christians in Early Pagan Accounts.' In *Others and the Construction of Early Christian Identities*, edited by Raimo Hakola, Nina Nikki and Ulla Tervahauta: 239–81. PFES 106. Helsinki: Finnish Exegetical Society, 2013.
Jacobs, Andrew S. 'Visible Ghosts and Invisible Demons: The Place of Jews in Early Christian *Terra Sancta*', In *Galilee through the Centuries: Confluence of Cultures*, edited by Eric M. Meyers: 359–75. Winona Lake, IN: Eisenbrauns, 1999.
———. 'The Lion and the Lamb: Reconsidering Jewish–Christian Relations in Antiquity.' In *The Ways that Never Parted: Jews and Christians in Late Antiquity and the Early Middle Ages*, edited by Adam H. Becker and Annette Yoshiko Reed: 95–118. Minneapolis: Fortress Press, 2007.
———. 'Jews and Christians.' In *The Oxford Handbook of Early Christian Studies*, edited by Susan Ashbrook Harvey and David G. Hunter: 169–85. Oxford: Oxford University Press, 2008.
———. 'Matters (Un-)Becoming: Conversions in Epiphanius of Salamis.' *Church History* 81 (2012): 27–47.
Jacobs, Ine. 'Production to Destruction? Pagan and Mythological Statuary in Asia Minor.' *AJA* 114 (2010): 267–303.
James, Liz. '"Pray Not to Fall Into Temptation and Be on Your Guard": Pagan Statues in Christian Constantinople.' *Gesta* 35 (1996): 12–20.
Jensen, Robin M. 'Saints' Relics and the Consecration of Church Buildings in Rome.' In *Studia Patristica, Vol. LXXI, Including Papers Presented at the Conferences on Early Roman Liturgy to 600 (14.11.2009 and 27.2.2010) at Blackfriars Hall, Oxford, UK*, edited by Juliette Day and Markus Vinzent (Leuven: Peeters, 2014): 153–69.
Jones, Siân. 'Identities in Practice: Towards an Archaeological Perspective on Jewish Identity in Antiquity.' In *Jewish Local Patriotism and Self-Identification in the Graeco-Roman Period*, edited by Siân Jones and Sarah Pearce: 29–49. JSPSup 31. Sheffield: Sheffield Academic Press, 1998.
Joslyn-Siemiatkoski, Daniel. *Christian Memories of the Maccabean Martyrs*. New York: Palgrave MacMillan, 2009.
Jürgens, Heiko. *Pompa diaboli: Die lateinischen Kirchenväter und das antike Theater.* TBAW 46. Stuttgart: W. Kohlhammer, 1972.
Kahlos, Maijastina. '*Comissationes et ebrietates*: Church Leaders against Banqueting at *Martyria* and at Tombs.' In *Ad itum liberum: Essays in Honour of Anne Helttula*, edited by Outi Merisalo and Raija Vainio: 13–23. Jyväskylä: University of Jyväskylä, Department of Languages, 2007.
———. *Debate and Dialogue. Christian and Pagan Cultures, c. 360–430.* Aldershot: Ashgate, 2007.
———. *Forbearance and Compulsion: Rhetoric of Tolerance and Intolerance in Late Antiquity.* London: Duckworth, 2009.
———. 'Introduction.' In *The Faces of the Other: Religious Rivalry and Ethnic Encounters in the Later Roman World*, edited by Maijastina Kahlos: 1–15. Cursor Mundi 10. Turnhout, Belgium: Brepols, 2011.
———. 'The Shadow of the Shadow: Examining Fourth- and Fifth-Century Christian Depictions of Pagans.' In *The Faces of the Other: Religious Rivalry and Ethnic Encounters in the Later Roman World*, edited by Maijastina Kahlos: 165–195. Cursor Mundi 10. Turnhout, Belgium: Brepols, 2011.

———. 'Rhetoric and Realities: Themistius and the Changing Tides in Imperial Religious Policies.' In *Politiche religiose nel mondo antico e tardoantico*, edited by Giovanni A. Cecconi and Chantal Gabrielli: 287–304. Collana Munera 33. Bari: Edipuglia, 2011.

———. 'Polluted by Sacrifices: Christian Repugnance at Sacrificial Rituals in Late Antiquity.' In *Ancient and Medieval Religion in Practice*, edited by Ville Vuolanto and Sari Katajala-Peltomaa: 159–71. Rome: Acta Instituti Romani Finlandiae, 2013.

———. 'The Emperor's New Images: How to Honour the Emperor in the Christian Empire.' In *Emperors and the Divine: Rome and Beyond*, edited by Maijastina Kahlos. Helsinki: Helsinki Collegium for Advanced Studies, forthcoming.

Kaldellis, Anthony. *Hellenism in Byzantium: The Transformations of Greek Identity and the Reception of the Classical Tradition*. Cambridge and New York: Cambridge University Press, 2007.

———. 'The Making of Hagia Sophia and the Last Pagans of New Rome.' *JLA* 6.2 (2013): 347–66.

Kalmin, Richard. 'Christians and Heretics in Rabbinic Literature of Late Antiquity.' *HTR* 87 (1994): 155–69.

———. *The Sage in Jewish Society in Late Antiquity*. New York: Routledge, 1999.

Kalvesmaki, Joel (ed.). *Guide to Evagrius Ponticus*. Available online at http://evagriusponticus.net (edition used: Spring 2015).

Kessler, Herbert L. 'The Sepphoris Mosaic and Christian Art.' In *From Dura to Sepphoris: Studies in Jewish Art and Society in Late Antiquity*, edited by Lee. I. Levine and Zeev Weiss: 64–72. JRASup 40; Portsmouth, RI: JRA, 2000.

Kimelman, Reuven. 'Identifying Jews and Christians in Roman-Syria Palestine.' In *Galilee through the Centuries: Confluence of Cultures*, edited by Eric M. Meyers: 301–33. Winona Lake, Indiana: Eisenbrauns, 1999.

King, Karen L. *What is Gnosticism?* Cambridge, Massachusetts: The Belknap Press of Harvard University, 2003.

Klauser, Theodor. 'Der Festkalender der Alten Kirche im Spannungsfeld jüdischer Traditionen, christlicher Glaubensvorstellungen und missionarischen Anpassungswillens.' In *Kirchengeschichte als Missionsgeschichte* I, edited by Heinzgünther Frohnes and Uwe W. Knorr: 377–88. München: Kaiser, 1974.

Klostergaard Petersen, Anders. 'The Notion of Demon: Open Questions to a Diffuse Concept.' In *Die Dämonen: die Dämonologie der israelitisch-jüdischen und frühchristlichen Literatur im Kontext ihrer Umwelt*, edited by Armin Lange and Herman Lichtenberger: 23–41. Tübingen: Mohr-Siebeck, 2003.

Klutz, Todd E. 'The Rhetoric of Science in *The Rise of Christianity*: A Response to Rodney Stark's Sociological Account of Christianization.' *JECS* 6.2 (1998): 183–4.

Knuuttila, Simo. *Emotions in Ancient and Medieval Philosophy*. Oxford: Clarendon Press, 2004.

Kohl, Heinrich, and Carl Watzinger. *Antike Synagogen in Galiläa*. Leipzig: Hinrichs, 1916.

Kraeling, Carl H. *Ptolemais: City of The Libyan Pentapolis*. Chicago: The University of Chicago Press, 1962.

Kraemer, David. 'Food, Eating, and Meals.' In *The Oxford Handbook of Jewish Daily Life in Roman Palestine*, edited by Catherine Hezser: 403–19. Oxford: Oxford University Press, 2010.

Krauss, Samuel. *Synagogale Altertümer*. Berlin: Harz, 1922; reprinted Hildesheim: Olms, 1966.

Krautheimer, Richard. *Three Christian Capitals: Topography and Politics*. Berkeley: University of California Press, 1983.

Kristensen, Troels M. 'The Display of Statues in the Late Antique Cities of the Eastern Mediterranean: Reflections on Memory, Meaning, and Aesthetics.' In *Debating Urbanism Within and Beyond the Walls A.D. 300–700: Proceedings of a Conference Held at the University of Leicester, 15th November 2008*, edited by Denis Sami and Gavin Speed: 265–91. Leicester: School of Archaeology and Ancient History, 2010.

Kühnel, B. 'The Synagogue Floor Mosaic in Sepphoris: Between Paganism and Christianity.' In *From Dura to Sepphoris: Studies in Jewish Art and Society in Late Antiquity*, edited by Lee. I. Levine and Zeev Weiss: 31–43. JRASup 40; Portsmouth, RI: JRA, 2000.

Lahire, Bernard. *The Plural Actor*, translated by David Fernbach. Cambridge: Polity, 2011.

Laiou, Angeliki E. (ed.). *The Economic History of Byzantium. DOP* 39. Washington, DC: Dumbarton Oaks, 2002.

Lampe, Peter. 'Die dämonologischen Implikationen von I Korinther 8 und 10 vor dem Hintergrund paganer Zeugnisse.' In *Die Dämonen: Die Dämonologie der israelitisch-jüdischen und frühchristlichen Literatur im Kontext ihrer Umwelt*, edited by Armin Lange, Hermann Lichtenberger, and K.F. Diethard Römheld: 594–9. Tübingen: Mohr Siebeck, 2003.

Lange, Armin, Hermann Lichtenberger, and K. F. Diethard Römheld (eds). *Die Dämonen: Die Dämonologie der israelitisch-jüdischen und frühchristlichen Literatur im Kontext ihrer Umwelt*. Tübingen: Mohr Siebeck, 2003.

Lapin, Hayim. 'Rabbis and Cities in Later Roman Palestine: The Literary Evidence.' *JJS* 50 (1999): 187–207.

Larsen, Lillian I. 'Re-Drawing the Interpretative Map: Monastic Education as Civic Formation in the *Apophthegmata Patrum*.' *Coptica* 12 (2013): 1–30.

Lavan, Luke. '*Fora* and *Agorai* in Mediterranean Cities during the 4th and 5th c. A.D.' In *Social and Political Life in Late Antiquity*, edited by William Bowden, Adam Gutteridge and Carlos Machado: 195–249. LAA 3.1. Leiden: Brill, 2006.

———. 'Political Talismans? Residual "Pagan" Statues in Late Antique Public Space.' In *The Archaeology of Late Antique 'Paganism'*, edited by Luke Lavan and Michael Mulryan: 439–77. Leiden: Brill, 2011.

Lazzarini, Lorenzo. 'La determinazione della provenienza delle pietre decorative usate dai Romani.' In *I marmi colorati della Roma Imperiale*, edited by Marilda De Nuccio and Lucrezia Ungaro: 223–66. Venice: Marsilio, 2002.

———. 'La diffusione e il riuso dei più importanti marmi Romani nelle province Imperiali.' In *Pietre e Marmi Antichi: natura, caratterizzazione, origine, storia d'uso, diffusione, collezionismo*, edited by Lorenzo Lazzarini: 101–22. Padua: CEDAM, 2004.

Lee, A. D. *Pagans and Christians in Late Antiquity*. London: Routledge, 2000.

Leemans, Johan. 'General Introduction.' In *'Let Us Die That We May Live': Greek Homilies on Christian Martyrs from Asia Minor, Palestine and Syria (c. AD 350 – AD 450)*, edited by Johan Leemans, Wendy Mayer, Pauline Allen, and Boudewijn Dehandschutter: 3–52. London: Routledge, 2003.

Lefebvre, Henri. *La production de l'espace*. Paris: Anthropos 1974. English translation: *The Production of Space*, translated by Donald Nicholson-Smith. Oxford: Blackwell, 1991.

Leibner, Uzi. *Settlement and History in Hellenistic, Roman and Byzantine Galilee. An Archaeological Survey of the Eastern Galilee*. TSAJ 127. Tübingen: Mohr Siebeck, 2009.

———. 'Settlement Patterns in the Eastern Galilee: Implications Regarding the Transformation of Rabbinic Culture in Late Antiquity.' In *Jewish Identities in Antiquity: Studies in Memory of Menahem Stern*, edited by Lee I. Levine and Daniel R. Schwartz: 269–95. TSAJ 130; Tübingen: Mohr-Siebeck, 2009.

——. 'Excavations at Khirbet Wadi Hamam (Lower Galilee): The Synagogue and the Settlement.' *JRA* 23 (2010): 220–37.
Leibner, Uzi, and Shulamit Miller. 'A Figural Mosaic in the Synagogue at Khirbet Wadi Hamam.' *JRA* 23 (2010): 238–64.
Lenski, Noel. *Failure of Empire: Valens and the Roman State in the Fourth Century A.D.* Berkeley: University of California Press, 2002.
Leone, Anna. *Changing Townscapes in North Africa From Late Antiquity to the Arab Conquest.* Bari: Edipuglia, 2007.
——. *The End of the Pagan City. Religion, Economy, and Urbanism in Late Antique North Africa.* Oxford: Oxford University Press, 2013.
Lepelley, Claude. 'Formes païennes de la sociabilité en Afrique au temps de Saint Augustin.' In *Sociabilité, pouvoirs et société*, edited by Françoise Thélamon: 99–103. *Actes du Colloque de Rouen 24/26 novembre 1983*. Rouen: Publications de l'Université de Rouen 1987.
——. 'The Survival and Fall of the Classical City in Late Roman Africa.' In *The City in Late Antiquity*, edited by John Rich: 50–76. London: Routledge, 1992.
——. 'Le lieu des valeurs communes: La cité terrain neutre entre païens et chrétiens dans l'Afrique romaine tardive.' In *Idéologies et valeurs civiques dans le Monde Romain: Hommage à Claude Lepelley*, edited by Hervé Inglebert: 271–85. Paris: Picard, 2002.
——. 'De la reaction païenne à la sécularisation: le témoignage d'inscriptions municipales romano-africaines tardives.' In *Pagans and Christians in the Roman Empire: The Breaking of a Dialogue (IVth–VIth Century A.D)*, edited by Peter Brown and Rita Lizzi Testa: 273–89. Wien: Lit Verlag, 2011.
Leppin, Hartmut. 'Christianisierung, Neutralisierung und Integration: Überlegungen zur religionsgeschichtlichen Entwicklung in Konstantinopel während des vierten Jahrhunderts.' In *Christentum und Politik in der Alten Kirche*, edited by Johannes van Oort, Otmar Hesse: 1–24. Leuven: Walpole, 2009.
——. 'Christianisierungen im Römischen Reich: Überlegungen zum Begriff und zur Phasenbildung.' *ZAC* 16 (2012): 247–78.
Lerer, Yoav. 'Tarshiha, Survey.' *HA/ESI* 123 (2011). Available online at http://www.hadashot-esi.org.il/report_detail_eng.aspx?id=1689&mag_id=118. Accessed 28 September 2015.
Levine, David A. 'The Roman Limekilns of the Bamboccianti.' *AB* 70 (1988): 568–89.
Levine, Lee I. 'Bet Šeʿarim in Its Patriarchal Context.' In *'The Words of a Wise Man's Mouth are Gracious' (Qoh 10,12). Festschrift for Günter Stemberger on the Occasion of his 65th Birthday*, edited by Mauro Perani: 197–226. SJ 32. Berlin: De Gruyter, 2005.
——. *The Ancient Synagogue: The First Thousand Years*, second edition. New Haven, CT: Yale University Press, 2005.
——. *Visual Judaism in Late Antiquity. Historical Contexts of Jewish Art.* New Haven, CT: Yale University Press, 2012.
Leyerle, Blake. 'Early Christian Perceptions of the Galilee.' In *Galilee through the Centuries: Confluence of Cultures*, edited by Eric M. Meyers: 345–57. Winona Lake, IN: Eisenbrauns, 1999.
Lichtenberger, Hermann. 'Demonology in the Dead Sea Scrolls and the New Testament.' In *Text, Thought, and Practice in Qumran and Early Christianity*, edited by Ruth A. Clements, Daniel R. Schwartz: 267–80. Leiden/Boston: Brill, 2009.
Liebeschuetz, Wolf. 'The View from Antioch: from Libanius to John Chrysostom to John Malalas and Beyond.' In *Pagans and Christians in the Roman Empire: The Breaking of a Dialogue (IVth–VIth Century A.D)*, edited by Peter Brown and Rita Lizzi Testa: 309–37. Wien: Lit Verlag, 2011.

Lieu, Judith. 'History and Theology in Christian Views of Judaism' in *Jews among Pagans and Christians*, Judith Lieu, John North and Tessa Rajak (eds). London: Routledge, 1992.
———. *Image and Reality. The Jews in the World of the Christians in the Second Century.* Edinburgh: T&T Clark, 1996.
———. *Neither Jew Nor Christian: Constructing Early Christianity.* London and New York: T & T Clark, 2002.
———. *Christian Identity in the Jewish and Graeco-Roman World.* Oxford: Oxford University Press, 2004.
Lim, Richard. 'People as Power: Games, Munificence, and Contested Topography.' In *Transformations of Urbs Roma in Late Antiquity*, edited by William V. Harris: 265–81. JRASup 33. Portsmouth, RI: Journal of Roman Archeology, 1999.
———. 'Christianization, Secularization, and the Transformation of Public Life.' In *A Companion to Late Antiquity*, edited by Philip Rousseau: 497–511. Oxford: Wiley-Blackwell, 2009.
———. 'Inventing Secular Space in the Late Antique City: Reading the Circus Maximus.' In *Rom in der Spätantike: Historische Erinnerung im städtischen Raum*, edited by Ralf Behrwald and Christian Witschel: 61–81. HABES 51. Stuttgart: Franz Steiner, 2012.
Limor, Ora. '"Holy Journey", Pilgrimage and Christian Sacred Landscape.' In *Christians and Christianity in the Holy Land: From the Origins to the Latin Kingdoms*, edited by Ora Limor and Gay G. Stroumsa: 321–53. Cultural Encounters in Late Antiquity and the Middle Ages 5. Turnhout, Belgium: Brepols, 2006.
Linder, Amnon. *The Jews in Roman Imperial Legislation.* Detroit, Michigan and Jerusalem: Wayne State University Press and The Israel Academy of Sciences and Humanities, 1988.
Lindqvist, Pekka. 'Less Antagonistic Nuances in the Early Jewish Attitude towards Christianity.' In *Encounters of the Children of Abraham from Ancient to Modern Times*, edited by Antti Laato and Pekka Lindqvist: 165–80. Studies on the Children of Abraham 1. Leiden: Brill, 2010.
Ling, Roger. 'Stuccowork.' In *Roman Crafts*, edited by Donald Strong and David Brown: 209–22. London: Duckworth, 1976.
Lizzi, Rita. *Senatori, popolo, papi: Il governo di Roma al tempo dei Valentiniani.* Bari: Edipuglia, 2004.
Loffreda, Stanislao. 'The Late Chronology of the Synagogue of Capernaum.' *IEJ* (1973): 37–42.
———. *Recovering Capernaum.* Jerusalem: Franciscan Printing Press, 1993.
Lugaresi, Leonardo. '*Regio aliena*: L'atteggiamento della Chiesa verso i luoghi di spettacolo nella città tradoantica.' *AntTard* 15 (2007): 35–46.
Luomanen, Petri. *Recovering Jewish–Christian Sects and Gospels.* VCSup 110. Brill: Leiden, 2012.
MacCormack, Sabina. 'Loca Sancta: The Organisation of Sacred Topography in Late Antiquity.' In *The Blessings of Pilgrimage*, edited by Robert Ousterhout: 7–40. Urbana: University of Illinois Press, 1990.
Machado, Carlos. 'Building the Past: Monuments and Memory in the Forum Romanum.' In *Social and Political Life in Late Antiquity*, edited by William Bowden, Adam Gutteridge and Carlos Machado: 157–192. LAA 3.1. Leiden: Brill, 2006.
———. 'The City as Stage – Aristocratic Commemorations in Late Antique Rome'. In *Les frontières du profane dans l'antiquité tardive*, edited by Eric Rebillard and Claire Sotinel: 287–317. Collection de l'École française de Rome 428. Rome: École française de Rome, 2010.
MacMullen, Ramsay. *The Second Church: Popular Christianity, A.D. 200–400.* WGRWS 1. Atlanta: SBL, 2009.

Magness, Jodi. 'A Response to Eric. M. Meyers and James F. Strange.' In *Judaism in Late Antiquity, Part Three, Where We Stand: Issues and Debates in Ancient Judaism. Volume Four: The Special Problem of the Synagogue*, edited by Alan J. Avery-Peck and Jacob Neusner: 93–120. HO, Section One 55; Leiden: Brill, 2001.

———. 'The Question of the Synagogue: The Problem of Typology.' In *Judaism in Late Antiquity, Part Three, Where We Stand: Issues and Debates in Ancient Judaism. Volume Four: The Special Problem of the Synagogue*, edited by Alan J. Avery-Peck and Jacob Neusner: 1–48. HO, Section One 55; Leiden: Brill, 2001.

———. 'Did Galilee Decline in the Fifth Century? The Synagogue at Chorazin Reconsidered.' In *Religion, Ethnicity, and Identity in Ancient Galilee*, edited by Jürgen K. Zangenberg, Harold W. Attridge and Dale B. Martin: 259–74. WUNT 210. Tübingen: Mohr Siebeck, 2007.

———. 'The Ancient Synagogue at Nabratein.' *BASOR* 358 (2010): 61–8.

———. 'The Pottery from the Village of Capernaum and the Chronology of Galilean Synagogues.' *Tel Aviv* 39 (2012): 238–50.

Magness, Jodi, Shua Kisilevitz, Karen Britt, Matthew J. Grey and Chad Spigel. 'Huqoq (Lower Galilee) and Its Synagogue Mosaics: Preliminary Report on the Excavations of 2011–2013.' *JRA* 27 (2014): 327–55.

Magness, Jodi, Shua Kisilevitz, Matthew Grey, Chad Spigel, Brian Coussens and Karen Britt. 'Huqoq – 2013.' *HA/ESI* 126 (2014). Available online at http://www.hadashot-esi.org.il/report_detail_eng.aspx?id=12648&mag_id=121, accessed 25 January 2015.

Maier, Harry O. 'Religious Dissent, Heresy and Households in Late Antiquity.' *VC* 49.1 (1995): 49–63.

Mango, Cyril. 'Antique Statuary and the Byzantine Beholder.' *DOP* 17 (1963): 53–75.

———. *The Art of the Byzantine Empire, 312–1453: Sources and Documents.* Toronto: University of Toronto Press, 1986.

Ma'oz, Z.U. 'The Synagogue at Capernaum: A Radical Solution.' In *The Roman and Byzantine Near East, Volume 2. Some Recent Archaeological Research*, edited by J. H. Humphrey: 137–48. JRASup 31: Portsmouth, RI: Journal of Roman Archaeology, 1999.

Maraval, Pierre. 'The Earliest Phase of Christian Pilgrimage in the Near East (before the 7th Century).' *DOP* 56 (2002): 63–74.

Markus, Robert A. *The End of Ancient Christianity.* Cambridge: Cambridge University Press, 1990.

———. 'How on Earth Could Places Become Holy? Origins of the Christian Idea of Holy Places.' *JECS* 2 (1994): 257–71.

Martin, Dale. *Inventing Superstition: From the Hippocratics to the Christians.* Harvard: Harvard University Press, 2004.

———. 'When Did Angels Become Demons?' *JBL* 129, no. 4 (2010): 657–77.

Martin, M. l'Abbé. 'Discours de Jacques De Saroug sur la Chute des Idoles.' *ZDMG* 29 (1875): 107–47.

Massey, Doreen. *For Place.* London: Sage, 2005.

Masterman, Ernest W. G. *Studies in Galilee.* Chicago: The University of Chicago Press, 1909.

Matthews, J. F. *The Roman Empire of Ammianus Marcellinus.* London: Duckworth, 1989.

Mattila, Sharon Lea. 'Inner Village Life in Galilee: A Diverse and Complex Phenomenon.' In *Galilee in the Late Second Temple and Mishnaic Periods, Volume 1: Life, Culture and Society*, edited by David A. Fiensy and James R. Strange: 312–45. Minneapolis: Fortress Press, 2014.

Mattsson, Axel. *Untersuchungen zur Epigrammsammlung des Agathias.* Lund: Håkan Ohlssons Boktryckeri, 1942.

Maxwell, Jaclyn L. *Christianization and Communication in Late Antiquity: John Chrysostom and his Congregation in Antioch*. Cambridge: Cambridge University Press, 2006.

Mayer, Wendy. 'Les Homélies de s. Jean Chrysostome en Juillet 399: A Second Look at Pargoire's Sequence and the Chronology of the Novae Homiliae (CPG 4441).' In *Byzantinoslavica* 60 (1999): 273–303.

———. *St John Chrysostom: The Cult of the Saints. Select Homilies and Letters Introduced, Translated, and Annotated by Wendy Mayer with Bronwen Neil*. New York: St Vladimir's Seminary Press, 2006.

Mazar, Benjamin. 'Excavations in Palestine and Trans-Jordan – Esh Sheikh Ibreiq.' *QDAP* 9 (1941): 212–15.

———. 'Beth She'arim.' *IEJ* 6 (1956): 261–2.

———. *Beth She'arim I. Report on the Excavations During 1936–1940: Catacombs 1–4*. Brunswick, NJ: Rutgers University Press, 1973.

Mazor, Gabriel. 'Beth She'an Project. City Center of Ancient Beth She'an (South).' *ESI* 6 (1988): 10–24.

———. 'Beth She'an Project 1988. Department of Antiquities Expedition.' *ESI* 7–8 (1989): 22–32.

McCail, Ronald C. 'The *Cycle* of Agathias: New Identifications Scrutinised.' *JHS* 89 (1969): 87–96.

McCollough, C. Thomas. 'Monumental Changes: Architecture and Culture in Late Roman and Early Byzantine Sepphoris.' In *The Archaeology of Difference. Gender, Ethnicity, Class and the 'Other' in Antiquity. Studies in Honor of Eric M. Meyers*, edited by Douglas R. Edwards and C. Thomas McCollough: 267–77. AASOR 60/61. Boston: ASOR, 2007.

McGuire, Meredith B. *Lived Religion: Faith and Practice in Everyday Life*. Oxford: Oxford University Press, 2008.

McInroy, Mark. 'Origen.' In *The Spiritual Senses: Perceiving God in Western Christianity*, edited by Paul L. Gavrilyuk and Sarah Coakley: 20–35. Cambridge: Cambridge University Press, 2011.

McKenzie, Judith S., Joseph A. Greene, Andres T. Reyes, Catherine S. Alexander, Deirdre G. Barrett, Brian Gilmour, John F. Healey, Margaret O'Hea, Nadine Schibille, Stephan G. Schmid, Wilma Wetterstrom, and Sara Whitcher Kansa, with contributions by Kate da Costa, Patrick Degryse, Kathy Eremin, Sheila Gibson, Owen Gingerich, and Elias Khamis. *The Nabatean Temple at Khirbet et-Tannur, Jordan. Volume 1: Architecture and Religion. Final Report on Nelson Glueck's 1937 Excavation*. AASOR 67; Boston: ASOR, 2013.

McLynn, Neil. *Ambrose of Milan: Church and Court in a Christian Capital*. Berkeley: University of California Press, 1994.

Meeks, Wayne. *The First Urban Christians: The Social World of the Apostle Paul*, second edition. Yale: Yale University Press, 2003.

Meir, Dafna, and Eran Meir. *Ancient Synagogues in the Golan Heights*. Jerusalem: Yad Yitzhak Ben-Zvi, 2013.

Merkt, Andreas. *Maximus I. von Turin: Die Verkündigung eines Bischofs der frühen Reichskirche im zeitgeschichtlichen, gesellschaftlichen und liturgischen Kontext*. Leiden: Brill, 1997.

Meslin, Michel. *La fête des kalends de janvier dans l'empire romain*. Collection Latomus 115, Bruxelles: Latomus, 1970.

Metz, René. *La consécration des vierges dans l'église romaine: Étude d'histoire de la liturgie*. Paris: Press Universitaires de France, 1954.

Meyers, Eric M. 'Recent Archaeology in Palestine: Achievements and Future Goals.' In *The Cambridge History of Judaism, Volume Three: The Early Roman Period*, edited by W. Horbury, W. D. Davies and J. Sturdy: 59–74. Cambridge: Cambridge University Press, 1999.

——. 'The Dating of the Gush Halav Synagogue: A Response to Jodi Magness.' In *Judaism in Late Antiquity, Part Three, Where We Stand: Issues and Debates in Ancient Judaism. Volume Four: The Special Problem of the Synagogue*, edited by Alan J. Avery-Peck and Jacob Neusner: 49–70. HO, Section One 55; Leiden: Brill, 2001.

——. 'Living Side by Side in Galilee.' In *Partings: How Judaism and Christianity Became Two*, edited by Hershel Shanks: 133–50. Washington D.C.: Biblical Archaeology Society, 2014.

Meyers, Eric M. and Dan Barag. 'Meiron.' In *Encyclopedia of Archaeological Excavations in the Holy Land III*, edited by Michael Avi-Yonah: 856–62. Oxford: Oxford University Press, 1977.

Meyers, Eric, A. Thomas Kraabel and James F. Strange. *Ancient Synagogue Excavations at Khirbet Shema', Upper Galilee, Israel 1970–1972*. AASOR 42. Durham: Duke University Press, 1976.

Meyers, Eric M. and Carol L. Meyers. *Excavations at Ancient Nabratein. Synagogue and Environs*. MEPR 6. Winona Lake, IN: Eisenbrauns, 2009.

——. 'A Response to Jodi Magness's Review of the Final Publication of Nabratein.' *BASOR* 359 (2011): 67–76.

Meyers, Eric M., Carol L. Meyers and James F. Strange. *Excavations at the Ancient Synagogue of Gush Halav*. MEPR 5. Winona Lake, IN: Eisenbrauns, 1990.

Meyers, Eric M., James F. Strange, and Dennis E. Groh. 'The Meiron Excavation Project: Archaeological Survey in Galilee and Golan, 1976.' *BASOR* 230 (1978): 1–24.

Meyers, Eric M., James F. Strange and Carol L. Meyers. *Excavations at Ancient Meiron, Upper Galilee, Israel 1971–72, 1974–75, 1977*. MEPR 3. Cambridge: ASOR, 1981.

Meyers, Eric M., James F. Strange, Carol L. Meyers, and J. Raynor. 'Preliminary Report on the 1980 Excavations at en-Nabratein, Israel.' *BASOR* 244 (1981): 1–25.

Miller, Stuart S. 'The Minim of Sepphoris Reconsidered.' *HTR* 86 (1993): 377–402.

——. 'Epigraphical Rabbis, Helios and Psalm 19: Were the Synagogues of Archaeology and the Synagogues of the Sages One and the Same.' *JQR* 94 (2004): 27–76.

——. *Sages and Commoners in Late Antique 'Erez Israel: A Philological Inquiry into Local Traditions in Talmud Yerushalmi*. TSAJ 111. Tübingen: Mohr Siebeck, 2006.

——. 'Review Essay. Roman Imperialism, Jewish Self-Definition, and Rabbinic Society: Belayche's *Iudaea-Palaestina*, Schwartz's *Imperialism and Jewish Society*, and Boyarin's *Border Lines* Reconsidered.' *AJSR* 31 (2007): 329–62.

Moralee, Jason. 'The Stones of St. Theodore: Disfiguring the Pagan Past in Christian Gerasa.' *JECS* 14:2 (2006): 183–215.

Moxness, Halvor. *Putting Jesus in His Place: A Radical Vision of Households and Kingdom*. Louisville: Westminster John Know Press, 2003.

Munro, Beth. 'Sculptural Deposition and Lime Kilns at Roman Villas in Italy and the Western Provinces in Late Antiquity.' In *The Afterlife of Greek and Roman Sculpture*, edited by Troels M. Kristensen and Lea M. Stirling. Ann Arbor: University of Michigan Press, forthcoming.

Murray, Michele. *Playing a Jewish Game: Gentile Christian Judaizing in the First and Second Century CE*. SCJ 13. Waterloo, Ont.: Wilfrid Laurier University Press, 2004.

Neusner, Jacob. *Judaism: The Evidence of the Mishnah*, second edition. BJS 129. Atlanta, Ga: Scholars Press, 1988.

Nisbet, Gideon. *Greek Epigram in the Roman Empire: Martial's Forgotten Rivals*. Oxford and New York: Oxford University Press, 2003.
O'Daly, Gerard. *Augustine's City of God. A Reader's Guide*. Oxford: Clarendon Press, 1999.
O'Donnell, James. *Augustine, Confessions: Commentary on Books 8–13*. Oxford: Clarendon Press, 1992.
O'Meara, Dominic J. *Platonopolis*: *Platonic Political Philosophy in Late Antiquity*. Oxford: Oxford University Press, 2003.
O'Shea, W. J. and T. D. Rover. 'Homily' in *NCE* second edition, Vol. 7: 62–4. Detroit: Gale/Thomson Learning, Inc, 2003.
Oakes, Penelope J., S. Alexander Haslam and John C. Turner. *Stereotyping and Social Reality*. Oxford: Blackwell, 1994.
Obermann, Julian. 'The Sepulchre of the Maccabean Martyrs.' *JBL* 50:4 (1931): 205–65.
Ostrasz, Antoni A. 'The Hippodrome of Gerasa: A Report on Excavations and Research 1982–1987.' *Syria* 66 (1989): 51–77.
Otten, Willemien and Nienke Vos (eds). *Demons and the Devil in Ancient and Medieval Christianity*. Leiden: Brill, 2011.
Otto, Rudolf. *Das Heilige: Über das Irrationale in der Idee des Göttlichen und sein Verhältnis zum Rationalen*. Breslau: Trewendt & Granier, 1917; reprint München, 2004.
Ousterhout, Robert (ed.). *The Blessings of Pilgrimage*. Urbana: University of Illinois Press, 1990.
Ovadiah, Asher. *Corpus of the Byzantine Churches in the Holy Land*. Bonn: P. Hanstein, 1970.
Polinskaya, Irene. 'Lack of Boundaries, Absence of Oppositions: The City–Countryside Continuum of a Greek Pantheon.' In *City, Countryside, and the Spatial Organization of Value in Classical Antiquity*, edited by Ralph M. Rosen and Ineke Sluiter: 61–92. Mnemosyne Supplementa 279. Leiden, Boston: Brill, 2006.
Porath, Yosef. 'The Caesarea Excavation Project – March 1992–June 1994: Expedition of the Antiquities Authority.' *ESI* 17 (1998): 39–49.
Prince, Gerald. *A Dictionary of Narratology*. Lincoln: University of Nebraska Press, 2003.
Pülz, Andreas. 'Ephesos in Spätantiker und Byzantinischer Zeit.' *FA* 53/XII (2009). Available online at http://farch.net, accessed 25 January 2016.
Radt, Wolfgang. 'Pergamon, 1986.' *AS* 37 (1987): 211–14.
Räisänen, Heikki. *The Rise of Christian Beliefs: The Thought World of Early Christians*. Minneapolis: Fortress Press, 2010.
Rajak, Tessa. 'The Rabbinic Dead and the Diaspora Dead at Beth She'arim.' In *The Talmud Yerushalmi and Graeco-Roman Culture I*, edited by Peter Schäfer: 349–66. TSAJ 73. Tübingen: Mohr Siebeck, 1998.
Ramsey, Boniface. *Ambrose*. London and New York: Routledge, 1997.
Rapp, Claudia. 'Desert, City, and Countryside in the Early Christian Imagination.' *Church History and Religious Culture*, 86/1 (2006): 93–112.
Rappaport, Roy A. *Ritual and Religion in the Making of Humanity*. Cambridge and New York: Cambridge University Press, 1999.
Rebillard, Éric. '"To Live with the Heathen, but not Die with Them." The Issue of Commensality between Christians and non-Christians in the First Five Centuries.' In Rebillard, Éric. *Transformation of Religious Practices in Late Antiquity*: 115–41. Farnham: Ashgate Variorum, 2013. (orig. '"Vivre avec les païens, mais non mourir avec eux". Le problème de la commensalité des chrétiens et des non-chrétiens [Ier-Ve siècles].' In *Les frontières du profane dans l'antiquité tardive*, edited by Éric Rebillard and Claire Sotinel, 151–76. Rome: École française de Rome, 2010).

230   Bibliography

——. *Christians and Their Many Identities in Late Antiquity, North Africa, 200–450 CE*. Ithaca: Cornell University Press, 2012.

Rebillard, Éric and Claire Sotinel (eds). *Les frontières du profane dans l'antiquité tardive*. Collection de l'École française de Rome 428. Rome: École française de Rome, 2010.

——. 'Introduction.' In *Les frontières du profane dans l'antiquité tardive*, edited by Éric Rebillard and Claire Sotinel: 1–14. Rome: École française de Rome 2010.

Reed, Annette Y. and Adam H. Becker. 'Introduction: Traditional Models and New Directions.' In *The Ways that Never Parted: Jews and Christians in Late Antiquity and the Early Middle Ages*, edited by Adam H. Becker and Annette Yoshiko Reed: 1–33. Minneapolis: Fortress Press, 2007.

Rees, B. R. *The Letters of Pelagius and his Followers*. Rochester, NY: The Boydell Press, 1991.

Retzleff, Alexandra G. 'John Chrysostom's Sex Aquarium: Aquatic Metaphors for Theater in Homily 7 on Matthew.' *JECS* 11:2 (2003): 195–207.

Riggs, David. 'Christianising the Rural Communities in Late Roman Africa.' In *Violence in Late Antiquity: Perceptions and Practices*, edited by H. A. Drake: 297–308. Aldershot: Ashgate, 2006.

Rosen, Klaus. 'Fides contra dissimulationem: Ambrosius und Symmachus im Kampf um den Victoriaaltar.' *JbAC* 37 (1994): 29–36.

Rosenblum, Jordan D. *Food and Identity in Early Rabbinic Judaism*. Cambridge: Cambridge University Press, 2010.

Rosenfeld, Ben-Zion, and Joseph Menirav. *Markets and Marketing in Roman Palestine*. JSJSup 99. Leiden: Brill, 2005.

Rousseau, Philip. 'Christian Culture and the Swine's Husks: Jerome, Augustine, and Paulinus.' In *The Limits of Ancient Christianity: Essays on Late Antique Thought and Culture in Honor of R.A. Markus*, edited by William E. Klingshirn and Mark Vessey: 172–87. Ann Arbor MI: University of Michigan Press, 1999.

——. 'Moses, Monks, and Mountains in Theodoret's Historia Religiosa.' In *Il monachesimo tra eredità e aperture*, edited by Maciej Bielawski and Daniël Hombergen. Rome: Centro Studi S. Anselmo, 2004.

Rouwhorst, Gerhard. 'The Emergence of the Cult of the Maccabean Martyrs in Late Antique Christianity.' In *More than a Memory: The Discourse of Martyrdom and the Construction of Christian Identity in the History of Christianity*, edited by J. Leemans: 81–96. Leuven: Peeters, 2005.

——. 'Raphaëlle Ziadé, Les Martyrs Maccabées: de l'histoire juive au culte chrétien. Les homélies de Grégoire de Nazianze et de Jean Chrysostome.' *VC Reviews* 66 (2012): 213–16.

Rubenson, Samuel. 'Christian Asceticism and the Emergence of the Monastic Tradition.' In *Asceticism*, edited by V. L. Wimbush and R. Valantasis: 49–57. Oxford: Oxford University Press, 1998.

Runesson, Anders. 'Architecture, Conflict, and Identity Formation: Jews and Christians in Capernaum from the First to the Sixth Century.' In *Religion, Ethnicity, and Identity in Ancient Galilee*, edited by Jürgen K. Zangenberg, Harold W. Attridge and Dale B. Martin: 231–257. WUNT 210. Tübingen: Mohr Siebeck, 2007.

Russell, Ben. *The Economics of the Roman Stone Trade* (Oxford Studies on the Roman Economy). Oxford: Oxford University Press, 2013.

Rutgers, Leonard V. 'The Importance of Scripture in the Conflict between Jews and Christians: The Example of Antioch.' In *The Use of Sacred Books in the Antique World*, edited by Leonard V. Rutgers, Pieter W. van der Horst, Henriëtte W. Havelaar and Lieve Teugels: 287–303. CBET 22. Leuven: Peeters, 1998.

Safrai, Zeev. 'The Communal Function of the Synagogue in the Land of the Israel in the Rabbinic Period.' In *Ancient Synagogues: Historical Analysis and Archaeological Discovery*, edited by Dan Urman and Paul Virgil McCracken Flesher: 181–204. StPB 47. Leiden, Boston and Köln: Brill, 1998.

———. *The Missing Century, Palestine in the Fifth Century: Growth and Decline*. Palestina Antiqua 9. Leuven: Peeters, 1998.

Salzman, Michele Renee. '*Superstitio* in the *Codex Theodosianus* and the Persecution of Pagans.' *VC* 41 (1987): 172–88.

———. *On Roman Time: The Codex Calendar of 354 and the Rhythms of Urban Life in Late Antiquity*. Berkeley: University of California Press, 1990.

———. 'Rethinking Pagan–Christian Violence.' In *Violence in Late Antiquity: Perceptions and Practices*, edited by H. A. Drake: 265–85. Aldershot: Ashgate, 2006.

Sanders, Ed P. *Judaism: Practice and Belief 63 B.C.E.–66 C.E.* London: SCM; Philadelphia: Trinity Press International, 1992.

Salzman, Michele. 'The Christianization of Sacred Time and Sacred Space.' In *Transformations of Urbs Roma in Late Antiquity*, edited by W. V. Harris: 123–34. JRASup 33. Portsmouth, RI: JRA 1999.

Sandwell, Isabella. *Religious Identity in Late Antiquity: Greeks, Jews and Christians in Antioch*. Cambridge: Cambridge University Press, 2007.

Saradi, Helen G. 'The Use of Ancient Spolia in Byzantine Monuments: the Archaeological and Literary Evidence.' *IJCT* 3 (1997): 395–423.

———. *The Byzantine City in the Sixth Century. Literary Images and Historical Reality*. Athens: Society of Messenian Archaeological Studies, 2006.

Saradi-Mendelovici, Helen G. 'Christian Attitudes Toward Pagan Monuments in Late Antiquity and Their Legacy in Later Byzantine Centuries.' *DOP* 44 (1990): 47–61.

Sauer, Eberhard. 'Not Just Small Change. Coins in *Mithraea*.' In *Roman Mithraism: The Evidence of the Small Finds. Papers of the international conference / Bijdragen van het internationaal congres, Tienen 7/8 November 2001*, edited by Guy De Boe and Marleen Martens: 327–53. AIVM 4. Brussels: I.A.P., 2004.

Schäfer, Peter. *The Jewish Jesus: How Judaism and Christianity Shaped Each Other*. Princeton: Princeton University Press, 2012.

Schatkin, Margaret. 'The Maccabean Martyrs.' *VC* 28 (1974): 97–113.

Scheibelreiter-Gail, Veronika. 'Inscriptions in the Late Antique Private House: Some Thoughts about their Function and Distribution.' In *Patrons and Viewers in Late Antiquity*, edited by Stine Birk and Birte Poulsen: 135–165. Aarhus, Denmark: Aarhus University Press.

Schlatter, Fredric W. 'The Text in the Mosaic of Santa Pudenziana.' *VC* 43.2 (1989): 155–65.

Schmitzer, Ulrich. 'Raumkonkurrenz. Der symbolische Kampf um die römische Topographie im christlich-paganen Diskurs.' In *Rom und Mailand in der Spätantike: Repräsentationen städtischer Räume in Literatur, Architektur und Kunst*, edited by Therese Fuhrer: 237–62. Topoi: Berlin Studies of the Ancient World 4. Berlin: De Gruyter, 2012.

Schor, Adam. *Theodoret's People: Social Networks and Religious Conflict in Late Roman Syria*. Berkeley: University of California Press, 2011.

Schulte, Heinrich. *Die Epigramme des Leontios Scholastikos Minotauros: Text, Übersetzung, Kommentar*. Trier: Wissenschaftlicher Verlag Trier, 2005.

Schwabe, Moshe, and Baruch Lifshitz. *Beth She'arim II: The Greek Inscriptions*. Brunswick, NJ: Rutgers University Press, 1974.

Schwartz, Seth. *Imperialism and Jewish Society: 200 B.C.E. to 640 C.E.* Princeton: Princeton University Press, 2001.

Setzer, Claudia. *Jewish Responses to Early Christians: History and Polemics 30–150 C.E* Minneapolis, Fortress Press, 1994.

Shephardson, Christine C. 'Controlling Contested Places: John Chrysostom's Adversus Iudaeos Homilies and the Spatial Politics of Religious Controversy.' *JECS* 15:4 (2007): 483–516.

Shorrock, Robert. *The Myth of Paganism: Nonnus, Dionysus and the World of Late Antiquity*. New York and London: Bloomsbury Academic, 2011.

Siegel, Rudolph E. *Galen on Sense Perception: His Doctrines, Observations and Experiments on Vision, Hearing, Smell, Taste, Touch and Pain, and Their Historical Sources*. Basel: S. Karger, 1970.

Silvas, Anna. *Gregory of Nyssa: The Letters*. Leiden: Brill, 2007.

Simon, Marcel. *Verus Israel. A Study of the Relations between Christians and Jews in the Roman Empire (135–425)*. New York: Oxford University Press, 1986.

Siniossoglou, Niketas. *Plato and Theodoret: The Christian Appropriation of Platonic Philosophy and the Hellenic Intellectual Resistance*. Cambridge: Cambridge University Press, 2008.

Sivan, Hagith. *Palestine in Late Antiquity*. Oxford: Oxford University Press, 2008.

———. *Galla Placidia: The Last Roman Empress*. Oxford: Oxford University Press, 2011.

Sluiter, Ineke, and Ralph M. Rosen, 'General Introduction.' In *City, Countryside, and the Spatial Organization of Value in Classical Antiquity*, edited by Ralph M. Rosen and Ineke Sluiter. Mnemosyne Supplementa 279. Leiden, Boston: Brill, 2006.

Smith, Jonathan Z. *Map Is Not Territory: Studies in the History of Religion*. Leiden: Brill, 1978.

———. *Imagining Religion: From Babylon to Jonestown*. Chicago: University of Chicago Press, 1982.

———. *To Take Place: Toward Theory in Ritual*. Chicago: University of Chicago Press, 1987.

Smith, Steven D. 'Agathias and Paul the Silentiary: Erotic Epigram and the Sublimation of Same-Sex Desire in the Age of Justinian.' In *Sex in Antiquity*, edited by Mark Masterson Nancy Sorkin Rabinowitz and James Robson: 500–516. Abingdon and New York: Routledge, 2015.

Sodini, Jean-Pierre. 'Marble and Stoneworking in Byzantium, Seventh–Fifteenth Centuries.' In *The Economic History of Byzantium*, edited by Angeliki E. Laiou: 129–46. DOS 39. Washington: Dumbarton Oaks, 2002.

Soler, Emmanuel. 'Sacralité et partage du temps et de l'espace festifs à Antioche au IVe siècle.' In *Les frontières du profane dans l'antiquité tardive*, edited by Éric Rebillard and Claire Sotinel: 273–86. Rome: École française de Rome, 2010.

Sorabji, Richard. *The Philosophy of the Commentators, 200–600 AD: A Sourcebook*. Vol. 1, Psychology (with ethics and religion). London: Duckworth, 2004.

Sorensen, Eric. *Possession and Exorcism in the New Testament and Early Christianity*. WUNT; Tübingen: Mohr Siebeck, 2002.

Sotinel, Claire. *Church and Society in Late Antique Italy and Beyond*. Aldershot: Ashgate, 2010.

———. 'La sphere profane dans l'espace urbain.' In *Les frontières du profane dans l'antiquité tardive*, edited by Éric Rebillard and Claire Sotinel: 319–49. Rome: École française de Rome, 2010.

Sperber, Daniel. *Roman Palestine 200–400: Money and Prices*, second edition. Ramat Gan: Bar Ilan University Press, 1991.

Spieser, Jean-Michel. 'La christianisation de la ville dans l'Antiquité tardive.' *Ktèma* 11 (1986): 49–55.

Spigel, Chad S. *Ancient Synagogue Seating Capacities: Methodology, Analysis and Limits.* TSAJ 149. Tübingen: Mohr Siebeck, 2012.

Stemberger, Günter. 'Die Umformung des palästinischen Judentums nach 70: Der Aufstieg der Rabbinen.' In *Jüdische Geschichte in hellenistisch-römischer Zeit. Wege der Forschung: Vom alten zum neuen Schürer*, edited by Aharon Oppenheimer: 85–99. Schriften des Historischen Kollegs: Kolloquien 44. München: R. Oldenbourg Verlag, 1999.

———. 'Christians and Jews in Byzantine Palestine.' In *Christians and Christianity in the Holy Land: From the Origins to the Latin Kingdoms*, edited by Ora Limor and Gay G. Stroumsa: 293–318. Cultural Encounters in Late Antiquity and the Middle Ages 5. Turnhout, Belgium: Brepols, 2006.

———. *Jews and Christians in the Holy Land* (Ruth Tuschling (trans.)). Edinburgh: T&T Clark 2000.

———. 'Rabbinic Reactions to the Christianization of Roman Palestine: A Survey of Recent Research.' In *Encounters of the Children of Abraham from Ancient to Modern Times*, edited by Antti Laato and Pekka Lindqvist: 141–63. Studies on the Children of Abraham 1. Leiden: Brill, 2010.

Stewart, Peter. 'The Destruction of Statues in Late Antiquity.' In *Constructing Identities in Late Antiquity*, edited by Richard Miles: 159–89. London: Routledge, 1999.

———. *Statues in Roman Society: Representation and Response.* Oxford: Oxford University Press, 2003.

Stirling, Lea M. 'Collections, Canons, and Context: the Afterlife of Greek Masterpieces in Late Antiquity.' In *Using Images in Late Antiquity*, edited by Stine Birk, Troels M. Kristensen, and Birte Poulsen: 96–114. Oxford: Oxbow, 2014.

Strack, Herman L. and Günter Stemberger. *Introduction to the Talmud and Midrash*, translated by Markus Bockmuehl, second edition. Minneapolis: Fortress Press, 1996.

Strange, James F. 'Synagogue Typology and Khirbet Shema.' In *Judaism in Late Antiquity, Part Three, Where We Stand: Issues and Debates in Ancient Judaism. Volume Four: The Special Problem of the Synagogue*, edited by Alan J. Avery-Peck and Jacob Neusner: 71–8. HO, Section One 55; Leiden: Brill, 2001.

Strange, James F., Thomas R. W. Longstaff, and Dennis E. Groh. 'Zippori – 1991.' *ESI* 13 (1994): 29–30.

———. *Excavations at Sepphoris, Volume I. University of South Florida Probes in the Citadel and Villa.* BRLJ 22. Leiden: Brill, 2006.

Sukenik, Eleazar. *Ancient Synagogues in Palestine and Greece.* London: British Academy, 1934.

Swartz, David. 'Bridging the Study of Culture and Religion: Pierre Bourdieu's Political Economy of Symbolic Power.' *Sociology of Religion* 57 (1996): 71–85.

Syon, Danny and Zvi Yavor. *Gamla II: The Architecture. The Shmarya Gutmann Excavations, 1976–1989.* IAA Reports 44. Jerusalem: IAA, 2010.

Talgam, Rina. *Mosaics of Faith: Floors of Pagans, Jews, Samaritans, Christians and Muslims in the Holy Land.* Jerusalem: Yad Ben-Zvi and University Park: Pennsylvania State University Press, 2014.

Taylor, Joan E. *Christians and the Holy Places: The Myth of Jewish–Christian Origins.* Oxford: Clarendon, 1993.

———. 'Parting in Palestine.' In *Partings: How Judaism and Christianity Became Two*, edited by Hershel Shanks: 87–104. Washington DC: Biblical Archaeology Society, 2014.

Tchalenko, Georges. *Villages antiques de la Syrie du Nord: Le massif du Bélus à l'époque romaine*, three vols. Paris: P. Geuthner, 1953–1958.

Testa, Emmanuele. *The Faith of the Mother Church: An Essay on the Theology of the Judeo-Christians*. SBF Collectio Minor. Jerusalem: Franciscan Printing Press, 1992.

Tilley, Maureen A. 'An Anonymous Letter to a Woman Named Susanna.' In *Religions of Late Antiquity in Practice*, edited by Richard Valantasis: 218–29. Princeton, NJ: Princeton University Press, 2000.

Tloka, Jutta. *Griechische Christen – christliche Griechen: Plausibilisierungsstrategien des antiken Christentums bei Origenes und Johannes Chrysostomos*. Tübingen: Mohr Siebeck, 2005.

Tsafrir, Yoram. 'The Classical Heritage in Late Antique Palestine: the Fate of Freestanding Sculptures.' In *The Sculptural Environment of the Roman Near East: Reflections on Culture, Ideology, and Power*, edited by Yaron Z. Eliav, Elise A. Friedland, and Sharon C. Herbert: 117–42. ISACR 9. Leuven: Peeters, 2008.

Urbano, Arthur. *The Philosophical Life: Biography and the Crafting of Intellectual Identity in Late Antiquity*. North American Patristic Society; Patristic Monograph Series, vol. 21. Washington, DC: The Catholic University of America Press, 2013.

Uscatescu, Alexandra and Manuel Martín-Bueno. 'The Macellum of Gerasa (Jerash, Jordan): From a Market Place to an Industrial Area.' *BASOR* 307 (1997): 67–88.

Ustinova, Yulia. *Caves and the Ancient Greek Mind: Descending Underground in the Search for Ultimate Truth*. Oxford: Oxford University, 2009.

van Fleteren, Frederick. 'Demons.' In *Augustine Through the Ages: An Encyclopedia*, edited by Allan D. Fitzgerald and John C. Cavadini: 266–8. Michigan: Grand Rapids, 1999.

——. 'Devil.' In *Augustine through the Ages: An Encyclopedia*, edited by Allan D. Fitzgerald and John C. Cavadini: 268–9. Michigan: Grand Rapids, 1999.

van Oort, Johannes. *Jerusalem and Babylon: A Study into Augustine's City of God and the Sources of his Doctrine of the Two Cities*. Leiden: Brill, 1990.

van Straaten, Folkert T. 'Ancient Greek Animal Sacrifice: Gift, Ritual Slaughter, Communion, Food Supply, or What? Some Thoughts on Simple Explanations of a Complex Ritual.' In *La cuisine et l'autel: Les sacrifices en questions dans les sociétés de la Méditerranée ancienne*, edited by Stella Georgoudi, Renée Koch Piettre and Francis Schmidt: 15–29. Turnhout: Brepols, 2005.

Vanderspoel, John. *Themistius and the Imperial Court, Oratory, Civic Duty, and Paideia from Constantius and Theodosius*. Ann Arbor: The University of Michigan Press, 1995.

Vermander, Jean-Marie. 'La polémique des apologistes latins contre les dieux du paganisme.' *RA* 17 (1982): 3–128.

Viansino, Giovanni. *Agazia Scolastico: Epigrammi*. Milan: Luigi Trevisini, 1967.

Viken, Gary. 'Pilgrims in Magi's Clothing: The Impact of Mimesis on Early Byzantine Pilgrimage Art.' In *The Blessings of Pilgrimage*, edited by Robert Ousterhout: 97–107. Urbana: University of Illinois Press, 1990.

Ville, Georges. 'Les jeux gladiateurs dans l'empire chrétien.' *MEFR* 72 (1960): 273–335.

Vincent, H. and Abel, F.-M. *Bethléem: le sanctuaire de la Nativité*. Paris: J. Gabalda, 1914.

Vinson, Martha. 'Gregory Nazianzen's Homily 15 and the Genesis of the Christian Cult of the Maccabean Martyrs.' *Byzantion* 64 (1994): 166–92.

Vitto, Fanny. 'Byzantine Mosaics at Beth She'arim: New Evidence for the History of the Site.' *'Atiqot* 28 (1996): 115–59.

von Fisenne, Friedrich. 'Das Mithräum zu Saarburg in Lothringen: Bericht über die Ausgrabungen im Sommer 1895.' *Jahrbuch der Gesellschaft für Lothringische Geschichte und Altertumskunde* 8 (1896): 119–75. Available online at https://archive.org/stream/jahrbuchdergesel08gese/jahrbuchdergesel08gese_djvu.txt, accessed 25 January 2016.

Waelkens, Marc. 'Marble.' In *Late Antiquity: A Guide to the Postclassical World*, edited by Glen W. Bowersock, Peter R. L. Brown and Oleg Grabar: 559–62. Cambridge, MA: Harvard University Press, 1999.
Walters, Vivienne J. *The Cult of Mithras in the Roman Provinces of Gaul*. EPRO 81. Leiden: Brill, 1974.
Waltz, Pierre, Guy Soury, Jean Irigoin and Pierre Laurens (eds). *Anthologie Grecque, Tome VIII. Anthologie Palatine. Livre IX, Épigrammes 359–827*. Paris: Les Belles Lettres, 1974 (reprinted 2002).
Warf, Barney and Santa Arias. 'Introduction: The Reinsertion of Space into the Social Sciences and Humanities.' In *The Spatial Turn: Interdisciplinary Perspectives*, edited by Barney Warf and Santa Arias: 1–10. Routledge Studies in Human Geography 26. London: Routledge, 2009.
Waterman, Leroy (ed.). *Preliminary Report of the University of Michigan Excavations at Sepphoris, Palestine, in 1931*. Ann Arbor: University of Michigan Press, 1937.
Webb, Ruth. *Demons and Dancers: Performance in Late Antiquity*. Cambridge MA and London, England: Harvard University Press, 2008.
Weber, Thomas and Ulrich Hübner. 'Gadara 1998 The Excavation of the Five-aisled Basilica at Umm Qays: A Preliminary Report.' *ADAJ* 42 (1998): 443–56.
Weismann, Werner. *Kirche und Schauspiele: Die Schauspiele im Urteil der Kirchenväter unter besonderer Berücksichtigung von Augustin*. Würzburg: Augustinus Verlag, 1972.
Weiss, Zeev. 'Sepphoris.' In *NEAEHL 4*, edited by Ephraim Stern: 1324–8. Jerusalem: IES, 1993.
——. 'Greco-Roman Influences on the Art and Architecture of the Jewish City in Roman Palestine.' In *Religious and Ethnic Communities in Later Roman Palestine*, edited by Hayim Lapin: 219–46. STJHC 5. Bethesda: University Press of Maryland, 1998.
——. 'Sepphoris (Sippori), 2005.' *IEJ* 55 (2005): 219–27.
——. *The Sepphoris Synagogue: Deciphering an Ancient Message through Its Archaeological and Socio-Historical Contexts*. Jerusalem: IES, 2005.
——. 'Sepphoris (Sippori), 2007.' *IEJ* 57 (2007): 215–29.
——. 'Sculptures and Sculptural Images in Urban Galilee.' In *The Sculptural Environment of the Roman Near East. Reflections on Culture, Ideology, and Power*, edited by Yaron Z. Eliav, Elise A. Friedland and Sharon C. Herbert: 559–73. Leuven: Peeters, 2008.
——. 'Sepphoris.' In *NEAEHL 5: Supplementary Volume*, edited by Ephraim Stern: 2029–35. ISACR 9. Jerusalem: IES, 2008.
——. 'From Roman Temple to Byzantine Church: a Preliminary Report on Sepphoris in Transition.' *JRA* 23 (2010): 196–218.
Weiss, Zeev and Ehud Netzer. 'Zippori – 1992/1993.' *ESI* 14 (1995): 40–46.
——. 'Sepphoris During the Byzantine Period.' In *Sepphoris in Galilee. Crosscurrents of Culture*, edited by Rebecca M. Nagy, Carol L. Meyers, Eric M. Meyers and Zeev Weiss: 81–89. Winona Lake, IN: Eisenbrauns, 1996.
——. 'Zippori – 1994–1995.' *ESI* 18 (1998): 22–7 (English), 31–9 (Hebrew).
Wenger, A. 'Restauration de l'Homélie de Chrysostome sur Eléazar et les sept frères Macchabées (PG 63: 523–530).' In *Texte und Textkritik. Eine Aufsatzsammlung in Zusammenarbeit mit Johannes Irmscher, Franz Paschke & Kurt Treu*, edited by Jürgen Dummer: 599–604. Berlin: Akademie-Verlag, 1987.
Westergren, Andreas. *Sketching the Invisible: Patterns of Church and City in Theodoret of Cyrrhus' Philotheos Historia*. PhD dissertation, Lund University, 2012.

White, L. Michael. *Building God's House in the Roman World: Architectural Adaptation among Pagans, Jews, and Christians*. Baltimore and London: The Johns Hopkins University Press, 1990.

Wilken, Robert L. *John Chrysostom and the Jews. Rhetoric and Reality in the Late 4th Century*. Berkeley: University of California Press, 1983.

——. 'Something Greater than Temple.' In *Anti-Judaism and the Gospels*, edited by William R. Farmer: 176–202. Harrisburg, PA: Trinity Press, 1999.

Witakowski, Witold (ed.). *Pseudo-Dionysius of Tel-Mahre. Chronicle. Part III*. Liverpool: Liverpool University Press, 1996.

Wood, Philip. *'We Have No King but Christ': Christian Political Thought in Greater Syria on the Eve of the Arab Conquest (c.400–585)*. Oxford: Oxford University Press, 2010.

Woyke, Johannes. 'Das Bekenntnis zum einzig allwirksamen Gott und Herrn und die Dämonisierung von Fremdkulten: Monolatrischer und polylatrischer Monotheismus in *1. Korinther* 8 und 10.' In *Gruppenreligionen im römischen Reich*, edited by Jörg Rüpke: 87–112. STAC 43. Tübingen: Mohr Siebeck, 2007.

Yannai, Yuval. 'The Gorna – A Basin from Beth She'an.' In *The 12th World Congress of Jewish Studies: Division B: The History of the Jewish People*, edited by Ron Margolin. Jerusalem: Magness Press, 1999.

Yarnold, Edward. *The Awe-Inspiring Rites of Initiation: The Origins of the RCIA*, second edition. Collegeville, MN: The Liturgical Press, 1994.

Yasin, Ann Marie. *Saints and Church Spaces in the Late Antique Mediterranean: Architecture, Cult, and Community*. Cambridge: Cambridge University Press, 2009.

Yegül, Fikret. *The Bath-Gymnasium Complex at Sardis*. AES 3. Cambridge, MA: Harvard University Press, 1986.

Yeivin, Ze'ev. *The Synagogue at Korazim: The 1962–1964, 1980–1987 Excavations*. IAA Reports 10. Jerusalem: IAA, 2000.

Younger, John G. 'Architectural Elements and Sculptures.' In *Excavations at Ancient Nabratein. Synagogue and Environs*, edited by Eric M. Meyers and Carol L. Meyers: 78–92. MEPR 6. Winona Lake, IN: Eisenbrauns, 2009.

Zangenberg, Jürgen K. 'Ein Dorf auf dem Hügel: Neue Entdeckungen des Kinneret Regional Project in der Synagoge von Horvat Kur, Galiläa.' In *Bauern, Fischer und Propheten: Galiläa zur Zeit Jesu*, edited by Jürgen K. Zangenberg and Jens Schröter: 131–44. Mainz: Von Zabern, 2012.

——. 'From the Galilean Jesus to the Galilean Silence: Earliest Christianity in the Galilee until the Fourth Century CE.' In *The Rise and Expansion of Christianity in the Three Centuries of the Common Era*, edited by Clare K. Rothschild and Jens Schröter: 75–108. WUNT 301. Tübingen: Mohr Siebeck, 2013.

——. 'Pure Stone: Archaeological Evidence for Jewish Purity Practices in Late Second Temple Judaism (Miqwa'ot, Stone Vessels).' In *Purity and the Forming of Religious Traditions in the Ancient Mediterranean World and Ancient Judaism*, edited by Christian Frevel and Christophe Nihan: 537–572. DHR 3. Leiden and Boston: Brill, 2013.

——. 'A Basalt Stone Table from the Byzantine Synagogue at Horvat Kur, Galilee. Publication and First Interpretation', in print for *Yizhar Hirschfeld Memorial Volume*, Yosef Patrich, Lea DiSegni, Orit Peleg-Barkat and Erez Ben Yosef (eds). Jerusalem: Israel Exploration Society, 2015.

Zangenberg, Jürgen K. and Stefan Münger. 'Horbat Kur: Preliminary Report.' *HA/ESI* 123 (2011). Available online at http://www.hadashot-esi.org.il/report_detail_eng.aspx?id=1746&mag_id=118, accessed 30 January 2016.

Zangenberg, Jürgen K., Stefan Münger, Raimo Hakola, Rick Bonnie and Patrick Wyssmann. 'Horvat Kur. Kinneret Regional Project – The 2011 Season.' *HA/ESI* 125 (2013). Available online at http://www.hadashot-esi.org.il/report_detail_eng.aspx?id=2230&mag_id=120, accessed 30 January 2016.

Zangenberg, Jürgen K., Stefan Münger, Raimo Hakola and Byron R. McCane, 'The Kinneret Regional Project Excavations of a Byzantine Synagogue at Horvat Kur, Galilee, 2010–2013: A Preliminary Report.' *HeBAI* 2 (2013): 557–76.

Ziadé, Raphaëlle. *Les Martyrs Maccabées: de l'histoire juive au culte chrétien. Les homélies de Grégoire de Nazianze et de Jean Chrysostome.* VCSup 80. Leiden: Brill, 2007.

Index

Achilles Tatius 41
acropolis 56
Agathias of Myrina 32–47
Agricola and Vitalis 89
Ambrose of Milan 5, 89, 91–5, 97–8, 101–5
Ammianus Marcellinus 28–9
Antioch 12, 23, 49–52, 56, 131
antiphons 94–5
Apostolos-Cappadona, Diane 84
Athanasius 6, 106, 112–13, 116
Augustine 14, 114–17, 151: *Against Faustus* 151; *Confessiones* 116; *De Civitate Dei* 114–16; *Tractatus in Ioannis Evangelium* 151
authority, of bishops 103–5

baptism 92–3
baptistery 93
Barsanuphius of Gaza 152
Barsauma 148
Basil of Caesarea 27, 44
basin (*labrum*) 173–6, 181
Bell, Catherine 96–8, 102, 104
bemah (platform): in synagogue *see* synagogue
bench: in synagogue *see* synagogue
Bethlehem 72, 75–6, 85–8
Beth She'arim 199–200
bodies, ritualized 96–7, 104
Bourdieu, Pierre 97–8, 102
Brakke, David 107, 113
Brown, Peter 19, 167
Brubaker, Rogers 14, 31
burial, *ad sanctos* 89
Buxton, Richard 55

Cain, Andrew 86, 87
Canivet, Pierre 61
Capernaum 141, 144, 155, 160–4, 168
Cato the Elder 195
cave (as abode of an ascetic) 61
cell (as abode of an ascetic) 56, 58, 62–3
Chancey, Mark 191
Chorazin 141, 160, 168, 180, 182
city: and countryside 49–50; and desert 56; and mountains 56; as a place of demons 106, 109–11
Clement of Alexandria 106, 109–11, 116
Coakley, Sarah 80
Codex Theodosianus 207
consecration, of virgins 89–105
Constantinople 32–4, 36–9, 44, 120
conversion: of Christians to Judaism 145; of Jews to Christianity 145–6
Council of Carthage 103
Cox Miller, Patricia 70, 79
Cresswell, Tim 1
cult of the saints 121
Cyril of Jerusalem 71–2, 77, 83

Daly, Lawrence J. 30
Delphi 61
de Luca, Stefano 163–4
demonology: early Christian 106–9; Jewish 108
demons: *pneuma akatharton* (unclean spirit) 108; positive and negative sense of 107–8; in public spaces, spectacles and the city 109–11, 116; realistic understanding of 110
desert 53, 106–7, 111–17: and mountain 55–6; *see also* desert fathers

desert fathers 50, 110
diakrisis pneumaton (discernment of the spirits) 109, 112
Diodore of Tarsus 52
domestic space/private space 35–40, 42
Dura Europos 181

Easter 91–2
Edessa 56
Egeria 69, 70, 73–5, 79, 82–3, 86–7, 162
ekphrasis 49
Eliezer ben Hyrcanus 144
Emilsson, Eyjólfur Kjalar 79
En-Gedi 181
Ephraim, Bishop of Cherson 42–4
Epiphanius of Salamis 146, 201
Errington, Malcolm R. 28
ethopoeia 49
Evagrius Ponticus 106, 110, 113–17

Fine, Steven 167
Fischer, Moshe 199
Frank, Georgia 69, 70, 88
Fredriksen, Paula 3, 144, 151

Galen 77–9
Galilee 168, 170, 172, 179, 187, 190–3, 196, 198–200, 204, 210–11
games (wrestling) 130
Gaşpar, Cristian 51–2
Gavrilyuk, Paul 80
Gentile Christian Judaizing 142–3
Goehring, James E. 50
Golan Heights 160, 172, 179, 181, 184
Greenhalg, Michael 210
Gregory the Great 95
Gregory of Nazianzus 44
Gregory of Nyssa 43–4, 72
Grey, Matthew J. 158–9
Guérin, V. 199

Hachlili, Rachel 174, 180
Hadley, James 84
Hammat Tiberias 180–1
heaven: various ascents to 57–8
Henry, Nathalie 94
heresy: orthodoxy and heresy in Early Christianity 152
Hesiod 32, 39, 44–5

hierarchy 96–7
Hoffman, Lawrence 167
Holy Sepulchre, Church of 75–6, 85–6
Homer 59
Horvat Kur 141, 156, 159–61, 168–88
Huqoq 141, 156, 158–61

identity: as socially constructed 150–1

Jacob 42, 44–5
Jacob of Sarug 208
Jacobs, Ine 205
James of Nisibis 56, 60, 63
Jeremiah 123–4
Jerome 70, 75–7, 84–8, 95
Jerusalem 70–2, 75–6, 80, 84–5, 88
Jew, a stereotype 124
Jewish–Christian relations 141–2, 145, 148; *see also* Gentile Christian Judaizing
Jewish Christians 153, 161–2
John Chrysostom 23, 49: exegesis on Jeremiah 123–4; homily 'On Eleazar and the seven boys' 118–22
Joseph of Tiberias 146, 201
Julian Saba 60–1
Justinian 33, 36–8, 42, 45

Kaldellis, Anthony 44
Kalendae Ianuariae 15–16, 18–19, 21
Khirbet Wadi Hamam 158, 174–6
Kinneret Regional Project 168, 184

Laer, Pieter van 208–9
Lahire, Bernard 14
Lange, Armin 107
Larsen, Lillian I. 50
Levine, David 209
Levine, Lee I. 182, 188
Libanius 48–52, 55, 57, 59, 63–5
Lichtenberger, Herman 107
Liebeschuetz, Wolf 12
Life of Antony 50
Lim, Richard 13
limekiln: production of lime 194–6; limekilns in Galilee 196–204
liturgy: of marriage 99; in synagogue 166–7
lived religion 150

Maccabees: the feast of the Maccabees 120, 123–4, 130–1, 134, 136–7; the homilies 'On the Maccabees' 121, 130–2; homily 'On Eleazar and the Seven Boys' 118–22
Maier, Harry 37
Malalas, John 44–5
Maraval, Pierre 82
marble: destruction and reuse of 192–6, 204–6
Marcellina 91
Markus, Robert 12
marriage: between Jews and Christians 145; *see also* liturgy, of marriage
Martin, Dale 108
Massey, Doreen 3
Maxwell, Jaclyn L. 131, 135
Mayer, Wendy 120
McInroy, Mark 80–1
Melania the Elder 72, 80, 86
menorah: menorah in Horvat Kur synagogue mosaic 173, 189
Meroth 185
Miller, Stuart S. 149, 153, 159
minim see rabbinic Judaism
Modechai, Aviam 165
monasteries: the economy of 164; in Galilee 163
monasticism: rise of 59–63
money: in synagogue *see* synagogue
mosaic: in synagogue *see* synagogue
Moses 55, 61
mountain 55, 59–60; *see also* desert
Mount Olympus 55
Mount Sinai 55

Nativity, Church of 75, 85, 87
Nazareth 146, 161–2
Nebo 74
neophytes 92–3
Nicarchus 40–1, 44
Nicetas of Remesiana 92
Nisibis 56
Nonnos of Panopolis 46–7

one-space model of divine and human realms 51, 65
Origen 42, 79–82, 88, 151
orthodoxy *see* heresy

Ory, Jacob 180
Otten, Willemien 107
Otto, Rudolf 166–7

Palladius 195
parting of the ways between Judaism and Christianity 142–3
Pascha 91–2
patronage 3
Paula 70, 75–6, 85–8
Paulinus of Nola 72–3, 86
Paul the Apostle 22, 62, 123, 126, 136
Paul the Silentiary 38
performance (of sacred) 167
Petrus Chrysologus 14–20, 27
Philo 79, 80
pilgrimage 89: in Galilee 162
Plato 40–1, 44, 59–60, 64
Plotinus 71, 79
pneuma akatharton (unclean spirit) *see* demons
polis see city
pontifex maximus 30
power, symbolic 97–8, 102–3
Prudentius 26–7
public space 2–4: the church's dominance of 2; statuary in public spaces 190; urban public space 3; *see also* demons

rabbinic Judaism: and Christianity 144; and *minim* 145, 153, 161; power and influence of 144–5, 152–3, 158–9; and synagogues 154, 158–9; as an urban movement 159
Rappaport, Roy A. 90
Rebillard, Éric 13, 18, 24
Römheld, K. F. 107
Rousseau, Philip 54–5

sacrifice, of virginity 99–101
S. Pudenziana, Rome 83–5
Sepphoris 144, 146, 155, 159, 197–8, 201–4, 210–11
Septuagint 42, 123
Shepardson, Christine 49
singing, antiphonal 94–5
Siniossoglou, Niketas 51
Slouschz, Nahum 179
Smith, Jonathan Z. 90, 167